THE
COMPLETE
STEPHEN
KING
UNIVERSE

THE COMPLETE STEPHEN KING UNIVERSE

A GUIDE TO THE WORLDS OF STEPHEN KING

Stanley Wiater,
Christopher Golden,
and Hank Wagner

 ST. MARTIN'S GRIFFIN ❧ NEW YORK

www.stmartins.com

Design by Phil Mazzone

Library of Congress Cataloging-in-Publication Data

Wiater, Stan.
    The complete Stephen King universe : a guide to the worlds of Stephen King / Stanley Wiater, Christopher Golden, and Hank Wagner.
        p.   cm.
    Includes index.
    ISBN-13: 978-0-312-32490-2
    ISBN-10: 0-312-32490-1
    1. King, Stephen, 1947– —Criticism and interpretation. 2. Horror tales, American—History and criticism. I. Golden, Christopher. II. Wagner, Hank. III. Title.

PS3561.I483Z918   2006
813'.54—dc22   2006041065

First Edition: June 2006

10 9 8 7 6 5 4 3 2 1

To Iris and Tanya—for fighting off the wolves so long, so well. I love you both. And to Stephen King, for inviting me to your party in 1979 and allowing me to stay.

—S.W.

To Connie, Nicholas, and Daniel, my fellow explorers. And for the man himself, Stephen King, who always holds the lantern high to light the path, and yet rejoices in the shadows cast by its illumination.

—C.G.

To my parents, who endured my antics as a child, and to Nancy and the kids, who endure my antics now that I'm "allgrownup." And to Stephen King, for all his wonderful stories.

—H.W.

CONTENTS

SECTION TWO

THE PRIME REALITY

PART I: DERRY

SECTION THREE

THE PRIME REALITY

PART II: CASTLE ROCK

SECTION FOUR

THE PRIME REALITY

PART III: JERUSALEM'S LOT AND KING'S MAINE

SECTION FIVE
The Prime Reality
Part IV: Tales of The Shop

SECTION SIX
Other Prime Reality Tales

SECTION SEVEN

The World of Richard Bachman

SECTION EIGHT

Tales From Beyond: Further Parallel Realities

ACKNOWLEDGMENTS

We would like to thank those people who had a hand in the creation of this book. First, our agent, Lori Perkins, who can truly say she was the mother of this particular (sometimes very particular) baby. And . . . .

Claudia Carlson
Richard Chizmar
Alan Clark
Marsha De Filippo
Julie Eugley
Lisa French
Kathi Kamen Goldmark
Beth Gwinn
Dave Hinchberger
Misty Jenese
Lisa Lenthall
Arthur Morey
Suzanne Moss
Micol Ostow
James Robert Parish
Susan Shankin
Bill Sheehan
Stephen Spignesi
Allan Taylor
Bev Vincent
Bill Walker

INTRODUCTION

The Worlds of Stephen King

Welcome, one and all, to *The Stephen King Universe*. It is an incredible place of grotesque terror, dark magic, and fearsome wonder, a great multiverse conjured from one individual's imagination. It is a vast and still growing kingdom, and its many pathways can veer off into the darkest regions, where it's all too easy to get lost without guidance.

That's why we're here. To be your guides.

And what about you? Why are *you* here?

Are you one of the faithful, one of those to whom Stephen King is referring in his author's notes when he uses the term "Constant Reader"? If so, have you read his writings only casually, or are you among those who have paid closer attention, and realized there is a pattern? Perhaps you've only recently begun to explore what we respectfully term "the Stephen King Universe." If so, you may not have realized that there is so much more to know: connections implied or revealed, stories hidden within stories, tales spun within tales.

The Stephen King Universe (SKU)—though it might more precisely be called a multiverse (a cluster of universes existing in parallel dimensions)—is a truly wondrous and monumental creation. This volume of the same name is not, however, a concordance, or an encyclopedia, nor is it exactly a critical examination. More accurately, it is a guidebook. Stephen King's body of fiction can be, in large part, broken down by category based upon the world, or reality, in which each tale takes place. The world of the *Dark Tower* series or *The Stand*. The world he created under his pseudonym, Richard Bachman. Or the world in which most of his work has taken place, the reality in which Derry and Castle Rock and 'Salem's Lot exist, which we have called herein The Prime Reality.

They are all interrelated. Characters and stories cross over from one to the next. More importantly, there is a seemingly eternal struggle between good and evil, chaos and order, taking place throughout the Stephen King Universe and its myriad parallel realities or dimensions.

This is your guidebook to all of them.

Herein, broken down based upon the parallel realities, you will find descriptions of the significant action of nearly every story, novel, or original screenplay King has written, along with discussion of the themes that recur throughout the author's work. In addition, however, we have created a sort of bible to reference every major individual and setting in the Stephen King Universe, including notes about the various characters' current whereabouts or activities.

The implications of that are vital.

Why would you need to know the current whereabouts of Ben Mears from 'Salem's Lot? That novel is more than two decades old. Simply put, 'Salem's Lot isn't truly over yet. It exists within the Stephen King Universe, an ever-changing fictional landscape that is constantly being altered because it is all of a piece, for, as noted, King has created—with a large portion of his audience not realizing it at the time of publication—an entire multiverse, a fully realized cosmology wherein every story and book is *somehow connected to every other story and book by the author.*

It's easy to make these connections once you start to look for them. Let's take a brief tour through the Stephen King Universe to demonstrate. The city of Derry, Maine, is an important hub of the SKU. Derry is mentioned in *The Running Man*, forging a link to The Worlds of Richard Bachman. Dick Halloran of *The Shining* passed through Derry during his stint in the U.S. Army. Derry is also home to It, whose presence is felt in *The Tommyknockers*, and to Mike Noonan, the main character of *Bag of Bones*, a book that also features Norris Ridgewick, formerly of the Castle Rock Police Department. Another resident of Derry is young Patrick Danville from *Insomnia*, who plays an integral part in the action of *The Dark Tower VII*. And yet another key character featured in DT VII—Father Donald Callahan—first appeared in *'Salem's Lot*. There are dozens upon dozens of subtle (and sometimes not so subtle) connections within King's work, but that is still only the tip of the iceberg.

King has, ever since beginning the *Dark Tower* epic while in college in the 1960s, been feeding into one larger, greater narrative: that of Roland, the Gunslinger. The *Dark Tower* series is, simply put, the core of the Stephen King Universe. Works as seemingly diverse as *It* (1986), *Insomnia* (1994), *Hearts in Atlantis* (1999), *The Eyes of the Dragon* (1987), *The Stand* (1978), and *The Talisman* (1983) are all vitally and directly connected.

Not yet convinced?

Then note the following quote from the author's afterword to *The Dark Tower IV: Wizard and Glass* (1997):

> I have written enough novels and short stories to fill a solar system of the imagination, but Roland's story is my Jupiter—a planet that dwarfs all the others (at least from my own perspective), a place of strange atmosphere, crazy landscape, and savage gravitational pull. Dwarfs the others, did I say? I think there's more to it than that, actually. I am coming to understand that Roland's world (or worlds) actually *contains* all the others of my making; there is a place in Mid-World for Randall Flagg, Ralph Roberts, the wandering boys from *The Eyes of the Dragon*, even Father Callahan, the damned priest from *'Salem's Lot*.

Stephen King has been choosing sides, you see, for decades. He has been inventing (and occasionally reinventing) his heroes and villains on a cosmic scale, across time and space and dimension, painting in broad strokes the outline of a battle for the fate of the multiverse—of the Stephen King Universe itself.

Now that *The Dark Tower* has concluded, we've seen the final battle for the fate of the Stephen King Universe . . . for now. But those who have followed Roland all the way to the Tower and yet are familiar with King's other works may still be left with questions unresolved about characters and connections. We'll touch on those here as well. After all, there is no doubt that Roland and his ka-tet (the group of characters whose destiny is bound together in the *Dark Tower* series), Ralph Roberts from *Insomnia*, the kids from *It*, Dennis and Thomas from *Eyes*, Ted Brautigan of *Hearts in Atlantis*, Mike Anderson of *Storm of the Century* (1999), and the cast of *Desperation* (1996)—and so many others—are allied, albeit perhaps unwittingly, against the evil forces that also inhabit the Stephen King Universe. These include the Crimson King, Flagg, It, Tak, Leland Gaunt, Andre Linoge, and many, many others.

These theories and ideas, certainties and possibilities, the connecting of various pieces to the puzzle, are, then, the fabrics of this volume. Like no other modern author, King has crafted a massive fiction, comparable in some ways to the great universes of Marvel and DC Comics—which, of course, were the work of hundreds of storytellers. And yet, amazingly enough, the Stephen King Universe is the work of *one person*. In the Chronology, we will provide a timeline of King's own life and work. We will also provide lists of recommended further reading and preferred Web sites dealing with this bestselling author and his work. For the most part, however, our primary goal is to present both the Constant Reader and the casual fan with a comprehensive overview of the creations of one of the most important writers in American history.

In essence, *The Stephen King Universe* is a travel guide for your sojourns into the Stephen King Universe.

In any undertaking of this magnitude, some hard and practical choices must be made. (For one thing, no one involved wanted a book that would be too large to lift off a desk without injury to the reader.) It should be noted that scattered herein you will find the words "apparently," "presumably," and other similar terms. In such cases, hypotheses were necessary, as no confirmation from our subject was available.

More important, however, were our discussions about what to include or exclude, how to present the information, what length to devote to an individual work, and so on. We focused on several fundamental questions:

1. WHAT DESERVES INCLUSION?

A question we struggled with time and again. Of course, all of King's published novels as of March 2006 are included. But there are some gray areas, as follows:

- Original screenplays for *Storm of the Century*, *Golden Years* (1991), *Cat's Eye* (1985), and *Sleepwalkers* (1992) are included as individual entries. Though we have a segment on film and television adaptations, whenever appropriate, in each chapter, we considered "official" or "in continuity" with the Stephen King Universe only the original print version, where one exists. For instance, parts of *Cat's Eye* are based upon stories that had been previously published, but one segment in particular was written specially for the film. Following our methodology, the original segment would be part of the Stephen King Universe, while the adapted segments would not, as we rely instead upon the originally published versions. Thus, *Sleepwalkers* and *Storm of the Century* are part of our official continuity, because they also had never previously appeared in another form. *Golden Years* proved a special challenge in determining what we would consider "official continuity." See that chapter for further explanation.

- Conversely, in the case of *The Dark Tower: The Gunslinger*, *The Stand*, and short stories such as "Blind Willie," which reappeared some time after their initial publication in an altered form, we consider the most recent versions as being in official continuity, since they have been updated by Stephen King himself.

- The author's unpublished or most obscure works are generally not included.

- King's early, short work is included only if he deemed it significant enough to be included in one of his collections.

- Though Tabitha King's novels include references to her husband's universe, and Peter Straub cowrote *The Talisman*—making the entire works of both authors tangentially a part of the Stephen King Universe—we limited our coverage to works actually written or, as in the case of *The Talisman*, cowritten by King himself.

2. HOW SHALL WE BREAK DOWN THE DISCUSSION OF EACH BOOK?

While we certainly wanted to examine the books themselves in open-minded fashion, we also deemed it important to discuss all of the significant characters and major elements of the Stephen King Universe as if the reader were truly entering that multiverse. In this way, we hoped to provide the proper feel, texture, and setting to those entries, so that instead of just reading about a character King created, the reader would become part of the Universe, and thus be learning about and discovering a person who truly exists (or existed, given that a great many of those who have populated the Stephen King Universe have died).

[NOTE: *Since the author himself is brought into the* Dark Tower *series as a pivotal character, and some of the action takes place in the "real" world, it follows that we are all a part of the Stephen King Universe.* You *are a character of Stephen King's imagination. He may not have created you, but he has certainly coopted you.*]

We also knew we had to mention the numerous film and television adaptations of King's works, though we didn't want to lose our focus on the literary medium. Indeed, there have already been several books written on that one aspect of King's career alone, and another could easily be created with the information we gathered.

For three decades, Stephen King has been creating worlds that are enthusiastically visited by literally hundreds of millions of readers. According to *Entertainment Weekly,* he is the most significant novelist of the second half of the twentieth century. While Tom Clancy and John Grisham have challenged and briefly even surpassed his position as America's most popular author at one time or another, no writer in modern times has had the staying power of Stephen King. His accomplishments in terms of worldwide sales and motion picture and television miniseries adaptations are, to say the least, extraordinary.

So phenomenal is his stunning success, in fact, that his literary accomplishments are frequently relegated to a position of less importance due to the staggering statistics (i.e. the number of novels he's written, total number of his books in print, his personal finances and charitable activities) that accompany his every endeavor. Though many critics would disagree that he has any place in the lofty halls of Literature or Art, others have lionized him as the greatest writer of purely American fiction of his generation, comparing him to such past American masters as Mark Twain, others consider him this century's version of the nineteenth-century British novelist Charles Dickens. This dichotomy has never been more fully realized than with the controversy that arose over his selection to receive a National Book Foundation Medal for Distinguished Contribution to American Letters in 2003. There were many who looked down their noses at the very idea that such a popular writer would be so honored—some in print—but many more who said, simply, "It's about time."

There is a *great* deal more going on in the work of Stephen King—on several levels—than at first seems apparent to the casual reader. You will discover this for yourself as you turn the page . . .

[NOTE: When referring to "the author" or "the novelist" we always mean, of course, Stephen King, not the authors of this volume.]

STEPHEN KING:

A Chronology

1947

Stephen Edwin King born September 21, in Portland, Maine, at Maine General Hospital. He is the son of Donald and Nellie Ruth (Pillsbury) King. The couple had previously adopted an older son, David King, in 1945.

1949

Donald Edwin King separates from Nellie, then deserts his family and is never heard from again.

1954–1958

Stephen King begins first attempts at writing stories, inspired by the science fiction movies and books that he reads. Early movie influences include *The Creature from the Black Lagoon* (1954) and *Earth vs. the Flying Saucers* (1956).

1959–1960

Stephen King discovers a box of science fiction and horror books that had once belonged to his father. Obtains first typewriter during this period, and begins to actively submit stories to genre magazines.

1962–1966

Stephen King attends high school in Lisbon Falls, Maine. During this period, he writes his first novel-length manuscript, *The Aftermath*. He also starts work on *Getting It On*, which would later be published under a pseudonym as *Rage* (1977).

1965

Stephen King publishes his first short story, "I Was a Teenage Graverobber," in *Comics Review*, a fanzine.

1966–1970

Stephen King attends the University of Maine at Orono, graduating with a B.S. in English. He writes a regular column for the university newspaper entitled "King's Garbage Truck."

While working at the university library, he meets Tabitha Jane Spruce (b. 1949), an aspiring poet and short story writer.

Makes his first professional sale in 1967, with the story "The Glass Floor" in the pulp magazine *Startling Mystery Stories*.

Completes two novel-length manuscripts, *The Long Walk* and *Sword in the Darkness*. *The Long Walk* would later be published as a Richard Bachman title, while *Sword in the Darkness* would never see print.

Stephen King begins making sales of his short fiction to various men's magazines, most notably to *Cavalier*.

1971

Stephen King marries Tabitha Spruce.

1971–1973

Stephen King teaches high school English at Hampden Academy in Hampden, Maine.

Completes early novel *Getting It On*, but is unable to sell it. Writes *The Running Man* over the course of a long weekend, but is unable to sell it. Begins work on a short story called "Carrie," which his wife encourages him to complete as a short novel.

1973

Sells *Carrie* to Doubleday and Co. publishers for a hardcover advance of $2,500.

Stephen King's mother, Nellie Ruth King, dies of cancer before the publication of *Carrie*.

1974

Writes *Roadwork*, which will later see print as a Richard Bachman book.

Carrie is published in hardcover by Doubleday. Paperback rights are sold for $400,000. King receives half, the other half going to Doubleday.

1975
'Salem's Lot is published by Doubleday.

1976
The movie version of *Carrie*, directed by Brian De Palma, is released by United Artists and becomes a surprise summer hit. The movie tie-in paperback edition of the novel becomes a bestseller.

1977
The Shining is published by Doubleday. On only his third published novel, the dust jacket copy proclaims Stephen King "the undisputed master of the modern horror story."

The first "Richard Bachman" novel, *Rage*, is published by New American Library, Stephen King's paperback publisher, as a mass-market paperback original.

King travels with his family to England for an aborted yearlong stay. There he begins a lifelong friendship with horror and suspense novelist Peter Straub, with whom he would later collaborate on *The Talisman* (1984) and *Black House* (2001).

1978
His first collection of short stories, *Night Shift*, is published by Doubleday.

The first version of *The Stand* is published by Doubleday. The "complete and uncut" edition would not appear until 1990.

Stephen King serves as writer-in-residence and instructor at the University of Maine at Orono.

1979
King attends the Fifth World Fantasy Convention in Providence, Rhode Island, as a Guest of Honor.

The Dead Zone is published by Viking Press after a contract dispute with Doubleday; it becomes his first book to rise to the number-one position on the *New York Times* bestseller list.

'Salem's Lot, directed by Tobe Hooper, is adapted as a miniseries for network television on CBS.

The second "Richard Bachman" novel, *The Long Walk*, is released by New American Library without fanfare as a paperback original.

1980

Firestarter is published by Viking Press.

The Shining, directed and adapted by filmmaker Stanley Kubrick, is released by Warner Brothers Studios.

1981

Danse Macabre, a nonfiction study of horror in the mass media, is published by Everest House.

Cujo is published by Viking Press.

Roadwork, the third "Richard Bachman" novel, is published in paperback by New American Library.

Receives Career Alumni Award from the University of Maine.

1982

Different Seasons, a collection of original novellas, is published by Viking Press.

The Dark Tower: The Gunslinger is published in a limited run by Donald M. Grant, Publisher. It becomes an instant collector's item.

Creepshow, a collection of graphic stories done in the style of the infamous E.C. Comics of the 1950s, is published by New American Library.

The Running Man, the fourth "Richard Bachman" novel, is published by New American Library as a mass market paperback original.

Creepshow is released as a motion picture by Warner Brothers Studios; directed by George A. Romero, it is the first produced screenplay by Stephen King from previously published short stories.

1983

Christine is published by Viking Press.

Pet Sematary is published by Doubleday.

Cycle of the Werewolf is released by Land of Enchantment, a specialty press, in a limited edition.

The Dead Zone, directed by David Cronenberg, is released as a motion picture by Paramount Studios.

Cujo, directed by Lewis Teague, is released as a motion picture by the Taft Entertainment Company.

Christine, directed by John Carpenter, is released as a motion picture by Columbia Pictures.

1984

The Talisman, coauthored with Peter Straub, is published jointly by Viking and G. P. Putnam's Sons.

The Eyes of the Dragon is self-published by Stephen King's own Philtrum Press.

Thinner, the fifth "Richard Bachman" novel, is published by New American Library, but this time in an original hardcover edition heavily promoted at the American Booksellers Association convention.

Children of the Corn, directed by Fritz Kiersch and based on the short story of the same name, is released as by New World Pictures. A series of loosely related sequels would follow.

Firestarter, directed by Mark L. Lester, is released as a motion picture by Universal Pictures.

1985

After years of successfully denying it, Stephen King admits in a local newspaper report to using the pseudonym Richard Bachman.

King writes and directs the feature *Maximum Overdrive*, based on his short story "Trucks," for Dino De Laurentiis in Wilmington, North Carolina.

Cat's Eye, directed by Lewis Teague, is released as a motion picture by MGM/UA; it is the second produced screenplay by Stephen King.

Skeleton Crew, his second major collection of short stories, is published by G. P. Putnam's Sons.

The Bachman Books, an omnibus collection of the first four Richard Bachman titles, is published by New American Library in simultaneous hardcover and trade paperback editions.

Silver Bullet, directed by Daniel Attias and based on the book *Cycle of the Werewolf*, is released as a motion picture by Columbia-EMI-Warner, for which Stephen King also wrote the screenplay.

1986

It is published by Viking Press.

Maximum Overdrive, the first movie both written and directed by Stephen King, is released by De Laurentiis Entertainment Group.

Stand by Me, directed by Rob Reiner and based on the novella "The Body," is released as a motion picture by Columbia Pictures.

1987

Misery is published by Viking Press.

The Eyes of the Dragon (revised version) is published by Viking Press.

The Tommyknockers is published by Viking Press.

Creepshow 2, directed by Michael Gornick, with a screenplay by

George A. Romero, is released as a motion picture by New World Pictures.

The Dark Tower II: The Drawing of the Three is published by Donald M. Grant, Publisher.

King writes an original teleplay called "Sorry, Right Number" for George A. Romero's syndicated television series *Tales From the Darkside*.

The Running Man, directed by Paul Michael Glaser, is released as a motion picture by Taft Entertainment Pictures. Credits read "based on the novel by Richard Bachman."

1988

Nightmares in the Sky, a collection of photographs by "f-stop fitzgerald" to which Stephen King includes only the introductory text, is published by Viking Press.

Carrie is transformed into a Broadway musical, opening at the Virginia Theater. It closes after only five regular performances.

1989

The Dark Half is published by Viking Press.

Pet Sematary, directed by Mary Lambert, is released as a motion picture by Paramount Pictures, with a screenplay by Stephen King.

1990

The Stand (complete version) is published by Doubleday.

Four Past Midnight, a collection of original novellas, is published by Viking Press.

Misery, directed by Rob Reiner, is released as a motion picture by Castle Rock Entertainment.

Stephen King's Graveyard Shift, a feature film directed by Ralph S. Singleton, based on the short story of the same name, is released by Columbia Tri-Star.

Stephen King's It, directed by Tommy Lee Wallace, airs on ABC as a television miniseries.

1991

Needful Things is published by Viking Press.

The Dark Half is released as a motion picture by Orion Pictures, adapted and directed by George A. Romero.

Stephen King's Golden Years airs on television as a seven-part series on CBS, with most of the episodes written by King.

Sometimes They Come Back, based on the short story of the same name, airs as a made-for-television feature on CBS network, directed by Tom McLoughlin.

The Dark Tower III: The Waste Lands is published by Donald M. Grant, Publisher.

1992

Gerald's Game is published by Viking Press.

Stephen King performs with his celebrity author rock band, the Rock Bottom Remainders, at the American Booksellers Association convention in Anaheim, California.

Stephen King's Sleepwalkers, with an original screenplay by Stephen King, directed by Mick Garris, is released as a motion picture by Columbia Pictures.

The Lawnmower Man, directed by Brett Leonard, is released as a motion picture by New Line Cinema. It bears so little resemblance to King's story that the author successfully sues to have his name removed from the title.

1993

Nightmares & Dreamscapes, his third major collection of short stories, is published by Viking Press.

Dolores Claiborne is published by Viking Press.

Needful Things, directed by Fraser Heston, is released as a motion picture by Columbia Pictures.

Stephen King's The Tommyknockers, directed by John Power, airs as a miniseries for ABC.

1994

Stephen King's The Stand airs as a miniseries for ABC, with a teleplay by Stephen King, directed by Mick Garris.

Insomnia is published by Viking Press.

The Shawshank Redemption, directed by Frank Darabont, is released as a motion picture by Columbia Pictures, based on the novella "Rita Hayworth and the Shawshank Redemption," which originally appeared in *Different Seasons*.

1995

Rose Madder is published by Viking Press.

The Mangler, directed by Tobe Hopper and based on the short story of the same name, is released as a motion picture by New Line Cinema.

Dolores Claiborne, directed by Taylor Hackford, is released by Columbia Pictures; it stars Kathy Bates, who had previously won an Academy Award for her performance in *Misery*.

Stephen King's The Langoliers, directed by Tom Holland and based on the novella that appeared in *Four Past Midnight*, airs as a miniseries on ABC.

1996

Desperation is published by Viking Press.

The Regulators (as by "Richard Bachman") is published simultaneously with *Desperation* by Dutton.

"The Man in the Black Suit" is given First Prize status in *Prize Stories 1996: The O. Henry Awards*, edited by William Abrahams. In its original magazine appearance in 1994, it won a World Fantasy Award.

Thinner, directed by Tom Holland, is released as a motion picture by Paramount Pictures.

Pet Sematary 2, directed by Mary Lambert, is released as a motion picture by Paramount Pictures.

1997

The Dark Tower IV: Wizard and Glass is published by Donald M. Grant, Publisher.

Quicksilver Highway, an anthology movie directed by Mick Garris that includes "Chattery Teeth," is broadcast as an original television feature on Fox.

Six Stories is published in a limited edition by Stephen King's own Philtrum Press.

Trucks, based on the story of the same name, directed by Chris Thomson, is broadcast as an original television feature on USA Network.

Stephen King's The Shining, directed by Mick Garris, airs on ABC as a miniseries, with a teleplay by Stephen King.

1998

Stephen King's The Night Flier, directed by Mark Pavia, which had premiered on HBO, is briefly released as a theatrical motion picture by New Line Cinema.

Storm of the Century, the script for "an original novel for television," is published by Pocket Books.

Storm of the Century, an original miniseries directed by Craig Baxley, airs on ABC, with a teleplay by Stephen King.

Stephen King writes an original teleplay (subsequently rewritten by Chris Carter) for Fox's *The X-Files*.

Apt Pupil, directed by Bryan Singer, based on the novella that originally appeared in *Different Seasons*, is released as a motion picture by Paramount Pictures.

Bag of Bones is published by Scribner.

1999

The Girl Who Loved Tom Gordon is published by Scribner.

The Rage: Carrie 2, directed by Katt Shea, is released as a motion picture by United Artists.

Hearts in Atlantis is published by Scribner.

On June 19, King is seriously injured in an automobile accident near Center Lovell, Maine, from which it will take him many months to recover.

Blood and Smoke, a collection of three stories, is published exclusively as an audio book by Scribner.

The Green Mile, directed and adapted by Frank Darabont, is released as a motion picture by Warner Bros. It is nominated for several Academy Awards.

2000

"Riding the Bullet," a never-before-published tale, is sold by King on the Internet, bypassing the use of "traditional" publishing methods, though in conjunction with a traditional publisher, Simon & Schuster.

The Plant, an epistolary novel in progress, is sold by King on the Internet, one section at a time, while it is being written. This time, King publishes online himself, without the intercession of a traditional publisher.

On Writing: A Memoir of the Craft, a nonfiction work, is published by Scribner.

2001

The Girl Who Loved Tom Gordon, adapted and directed by George A. Romero, goes into production as a motion picture.

Black House, the sequel to *The Talisman*, again written in collaboration with Peter Straub, is published by Random House.

2002

The miniseries *Rose Red* appears on ABC.

The miniseries *Firestarter: Rekindled* appears on the Sci Fi Channel.

The Dead Zone television series premieres on USA.

The television remake of *Carrie* premieres on NBC.

From a Buick 8 is published by Scribner.

Everything's Eventual: 14 Dark Tales is published by Scribner.

2003

The "revised and expanded" edition of *The Gunslinger*, subtitled *The Dark Tower I*, is published by Viking.

The Dark Tower V: Wolves of the Calla is published by Donald M. Grant, Publisher.

King begins a semiregular column appearing on the back page of *Entertainment Weekly* called *"The Pop of King."*

2004

The miniseries *Kingdom Hospital* appears on ABC.

The Dark Tower VI: Song of Susannah is published by Donald M. Grant, Publisher.

The Dark Tower VII: The Dark Tower is published by Donald M. Grant, Publisher.

A new television adaptation of *'Salem's Lot* appears on TNT.

The movie version of *Riding the Bullet*, adapted and directed by Mick Garris, premieres.

A pop-up version of *The Girl Who Loved Tom Gordon*, based on the novel by King, with text adaptation by Peter Abrahams, illustrations by Alan Dingman, and paper engineering by Kees Moerbeek, is published by Little Simon, a division of Simon and Schuster.

Faithful: Two Diehard Boston Red Sox Fans Chronicle the Historic 2004 Season, cowritten by Stewart O'Nan and Stephen King, is published by Scribner.

Secret Window, starring Johnny Depp and John Turturro, adapted and directed by David Koepp, premieres. It is based on the short story "Secret Window, Secret Garden."

2005

Winterfall LLC, creator of the celebrated *Hard Case Crime* line of pulp-style paperback crime novels, announces in February that a new book by Stephen King called *The Colorado Kid* will be the lead title of the line's second year. The book is scheduled to appear in October 2005.

Desperation, a TV miniseries adapted and directed by Mick Garris, is scheduled to appear on ABC in 2006.

SECTION ONE

The Worlds of
The Dark Tower
and *The Stand*

he *Dark Tower* series is the core of the Stephen King Universe, and the axis upon which our entire thesis for this book rotates. Though the majority of the author's work takes place in the parallel reality dimension that contains King's fictional towns Castle Rock, Derry, and others, the parallel reality of Roland the Gunslinger—and by extension that of *The Stand*—is much more fundamental.

Just as, in the series itself, The Dark Tower is the point of time, space, and reality where all dimensions meet, the spindle of creation, so are most of King's works then an outcropping of the *Dark Tower* series, which was conceived as early as 1970. Nearly all of King's heroes and all of his villains, scattered across the various parallel realities, are involved in a single cosmic conflict, with the Tower as the ultimate prize.

Although Stephen King worked on the *Dark Tower* series for three decades, consciously and unconsciously weaving it in and out of his other writings, a great many of his readers are likely to have missed its prominence. Just as the Tower itself binds all realities together, this series of stories and concepts is the center of the Stephen King Universe, the many fictional worlds he has created.

And it all started with a poem.

King read Robert Browning's "Childe Roland to the Dark Tower Came" (1855) for a class assignment in his sophomore year (1967/68) at the University of Maine at Orono. In March of 1970, the year he graduated, he began the first novel in the series, *The Gunslinger*. He continued to work on that novel over the course of the next twelve years, even while he was writing some of his best-loved works, including *'Salem's Lot* (1975), *The Shining* (1977), and *The Stand* (1978).

Did he realize, then, at the start of the process, that it would be all of a piece, all bits of a single story? Perhaps. Perhaps not.

But it is. In the fourth volume, *Wizard and Glass* (1997), he at last came to that conclusion. In the afterword, he states:

> I have written enough novels and short stories to fill a solar system of the imagination, but Roland's story is my Jupiter—a planet that dwarfs all the others . . . I am coming to understand that Roland's world (or worlds) actually *contains* all the others of my making; there is a place in Mid-World for Randall Flagg, Ralph Roberts, the wandering boys from *The Eyes of the Dragon*, even Father Callahan, the damned priest from *'Salem's Lot*.

In the latter volumes, the truth of this collision of worlds becomes incarnate, as characters from *'Salem's Lot*, *Hearts in Atlantis*, and others all enter into the saga as significant characters, all from different worlds, and as Stephen King himself is drawn into the series as a character, the author a part of his own magnum opus. It is all of a piece.

Herein, we shall discuss the books in this series and those related to it, how they are interrelated and interconnected, and how they touch upon and are likewise touched upon by other of the author's works.

The history of the *Dark Tower* series is this:

In a place called Mid-World—which might be the future of a world much like our own, or a separate reality entirely—the land is divided into Baronies, some ruled by an honorable rank of men called gunslingers, much like knights. One of the jewels of Mid-world is Gilead, whose lord is Steven Deschain, a gunslinger descended from the bloodline of Arthur Eld, who had united much of Mid-world in ancient times (King Arthur, of course).

But during Steven's time, a new threat arises. John Farson, called "the good man," has begun to incite a rebellion among the peasantry and even some nobility against the Affiliation, the governments of the various Baronies that have banded together. Traitors and spies abound. Marten, a wizard advisor of Steven's, seduces the lord's wife and flaunts that intimacy in front of Steven's son, Roland, a gunslinger-in-training. (In order to become gunslingers, the young students have to best their teacher in battle.) Marten hopes to force Roland to an early test against his teacher so that he will fail, and be killed or banished from Gilead.

Marten's scheme works, but only partially, for Roland does best his instructor in single combat.

Roland is shocked to find that his father is aware of Marten's machinations, and Steven prevents him from going after Marten. He tells his son that Marten is working with Farson (though in fact Marten will eventually be revealed to BE Farson), and in order for him to be certain Roland is safe, Steven sends his offspring incognito to a seaside Barony called Mejis, along with his two best friends—Cuthbert and Alain—neither of whom are full gunslingers yet.

In Mejis, however, they find that Farson's plans have stretched even further, and the local authorities are in league with the rebellion. It is evident that Farson, though pretending to be the hero of the people, has had sinister intentions all along. Soon enough, a dark magician called Walter shows up in Mejis; the mage apparently works for both Farson and Marten. Once again, however, it seems this creature has many faces, and is in fact yet another facet of the same man. Walter is Farson and Farson is Marten, all one and the same. There are many other faces to this being, whom we may alternately refer to as "Flagg" or "Legion."

Roland falls in love with Susan Delgado in Mejis, and though their love is doomed (as is Susan), it will be the one real love of his life. During his time by the sea, Roland comes into possession of a glass ball, a powerful magical tool that is part of Maerlyn's Rainbow. In it, he sees a vision of the future, much of which he cannot remember later. One thing remains clear to him: the Dark Tower at the center of all things, the spindle upon which reality turns, has been somehow tainted. It is being corrupted, and Roland decides instantly that he must devote his life to a quest to save the Tower.

Before he may do that, however, he returns to Gilead, where he is tricked by a witch into killing his own mother. The time subsequent to that is shrouded in mystery. All that is known is this: Farson's efforts cause the destruction of the Affiliation and the devastation of Gilead, which only hastens the changes that are coming to the entire world. The world, as Roland says so often, is moving on. It is ending, growing barren and empty. The only way to stop that is to save the Tower, and so Roland and his friends set off on a quest to find it. During that mission, all of his associates, his *ka-tet*, die, until only he remains.

Many years later, he catches up with Walter, the man in black, and learns a little about the true nature of the Tower. Thereafter, he begins gathering a new *ka-tet* from various worlds connected to his own: Eddie and Susannah Dean and Jake Chambers become gunslingers in their own right over the course of the quest.

The new *ka-tet* faces many adventures and hardships during their time together. They cross over from one world to another and then back, through thin places between those worlds. In the New York City that Jake is from there is a rose that is the physical embodiment of the Tower before it became tainted. The agents of chaos, or of the Beast that now guards the Tower, the Crimson King, want it destroyed; Roland and the others will have to save it.

They meet Flagg on their journey, and it is revealed that he is also Marten (Walter/Farson/Legion), who serves the Crimson King. As noted, the specific chronicle of Roland is the centerpiece, but a great many of King's other works have direct or indirect ties to it. Flagg originally appeared in King's landmark novel *The Stand*, still widely considered to be among his best. In that book, a U.S. military research facility investigating biowarfare accidentally unleashes a virus that kills 99.4% of the population of the Earth. In America, the survivors are plagued with dreams of a kindly old woman serving the side of light, and a dark man with blazing red eyes who serves the cause of darkness. This is Flagg. Over the course of the novel, the survivors join one side or the other, and eventually those serving light must make a final stand against those serving darkness. Flagg is defeated, and society and civilization begin again.

At the time of *The Stand*'s publication, Flagg's part in Roland's story was unclear. In fact, the next time Flagg appeared as a major figure was in *The Eyes of the Dragon* (1987). In that fairy-tale-like story, Flagg is a wizard serving a king in a medieval landscape filled with magick, a land that seems somewhat similar to but not necessarily the same as that of Roland the Gunslinger. (Flagg was noted to have returned to that particular city many times over the ages.) The heroes of that tale eventually defeat Flagg but he escapes, prompting two of them, Thomas and Dennis, to go on a hero's quest to destroy the wizard. That is a story as yet untold.

In the novella "The Little Sisters of Eluria," King clearly connects Roland's world with that of *The Eyes of the Dragon*, unmistakably making them one and the same. In *The Dark Tower IV*, Roland and his *ka-tet* pass through a parallel dimension that is clearly that of *The Stand*, just before they finally meet Flagg face to face.

A major theme of the *Dark Tower* series is that due to the machinations of The Crimson King, the "beams" of power that emanate from the Tower and hold all time, space, and reality together are being broken down and corrupted. This phenomenon has affected all of those realities, causing the barriers between them to begin breaking down and allowing for some travel from one to the next.

Consider these few examples:

- In *Insomnia* (1994), a young boy has a vision of Roland, and the main characters find themselves up against the Crimson King. They save the life of that boy, who is going to be vital to Roland's battle against the Crimson King. If Patrick Danville dies, the Tower will fall. Thus, Ralph and Lois and Patrick Danville are allied with Roland against the forces of chaos represented by the Crimson King and Flagg, among many others.

- Roland recalls having met Dennis and Thomas, from *The Eyes of the Dragon*, who are on a mission to destroy Flagg.

- Father Callahan, of *'Salem's Lot*, plays a major role in the final three volumes of the *Dark Tower* series, though Callahan is from a world that is clearly not that of the series.

- In *It* (1986), there is a great deal of discussion about the Turtle (a benevolent being in opposition to the Crimson King), a clear reference to Roland's saga.

- In *Hearts in Atlantis*, it is revealed that the Crimson King employs humans with psychic abilities as "breakers," forcing them to use their mental powers to aid in the shattering of the Beams that bind the worlds together, the center of which is the Dark Tower. Once the Beams are shattered, the Tower would come completely into the Crimson King's control and he would then be able to manipulate all realities to his liking.

- Also in *Hearts in Atlantis*, there is a very oblique reference (see "*Hearts in Atlantis*") that indicates that Randall Flagg himself is interfering in the lives of the characters in the book. His purpose is unclear, but is likely related to their relationship to the "Breaker" they meet early in the story. It seems likely that the protagonists of the book may also find themselves allied with Roland and his comrades in the final battle.

- In *Rose Madder* (1995), the world that exists inside the painting seems likely to be Roland's world, as there are references to the City of Lud.

- In *Black House* (2001), the sequel to 1983's *The Talisman* (both co-authored with Peter Straub), Jack Sawyer runs afoul of Breakers and the Crimson King.

All of this reinforces the idea that all beings in the various parallel realities of the Stephen King Universe—his main protagonists and antagonists in particular—are involved in one enormous struggle for the fate of the Dark Tower. Within the Dark Tower series, King introduces the idea that the Beams have cosmic guardians whose avatars are animal in nature, including "the Turtle," a cosmic being who actually plays a part in *It*. In another form, the lingering power of the Turtle plays a vital role in the final arc of the series.

With all of the connections above in place, one might then move further out into King's works, making the links to the various stories set in Castle Rock, Derry, and Haven. Take, for instance, *The Tommyknockers* (1987). With references to John Smith of *The Dead Zone* (1979), it is tied to all of the Castle Rock books and stories. With mentions of Derry, it is linked to *It* and *Insomnia*, and therefore to the *Dark Tower* saga. There are more associations, but the foregoing simply serves to illustrate that all of King's stories are indeed of a piece, and that the *Dark Tower* series, as noted, is the center. These heroes and villains—almost all of King's central characters—are merely soldiers and pawns, or at the very least innocent bystanders, in the grand battle to determine the ultimate fate of the Tower.

What follows is a guide to each individual work in the corner of the Stephen King Universe that contains the parallel realities of the *Dark Tower* series and *The Stand*. Each segment includes a discussion of the work in question and a guide to the key characters, as well as places or items, where appropriate.

1

THE DARK TOWER: THE GUNSLINGER

(1982)

**revised edition (2003)

The man in black fled across the desert, and the gunslinger followed."

So begins Stephen King's longest work. Not *The Gunslinger* itself, but *The Dark Tower*, the series of which this novel is merely the first installment.

It is within the pages of this first installment, however, that the many threads of the Stephen King Universe begin to be drawn together. The quest of Roland—whose journey and epic significance to his world give him numerous opportunities to explore other parallel universes, traveling through space and time—mirrors our own quest to understand the Stephen King Universe as a whole.

As the story goes—becoming its own sort of myth, in a way—King began the saga of Roland the gunslinger in March 1970, and continued to return to it when the tale called to him over the course of the ensuing twelve years. It was inspired by Robert Browning's epic romantic poem, "Childe Roland" (1855), which was in itself inspired by the legends surrounding the August 15, 778, death of the real-life Count Roland, nephew of Charlemagne.

The Gunslinger is comprised of five long chapters, all of which were published in *The Magazine of Fantasy & Science Fiction* between 1978 and 1981. The story defies genre classification, melding horror, fantasy, science fiction and mystery together into what King designed to be a sort of romantic epic, but which became far more.

Roland's world may once have been similar to our own, but what civilization there once was has been all but forgotten. The old society, crumbled so long ago that it is little more than myth, was then replaced by a feudal system reminiscent of mythical England before Arthur brought unity to that land. The equivalent of the King Arthur myth in our world is the tale of a man called Arthur Eld in Roland's. Roland is the last surviving descendant of Arthur Eld.

In the time of Roland's youth, the land of Mid-World was organized into a collection of Baronies called the Affiliation, but we learn that all of that has passed on; the world is deteriorating rapidly, and much of what remains is barren wasteland. Time and space have little meaning, making compasses useless. Roland has lived for an indeterminate period of time, and while not immortal, it seems now that with the slippage of time, age means little.

As a hero, Roland is perhaps King's most single-minded, implacable creation. When we first meet him, he has long since lost everything that ever meant anything to him. The world, as we are reminded time and again, has moved on (though it will be some time in the series before King begins to explain precisely what that means). Roland pursues the sinister man in black, a wizard called Walter, not merely to punish him for his offenses, but to discover more about the Tower itself. The Tower is revealed to be the cornerstone of all existence, holding the meaning to life and the universe (or the multiverse). Roland hopes that at the Tower, he will find . . . what, exactly? Answers? Enlightenment? An odd thing, really, for such a single-minded hero to seek enlightenment, for one so stolid and hardened to search for the secrets of the universe.

Yet that is what we have here. King doesn't let Roland dwell too much on the metaphysical nature of his quest, but it's there just the same.

And Roland is effective. It is only logical to extrapolate from the dialogue between Roland and Walter at the end of *The Gunslinger* that a powerful entity has recognized in Roland the potential to do precisely what he plans. Interestingly enough, however, the force does not appear determined to stop him. And why should it? Nothing can interfere with *ka*, the word, in Roland's world, for destiny.

There is more to Roland than even he knows.

As the narrative evolves, Roland must struggle with the focus and callousness he was taught as a gunslinger, as well as his great capacity for love, a part of him that he regularly denies. Still, he places his quest above all else, even at the cost of the life of the boy, Jake Chambers.

But Roland is a product of his world, a place that had already "moved on" (begun to deteriorate, suffering greatly from natural—or perhaps forced—entropy) when he was a boy, but now has broken down even further. It seems that all that is good and noble has gone out of the world. Just as another modern version of the romantic epic hero, Luke Skywalker of *Star Wars*, is the last of the Jedi Knights, so is Roland the last of the gunslingers, until, like Skywalker, he himself searches out, discovers, and begins to train more.

King's boyhood home, Durham   DAVID LOWELL

But while George Lucas's creations take the stage a long time ago in a galaxy far, far away, King's characters feel much closer to home. There are startling similarities between Roland's world and what we'll call the Prime Reality, in which novels such as *The Shining* (1977) and *'Salem's Lot* (1975) take place. Some time in the past—as evidenced by old songs and artifacts and the words of Walter—Roland's world was almost identical to the Prime Reality of the Stephen King Universe, the one that includes Castle Rock and Derry.

PRIMARY SUBJECTS

ROLAND: A member of the warrior caste called gunslingers, Roland is the son of Gabrielle and Steven, the rulers of Gilead, the Barony where Roland grew up. Gilead was the shining star in the Affiliation, a group of baronies that made up the core of Mid-World civilization. Thanks to the machinations of the sorcerer Marten (a.k.a. Walter, a.k.a. the man in black), the Affiliation was shattered and civilization crumbled. The world moved on, suffering the predations and deterioration of entropy. The gunslingers died off or were killed. Roland is the last of them.

Roland's quest, at first, is twofold: first, to find the man in black and have vengeance upon him for his evil doings, and second, to journey to the Dark Tower, and there find the answers to the questions of the universe, including the very nature of reality itself. His quest to find the Tower is not merely for curiosity's sake, however. He believes it to be his destiny—his *ka*—and also believes that the universe is unraveling because of some malevolent force gnawing at the Tower and at the Beams that bind all of reality together, and that this must be stopped.

During this journey, Roland meets Jake Chambers for the first time. Jake is one key to the evolution Roland must undergo on his journey, but when he is faced with the choice of letting the boy die or losing the trail of the man in black, he chooses to pursue his quarry, and Jake dies. For now.

Later, Roland spends ten years entranced by the man in black on a mountaintop, after Walter has told his fortune. Roland's quest, though he has already been at it for a very long time, is merely beginning.

WALTER/MARTEN/FLAGG: Also known as Walter O'Dim and the man in black. Though we are not yet aware of it, Walter is merely one face for a being we refer to (as King has referred to him) as Legion. He is also Marten Broadcloak and Randall Flagg, among others.

Walter is a powerful sorcerer who manipulates and topples rulers, spreads his influence, and perpetuates evil in the service of a Master we are not yet familiar with. Walter manipulates Roland's life and leads him on a chase across the desert and to the mountains, where he reads Roland's fortune and gives him a psychic vision revealing the true nature of the secrets within the Tower, before apparently dying himself, having served his purpose.

As Marten, he was a sorcerer and enchanter who manipulated Roland's father, Steven, and seduced the man's wife, a series of events that led to the ruin of Gilead. As Flagg, he has performed many heinous deeds throughout the multiverse.

THE CRIMSON KING: Though we see very little of the Crimson King at the outset of Roland's tale, it is implied that he is the gunslinger's true enemy, and all others merely his servants.

JAKE CHAMBERS: Jake is not from Roland's reality, but rather, some other dimension. After he is murdered by being pushed in front of a car in his own reality, he is somehow transported to Roland's world, where he briefly joins Roland on his quest. When Roland is forced to choose between catching the man in black or letting Jake fall to his death, however, Roland lets the boy die.

Jake will return, though, for he has a continuing role to play in the journey of the gunslinger.

STEVEN DESCHAIN: Father to Roland, husband to Gabrielle, lord of Gilead, he is betrayed by his wife and his confidant, Marten. It costs him his life.

CORT: Cort is the instructor who teaches the boys of Gilead everything they need to know to become gunslingers. He teaches them how to use their weapons, as well as hand-to-hand combat and strategy. In order to "graduate," a gunslinger must defeat Cort in brutal single combat. If the young man cannot defeat his teacher, he is banished from Gilead. Roland becomes the youngest gunslinger ever to defeat his teacher.

CUTHBERT: During their youth, Cuthbert was Roland's best friend. In time, he became a gunslinger. Cuthbert was part of Roland's original *ka-tet* and would one day become a casualty of his quest for the Tower.

DAVID: In order to defeat Cort and take his place among the ranks of gunslingers, Roland must choose a single weapon. He selects his falcon, David.

GABRIELLE: Roland's mother, Gabrielle, is wife to the ruler of Gilead. She betrays her husband by sleeping with Marten, the enchanter. She is later accidentally killed by her own son.

HAX: A cook in the service of Roland's father, he turns out to be a traitor, and is hanged by the Gilead authorities. Roland attends the execution.

SUSAN: The one girl Roland ever loved, Susan was a part of his life many years ago. She was burned to death in Mejis, a tragedy of which we shall learn more in subsequent volumes.

THE TOWER: The Tower is the axis upon which all time and space, all of reality, spins, and from which the Beams that bind reality together, just like spokes from a wheel, emanate. It is Order placed upon the necessary and infinite Chaos of the multiverse. Within the physical existence of the Tower lies all the knowledge, magickal and otherwise, in existence. Roland is determined to find it.

THE DARK TOWER:
THE GUNSLINGER: TRIVIA

- *The Gunslinger* was originally published in a limited hardcover edition of ten thousand copies. Perhaps because King deemed it so very different from his other work, years passed before it became available to the general public in any other edition.

- The revised edition of *The Gunslinger* was published in 2003. In addition to adding length and texture to the original, King altered and clarified certain story elements, providing fresh hints regarding the overall mythology of the series.

2

THE DARK TOWER II: THE DRAWING OF THE THREE

(1987)

In the first volume of the *Dark Tower* series, 1982's *The Gunslinger*, Stephen King introduced his loyal readership to Roland of Gilead. At the time of its release, initially only a limited edition, the first book was an oddity, a fantasy novel with a western motif by the acknowledged master of horror. Even five years later, when this second volume was released, also only in a limited edition, readers were unaware that King had embarked upon the greatest literary journey of his career.

In the comparatively brief first volume, *The Gunslinger*, we are introduced to Roland as he travels across the desert in pursuit of "the man in black," who turns out to be a wizard named Walter. Walter had a part in the destruction of the entire civilization Roland had known throughout his life, including the society and nobility of the barony of Gilead, of which Roland's father was lord. The gunslinger set out after that destruction on a quest to find the Dark Tower, which others insist is only a myth but that Roland believes is not only real, but holds the secrets of the universe. At the Tower he believes he will find an explanation for the manner in which his world has fallen apart or "moved on," as he so often thinks of it.

Believing that Walter can offer information about the Tower, and in an effort to have revenge upon the wizard, he tracks the man in black and finally confronts him. Walter did provide certain information about the Tower, though all of it vague, and told Roland's fortune, again vaguely, before dying. At the end of that premiere installment, Roland was still on his quest.

King's West Broadway mansion in Bangor   VINTAGE POSTCARD

The Drawing of the Three was first released in 1987 in a limited edition from Donald M. Grant, Publisher—which has published the hardcover editions of each of the books in the series—and in 1989 in a trade paperback version from Plume Books. While *The Gunslinger* introduced us to Roland, his quest, and the basic concepts of his world, this second volume does not really advance him along his journey very much. Rather, it spends its time doing precisely what the title implies, drawing together his team, in the same way that bands of adventurers have gathered around heroes throughout myth and popular fiction. They are Robin Hood's Merry Men. They are the apostles. They are the X-Men.

They are *ka-tet.*

For that is what *The Drawing of the Three* is really about, though we, as readers, don't quite understand it early on. In Roland's world, *ka-tet* means a great many things, one of which is family. It can be a group of people—usually without actual blood relationships—bound together by duty, obligation, love, and common objectives. But in many ways, it is even more vital and real than family, because there are other definitions of *ka-tet*. More than those aforementioned values, it is a group of people bound together by destiny. Fate has inextricably linked them together, for better or worse. This may define an alliance, or it may explain the hatred of sworn enemies—they are destined to oppose one another until one falls.

In this case, however, we are speaking of the former.

Over the course of this volume, Roland travels from his reality (or dimension) into others through mystical portals that appear inexplicably on the beach, placed there by some unknowable universal force (referred to later in the series as "the White") that is attempting to help him. By way of these portals, he enters the minds of individuals in other worlds, and can assert control over them physically. He is even able to bring things back from those worlds. Things . . . and people.

He visits three variant realities in this fashion—or, quite possibly, simply three different time periods of the same reality. During these trips, Roland abruptly abducts two people who will in time become part of the new order of gunslingers, part of his new *ka-tet*.

Eddie Dean comes from a New York City in 1987. Odetta Holmes, a legless woman with multiple personality syndrome, comes from a New York in 1963. The third person drawn, as per the title, is apparently Susannah, Odetta's other personality.

Roland visits a third reality, however. There he jumps into the mind of a murderer named Jack *Mort*—which of course means "death"—mentally inhabiting his body just as he did Eddie's and Odetta's before drawing them through. Mort thinks of himself as "the pusher." But it isn't drugs he pushes, it's people.

In fact—and here is the kind of thing that in the world of *The Dark Tower* cannot be coincidence—Mort is responsible for the injury that caused Odetta's multiple personalities to develop, as well as a second incident that led to the loss of her legs. Further, Mort is responsible for the death of Jake Chambers.

As detailed in the entry for *The Gunslinger*, Jake is a young boy from a parallel reality Earth (which we later discover is the same reality from which Eddie Dean hails) who was pushed in front of a car and died in his reality . . . only to somehow awaken in Roland's. Impossible to explain, and yet true. For a time in the first volume he was Roland's traveling companion, but at a crucial moment the gunslinger was forced to decide whether to save Jake's life or finally catch up with the man in black. He let Jake die.

It is a deed over which he agonizes, the guilt eating at him. Here in the second volume, Roland has a chance to undo that wrong. This redemptive action will set up a maddening incongruity between the two dimensions that Roland must deal with in volume three.

There is already an implication here that Jake will become a member of the newly developed *ka-tet;* indeed, he will. Already it seems that the members of this *ka-tet* are intrinsically linked to one another.

Through Roland's intervention, Odetta is able to unify her two disparate personalities, merging to become one woman, named Susannah Dean, as she now considers herself Eddie's wife: another link in the chain that binds them together.

Though Roland's quest seems to grind to a halt during the events of this story, Roland himself continues to grow as an individual. He is a cold, practical, single-minded man, and yet the presence of Eddie and Susannah forming a new *ka-tet* begins, even here, to bring about a change in Roland. He does not become softer—that would be the death of him. He does, however, become more aware of what is happening around him, and of the feelings of those with whom he is now forever linked.

Still, it is clear that his quest for the Tower supersedes any such humane concerns. As we are told time and again, nothing is too precious to be sacrificed in favor of the quest.

We have posited that the quest does not truly advance in this story. This is not entirely true. Roland begins this story on the beach, and he spends most of the book there, walking along the shore in a direction his instincts tell him is the right one. At intervals along the way, he comes upon the doors through which the three are drawn. Even thereafter, they continue on their way.

But although they cross many miles of ground, that in itself does not feel like progress. The progress in this tale is almost entirely internal. External, yes, in that Roland builds his *ka-tet* with Eddie and Susannah, but internal in that the only real progress is in the *preparation* to reach the Tower. The team is molded, the bonds are formed, almost as though these were necessary rituals.

What all of this accomplishes, in a more concrete way, is the formulation of identity for all three characters. Roland, the last gunslinger, seeks to redefine himself in a world that has moved on, and has no more use for his kind. He seeks to find the truth about his virtue, the answer to his own questions about what kind of man he really is, in the aftermath of Jake's death in the first volume.

Eddie, for his part, strives to find the identity at his core, beneath the despicable surface of the drug-addicted loser dependent on an enabling relationship with his brother. He strives to find within him the man he knew that he could be, and he does.

Odetta/Susannah's quest for identity is, of course, the most obvious of the three. Her split personalities—the erudite, wealthy Odetta Holmes and the vulgar, furious and uneducated Detta Walker—are both aspects of her self, but she is not a whole being until those aspects are united in Susannah Dean.

Their identity quests are individual, but could not be realized without one another. This is yet another facet of *ka-tet*. Separately, their paths were unclear, their wills—with the exception of Roland's—wavering. But together they become strong, the whole feeding strength and purpose back into the parts, the individuals.

Finally, as to the Tower itself, and the nature of the Stephen King Universe as a whole, within *The Drawing of the Three*, we actually learn very little of those things. Which is, perhaps, to be expected in what is only the second volume of a much longer story.

THE DRAWING OF THE THREE: PRIMARY SUBJECTS

ROLAND: The last survivor of an order of warriors called gunslingers, Roland is the son of the lord and lady who ruled the Barony of Gilead. Gilead and all the Baronies of the Affiliation lie in ruins. The destruction of Gilead and the circumstances surrounding the deaths of many of his family and friends are unclear at this point. Roland is on his own, and must begin again by gathering a new breed of gunslingers, gunslingers that he himself must train.

As he travels along the beach, he encounters doors into other dimensions, from which he brings back both Eddie Dean and the woman who will become known as Susannah Dean. They are to be the new gunslingers, and members of Roland's *ka-tet*, who join him on the quest for the Dark Tower that consumes his every thought.

The quest is his fate and his destiny. It is the only reason he draws breath. Roland continues on his quest with his new companions, and the Tower draws ever closer.

EDDIE DEAN: The first to be drawn by Roland into the gunslinger's own world, Eddie Dean is a junkie living in New York City. He seems weak at first, due to his reliance on drugs and his fear of drug lord Rico Balazar. But the death of his brother and his experiences in Roland's world strip away that outer shell to reveal a strong and dangerous man within.

Eddie finds himself dealing with a torrent of emotions due to the presence of the other new arrival, a woman who suffers from multiple personality disorder. He begins to fall in love with one of her personae, Odetta Holmes, even while he is terrified—and rightly so—of her other, Detta Walker. Eventually, however, the woman's two personalities are merged into Susannah, who becomes Eddie's wife.

While there is a time when he is so furious at Roland he is tempted to kill him, Eddie comes to terms with his destiny, and now dedicates himself to the quest.

SUSANNAH DEAN: As noted, Susannah began her life as Odetta Holmes. As a young girl, a man named Jack Mort dropped a brick on her head. As a result, she developed a second personality, that of a crass, vicious woman named Detta Walker. Later, after Mort pushes her in the path of a subway train and she loses her legs as a result, her mental condition becomes even worse.

Only through the efforts of Eddie and Roland is Odetta able to merge her two selves into the woman named Susannah Dean. She now considers herself married to Eddie, and has also dedicated herself to the quest, and to the *ka-tet* that the three of them have formed.

JAKE CHAMBERS: A boy from an alternate version of New York City, Jake was pushed in front of a car and died, only to mysteriously awaken in Roland's reality. Joining the gunslinger on his quest, Jake becomes his sidekick, only to die when, forced to choose between catching the wizard called Walter or saving Jake, Roland chooses the former, letting Jake die.

Later, when Roland has traveled to Jake's reality (after a fashion, as only his mind and spirit are there) at a time before the boy's first death, the gunslinger psychically enters the body of Jack Mort, "the pusher." Roland soon realizes that Mort is the man who will later push Jake in front of the car that kills him that first time. Roland kills Jack Mort, creating a glitch in the time-space continuum. If Mort is dead, then Jake will never be pushed in front of the car and die, will never wake up in Roland's world, and Roland will never be forced to choose between saving him or finally catching the wizard. It is a paradox that will later cause a great deal of trouble for both Roland and Jake.

JACK MORT: Mort is a twisted man who is a sort of serial pusher, shoving people in the path of speeding cars or subway trains. Some of his victims, including Jake Chambers, die. Others, such as Odetta Holmes, aren't that fortunate. (Her legs are severed when she is hit by a subway train.)

Mort is one of the three people Roland mentally "enters" and is able to control. Just before he abandons Mort's body, Roland forces the killer to jump in front of a speeding train. Thus, Mort faces death in the same manner as had his victims.

FLAGG: A creature of magic who appears to be a sorcerer, though Roland thinks he might actually be a demon disguised as a man. Years earlier, Roland saw Flagg near the end of the chaos that destroyed the realm of his birth, but that story has yet to be told in full.

THE DRAWING OF THE THREE: TRIVIA

- Rico Balazar, the drug dealer Eddie Dean is working for when we first meet him, is purportedly involved with a Mafiosi thug named Ginelli. Ginelli appears in a much more prominent role in *Thinner* (1984).

- Thomas and Dennis, the boys from *Eyes of the Dragon* (1987), are remembered by Roland in this volume. The gunslinger recalls having seen the creature called Flagg near the end of the chaos that destroyed the realm of his birth, and that Dennis and Thomas were in pursuit of him. This was the first indication that the *Dark Tower* saga and *Eyes* are closely linked.

3

THE DARK TOWER III:
THE WASTE LANDS

(1991)

While previous volumes in the *Dark Tower* series concern themselves almost exclusively with Roland's quest, in *The Waste Lands*, King at last begins to elaborate a bit on the world of Roland's birth. There is, of course, a great deal more than that going on here—chief among them the solidifying of the relationships among the main characters and their development as gunslingers. However, the bits and pieces supplied to readers regarding the nature of this world are also vital.

The Waste Lands first appeared in 1991 in a limited-edition hardcover from Donald M. Grant, Publisher. With this third volume, however, there was very little wait before the trade paperback appeared. This new speed seems to be reflective of the quickening pace at which King now returned to the story of the last gunslinger. Though there were still years between each book, they were coming faster, as both author and character drew nearer to their final goal.

To quote the author, "The Tower draws ever closer."

Which is odd, actually, when one examines King's revelations about Roland's world in *The Waste Lands*. It is, in fact, an extraordinary domain. Thousands of years earlier, when the world first began to break down, it was apparently repaired and maintained by the civilized race of that time, remembered in Roland's era as The Great Old Ones. They did not create the world, it is said, but they seem to have re-created it.

To do this, they built a technological marvel, apparently tapping into the natural energies of the planet, and perhaps the supernatural energies as well. With the Tower as focal point, or nexus, they built twelve portals to other dimensions—apparently the source of the power needed for their herculean task—to shore up the strength of the Beams that bind all reality together. The Beams all intersect at a central point.

The Tower.

Once upon a time, the twelve portals were at equal distances all around the world. But since that time, the world has moved on.

The world *is still moving on.*

Which brings us to the most mind-boggling element of all of this: the portals and beams and the huge cyborg animal guardians left to guard those entrances are farther away than they once were, and they are all breaking down. Entropy is winning the day. As a result, the power of the Beams is waning, and the very thing that they were created to prevent is happening, increasingly quickly now.

The world, like those mechanical constructs, is running down, rusting. And at the same time, it is spreading. Impossible as it may seem to us, Roland's world is quite literally growing and expanding. A distance that was once a thousand miles might now be twenty times that. This is apparently a direct result of the Tower weakening, or being tainted by the machinations of the forces of darkness or chaos represented by the Crimson King.

The Beams are weakening, eroding, and unless the process can be reversed, the Tower will fall and all of reality will be destroyed. In Roland's quest for the Tower, the destination has always been the focal point of the journey. Yet it is clear that there are those who would like to keep him from the Tower because he would, no doubt, do whatever possible to restore it and the Beams. He may be the last hope of the multiverse.

Due to this expansion, to the world "moving on," Roland has been on his quest for more than twenty years. In that time, we discover, he has lost all those friends remaining to him. When he set about his task, he was not alone. Which of his former comrades-at-arms were with him is at this point in the tale unclear, but they are dead now.

Within this installment, King introduces us to fascinating and complex ideas about this world, and implies connections and relationships, without ever slowing down the pace of the quest itself. In addition to the bizarre nature of the world's condition, there is the time paradox that is slowly driving Roland insane. By killing Jack Mort in the previous volume (1987), Roland prevented Mort from killing Jake Chambers, which means that Jake never died, was never transported to Roland's world, never met Roland, and was never sacrificed by Roland so that the gunslinger could finally catch up to the man in black.

Though Roland once allowed Jake to fall to his death, he has now seemingly redeemed himself. However, Roland and Jake, in their respective worlds, are each being driven mad by the fact that they each retain two sets of memories, from the dual realities in which Jake both died and did not die. Once again, King takes a complex idea and turns it into yet another obstacle on the road to the Tower.

King's home, Bangor   DAVID LOWELL

But *ka*—which means "destiny" in Roland's world—is more powerful than that obstacle. In order to save Roland from going insane, they realize that Jake must be drawn back into Roland's world. When we see Jake, he is also going a bit crazy because, like Roland, he has two sets of conflicting memories that are interfering with his life. However, *ka* draws him inexorably toward the place where he will cross over into Roland's world once more. During that time, he comes to an empty lot wherein grows a single, perfect rose. This flower seems destined to play a major role in the future of the story, as Jake is convinced that the rose must be protected. Roland seems to believe that the rose is, somehow, an incarnation of the Tower itself.

Jake, at last, is drawn into Roland's realm again, and he and Roland finally have peace in their minds. Yet even after this is accomplished, the *ka-tet* is not complete. That is only achieved with the arrival of Oy, a furry little creature whom Jake takes to right away. Oy is a billy-bumbler, a species of animal known on Roland's world for their ability to mimic human speech in an almost parrotlike fashion. Yet Oy seems to know what he's saying at times.

Together, the five of them forge on, and we learn more about Roland's world—this land that is moving on, apparently to its eventual demise. Few children are born. Memories of the past have grown vague and unclear. Those who yet survive respond in a variety of ways. Some, like those at the River Crossing settlement, exist in peace. Others, like the Pubes and Grays in the city of Lud (also discussed in *Rose Madder*), continue to feud decades after they have forgotten what the conflict is about.

Before they reach Lud, however, Roland's *ka-tet* come upon a downed airplane. Within that craft they find the remains of David Quick, a widely renowned outlaw prince of local legend. But the plane is even more interesting, coming, as it does, from the World War II Germany of Jake and Eddie and Susannah's world. Crossing over is not nearly as uncommon as we might once have believed, a fact that becomes more and more clear.

We also learn more about the nature of *ka-tet*, in that all three of Roland's gunslingers-in-training have at one time read a book called *Charlie-the-Choo-Choo*, which, unbeknownst to them, is directly connected to this grand adventure they now share. Also, though Eddie didn't really remember, he and Jake crossed paths once before, when Eddie was not much older than Jake is now. That kind of time paradox is the nature of the Tower, but it also establishes one fact for certain: Jake and Eddie and Susannah all come from different times in the same world or dimension. Or the same "level of the Tower," as Blaine the Mono notes later.

The city of Lud is a nightmarish place, where the last remaining residents are split into two groups. The Grays are led by the Tick-Tock Man, who is later revealed as Andrew Quick, descendant of the legendary David Quick. The Tick-Tock Man's followers include the vicious Gasher, who steals Jake away from the *ka-tet* briefly.

While Roland and Oy go to rescue Jake, Eddie and Susannah seek the Cradle, or train station, of Lud, where they encounter the psychotic, split-personality train, Blaine the Mono. On the way, they are forced to deal with the Grays' enemies, the Pubes, who are killing themselves off in a mournful, despairing kind of lottery.

The Grays are nearly all dead, including Gasher, but unbeknownst to Roland and Jake, the Tick-Tock Man survives, and is recruited by a mysterious demon-sorcerer who introduces himself as Richard Fannin, and also states that he has been known as Maerlyn or the Ageless Stranger.

This is the moment where the dominoes begin to fall, where the tale of the Dark Tower begins to draw together with all the other chronicles in the Stephen King Universe. For Richard Fannin is very clearly the same being as Randall Flagg, of *The Stand* (1978) and *The Eyes of the Dragon* (1987). Fannin notes that one of his other followers worshipped him with the words "my life for you," which is right out of *The Stand*.

King will soon make it clear that Flagg has been Roland's enemy from the beginning, as he has many names and faces. He is Legion, and has opposed Roland in the guise of Marten Broadcloak and Walter O'Dim in the past.

This installment concludes with a cliffhanger, as the *ka-tet* are traveling along the path of the Beam, toward the Tower, aboard a suicidal train who will carry them to their deaths if they fail to stump him in a game of riddles.

THE WASTE LANDS: PRIMARY SUBJECTS

ROLAND OF GILEAD: The gunslinger, son of the last Lord of Gilead. He has been on a quest for the Dark Tower over the course of many years, and has lost everything and everyone he cared about in that time. However, he has also gathered a new *ka-tet* about him, those who will become a new rank of gunslingers. With them, his quest for the Tower continues. As this portion of his tale comes to a close, he and his friends are trapped onboard Blaine the Mono, a sentient, insane monorail train.

EDDIE DEAN: Eddie was a drug addict on his world before Roland fetched him through dimensions. At first, his participation in Roland's quest is against his will. Now, though, Roland's search has become Eddie's. He is the husband of Susannah. Eddie does not realize it until much later, but when he was a boy, he came into contact with Jake Chambers. This establishes that Eddie and Jake are from the same dimension, though not from the same time. Despite his fears and reservations, Eddie is becoming a gunslinger.

SUSANNAH DEAN: Like her husband, Eddie, Susannah is drawn from another time and place to become part of Roland's quest. She has since taken up the quest as her own. In attempting to distract an invisible demon from their efforts to bring Jake Chambers over into Roland's world, Susannah is raped by the monster. Legless, bound to her wheelchair, she nevertheless is becoming a gunslinger.

JAKE CHAMBERS: Once, Roland let Jake die. Later, he saved the boy before that death ever occurred. This created a time paradox that nearly drove them both mad. With help from Eddie and Susannah, Roland draws Jake back into his world, eliminating the paradox. Jake is now an integral part of the *ka-tet* and the quest for the Tower.

OY: One of a breed of creatures called billy-bumblers, Oy becomes part of the group by sheer accident. Later, he saves Jake's life, and possibly Roland's as well, in battle with the Tick-Tock Man and Gasher.

BLAINE: An insane monorail train with a fondness for riddles. It is currently racing toward its destruction, with Roland and his *ka-tet* aboard.

LITTLE BLAINE: The "sane," smaller voice of the monorail; another personality of its artificial intelligence.

RICHARD FANNIN: Also known as the Magician or the Wizard, Maerlyn, and, quite obviously, given his conversation with the Tick-Tock Man, as Randall Flagg. A being of terrible power, he is Roland's nemesis.

TICK-TOCK MAN: Andrew Quick, son of the legendary giant David Quick, who apparently originated in another world and came to Roland's.

He controlled most of the City of Lud before Roland, Jake, and Oy came his way. Oy and Roland did him some damage, and he appears to be dead, until Flagg discovers him. Currently, the Tick-Tock Man serves Flagg.

SHARDIK AND THE GUARDIANS: Like the Turtle, Shardik the Bear is one of the Guardians of the Portals of the Beam. The Beams are bands of invisible energy that hold the world, and possibly all worlds, together. At their epicenter is the Tower. Each of the Beams has a Guardian at its termination point. In Roland's world, there are cybernetic Guardians built to represent their more cosmic counterparts. One of these is Shardik, which goes mad and is destroyed by Roland's *ka-tet*.

CUTHBERT: A childhood friend of Roland's, and later a gunslinger. Cuthbert is dead, but the manner of his demise is not revealed in this volume.

ALAIN: A childhood friend of Roland's, and later a gunslinger. Alain is dead, but the circumstances of his death are not revealed in this volume.

THE WASTE LANDS: TRIVIA

- In a small bookstore, Jake Chambers meets the proprietor, a man with the resonant name Calvin Tower, and buys the book *Charlie the Choo-Choo*, which will also resonate with other members of Roland's *ka-tet*. In the shop, a man reading a book called *The Plague* makes jokes about "the end of the world" (perhaps meant to echo *The Stand*), but more importantly, Mr. Tower congratulates Jake on his willingness to "saddle up and light out for the territories," most certainly a reference to *The Talisman*.

4

THE DARK TOWER IV: WIZARD AND GLASS

1997

In 1997, Donald M. Grant, Publisher released the fourth volume of the *Dark Tower* series, with Stephen King once again returning to the fantastic world of Roland of Gilead. This time, however, the trade paperback edition was not far behind at all. The clamor for the next segment in the story—the tale that is at the center of the Stephen King Universe, that binds it all—had grown so loud that getting it into readers' hands had become vital.

Wizard and Glass serves many purposes (though only one master, of course). The book continues the journey of Roland's new *ka-tet*, but perhaps more importantly, it tells the tale of his very first *ka-tet*, comprised of his good friends and fellow gunslingers (though they were but children at the time) Cuthbert and Alain and the only woman he ever truly loved, Susan Delgado.

Wizard and Glass is a history, then.

But it is also very much a Western. In truth, it is only when reading this fourth volume that one comes to realize that *all* of Roland's stories are westerns. The slow mutants or Blaine the Mono or robot bears or demons and sorcerers might throw one off the track of the sagebrush genre, but in the end, they really are all classic western stories, the kind of thing John Ford might have directed if he and King had ever had the opportunity to work together.

While *Wizard and Glass* is the fourth installment in the series, in so many ways, it is also the real beginning of everything. It is here that we learn more of Roland's backstory than perhaps we ever hoped King would share. His father, Steven, was a gunslinger, a member of the elite ruling class of the many baronies that made up the Affiliation, which itself had descended over many centuries, so legend had it, from King Arthur himself. Arthur, Maerlyn, Excalibur, all these are known to Roland's world, though in this reality he was called Arthur Eld.

Marten, having seen that Roland might be a roadblock to the plans he seems to share with the would-be usurper of the Affiliation, John Farson, seduces Roland's mother and allows the boy to discover them. Marten knows that Roland will try to "graduate" early, to win the title and weapons of a gunslinger. He hopes that Roland will fail and be sent west.

Roland does not fail. He becomes the youngest gunslinger in Gilead's history.

When confronted by his father, Roland is horrified to learn that his mother's infidelity has not escaped the man's attention; he also learns that his father has allowed it to go on because there are greater issues at hand. The barony itself is at stake. In fact, all of the baronies are in jeopardy. A dark time is coming in which Farson will bring war to the land, and Steven Deschain, Roland's father, wants his son out of danger.

Roland is dispatched, along with Cuthbert and Alain, to the oceanside town of Mejis. It is supposed to be for their safety. Instead, they uncover a plot against the old ways, and in favor of John Farson. Over the course of the conflict that ensues, they find a glass ball with great power, one of the last surviving pieces of Maerlyn's Rainbow. The great enchanter had once owned a great many of these powerful objects, in all the colors of the rainbow.

It is when the ball is in Roland's possession—and he in its (for the ball has a horrible hold on those who behold it)—that he has his first real glimpse of the Dark Tower, and the future that awaits him and his *ka-tet*. Most of it, he forgets. But he knows, from that point on, that there is a sickness at the tower, which is the center and sum of everything. Only by curing that sickness and destroying whatever had tainted it can he right all the things that are going wrong with the world. If he succeeds he can pull the skeins back together, reverse the process by which the world is "moving on."

In the end, having triumphed over their enemies in Mejis—at the horrible price of Susan Delgado's life—Roland and his friends moved on, very soon setting about the quest that Roland will pursue for the rest of his life and that the others will follow until they die. But before that search begins, Roland suffers a horrible blow. In a cruel twist of fate—manipulated by magic—he ends up murdering his own mother, a sin for which he can never forgive himself.

Wizard and Glass, as noted, is many things, however. Tragedy is one of them. Western is another. But it is also a love story. The romance and passion of Roland's relationship with Susan is related so powerfully that their rightness for one another is undeniable.

"*Ka* like a wind" is a statement that is repeated time and again in this book, and it is ever so accurate. King's romantic relationships—such as that between Ben and Susan in *'Salem's Lot* (1975) and between Fran and Stu in *The Stand* (1978)—are always sweet, and natural and real. But never so real as here, never so intense and undeniable as within these pages.

Finally, then, with the sacrifice of Susan, the murder of his mother, and his vision of the future, we truly begin to see the heart of Roland the gunslinger, Roland of Gilead, who had once, in the village of Tull, slaughtered the entire populace and seemed so inhumanly cold.

We see, also, that in order to be more than a cold-hearted killer, to be human, Roland must surround himself with friends, with *ka-tet*, with those doomed to join him on his quest. There are previous comparisons, but now we see, truly, why Eddie Dean, with his sharp wit and hot temper, reminds Roland so much of Cuthbert; and why Susannah, with her gentle smile belying the cold steel mind within, recalls Alain.

Then there's the boy, Jake, who appears, even more than the others, destined for an ending of unspeakable pain and horror.

There is so much contained in this one narrative, and well it should be, given that it offers so much, and establishes the foundations of the chronicle that will bring King's multiverse together. When Roland's *ka-tet* pass through a "thinny," a place where the barrier between parallel worlds is thin, they wind up in the world of *The Stand*.

It is not the world Jake or Eddie or Susannah come from, but because the world is moving on, because the Tower is being slowly corrupted, the barriers between worlds are thinning even further. Which means that the superflu, Captain Trips, can begin to make its way through those barriers.

King's worlds—his universes—are colliding.

Nowhere is this more evident than in the presence here of Randall Flagg. His identity was hinted at in *The Waste Lands* (1991). Here, all pretense is dropped. Flagg, it appears, has been Roland's enemy all along. Not only is Flagg also Marten, the enchanter, but he is Maerlyn as well. He is Walter, the man in black, and he is Flagg.

"All hail the Crimson King," says some of the graffiti in the world where people are torn between Mother Abagail and Randall Flagg. And we are only beginning to learn that the creature we know as Flagg and Marten and Walter and so many other names is perhaps the Crimson King's most loyal and powerful servant.

In *Insomnia* (1994), we are told by a small boy that Roland is also a king, and that he will come into final conflict with the Crimson King. This seems to be inevitable now, for Roland is, after all, the last descendant of King Arthur.

In the end, of course, Roland and his *ka-tet* are back on the path of the Beam, back on the road west, heading for the Dark Tower. King tells us that they will come to a dark land called Thunderclap, where other threads, other stories, other universes may intertwine.

The world moves on again.

The final conflict is yet to come.

WIZARD AND GLASS: PRIMARY SUBJECTS

ROLAND DESCHAIN: The gunslinger has now completed the gathering of his new *ka-tet*, a band of raw gunslingers drawn from other worlds who join him for the final leg of his quest. Roland, we have learned, is the son of the last Lord of Gilead, a descendant of Arthur Eld, an ancient king who united the baronies as an Affiliation.

As a teenager, soon after becoming a gunslinger, Roland was sent by his father to the barony of Mejis, where he met and fell in love with Susan Delgado. In Mejis, he and his friends foiled a plot by the locals to aid the efforts of John Farson to destroy the Affiliation. It is also there that he came into contact with the powerful glass ball that is part of Maerlyn's Rainbow. That sorcerous object gave him glimpses of the future, starting him on his quest for the Dark Tower.

Many years later, with his new *ka-tet*, Roland begins to learn just how serious the threat of the Dark Tower's corruption is, not merely to his world, but to all worlds. He finally meets Flagg face to face, unaware at this time that Flagg has always been his enemy, only under other guises.

EDDIE DEAN: Eddie is the member of the *ka-tet* who figures out how to destroy Blaine the Mono, saving all of their lives just in time. He is drawn out of another time and place to become part of Roland's quest. At first it is against his will. Now, though, Roland's quest has become Eddie's.

SUSANNAH DEAN: Like her husband, Eddie, Susannah is drawn from another time and place to become part of Roland's quest. She has since taken up the search as her own. Susannah holds a dark secret from her husband that only Roland knows—she is pregnant, and her offspring might be Eddie's, or it might be that of a demon that raped her.

JAKE CHAMBERS: Once, Roland let Jake die. Later, he saved the boy before that death ever occurred. This created a time paradox that nearly drove them both mad. However, Jake is now an integral part of the *ka-tet*.

OY: One of a breed of creatures called billy-bumblers, Oy becomes part of the group by sheer accident. Later, he saves Jake's life, and possibly Roland's as well. It has become clear, thanks in part to the actions of Flagg, that Oy is an important part of this *ka-tet* as well.

BLAINE: An insane monorail train that runs from Roland's world and into another dimension where a plague called Captain Trips has decimated the population. It has a fondness for riddles. Eddie eventually drives it deeper into madness, resulting in its destruction.

LITTLE BLAINE: The "sane," smaller voice of the monorail; another personality of its artificial intelligence.

STEVEN DESCHAIN: The son of Henry the Tall, Steven is descended from Arthur Eld himself. He is rightful Lord of the Barony of Gilead at the time of its destruction and his death. The details of those dark times are still unclear.

CUTHBERT ALLGOOD: One of Roland's closest friends; they are together in Mejis when Roland first learns of the Dark Tower, and the danger to all things posed by its deterioration. Cuthbert later joins Roland on his quest, but dies before completing it.

ALAIN JOHNS: One of Roland's closest friends; they are together in Mejis when Roland first hears of the Dark Tower, and the danger to all things posed by its deterioration. Alain later joins Roland on his mission, but dies before completing it.

SUSAN DELGADO: A young girl living in the village of Hambry in the barony of Mejis, Susan falls in love with Roland, though she has been promised to the mayor of Hambry, Hart Thorin. She breaks that promise by becoming Roland's lover. In the end, thanks in great part to the hideous actions of her cruel aunt, Cordelia Delgado, Susan is burned to death by the townspeople for her actions, both real and imagined.

RHEA: A witch who lives on the outskirts of Hambry, Rhea is the keeper of one of the pieces of Maerlyn's Rainbow for a time. Despite her magic, it corrupts her, sucking the life out of her. Rhea does not die then, however, and the circumstances of her death have yet to be revealed. After the events in Hambry, she uses her magic to manipulate Roland into murdering his own mother. He sees her again, but those events have yet to be revealed.

ELDRED JONAS: The leader of a trio of hired guns called the Big Coffin Hunters, Eldred Jonas once dreamed of being a gunslinger. He failed the final test, however, and like all those who did, was sent west, excommunicated, in a sense, from the Affiliation. Though he is eventually killed by Roland of Gilead, it is interesting to note that, according to his associates, Jonas bragged of having traveled to other worlds through "special doors."

SHEEMIE: A slow boy who lives in Hambry, he is a friend to Roland and Susan and the others, part of their *ka-tet*. They are later parted, but Roland will meet him again.

JOHN FARSON: A mysterious figure, often referred to but never seen. He leads the revolt against the Affiliation. However, it will be revealed that Farson is also Walter/Marten/Flagg/Legion.

WALTER: At first, Walter appears to be a servant of John Farson's. Walter first crosses paths with Roland (or nearly does) in Hambry. Later, of course, it is Walter whom Roland pursues across the desert. Walter seemingly dies on the mountain after giving Roland prescient visions. Over the course of this saga, it is revealed that Walter, Farson, Flagg, and Marten are all one and the same.

MAERLYN'S RAINBOW: It is said that Maerlyn has thirteen objects of power, one for each of the Twelve Guardians of the Portals, and one for the nexus point of the Beams that connect those, the nexus point, of course, being the Dark Tower. These objects are glass balls, most of which have apparently been destroyed. By looking into one of them, however, Roland is given a vision of the Dark Tower, and of the future.

WIZARD AND GLASS: TRIVIA

- Oatley, the town where Clay Reynolds and Coral Thorin meet their eventual end, shares the same name as a town in *The Talisman*, where Jack Sawyer is essentially held prisoner by the owner of the local bar.

- As a way of thanking his Constant Readers for purchasing the novels *Desperation* and *The Regulators*, a small (59-page) excerpt from a yet-to-be-completed *Wizard and Glass* was included as a complementary gift at the time of the publication of the two books in 1996. The miniature paperback is now a collector's item.

- In the 1998 novella *The Little Sisters of Eluria*, part of the saga of The Dark Tower, King establishes that the witch, Rhea, has sisters, one of whom is likely Rhiannon, who is mentioned in *The Eyes of the Dragon* (1987), which also takes place in the same plane of reality as Roland's story.

5

THE DARK TOWER V: WOLVES OF THE CALLA

(2003)

Stephen King's Constant Readers were able to rejoin Roland, Eddie, Susannah, Jake, and Oy on their journey to the Dark Tower when, on November 4, 2003, Donald M. Grant and Scribner jointly published the fifth installment of King's epic Dark Tower series, *Wolves of the Calla*, complete with twelve full-color illustrations by noted comic book/fantasy artist Bernie Wrightson.

The six-year period between installments had been an eventful one for King, seeing him switch publishers, experiment with e-commerce, and, most importantly, survive a terrible accident in which he was struck by a van and nearly killed. King's accident gave him a greater sense of urgency about completing his epic. Deciding to see the series straight through until its conclusion, he finished first drafts of the last three volumes over a period of roughly a year, from August of 2001 through the end of October 2002.

King also decided to substantially revise the first *Dark Tower* book, *The Gunslinger*, to bring it more in line with the series as it had developed over the years in terms of concepts, characters, and themes. By the time King had finished reworking the book, he had made subtle changes on nearly every page, added three scenes, and excised false starts that failed to develop meaningfully in subsequent books.

Sporting a new preface, the revised *Gunslinger* was released in June 2003. In addition to that book, Viking released new hardcover editions of *The Drawing of the Three, The Waste Lands*, and *Wizard and Glass*, all featuring new introductions from King. They also featured more uniform jackets, featuring a stylized keyhole on the top spine of each volume. The last three volumes of the series also sported these new designs.

It was in the new *Gunslinger* and in *Wolves of the Calla* that King also introduced subtitles to the series. *The Gunslinger* was now subtitled "Resumption"; *The Drawing of the Three* "Renewal"; *The Waste Lands* "Redemption"; and *Wizard and Glass* "Regard." Drawing inspiration from the John Sturges classic *The Magnificent Seven, Wolves of the Calla* was aptly subtitled "Resistance."

Readers can almost feel King rounding a metaphorical corner in *Wolves*, gathering speed as he heads toward the long-awaited conclusion of this massive epic. After three decades, the end was finally in sight. As *Wolves* commences, Roland and his *ka-tet* are still on the path of the beam. Their quest has led them to Calla Bryn Sturgis, an agricultural town beyond the forests of Mid-World and in the shadow of the ominous dark city of Thunderclap. As they approach the city, they are met by a group of desperate townspeople who beg them for help against a foe so implacable that many in the town have long since given up hope. Among this delegation is a familiar face from King's canon, the unfortunate Father Donald Callahan, former resident of Jerusalem's Lot, Maine.

The townsfolk of the Calla fear an army of beings they refer to as wolves, which attack from Thunderclap once each generation to abduct their children. Not just any children, mind you, but one half of each pair of the twins who live there in surprising numbers. Months after their abduction, the victims are returned to the village, robbed of some vital spark, doomed to grow into slow-witted, short-lived giants. Having seen signs that the wolves' next invasion is imminent, the people of the Calla beseech the gunslingers to help them.

Bound by their code, the gunslingers have no choice but to cast their lot with the villagers. What follows is a period of preparation and soul-searching, as hidden depths and hideous duplicity are discovered within the group. The day the wolves reappear, they find a newly defiant population willing to do battle to protect their progeny, even if that entails the ultimate destruction of the entire village.

Always a powerful storyteller, King really hits his stride in *Wolves*, which, as he acknowledges in an Author's Note, is essentially a Western draped in the clothing of the fantastic. King works the tropes like a master, delivering a gripping and satisfying tale, simultaneously positioning his characters for the final battle to come. Along the way, he pays homage to several diverse works of fiction, among them *The Lord of the Rings*, and the movies *The Magnificent Seven* and *2001: A Space Odyssey*, further strengthening the links between this and past works.

WOLVES OF THE CALLA: PRIMARY SUBJECTS

ROLAND: The last gunslinger in Mid-World, Roland Deschain has assembled a ka-tet consisting of Eddie Dean, Susannah Dean, Jake Chambers, and Oy, a doglike creature known as a billy-bumbler. Traveling the Way of the Beam toward the Dark Tower, the quintet are asked by the people of Calla Bryn Sturgis to assist them in fending off an invading army. Bound by the code of his kind, the gunslinger agrees to help them.

The Roland readers encounter in *Wolves* might surprise those who've read the first four volumes, as the gunslinger proves himself as much a psychologist and a politician as a man accustomed to dealing in lead. This Roland is also more tender (he takes a lover, Rosalita Munoz) and more fragile (his arthritis, which he calls "the dry twist," threatens to cripple him).

Roland organizes the people of the Calla to fight the wolves, laying out strategy for the battle even as he tries to discern just what kind of enemy he's actually facing. He also manages to take time out from his preparations to "go todash" (a kind of astral projection) to 1999 New York, where he visits the empty lot at the corner of Second and Forty-Sixth street, and sees "the rose" for the first time. The rose, as readers of earlier volumes are aware, is believed to be a physical embodiment of all realities.

EDDIE DEAN: Eddie is growing increasingly worried about the woman he calls his wife, Susannah. But, distracted by the Calla's plight and the imperiled rose, Eddie cannot focus on her problems as much as he would like. Always a fast talker, Eddie plays a crucial role in convincing a reluctant Calvin Tower to sell the vacant lot where the rose grows to Roland's *ka-tet* instead of the Sombra Corporation, which represents the interests of the Crimson King.

JAKE CHAMBERS: Jake uncovers the treachery of his best friend Benny's father, Ben Slightman, and Andy the robot. He also acquits himself admirably in the fight against the Wolves. More and more, he gives the *ka-tet* the appearance of a family, with Roland as his father, Eddie as his brother, and Susannah as his sister or mother figure.

SUSANNAH DEAN: Raped by a demon in an encounter described in *The Waste Lands*, Susannah starts to show signs of being pregnant even though she's still having her period. One sign is her odd cravings—at night, she sneaks off from camp to hunt and eat all sorts of small wildlife. Roland is aware of this, but says nothing to the others. Another disquieting development for Susannah is that she's begun to manifest yet another identity, which calls itself Mia. Mia becomes an increasingly powerful influence on Susannah, who is in fact pregnant with an entity Mia refers to as "her chap."

Susannah is a vital member of the *ka-tet*, perhaps its very heart and soul. In *Wolves*, she suggests using her inherited wealth to purchase the vacant lot in New York City where the rose grows from Calvin Tower. Despite looking as if she is ready to give birth at any moment, Susannah fights valiantly alongside the Sisters of Oriza, helping to rout the Wolves. At battle's end, Mia takes over, forcing her host to slip away to the Cave of Voices, where she enters a doorway to 1999 New York City. Susannah's continuing story forms the backbone of Volume 6 of the series, *Song of Susannah*.

OY: A doglike creature known as a billy-bumbler, Oy is devoted to Jake. Oy accompanies Eddie and Jake on their trip to 1977 New York. The animal is a valued member of the *ka-tet* who alerts Jake to Ben Slightman's treachery, and also fights valiantly in the battle against the Wolves.

THE SISTERS OF ORIZA: A small band of women in Calla Bryn Sturgis who are skilled in the art of throwing lethal disks, they preserve the tradition begun by Lady Oriza, who used one of the "dishes" to behead the outlaw prince known as Grey Dick. There seems a fateful connection between the plates thrown by the Sisters of Oriza and the "forspecial" plate that Susannah broke as a young girl, a significant event in the development of her multiple personality disorder.

THE NUMBER NINETEEN: In *Wolves*, the *ka-tet* becomes obsessed with this number, and starts to see it everywhere, whether it be the number of letters in a name, or a room number. The number nineteen is significant because that is the age at which Stephen King first conceived the idea for the *Dark Tower* series, inspired by Robert Browning's poem, Tolkien's epic *The Lord of The Rings*, and, later, Sergio Leone's film *The Good, the Bad, and the Ugly*. The number nineteen also figures in the day King was almost killed by an oncoming vehicle: June 19, 1999.

THE TET CORPORATION: Confronting Jack Andolini in Calvin Tower's bookstore in 1977 New York City, Eddie impulsively tells him to inform his boss Salazar that Tower has decided not to sell his vacant lot up the street to the Sombra Corporation, but rather to the Tet Corporation, which doesn't exist at that time. It will, however, exist shortly in the future, a venture organized by John Cullum, Moses Carver, and Aaron Deepneau.

FATHER DONALD CALLAHAN: Known to the townsfolk as "the Old Fella" or "Pere Callahan," Don Callahan came to End World from another reality, one in which the events described in *'Salem's Lot* actually took place. In *Wolves*, he tells the story of his life from his departure from the Lot to the time he came to Calla Bryn Sturgis, the mysterious globe known as Black Thirteen in his possession. Father Callahan spent many years hunting vampires until he "died," much like Jake Chambers, and found himself in Roland's world. He eventually becomes an integral part of Roland's *ka-tet*.

CALLA BRYN STURGIS: A small town on the River Whye, near the edge of End World. Roughly every twenty years, Calla Bryn Sturgis is attacked by a legion of cloaked invaders mounted on horses. The invaders have one goal, to kidnap the children of the town and spirit them to Thunderclap, presumably as slave labor (the truth is far more horrible). Many of the children taken are never seen again; those who return are, in the parlance of the locals, "roont," turned into slow-witted giants with an unnaturally short life span. Encouraged by the presence of Roland and his *ka-tet*, the current residents make a stand against the Wolf riders, and soundly defeat them.

ANDY THE ROBOT: This seven-foot-tall messenger robot has seemingly always lived in Calla Bryn Sturgis. It is he who tells the townspeople of the imminent arrival of the wolves. Seemingly benign, Andy, a product of North Central Positronics, is actually an ally of the Wolf riders. When Eddie discovers the truth about Andy, he renders him useless in a scene reminiscent of the one in *2001: A Space Odyssey* when astronaut Dave lobotomizes Hal, the computer that runs his ship.

CALVIN TOWER: The owner of The Manhattan Restaurant of the Mind, a New York bookstore, and of the vacant lot where grows the all-important rose. Sombra Corporation has an option on the land, which expires in a few short days.

AARON DEEPNEAU: Clavin Tower's best friend and attorney, he can often be found in Tower's bookstore, playing chess with the owner.

ENRICO BALAZAR: A representative of the Sombra Corporation, Balazar tries to purchase Calvin Tower's vacant New York City lot from him in 1977. Balazar, who sends his representative Jack Andolini to secure the property, is frustrated by the abrupt appearance of Jake Chambers in Tower's bookstore. Balazar is a mobster who, in another where and when, came into conflict with Eddie Dean and his older brother, Henry. Balazar also played a key role in Jake's death in another reality; it was his car that killed the boy.

JACK ANDOLINI: Representing Enrico Balazar, Andolini puts the squeeze on Calvin Tower to force him to sell his vacant lot to the Sombra Corporation. Confronted by Eddie Dean, Andolini backs off, but later engineers the destruction of the bookstore through an act of arson.

THE SOMBRA CORPORATION: A corporation with offices in New York, Chicago, Detroit, Denver, Los Angeles, and San Francisco, it is actually a front for the Crimson King's activities. The Sombra Corporation arranges a lethal ambush against Father Donald Callahan.

THE WOLVES: Once a generation, a small army descends from Thunderclap to kidnap the children of Calla Bryn Sturgis. Known as Wolves because of their fierce, wolflike faces, the hooded, green-cloaked army uses horses for transportation. Over the generations, they have met with little resistance. In what turns out to be their last foray against the Calla, however, they face a populace inspired and trained by Roland's *ka-tet*, which has now added Father Donald Callahan to its number. The wolves, which are revealed to be robots, are routed by the *ka-tet* and the townspeople.

RICHARD PATRICK SAYRE: The executive vice president of the Sombra Corporation and a minion of the Crimson King, he engineers the trap that results in Father Donald Callahan's entry into Roland's world. He later works to see that Mia's Chap is safely delivered.

STEPHEN KING: An author whose name appears on the deli board at Calvin Tower's bookstore, replacing the name that Jake originally recalled seeing there (King favorite John D. MacDonald). His name appears on a rare book owned by Calvin Tower called *'Salem's Lot*, which describes Father Donald Callahan's experiences in the vampire-infested town of Jerusalem's Lot, Maine.

WOLVES OF THE CALLA: TRIVIA

- In previous volumes, the children's book *Charlie the Choo-Choo* was written by Beryl Evans. But in this novel, they discover that the same book was penned in another reality by a woman named Claudia y Inez Bachman, significant because the letters of her name add up to nineteen, a number that resonates all through the final volumes. Also, of course, King wrote half a dozen novels under the pseudonym Richard Bachman, whose wife was said to be named Claudia.

- Also on the subject of books, one of the inhabitants of Calla Bryn Sturgis is a rancher named Wayne Overholser, who in another reality (in our world, which King calls the Keystone world) was a highly regarded author of Western novels.

6

THE DARK TOWER VI:
SONG OF SUSANNAH

(2004)

More like a poem than a song, the sixth novel of King's *Dark Tower* series is divided into thirteen stanzas, which are capped by a shocking coda. Although only spanning a one-day period in the lives of Roland and his *ka-tet*, the book chronicles several crucial developments.

At the end of their epic battle with the Wolves on the outskirts of Calla Bryn Sturgis, Roland, Eddie, Jake, Oy, and Don Callahan suddenly notice that Susannah is no longer on the scene. Following her trail to the Cave of Voices, they soon realize that Susannah (now dominated by the entity that calls itself Mia) has used the power of Black Thirteen to flee Mid-World for the New York City of 1999.

Enlisting the aid of Manni senders, a local group of religious mystics, the remaining members of Roland's *ka-tet* enter the Doorway Cave to pursue their comrade. They decide to split up, with Roland and Eddie pursuing Susannah in 1999, and Jake and Father Callahan seeking Calvin Tower (saving the Dark Tower depends not only on rescuing Susannah but also on securing the vacant lot Calvin Tower owns—the lot is the home of a single rose—before he loses it to the Sombra Corporation) in 1977. They discover, however, that the magic they are utilizing is not reliable, or that *ka* has other plans, as, against their original intentions, Father Callahan, Jake, and the billy-bumbler Oy are sent to 1999 New York City while Roland and Eddie are sent to 1977 Lovell, Maine.

The next twenty-four hours are very eventful.

Successfully reaching 1999 Manhattan, Susannah/Mia has only one desire, to give birth to her "chap" at a predetermined location in the East 60s. Susannah-Mia, who in a struggle to cope with each other and with an alien environment (a mostly mental struggle reminiscent of that which takes place between Gary Jones and his nemesis, Mr. Gray, in 2001's *Dreamcatcher*), eventually "go todash" to Castle Discordia on the border of End-World. In that stronghold of the Crimson King, Mia reveals her origins to Susannah.

In Maine, the Gunslinger and Eddie attempt to track down New York City bookstore owner Calvin Tower, who is being hunted down by mobster Enrico Balazar and his gang, who first appeared in Eddie's version of New York in *The Drawing of the Three*. Along the way, they participate in a gunfight, meet a pragmatic caretaker named John Cullum, and encounter a thirty-year-old writer named Stephen King.

Subtitled "Reproduction," the sixth installment of King's magnum opus stops short with the biggest cliffhanger of King's career. After being treated to a coda containing excerpts of King's diary from 1977 through 1999 in which he describes his experiences in writing Roland's story, readers encounter a press clipping from the *Portland Sunday Telegram* dated June 19, 1999, whose headline proclaims:

STEPHEN KING DIES NEAR LOVELL HOME

POPULAR MAINE WRITER KILLED

WHILE TAKING AFTERNOON WALK

SONG OF SUSANNAH: PRIMARY SUBJECTS

ROLAND: Traveling to 1977 Maine from Calla Bryn Sturgis, Roland, accompanied by Eddie, finds himself trapped in a small grocery store/service station, under attack by Jack Andolini and a small army of thugs. While escaping that trap, they make the acquaintance of John Cullum, who will come to play a large role in their destinies.

Roland and Eddie eventually locate Calvin Tower, the man they traveled from Mid-World to meet, then make a detour to meet a man they've be-come intrigued by, a young writer named Stephen King, the author of 'Salem's Lot, a novel that is purportedly fiction yet tells a story that features their friend Father Donald Callahan, describing his unfortunate experiences in that selfsame town. Roland discovers that King has begun chronicling his life and wonders if the author is his creator or if he is simply tapping into the knowledge somehow to tell the story of the gunslinger's quest for the tower.

EDDIE DEAN: Eddie accompanies Roland to 1977 Maine, and is wounded in the leg during the gun battle at the grocery store. With John Cullum's help, he and Roland locate Calvin Tower. Eddie strong-arms Tower into selling the vacant lot to the Tet corporation. As a way of compensating him, he advises Tower to invest in Microsoft. Roland does some field surgery on Eddie, who quickly recovers from his wound. On a hunch, the pair travel to meet the thirty-year-old author of 'Salem's Lot, Stephen King.

JAKE CHAMBERS: Jake and Donald Callahan travel to 1999 New York, and track Susannah first to her hotel room (Room 1919, where they se-cure Black Thirteen), then to an eating establishment called the Dixie Pig. As the book draws to a close, they prepare to mount a rescue operation.

FATHER DONALD CALLAHAN: Now a part of the *ka-tet*, Calla-han travels to 1999 New York with Jake. After discovering Black Thirteen, Callahan (thanks to Oy) also finds the small scrimshaw turtle originally hid-den in the lining of the bowling bag used to carry the orb. He knows instinc-tively it is the Turtle Maturin (Guardian of one of the Beams, perhaps the most vital of them all), and that it is an object of great power. As Callahan stands outside the Dixie Pig with Jake, some part of him surely must suspect that he will meet his destiny, revealed in The Dark Tower, inside.

SUSANNAH/MIA: Susannah/Mia uses Black Thirteen to travel to New York City on June 1, 1999, her primary goal to hook up with the minions of the Crimson King to ensure the safe birth of her "chap." Now truly a hybrid entity, Susannah sprouts legs upon arriving. Over the course of the novel, Susannah and Mia come to know each other. Mia's primary concern is her chap; Susannah also begins to feel motherly emotions toward the being growing inside her. Thus, in the end, she allows Mia to deliver the body they share to the Dixie Pig.

RICHARD PATRICK SAYRE: Employee of the earthly Sombra Corporation and servant of the Crimson King, his goal is to ensure that Mia's chap is born.

JACK ANDOLINI: When Roland and Eddie arrive in Maine, Andolini is waiting for them. Andolini, who was in that state searching for the incautious Calvin Tower, is not successful in his attempt to capture the gunslingers.

JOHN CULLUM: A local caretaker and handyman, John is shopping at the grocery store where Roland and Eddie arrive after going todash to 1977 Maine. John escapes from the grocery with the gunslingers, and offers them shelter for a time. He then helps them locate Calvin Tower.

THE TET CORPORATION: The corporation that Eddie "created" off the top of his head while in Calvin Tower's bookstore. Eddie signs the agreement between Calvin Tower and Tet Corporation on behalf of that legal entity, even though it does not yet exist.

CALVIN TOWER: An inveterate book lover and owner of the vacant lot, Tower reluctantly sells the lot to the Tet Corporation after Eddie browbeats him into it. The former Calvin Toren is more than he seems, however, as he shows an awareness of Roland's quest and family history.

AARON DEEPNEAU: Tower's best friend and attorney, he drafts the agreement between the bookseller and the Tet Corporation, transferring the ownership of the vacant lot to that entity for one dollar. Deepneau's role in Roland's quest has only begun, however.

STEPHEN KING: Living in Maine in 1977, the young writer is confronted by something he never thought he'd encounter—a character he created named Roland the Gunslinger, standing before him in the flesh (he doesn't recognize Eddie, because he hasn't thought him up yet). Speaking with King, Roland and Eddie realize just how important this man is to their quest. After securing the author's permission, Roland hypnotizes King. In that state, King reveals his knowledge of the Dark Tower, the beams, and the Crimson King. He tells a story that makes it clear that he's had the attention of the Crimson King since he was seven years old.

Before releasing King from his trance, Roland instructs him to tell their story until he tires. "When you can't tell any more, when the Turtle's song and the bear's cry grow faint in your ears, then you will rest. And when you can begin again, you will begin again."

GAN: Apparently God. Under hypnosis, King says, "I'm Gan, or possessed by Gan, I don't know which, maybe there's no difference." King says he stopped writing Roland's story at certain points because he didn't want to "be Gan," the source of *ka*. Every time King returns to the saga, some part of him feels the eye of the Crimson King on him.

THE BLACK TOWER: The skyscraper that stands at 2 Dag Hammarskjold Plaza in New York City.

HENCHIK: The Manni leader in Calla Bryn Sturgis, he helps the remaining members of Roland's *ka-tet* in traveling to 1999 New York City and 1977 Maine. The Manni are an End World religious group known for traveling between worlds.

WALK-INS: Shortly after John Cullum meets Roland and Eddie, he asks them, "Are you walk-ins?" Seeing they are puzzled by his question, the caretaker/handyman explains that "Walk-ins're people who just appear. Sometimes they're dressed in old-fashioned clothes, as if they came from . . . ago, I guess you'd say." The walk-ins have appeared in the Maine towns of Waterford, Stoneham, East Stoneham, Lovell, Sweden, and Denmark. These strange people first started arriving around the time a young writer named Stephen King arrived in Lovell. Some might speculate that the walls between realities have grown thin in that region of Maine.

BLACK THIRTEEN: An object of ancient power, it was given to Father Donald Callahan by Randall Flagg when the priest crossed over to Roland's world. Realizing its power, Callahan hid the orb in a church he built in Calla Bryn Sturgis. Taken from its resting place when Roland and his gunslingers came to town, the object was used by Susannah/Mia to transport her to 1999 New York City.

The object having served its purpose, Susannah/Mia stored it in her hotel safe, where it was discovered by Jake and Don Callahan. The pair stored the orb in a locker deep beneath the World Trade Center. As they are leaving the site, Callahan notes that it is "safe until June of 2002, unless someone breaks in and steals it."

Jake replied, "Or if the building falls down on top of it," a chilling reference to the terrorist attack that destroyed New York City's Twin Towers on September 11, 2001.

SONG OF SUSANNAH: TRIVIA

- References arise in *Song of Susannah* to *can-toi*, *can-tah*, and *can-tak*, words that are ascribed to various types of beings in King's universe. King's regular readers will be familiar with the words from the novel *Desperation*. The *can-tah* are "little gods," such as the carving of Maturin that Jake and Father Callahan make use of in the Dixie Pig, objects of power. The *can-tak* are "big gods," such as the evil Tak in *Desperation*, and the *can-toi* are a third group comprised mostly of various lackeys to these "gods," including the human-taheen hybrids of *Song of Susannah* and the Low Men from that book and from *Hearts in Atlantis*.

7

THE DARK TOWER VII:
THE DARK TOWER

(2004)

On Tuesday, September 21, 2004, King's fifty-seventh birthday, Donald M. Grant and Scribner simultaneously published editions of the 845-page conclusion to his epic *Dark Tower* saga, ending a journey that took thirty-four years and 3,872 pages to complete. An author and his creations had finally reached their common goal.

And what a goal. After all of the struggle, the pain, the blood, the sacrifice, what does Roland find when he finally reaches the Tower? He discovers that the Tower embodies the whole of his life, his triumphs, his tragedies, his successes and failures, all the things that make him the man he is today. He briefly visits his past and finds out that he is being prepared to reembark on his journey, this time with the hope of finding redemption. Thus, the story that began with one of the most memorable lines in modern fantasy fiction—"The man in black fled across the desert, and the gunslinger followed."—ends that way as well. We probably shouldn't have been surprised, since we were told as early as *The Waste Lands* that "Ka was a wheel, its one purpose to turn, and in the end it always came back to the place where it had started."

In an Author's Note at the end of the novel, King says:

> You may not like what Roland found at the top, but that's a different matter entirely. And don't write me angry letters about it, either, be-

cause I won't answer them. There's nothing left to say on the subject. I wasn't exactly crazy about the ending, either, if you want to know the truth, but it's the right ending. The only ending, in fact. You have to remember that I don't make these things up, not exactly; I only write down what I see.

The book elicited a mixed response from critics. Writing in the October 17, 2004, issue of *The New York Times Book Review*, in an article titled "Pulp Metafiction," Michael Agger wrote:

> At this point, readers of the series will be howling at the simplification of their heroes, but the whole project eludes description—it's a double-black-diamond ski run for fantasy nerds. There are the multiple worlds, the multiple names and characters who die and come back to life in different times and places. Even King can be overwhelmed.

The Washington Post critic Bill Sheehan had another take on the book. In his review, called "The Return of the King," Sheehan stated:

> Although King's detractors—a vocal, often contentious bunch—will doubtless disagree, *The Dark Tower* stands as an imposing example of pure storytelling. King has always believed in the primal importance of story, and his entire career—encompassing forty novels and literally hundreds of shorter works—is a reflection of that belief. On one level, the series as a whole is actually about stories, about the power of narrative to shape and color our individual lives. It is also, beneath its baroque, extravagant surface, about the things that make us human: love, loss, grief, honor, courage and hope. On a deeper level still, it is a meditation on the redemptive possibility of second chances, a subject King knows intimately. In bringing this massive project to conclusion, King has kept faith with his readers and made the best possible use of his own second chance. *The Dark Tower* is a humane, visionary epic and a true magnum opus. It will be around for a very long time.

We agree with the second interpretation. As King notes, many may not like the ending, but it is appropriate. After all, the true test of fiction is whether it rewards rereading—novels are meant to be revisited, reinterpreted, and reexperienced. By having Roland reembark on his adventure, King at once tacitly acknowledges that fact, even as he invites us to once again make the journey with him.

THE DARK TOWER: PRIMARY SUBJECTS

ROLAND: In *The Dark Tower*, the last gunslinger finally reaches the end of his centuries-long quest, but only after witnessing the death of several members of his *ka-tet*. Although not alone as he makes his final approach to the Dark Tower, he is the only member of the *ka-tet* to actually enter the structure.

Still in 1977 Maine at the end of *Song of Susannah*, Roland and Eddie reunite with John Cullum, and recruit him to assist Aaron Deepneau in gaining the cooperation of Moses Carver, Susannah's godfather, in setting up the Tet Corporation. Returning to Mid-World after eliminating Jake's pursuers at the Dixie Pig, the gunslinger and his *ka-tet* decide they must perform two tasks: first, liberate the Breakers enslaved by the Crimson King, and second, protect Stephen King's life at all costs. They achieve these goals, preventing the fall of the Tower, but only through great sacrifice.

His *ka-tet* dwindling, Roland finds himself back on the road to the Dark Tower, accompanied by Susannah and Oy, and pursued by his son, Mordred. By the time he reaches the Tower, Susannah has left him, and Oy and Mordred are dead. Although joined by Patrick Danville as he makes his final approach, only Roland enters the Dark Tower. There he finds his destiny.

Though Roland's evolution into the paternal figure of this *ka-tet* and the reawakening of his emotional self made it possible for him to reach the Tower, his love for his companions never makes him waver from his quest. In the end, however, he calls out the names of all of the good and loyal people in whose name he approaches the Dark Tower.

EDDIE DEAN: Eddie returns to Mid-World, only to be cut down by a bullet in the battle to free the Breakers held by the Crimson King at Devar-Toi. Eddie lingers for many hours after being shot, telling Jake he must protect Roland from Mordred and Dandelo.

JAKE CHAMBERS: As *The Dark Tower* commences, Jake and Don Callahan lay siege to the Dixie Pig. Jake survives that battle, and the battle at Devar-Toi, but dies protecting Stephen King, absorbing much of the impact from the van that strikes him and the writer. Like Eddie, he dies with a warning about Dandelo on his lips.

SUSANNAH DEAN: Susannah watches as Mia bears the child she carried, known as Mordred. Seeing Mordred for what he really is, she wounds him as she escapes her captors. Reunited with her *ka-tet*, she participates in the battle at Devar-Toi, and watches helplessly as her husband, Eddie, dies a slow death. Although she is with Roland as he nears the Dark Tower, she is not destined to enter the structure herself. Realizing the extent of Patrick Danville's talent, she asks him to draw her a doorway that will enable her to leave Mid-World. She does so, entering another reality where another Eddie awaits her, an Eddie with a little brother named Jake. We are left with the impression that this alternate version of Roland's *ka-tet* will have a peaceful, happy life.

MIA: After bearing Mordred, she is literally consumed by her monstrous child.

RICHARD PATRICK SAYRE: A minion of the Crimson King, he is killed by Susannah after ensuring that Mia gave birth to Mordred.

OY: Although he mourns Jake, Oy honors his master's last request to protect Roland by distracting Mordred at a key moment. Unfortunately, his actions cost the billy-bumbler his life, as Mordred impales him on a tree limb.

JOHN CULLUM: Enlisted by Roland and Eddie to assist Aaron Deepneau in forming the Tet Corporation, Cullum joins with Deepneau and Holmes family friend Moses Carver to form what becomes known as the *ka-tet* of the rose. Cullum successfully carries out their wishes, creating an organization that exists to thwart the plans of the evil Sombra Corporation. John Cullum dies in 1989 at the hands of the Crimson King's Low Men.

IRENE TASSENBAUM: On the scene of King's accident on June 19, 1999, Irene becomes involved in Roland's quest when she agrees to drive him to New York City. On the way to New York, they rent a hotel room in Harwich, CT, Bobby Garfield's hometown. She leaves the scene shortly after bringing him to visit the Tet Corporation, forever changed because of the time she spent with Roland.

FATHER DONALD CALLAHAN:
Callahan dies a noble death battling Low Men and vampires in the Dixie Pig. His bravery buys him redemption for the cowardice he displayed in *'Salem's Lot*.

MORDRED DESCHAIN:
The son of Susannah/Mia, Roland, and the Crimson King. In *The Gunslinger*, Roland had consensual sex with an invisible demon in payment for information given to him by an oracle. Somehow the seed he spent in that encounter was saved by the demon and later, when Susannah was raped by a demon, she was impregnated with it. At some point after Susannah was impregnated by the demon, the Crimson King "reimpregnated" her so that his genetic material also became part of the mix. Thus Mordred has two fathers, Roland and the Crimson King. Given that Susannah has the second personality of Mia inside her, Mordred also has two mothers.

Although born in human form, Mordred's true shape, reminiscent of It, is that of a heinous giant spider. Mordred's first act after birth is to kill his mother Mia. Possessed of a deep hatred of his White Father, Roland, the rapidly maturing Mordred follows him, looking for an opportunity to kill him. Although Mordred easily dispatches Randall Flagg, establishing his ferocity and lethality, he is unable to kill Roland and fulfill the wishes of his Red Father, the Crimson King. Mordred dies at the hands of Roland.

RANDALL FLAGG:
Intending to use Mordred to gain access to the Dark Tower, Flagg (a.k.a. Walter O'Dim, a.k.a. Marten Broadcloak) confronts the beast in a subterranean lair in which he is hiding. Mordred easily overcomes Flagg's defenses and forces him to rip out his own eyes and tongue before devouring him.

DEVAR-TOI:
Also known as Algul Siento, Pleasantville, and Blue Heaven, Devar-Toi is home to roughly three hundred Breakers (humans with various psychic abilities who work on behalf of the Crimson King to destroy the Beams that emanate from the Dark Tower). Kept in the dark about what

they're doing, the Breakers, misfits in their respective worlds, have it relatively good in Devar-Toi, and thus have little desire to be "freed." Devar-Toi is managed by a taheen named Finli and an ex–Attica prison guard named Pimli Prentiss. Prentiss fires the bullets that take Eddie Dean's life.

TED BRAUTIGAN:
The most powerful Breaker at Devar-Toi, Ted is the leader of the resistance there. When Ted first lays eyes on Jake, he mistakes the boy for Bobby Garfield. Ted tells the gunslingers what he suspects regarding the reason the children of Calla Bryn Sturgis were kidnapped— that their brains provided food to increase the Breakers' powers.

Ted, Dinky Earnshaw, and Sheemie are instrumental in helping the gunslingers engineer the downfall of the prison camp. He is last seen leading his fellow Breakers toward Calla Bryn Sturgis, where they hope to start a new life.

DINKY EARNSHAW:
Dinky, who first appeared in the King novella "Everything's Eventual," was captured by the Crimson King's low men and brought to Devar-Toi, where he met up with his co-conspirator, Ted Brautigan.

SHEEMIE RUIZ:
An acquaintance of Roland, the somewhat dim-witted Sheemie made prior appearances in *The Gunslinger* and *Wizard and Glass*. One of the residents of Devar-Toi, Sheemie has the power to transport himself and others over great distances, a power he uses to assist Ted Brautigan in his efforts to free the Breakers of Devar-Toi. Sheemie's power transports Jake, Oy, and Roland to 1999 Keystone Earth Maine to save Stephen King. He later dies from an infected foot wound sustained during the battle of Devar-Toi.

AARON DEEPNEAU:
Together with John Cullum and Moses Carver, he formed what came to be known as the *ka-tet* of the rose. The trio proved to be the driving force behind the creation of the Tet Corporation, whose main goal was to stand in the way of the evil Sombra Corporation. He dies in 1992 from cancer. Nancy Deepneau, his grandniece, carries on his work as an employee of the Tet Corporation.

THE TET CORPORATION: The end result of the formation of the *ka-tet* of the rose, its New York headquarters was built on the site of a formerly vacant lot on Second Avenue and Forty-sixth Street in New York City. In its lobby lives the fabled rose, protected against those who seek to destroy it. Roland travels to New York to visit the leaders of the Tet Corporation. Cullum and Deepneau are gone, but a surprisingly hardy Moses Carver (he's 100 years old in 1999) still works there. Roland is given some key intelligence by the Tet Corporation, information that aids him in pursuing his quest for the Dark Tower.

MOSES CARVER: One hundred years old in 1999, Moses is the last living member of the *ka-tet* of the Rose. Meeting Roland is the fulfillment of a lifelong dream of the old man, Susannah's godfather. He likens Roland's gun to King Arthur's sword Excalibur.

THE CALVINS: Tet Corporation scholars, they spend their days reading Stephen King's works, trying to glean important information about the Dark Tower. They tell Roland that *Insomnia* is the most important of King's non-Tower books, and that he should be on the lookout for Patrick Danville.

THE THREE KINGS: Known as Feemalo, Fimalo, and Fumalo (calling to mind "Jack and the Beanstalk"), these three entities, representing the id, the ego, and the superego, all look like Stephen King circa 1977. Their attempts to delay Roland and Susannah fail, as the gunslingers kill Feemalo and Fumalo. Roland leaves Fimalo behind to warn Mordred off, saying, "And tell him that he if comes forward, I'll kill him as I intend to kill his red father."

DANDELO: A final obstacle for Roland and Susannah to overcome on the road to the Dark Tower, this creature feeds off misery. One of its main sources of sustenance is young Patrick Danville, kept imprisoned in its basement. He initially appears to the duo as a harmless old man named Joe Collins. Before Susannah kills Dandelo, he briefly shows the face of a deranged clown.

PATRICK DANVILLE: The same boy whose fate was at stake in *Insomnia*. Patrick is imprisoned by Dandelo, who feeds off the boy's misery. He is freed by Roland and Susannah, and accompanies them as they approach the Dark Tower. A gifted artist, Patrick can change reality through his drawings. First, he heals a cancerous sore on Susannah's face by drawing her countenance, then erasing her malady. Then Patrick draws a doorway that allows Susannah to leave Mid-World. Finally, he crafts an uncanny likeness of the Crimson King, which he then erases entirely but for the King's red eyes, eliminating him as a threat. Roland does not allow Patrick to enter the Dark Tower. Instead, he instructs him to seek out Dandelo's service robot Stutterin' Bill, who might be able to take him to a door that opens on Patrick's America.

STEPHEN KING: The author, who lives on "Keystone Earth," plays a rather passive role in the Dark Tower. On his way to his death by automobile accident at the hands of Bryan Smith, King is saved from his fate by the intervention of Jake Chambers, who absorbs the killing force of the van's impact. Thus spared, King begins a slow recuperation, eventually mustering the determination to finish writing the *Dark Tower* saga, allowing Roland to meet his fate. After the accident, the stiffness and pain that have plagued Roland are transferred to King.

BRYAN SMITH: The hapless driver of the minivan that struck Stephen King on June 19, 1999. By writing about him in *The Dark Tower*, King reinforces the feeling he had after the accident that he had somehow been struck by one of his own characters.

THE CRIMSON KING: Roland's adversary tries to gain access to the Dark Tower, but is denied entrance. Taking up a position on a balcony outside the Tower, he tries to ward off the approaching gunslinger with explosives called, à la Harry Potter's "snitch," sneetches. The Crimson King is rendered harmless by Patrick Danville, who draws a picture of him, then erases it, except for the King's glowing red eyes. Those eyes remain hovering over the balcony where the King once stood.

THE DARK TOWER: Once Roland enters the structure, the meaning of the book's subtitle, "Resumption," becomes clear. After witnessing bits and pieces of his life on various levels of the Tower, Roland finds himself at its peak, ready to resume his pursuit of the man in black across the desert. It is clear he has lived this quest many times, but always lost the Horn of Eld in the battle that wiped out all of the other gunslingers. This time, however, he has managed to retain the Horn, and so perhaps with the Horn and the benefit of the hard lessons he's learned, Roland may finally find peace.

THE DARK TOWER: TRIVIA

- The creature called Dandelo survives by consuming the misery of others and is a trickster who appears to his prey as a kind of distorted clown. King has said publicly that Dandelo and Pennywise the Clown from *It* are not one and the same. However, it seems likely that the two are in some way related, at least as the same sort of creature.

- The robot, "Stutterin' Bill," is quite reminiscent of the character from *It*, and though the connection is never explained, it is there nevertheless.

- Turtleback Lane, where the story's King has his vacation home in Lovell, Maine, clearly gets its name from Maturin, Guardian of the Beam, the Turtle who legend says carries the world upon his back. In addition, that home is called Cara Laughs. The main action of King's *Bag of Bones* takes place in a similar vacation home named Sara Laughs, clearly an alternate-reality version of the same structure.

8

THE EYES OF THE DRAGON

(1982)

*T*he *Eyes of the Dragon* is a strange addition to the canon of Stephen King. It is a book for young readers, though older audiences will be no less entertained. As the story goes, King's daughter, Naomi, complained to her father that he never wrote anything she would want to (or be allowed to?) read. Thus, King set out to do just that, and dedicated the book to both Naomi and to Ben Straub, son of his longtime friend and twotime collaborator, Peter Straub. Indeed, the Ben and Naomi characters in the book are quite obviously named after the then-children the tale was dedicated to.

This novel is a fairy tale, told in a serious and yet somehow whimsical voice. It is a story of long ago, a story told at bedtime, perhaps. It has magic and kings and clever princes, intrigue and poisons and brave young girls.

The Eyes of the Dragon is the story of a kingdom and two young princes, Peter and Thomas. When the court magician, the evil Flagg, kills their father, he arranges for it to appear as though the elder prince, Peter, did the deed. Peter is a shrewd young man, and he would have inherited the throne and like as not tossed Flagg out of the kingdom of Delain moments after being crowned.

But Flagg prepared for that eventuality. He cut Thomas, the younger prince, out of the pack. Thomas has always felt that in their father's eyes he could not live up to his older brother's example. Flagg plays on that until Thomas is almost entirely his creature. When Peter is framed for the king's murder, though Thomas knows it is Flagg who is responsible, the younger brother does not make any attempt to help the elder.

Thomas becomes monarch, and Peter is imprisoned at the top of the Needle, a narrow tower that stands at the center of the kingdom. Peter forges an ingenious and extraordinarily patient scheme to escape—a plan that could only be found in a fairy tale. He uses the tiny working loom in his mother's old dollhouse, and a small number of threads stolen every day from the napkin that comes with his lunch, to weave a lengthy rope. It takes many years to complete, of course.

When the time finally comes for him to make his escape, he has help from some of those who still believe in him. At the same time, Thomas is at last tired of living with the horrible guilt of what he knows, and has determined to defy and hopefully destroy Flagg. In the end, the kingdom is at peace once more, with Peter as ruler, and his friends Naomi and Ben live "happily ever after." Thomas and Dennis (who had been his butler) go out across the land in search of Flagg, who escaped. They are determined to find him and put an end to him once and for all. The results of that quest are not revealed in the story (though the boys' hunt for Flagg is referred to in the *Dark Tower* series).

There are many interesting facets of this story. Primary among them is this: though Thomas shares the role of protagonist with Peter, and it appears to be a narrative in which the younger brother, falsely made monarch, will rise to the occasion and make all things right, Thomas does *not* emerge the hero. The account does not follow that path, but remains, in Thomas's case, a rather sad one. He may share the role of protagonist, and he may be the one to turn the tables on Flagg, but he is *not* a hero.

There is no doubt that *Eyes* is fashioned as a fairy tale. However, it is also far more than that. Not only does it contain a number of adult elements, including a discussion of the sexual practices of the ruler of Delain, but it also has strong ties to the rest of the Stephen King Universe, links that have become stronger as time has passed, and additional material has been added to the fabric of the tapestry King has created.

The most obvious of these is Flagg. The author's most ubiquitous villain, Flagg also appears in *The Stand* (1978) and the *Dark Tower* series (1982–2004), specifically, and in several other places as well (though disguised), including 1999's *Hearts in Atlantis*. Interestingly enough, though we first spotted him (or at least, first know him) as the Walkin' Dude from *The Stand*, in *Eyes* it is revealed that he has spent a great deal of time in *this* world. He has returned, for many decades at a time, century after century, to plague the kingdom of Delain.

Why Delain? What is its special fascination for Flagg? Readers are given insight into this in volume seven of the Dark Tower series, where King explains that it was Flagg's hometown.

Thomas and Dennis, and their quest in pursuit of Flagg, are mentioned by Roland in the *Dark Tower* series, but that is not enough to be 100 percent certain that Roland's world and the world of *Eyes* are one and the same. The author went to great length to establish that certainty, however, and only recently. For the 1998 novella collection *Legends*, he penned an entry entitled *The Little Sisters of Eluria*. Therein, Roland the Gunslinger meets a boy who is from Delain, a kingdom Roland knows of, and that he expects to pass through on his quest.

As such, one could very easily look at *The Eyes of the Dragon* as a segment of the Dark Tower series, a part of that story just as important, if not more so, than such other "linked" works as *The Stand* (1978), *Insomnia* (1994), and *'Salem's Lot* (1975).

THE EYES OF THE DRAGON: PRIMARY SUBJECTS

PETER: The older son of King Roland of Delain, he becomes king briefly upon his father's death, only to be framed for the murder by Flagg. He spends years as a prisoner, until his own ingenious plan for escape and his friends' determination to free him combine to not only give him liberty, but to reveal Flagg as the true villain.

It is presumed that Peter is still king of Delain.

THOMAS: The younger son of King Roland, Thomas is disaffected and jealous, and is manipulated into becoming Flagg's puppet after his brother is imprisoned. Thomas proves to be a very poor king, but he eventually rebels against Flagg, almost destroying him in vengeance for the murder of King Roland. When Peter again becomes ruler and Flagg flees Delain, Thomas and his former butler, Dennis, set off after the wizard in hopes of destroying him once and for all.

It is unknown whether they ever managed to catch up with Flagg, though the sorcerer himself is now dead.

FLAGG: An ancient wizard, possibly a demon, Flagg has existed for millennia. He has plagued Delain time and again for much of that time. His latest scheme in the kingdom involved his killing of King Roland and his plot to frame the king's son, Peter, so as to control the kingdom and bring about its ruin through his manipulation of Peter's younger brother, Thomas.

Flagg's plan eventually fails, and he flees the kingdom.

He continued to plague others across many worlds until he was slain by Roland of Gilead.

KING ROLAND: Once the king of Delain, Roland was good, but not very bright. He was the father of Peter and Thomas. His wizard and adviser, Flagg, plotted against him, and finally murdered him. No relation to Roland of Gilead.

DENNIS: The son of Brandon, Dennis is born into service to the royal family of Delain. As Brandon was King Roland's butler, so Dennis is butler first to Peter, and later to Thomas. When Peter is eventually freed, Dennis joins Thomas on his quest to find and destroy Flagg.

They remain on their quest.

BEN STAAD: Though not of a noble family, Ben Staad is King Peter's best friend as a child, and throughout their lives. He is one of the prime movers involved in the effort to free Peter from the Needle. Eventually he marries Naomi.

It is presumed that he yet lives in Delain, and remains the king's close friend and confidant.

NAOMI REECHUL: The daughter of a noble family who have fled Delain in fear of Flagg, Naomi becomes part of the effort to free Peter from the Needle, and falls in love with Ben Staad along the way. They are eventually married. It is presumed that she still lives in Delain.

ANDERS PEYNA: Once upon a time, Peyna was the Judge General of Delain. It is he who, upon seeing Peter crying at news of his father's death, thinks those tears imply guilt in the king's murder, and orders a trial. But Peyna comes to believe that he may have made a mistake, and is instrumental in helping to free Peter years later.

It is presumed that Anders Peyna still resides in retirement somewhere in Delain.

SASHA: The queen of Delain, she is the mother of Peter and Thomas, but dies giving birth to her second son. Her death is no accident, but, rather, is engineered by Flagg.

NINER: A dragon slain by King Roland, whose head is displayed upon the wall of the king's private chamber. There is a secret passage behind the wall from which one can see into the chamber through the dragon's eyes.

THE EYES OF THE DRAGON: TRIVIA

- In *The Eyes of the Dragon*, King mentions a witch named Rhiannon of the Coos. Much later, in *Dark Tower IV* (1997), we are introduced to a nasty, vicious witch called Rhea of the Coos. In the 1998 novella *The Little Sisters of Eluria*, Roland thinks about Rhea "and her sisters," yet another link to tie *Eyes* to the Tower.

- King mentions that Flagg is reading from a book of darkest magic, bound in human skin, which was written by a "madman" named Alhazred. This is an obvious nod to horror grandmaster H. P. Lovecraft, whose own book of darkest magic, the *Necronomicon*, was also supposedly written by a madman named Alhazred.

9

THE TALISMAN

(1984)

It's a mind-bending endeavor, attempting to incorporate *The Talisman* into the Stephen King Universe. In some ways, it should not be done at all. The simple fact that King did not author the book alone, but in full collaboration with his friend and colleague Peter Straub—a masterful writer in his own right—should disqualify the novel. But given that its sequel, *Black House*, ties the events of this book closely to *The Dark Tower* series, it must be included herein.

What that means is that by virtue of the logic we've followed throughout this volume, the entire works of Peter Straub could conceivably be connected to the SKU as well. Of course, that is a sort of mysterious logic that King has employed in his fiction. We could continue: since Straub has a character in his novel *Mystery* who is essentially the Shadow, we might include all of the early Shadow pulps as well.

Obviously, we must draw the line somewhere. Logic dictates that it be drawn cleanly between the two authors of this novel. So, while King and Straub coauthored *The Talisman*, it will be in its relation to the overall Stephen King Universe that we address that work, and only in that context.

The Talisman, for all its classic Americana—a King trademark—is a quest novel in the grand fantasy tradition of such fiction. A teenager named

Jack Sawyer discovers that his mother, Lily Cavanaugh, is dying of cancer. Almost simultaneously, however, he encounters Speedy Parker, an elderly African-American blues musician turned maintenance man. Parker reveals to Jack that he has a destiny that could lead him to find a cure for his mother's ailment.

Jack is supposed to travel across the country, from coast to coast, to find the mystical icon known as the Talisman. It is an object of extraordinary power that contains within itself a sort of microcosm of all time and space. With it, Jack can cure his mother. In his travels, Jack is able to "flip" back and forth between the "real" world and a place called "the Territories," a parallel reality in which there are many people who are doppelgangers—or "twinners"—of people in Jack's world.

The queen of the Territories is also dying, for she is Lily Cavanaugh's twinner.

Traveling in both worlds, Jack must retrieve the Talisman and bring it home. In that way, it is also a classic journey. The authors are at pains to reveal that one of the major inspirations for the book is the work of Mark Twain, the classic American novelist. Twain's *Tom Sawyer* (1876) and *Huckleberry Finn* (1885) are clearly the precedents upon which this book is dependent. Jack's last name, after all, is Sawyer. The novel ends with a quote from Twain. And Lester "Speedy" Parker begins as a character who might easily have been torn from the pages of Twain's stories.

Twain is not the only literary influence, however. It seems that the authors thought to throw in a bit of Charles Dickens as well. His *Oliver Twist* (1839) shares certain elements with the sections of *The Talisman* in which Jack and his friend Wolf are forced to become "guests" at a home for wayward boys called the Sunlight Gardener Home. The way the older boys treat the younger, or more recently arrived, kids, and the way Gardener deals with the local authorities, is quite Dickensian in nature.

Indeed, there are a great many classic elements in this novel, right alongside the very new, the very Straub, and the very King. Among the elements that are "very King" is all the talk of multiple dimensions and the thinning of certain places between them. Although in *The Dark Tower: The Gunslinger* (1982), it was clear that Jake had come from another, parallel world, it was not until much later, after *The Talisman*, that the concept of "thinnies" or places where the barriers between dimensions are worn down and can be traveled through began to show up. And yet this idea plays a significant role here.

Even more significant, however, is that this was the place where King (with Straub) first explored in earnest the idea of infinite dimensions. This has become not only a fundamental building block of King's work ever since, but the major premise for the book you now hold in your hands.

Moreover, beyond Jack's universe and the Territories, *The Talisman* also contains thinly veiled references to the Dark Tower. The place where the Talisman is located, and which only people who are unique in the multiverse (as is the Talisman) can enter, is called "the black hotel." But when Jack touches the Talisman and the world around him rapidly shifts through hundreds of variations, one of those permutations seems to be the Dark Tower of Roland's world.

In essence, *The Talisman* is a book about youth, hope, and innocence.

THE TALISMAN: PRIMARY SUBJECTS

JACK SAWYER: The son of a Hollywood agent and a movie starlet, Jack Sawyer led a pretty privileged life in California. Even as a child, though, strange things happened around him. He registered them, but they didn't have any impact for some time. His father, Phil Sawyer, died, and later, his mother, Lily Cavanaugh Sawyer, brought him to Arcadia Beach in New Hampshire, to an old hotel called the Alhambra, where Jack learns that his mother is dying of cancer.

There, in New Hampshire, Jack meets a man named Lester "Speedy" Parker, who reveals to him (or, more accurately, reminds him of) the existence of a place called the Territories, an alternate, almost medieval dimension. Jack learns that there are people in the Territories who are essentially alternate versions of people in the "real" world. Speedy calls those people "Twinners."

Jack's twinner, Jason, was the son of the queen of the Territories, Laura DeLoessian, but Jason was killed very young, due to the machinations of the villainous Morgan of Orris. Jack soon learns that Queen Laura is also dying.

Spurred on by Speedy, and his fear for his mother, Jack sets off on a quest to retrieve a magical Talisman, which Speedy tells him will save the lives of both of his "mothers." Meanwhile, his father's former business partner, Morgan Sloat, has been working to control the Territories for years, and now tries to prevent Jack from retrieving the Talisman.

"Flipping" back and forth between his own world and the Territories, Jack travels across the United States until he reaches a place referred to as "the black hotel," wherein the Talisman is kept. He has many and grand adventures on the way, and eventually retrieves the Talisman. With it, he saves the lives of both his mother and Queen Laura of the Territories.

LILY CAVANAUGH: B-movie queen Lily Cavanaugh married Phil Sawyer, an aspiring Hollywood agent. They become the parents of a boy named Jack. After her husband's death, Lily must raise Jack and thwart the interests of her late husband's sleazy former business partner, Morgan Sloat. When Lily discovers she is dying of cancer, she takes Jack to the Alhambra Hotel in New Hampshire, after the summer tourists have gone home.

Lily remains there for some time. Despite her fatal disease, there is always a spark of hope in her. She doesn't really understand about the Territories, and what her husband and Sloat had been up to, but she knows it was something incredible. She also knows that Jack is linked to it somehow. So when he tells her that he's leaving to find a way to cure her, somehow, she has faith. Or at least she has hope.

However, in Jack's absence, Morgan Sloat does his best to break Lily down. She refuses to give in. Eventually, Jack brings the Talisman back and heals her cancer.

WOLF: A werewolf from the Territories, he is a gentle soul save for the times when the full moon is upon him. Even then, however, his instinct is always to protect the "herd." In the Territories, the "wolfs" are all almost all shepherds, and the herd is sacred. To this particular Wolf, Jack becomes the herd.

Wolf dies to protect him.

MORGAN SLOAT: A Hollywood agent, Sloat once was the business partner of Phil Sawyer. Sloat is an envious, insidious man who discovers the mystery and magic of the Territories and does his best to abuse that knowledge and turn the Territories into his own kingdom. He has even greater ambitions, including the proprietorship of the Talisman and the total control of infinite reality. He kills Phil Sawyer and several other people along the way, and would have liked to have done in young Jack Sawyer if he'd had the chance.

Sloat dies in final battle with Jack over the Talisman on a stretch of California beach.

MORGAN OF ORRIS: Also known as Morgan Thudfoot, this vicious man is the twinner of Morgan Sloat. In the Territories, he is very powerful, and intends to overthrow Queen Laura.

He dies when his twinner does.

RICHARD SLOAT: The son of Morgan Sloat, Richard was Jack's best childhood friend. He also saw strange things as a boy, but rather than pursue them, as Jack has, he closes his mind off to such things and becomes an ultrarealist, until Jack draws him into his adventures in the Territories. There, Richard aids Jack in his quest. Eventually, parentless, Richard is taken in by Lily Cavanagh. In 2001's *Black House*, readers were informed that Richard went on to found his own law firm, Sloat & Associates, Ltd.

LESTER "SPEEDY" PARKER: Speedy, whose twinner is a man responsible for law and justice in the Territories, is a figure of some mystery. He plays an important role in finding Jack in New Hampshire and clarifying his quest, and gives him the potion that allows him to "flip" between worlds at first. He later aids Jack with advice during the journey.

PARKUS: The twinner to Speedy Parker, Parkus is essentially the marshal in charge of peace and justice in the Territories. It is presumed that he remains there, and still retains that position.

PHIL SAWYER: Jack Sawyer's father, he is one of the first to discover the Territories. Phil is murdered on the instructions of his business partner, Morgan Sloat. His twinner is Prince Philip Sawtelle, who dies in the Territories at about the same time.

OSMOND: The right-hand man of Morgan of Orris, he is the twinner of Sunlight Gardener. Osmond is a vicious, sadistic man. He dies in the final battle on the beach in California.

QUEEN LAURA DELOESSIAN: The Queen of the Territories, Laura DeLoessian is much loved by her people. Thanks to the machinations of Morgan of Orris, she falls ill and would have died if Jack Sawyer, the twinner of her dead son, had not saved her by fetching the Talisman.

It is presumed that Queen Laura still rules the Territories.

SUNLIGHT GARDENER: Osmond's twinner, Gardener is an evangelist who runs a home for wayward boys that in reality is nothing more than a slaving operation. The sadistic preacher dies during the final conflict on the beach in California.

JASON: The late son of Queen Laura of the Territories, Jason was Jack Sawyer's twinner. It was widely considered that he would return to live again, in messianic fashion, to save the Territories. Those who met Jack during his quest often thought he was Jason reborn.

THE BLACK HOTEL: The structure that houses the Talisman before Jack removes it, the black hotel might also be an alternate-reality version of the Dark Tower.

THE TALISMAN: TRIVIA

- The two-headed parrot, called EAST-HEAD and WEST-HEAD in *The Talisman*, might well be the same creature owned by Flagg in *The Eyes of the Dragon* (1987). Just a thought.

- Filmmaker Steven Spielberg has held the screen rights to the novel almost since its publication. As of this writing, the film version is in preproduction with Spielberg as producer.

10

BLACK HOUSE

(2001)

At the end of 1984's *The Talisman*, the then-thirteen-year-old Jack Sawyer had just successfully completed his quest to save his dying mother's life by obtaining the Talisman, the axis of all possible worlds. There ended, as the coauthors of that book indicated, the history of Jack the boy, as he had just taken the first steps on the road to becoming a man.

Over the next several years, fans often raised the topic of a sequel, but answers about Jack's life subsequent to 1984 were not forthcoming until April 1999, when Stephen King and Peter Straub met to begin outlining a new Jack Sawyer adventure. Although plans to commence the writing of the book were interrupted by King's accident in June 1999, the duo was able to begin writing in February 2000. *Black House* was finally published in the late summer of 2001, four days after 9/11.

Structurally, *Black House* is more reminiscent of *Insomnia* than *The Talisman* because of its slow movement from the "real" to the fantastic, and in the fact that its characters (who, like Ralph Roberts and Lois Chase, face off against King's major villain, the Crimson King) are merely pawns in a much larger cosmic chess game. It also differs from *The Talisman* in that the writing is more seamless—the authors have stated publicly the great lengths they went to to conceal their specific contributions to the text, and it shows. The book also has the advantage of being written by two more mature, more seasoned authors. Despite their already immense talents, and their considerable success, they continued to mature as writers. A good example of this is their use of an omniscient narrator for certain portions of the book, another tip of their hat to Charles Dickens's *Bleak House*—somewhat distracting at first, it turns out to be a wise choice, even providing the authors with a chance to engage in some self-deprecating humor.

Although serial killers in Wisconsin are squarely in Straub territory, it's clear that the book is set in the Stephen King universe. (Per publicity materials, the ties to the *Dark Tower* novels were Straub's idea.) Besides the Crimson King, there are mentions of Breakers and of Ted Brautigan, a concept and character introduced in King's *Hearts in Atlantis*. Interestingly, a link is forged between King's and Straub's realities when Milton Wanderley, brother of Don Wanderley from Straub's novel *Ghost Story*, is mentioned in passing. So *Black House* settles some questions about continuity in the Stephen King universe, and raises others.

Might another sequel be in the offing? Well, Peter Straub has said that "Given the tendency of fantasy novels to parcel themselves out in units of three, it would be entirely reasonable to propose a third part to the *Talisman* series." Indeed, Straub has publicly expressed his willingness to work with King on a third book. Whether such a book will appear in the future seems to depend mainly on King's desire to tackle such a project.

BLACK HOUSE: PRIMARY SUBJECTS

JACK SAWYER: Although still drawn to adventure, the Jack Sawyer readers first encounter in *Black House* remembers nothing of the time he spent in the Territories—a true child of the seventies and eighties, the adult Jack has thoroughly repressed all memories of his harrowing adventures in that strange land. In the ensuing years, Jack has become, to use his own term, a famous "coppiceman," an LAPD detective whose exploits have garnered him considerable attention in the national press. At several points in the novel, it's made clear that his success has everything to do with the time he spent in the Territories, and with his experiences with the Talisman itself.

One of Jack's greatest professional triumphs occurred in the small Wisconsin town of French Landing, where he uncovered a killer who had slaughtered a prostitute in Los Angeles. Jack's visit to the town left a deep impression on him, so deep that he retired there shortly after the case was solved. Jack looked forward to a peaceful retirement, but, alas, that was not to be.

French Landing is being terrorized by the Fisherman, a serial killer who preys on young children, dismembering and cannibalizing them. Baffled by the lack of leads, local law enforcement asks Jack for his assistance. Initially reluctant, Jack is finally convinced to help by an innate sense of responsibility and by the prodding of his friend Henry Leyden, a blind DJ who fills the role of Jack's guide and mentor in the physical absence of *The Talisman*'s Speedy Parker. Immersing himself in the case, Jack realizes that the killings are only the tip of the iceberg when it comes to the evil present in French Landing. Discovering this, he once again finds himself involved with the Territories, where the Fisherman, who serves the cosmic villain known as the Crimson King, disappears with his victims. Jack's quest leads him to the mysterious Black House, a portal to the Territories, where he will embark on the next phase of his life.

LILY CAVANAUGH: Jack's mother, actress Lily Cavanaugh, has been dead for several years as of the time the events described in *Black House* occur. Jack's musings in the novel reveal that Lily died approximately five years after the events described in *The Talisman*, from a relapse of her cancer.

CHARLES BURNSIDE: Also known as "the Fisherman," "Burny" is an aging serial killer who resides in the Maxton Elder Care facility in French Landing. Although infirm, the killer is imbued with new vigor and talents when he is possessed by Mr. Munshun, a servant of the Crimson King. One of these talents is teleportation, which allows Burnside to leave Maxton undetected in search of his chosen prey, young children whom he kidnaps, dismembers, and devours.

Through Munshun, Burnside finds himself in the employ of the Crimson King, who is always in the market for breakers, children whose wild talents can be used to weaken the beams of the Dark Tower. Burnside finds a particularly powerful breaker in French Landing, a young man named Tyler Marshall. Burnside's kidnapping of Tyler causes Jack Sawyer to become more involved in the Fisherman murders, ultimately leading to Burnside's demise. Burnside manages to wreak a good amount of havoc before he passes on, however; he is responsible for the deaths of several children, and for the murder of Henry Leyden.

HENRY LEYDEN: Alias George Rathburn, alias the Wisconsin Rat, alias Henry Shake, alias Symphonic Stan, Leyden is a blind man with an affinity for music of all kinds. He also is Jack's best friend in French Landing. Henry is a parental figure for Jack, filling the roles formerly played by Jack's mother, Lily, and Lester "Speedy" Parker, Jack's mentor from the Territories.

Henry, who encounters Charles Burnside when he DJs an event at the Maxton Elder Care facility, eventually realizes that Burnside is the killer after listening to a tape of the killer's voice provided to him by Jack. Henry is killed by Burnside, but not before he wounds the killer. Ty Marshall later exploits that wound to dispatch Burnside in a truly grisly manner.

DALE GILBERTSON: The chief of police of French Landing, Dale is Henry Leyden's nephew. Dale becomes friendly with Jack after working with him on the Thornberg Kinderling murder case, eventually selling him his family homestead when Jack decides to settle in French Landing. It is partly a desire to help Dale, who is in way over his head, that draws Jack into the Fisherman case.

JUDY MARSHALL/SOPHIE: In Jack's world, Judy Marshall is the distraught mother of Tyler Marshall, the Fisherman's last kidnapping victim. Judy is being driven crazy by her son's disappearance, and by her connection to her twinner in the Territories, Queen Sophie, successor to Queen Laura DeLoessian. Trying to warn Judy, Sophie has instead brought her to the brink of insanity.

When Jack first meets Judy, he is strangely drawn to her; when he meets her twinner, Sophie, he instantly falls in love with her. As *Black House* concludes, Jack is convalescing in the Territories under the care of Sophie and Speedy Parker.

TYLER MARSHALL: Tyler is perhaps the most powerful Breaker ever to live, perhaps even more powerful than the legendary Ted Brautigan. His kidnapping by Charles Burnside, a serial killer possessed by a minion of the Crimson King, attracts Jack Sawyer's interest, ultimately leading to the downfall of the Crimson King's plans to use Tyler to break the Beams that hold reality together.

Ty proves very resourceful, eventually bringing about the demise of his captor despite being shackled.

THE HEGELIAN SCUM: A gang of highly educated bikers, also known as the Thunder Five, who live on the outskirts of French Landing. They become involved in the Fisherman case when the madman kidnaps the daughter of one of their number, Armand "Beezer" St. Pierre. The gang loses one of its members, Mouse, when they assist Jack in his assault on the Black House.

THE BLACK HOUSE: In Random House's promotional materials, Peter Straub says, "As Shirley Jackson would say, Black House is not sane." Like the Black Hotel from *The Talisman*, the Black House is a portal to other worlds. The house is located on the outskirts of town, but is not easily located unless one is looking for it. Even then, it is difficult. Fortunately, Jack Sawyer and the Thunder Five locate the house, which they come to realize is a doorway to the reality where Mr. Munshun has taken Ty Marshall.

THE CRIMSON KING: Also referred to as Abbalah in *Black House*, the Crimson King is the force behind the effort to bring down the Dark Tower.

It is revealed in *Black House* that the king has spent the last two centuries gathering a massive group of "Breakers" (i.e., those who display wild talents such as precognition, telepathy, and telekinesis) together. The king uses them to hasten the destruction of the Beams that hold reality together. In *Black House*, the king seeks to secure the cooperation of Ty Marshall, potentially the most powerful Breaker besides Ted Brautigan.

BLACK HOUSE: TRIVIA

- Speedy Parker, Jack Sawyer's old friend and mentor, is revealed to be a gunslinger from the world of Roland of Gilead.

- *Black House* was heavily influenced by Charles Dickens's *Bleak House*, from which Jack reads aloud to the blind Henry Leyden at one point in the novel.

11

HEARTS IN ATLANTIS

(1999)

*H*earts in Atlantis is truly a milestone for Stephen King, coming at a point in his long career when many authors might no longer be capable of anything resembling a milestone.

In this volume, King achieves something that might have seemed impossible upon conception: he has written his most ambitious literary novel—an exploration of the many facets of the Vietnam War era and the way it has tarnished America's idea of itself—and yet this is also a novel filled with wonder and terror and a significant and tangible connection to his most fantastic and epic work, the *Dark Tower* series (1982–2004).

Though still a novel in the sense that it does relate a singular narrative, *Hearts in Atlantis* is also experimental. It begins with a segment called *Low Men in Yellow Coats* which, at 243 pages, is a novel unto itself. Set in 1960, it deals with the coming of age of Bobby Garfield, a Connecticut boy who finds, much to his surprise, that his best pal, Carol Gerber, is, in fact, his girlfriend. But it is also the story of Ted Brautigan, who takes a room on the upper floor of the boardinghouse where Bobby lives with his mother, Liz.

Ted and Bobby form an odd friendship, based mainly around the fact that Ted doesn't treat him like a kid as well as their shared love for books. Bobby also must keep the secret that Ted is on the run from the Low Men in Yellow Coats. At first Bobby isn't sure if Ted is quite sane, and Liz wonders if Ted might be a pervert (because she is dealing with her own issues with a boss who is a sexual predator, her cynicism is perfectly understandable).

Both Bobby and Carol are forced to grow up in this tale. Carol is hurt by local bullies, and Bobby pays them back in spades. After a horrible confrontation with Bobby's mother, Ted is almost handed over to the low men and is forced to leave town.

Tragically, the low men catch up to Ted anyway, and Bobby is given the choice of trying to help and being taken along with Ted, or standing by and doing nothing. He chooses not to fight, and his life is changed forever. His youthful spirit and faith in himself are taken away. He becomes a juvenile delinquent, his life on an ugly path. The Garfields move, and Bobby's already-damaged relationships with Carol and with his best friend, Sully, wither. For some time, Bobby and Carol keep up writing to one another, but even that ends. Bobby believes that his destiny is a dark one.

Only when Bobby receives a note from Ted, forwarded by Carol, does he appear to have a change of heart. To understand that, however, it is necessary to really know Ted. Here is where the story veers into *The Dark Tower* territory and connects itself to the Stephen King Universe as a whole.

The low men are not human. Rather, they are supernatural shepherds of a sort, or trackers, who work for the Crimson King, the evil being who hopes to destroy the tower, and in that way all reality. The multiverse is bound together by Beams (made of energy or possibility or something else entirely), and the Tower's integrity is assured by those very Beams. Ted is a Breaker. He has certain mental abilities that when focused could help to shatter the Beams. In fact, the Crimson King enslaves him to do just that before he escapes to Bobby Garfield's world and time. In the end, he is recaptured by the low men, who bear a red eye upon their persons, the symbol of the Crimson King.

When Bobby receives that note, he realizes that Ted has escaped from the Court of the Crimson King again. There is hope. To illustrate that, Ted includes several rose petals, which have an effect on Bobby even he does not understand.

But *we do*. The implication is that those petals are from the rose of creation, which is an incarnation of the Dark Tower (and therefore all reality) itself, and which Roland and his friends are going to have to protect in that book series.

Hearts in Atlantis is a remarkable work for many reasons already stated. There is another, however. Though King's most mainstream book, it also has undeniable connections to other of his writings, such as those mentioned above, and a great many echoes of others.

The relationship between Bobby and Ted Brautigan, for example, is a very sweet mirror image of the horrifying relationship between Todd Bowden and Kurt Dussander in the 1982 novella *Apt Pupil*. In both narratives, a boy and an old man use the charade of the youth reading to the man due to his failing eyesight to cover up the truth from the boy's parent(s). And yet, the end results in each account could not be more different.

Ted's powers are similar, in some ways, to those of John Smith in *The Dead Zone* (1979). Ted's dialogue is laced with King references, including a joke about the library police (a nod to the novella *The Library Policeman* from *Four Past Midnight*, 1990), a paraphrasing of *The Dark Tower* refrain "there are other worlds than this," and an exact quote from *Storm of the Century* (1999)—"Give me what I want and I'll go away"—which seems quite intentional.

The Stephen King Universe is a tapestry being constantly woven with new colors and yet all of a piece. None of the author's works reveals that as completely as *Hearts in Atlantis*. For there is one other important connection to the author's fictional panorama, one that many readers will likely have missed. But we'll get to that shortly.

First, we move on to the second part of this epic, the title story, *Hearts in Atlantis*. At 150 pages, it is the second longest piece in the book, and it stands out as one of the most obviously autobiographical works of King's career. That is not to say that King wasted a semester of his college career playing the card game Hearts, as happens in this tale. But this narrative introduces us to Pete Riley, a freshman in 1966 at the University of Maine at Orono. No coincidence that King was also a freshman at Orono that year. It is, in its way, just as much a coming-of-age story as *Low Men in Yellow Coats*, but a different kind of age.

We think we lose our innocence when we become teenagers. Perhaps, as this story implies, that loss comes later. In this novella, Pete Riley and his friends get themselves wrapped up in a GPA-destroying obsession that causes some of them to fail academically and to be expelled. But there's no safety net for them. Those who are asked to leave are likely to be sent off to Vietnam; those sent to Asia during the war have a good chance of coming home in a body bag.

But the game of Hearts goes on.

Over the course of that semester, a distant war in Vietnam is brought to their attention. Despite their normal human faults, the students find enlightenment of a sort, and realize the horrible injustice of that war, but almost by accident. Few of the characters in this piece are actively seeking a cause, and yet it finds them.

The title novella may be completely a work of fiction, but it rings all too true. King has re-created this troubled era quite convincingly.

In this segment, Pete Riley is attracted to Carol Gerber, through whom we learn a bit more about Bobby Garfield. She has lost touch with him, and in high school, she and Bobby's best friend, John Sullivan, became romantically involved. But Sully is off fighting in Vietnam, and Carol is becoming a vocal antiwar protester. She is inspired by the way Bobby Garfield once lifted her in his arms, after she had been attacked by local boys, and carried her up the hill to his house, though she was even bigger than he was. She believes that somebody has to be there to help when injustice is being done. Though her relationship with Pete does not last, she has begun on a path that will lead to tragedy.

For the third installment, *Blind Willie*, the book jumps ahead to 1983 and focuses on Willie Shearman, who had been one of the boys who attacked Carol back in 1960. Willie never got over the guilt of what they did to her: he held her while a friend hit her with a baseball bat, hard enough to dislocate her shoulder. As a boy, he also stole Bobby Garfield's baseball glove, an item that takes on a talismanic importance.

In Vietnam, Willie saves John Sullivan's life, but that isn't enough. He hasn't done nearly enough penance, to his mind. He is injured, and temporarily blinded, but that isn't enough. Now, in 1983, Willie goes through a vastly complex series of ruses and identities to hide the truth: he suffers from a temporary blindness for several hours *every afternoon*. He has no job, save for begging for money in the guise of a blind vet named "William Garfield," and yet he has a life at home with a wife who loves him. Willie writes a message of apology thousands of times, a little each day. He gives a large portion of his income to the church, all to try to make up for what he once did.

He pays off the police to leave him alone while he is panhandling, but one of the cops is becoming trouble. By the end of the tale, it appears as though Willie will take on yet another identity to kill the cop. Such a deed would not be his, and therefore it wouldn't interfere with his penance.

In this segment, we learn a great deal more about Carol's fate through newspaper clippings that Willie keeps. She becomes involved with a militant antiwar group that plants a bomb at a college lecture hall. There aren't supposed to be any people in the building, but there are. Carol tries to stop it, but is pulled away by Raymond Fiegler, the leader of the group and probably her lover.

People die. The group is blamed, and is hunted down by the authorities. Eventually, in a confrontation with police, Carol supposedly dies in a house fire.

The fourth part of the book, *Why We're in Vietnam*, turns the focus to John Sullivan, and the year to 1999. Horribly wounded in the incident during which Willie Shearman saves his life, Sully has never been the same. In this short tale, we learn that he has been haunted since even before that incident by the ghost of an old Vietnamese woman whose life he could have saved, but didn't. She was murdered by another American soldier by the name of Ronnie Malenfant (a character who also appears in the novella *Hearts in Atlantis*).

In this section of the book, Sully is stuck in traffic on the way back from yet another funeral of a fellow veteran. He reminisces about a great many things, including the horrors of war and the fallout for veterans, both emotional and physical (e.g., the effects of Agent Orange). This story ends with yet another extraordinary moment. *Things* begin to fall from the sky, with no rhyme nor reason as to what exactly is falling: pianos and lawn mowers and ironing boards; anything you can imagine. And Bobby Garfield's old baseball glove, with a note inside it.

Only none of that actually occurs. What happens is that John Sullivan has a heart attack in his car during a traffic jam, and dies. But he dies with Bobby Garfield's baseball glove on his hand.

Finally, also in 1999, the book ends with *Heavenly Shades of Night Are Falling*, a brief sequence that brings the narrative back to Harwich, the little town where all of the central characters grew up, and to Bobby Garfield. He returns home for Sully's funeral. Bobby's a carpenter now, living in Philadelphia, with a wife and children. But he harbors the tiny hope that Carol is alive, because he's had a message from Ted Brautigan.

Carol *is* alive, of course, though she teaches at Vassar College under an assumed name and identity. And the message is for both of them. Sully's executor sends Bobby his old baseball glove, because on it is somehow inscribed, in Ted Brautigan's handwriting, Garfield's *current* address. Impossible, but true. Inside the glove is a sheet of paper torn out of a book that Ted and Bobby had loved in 1960, with the words "tell her she was as brave as a lion," referring to the time Ted fixed Carol's dislocated arm. And with an inscription familiar to Carol from her Vietnam days. Translated, it says, "Love plus peace equals information."

This final segment also reveals, albeit subtly, that other connection mentioned here earlier. Bobby doesn't notice Carol at the service for Sully because she does not want to be seen. Someone, a very dangerous and clever someone, taught her, once upon a time, how to remain unseen, how to be *dim*. Being dim, as we know from *The Eyes of the Dragon* (1987), is a trick of the dark sorcerer Randall Flagg, who also appears in *The Stand* (1978) and the *Dark Tower* series. Carol was involved with Raymond Fiegler, the leader of the protesters. Flagg has been shown to have many aliases over the years, and a number of them have also had the initials R. F. Raymond Fiegler is undoubtedly also an alias for Randall Flagg.

In the conclusion to *Hearts in Atlantis*—thanks to Ted, and to Sully's death—Bobby and Carol are brought back together to ponder the fundamental question of this novel. Earlier, a character laments that once upon a time, we had a chance to change the world, and "we blew it." The sentiment is shared as if it is *too late* now.

Or is it?

"People grow up," Carol tells Bobby firmly in the book's closing sequence. "They grow up and leave the kids they were behind."

"Do they?" Bobby asks.

The answer that is implied is this: not really. Not in their hearts.

HEARTS IN ATLANTIS: PRIMARY SUBJECTS

BOBBY GARFIELD: Bobby resides in Harwich, Connecticut, as a boy. During these formative years, he is best friends with John Sullivan and Carol Gerber, who is his first love. He and his mother, Liz, live in a boardinghouse. During the summer of 1960, a new boarder named Ted Brautigan moves in. Ted and Bobby become friends, though Bobby is only a boy, and although Ted is hiding out from people he calls "low men in yellow coats." Those low men turn out not to be human, and when he comes into contact with them, Bobby is forced to make a choice: fight for Ted and be captured with him, or stay out of it. He chooses not to get involved, and that decision sours his life for several years—up until the time he hears from Ted again, and realizes that Ted has escaped once more.

Today, Bobby Garfield lives outside of Philadelphia with his family. He is a carpenter by trade.

CAROL GERBER: In the summer of 1960, Carol is in love with her best friend, Bobby Garfield. During that same season, she is brutally beaten by several local boys, and Bobby takes vengeance upon the leader of the thugs. Later, after Bobby has moved out of Harwich, she dates his best friend, John Sullivan, for some years. In 1966, she attends the University of Maine at Orono, where she meets Pete Riley. Carol breaks off with Sully and dates Pete briefly, even as she becomes entrenched in the antiwar movement spawned by the crisis in Vietnam. Later, she becomes close to a man named Raymond Fiegler (who is also the creature known as Randall Flagg) and a group of militant antiwar protesters who plant a bomb that ends up taking lives.

Though she tries to stop it, Carol becomes a fugitive along with the others. She is believed to have died in a house fire with several of them, but survives, and resurfaces sometime later with a new identity as Denise Schoonover.

Today, under that new name, she lives in Poughkeepsie, New York, and is a professor at Vassar College.

JOHN SULLIVAN: As children, John Sullivan, or Sully-John, and Bobby Garfield are best friends. The events of the summer of 1960 so alter Bobby's behavior that their friendship is irrevocably damaged. After Bobby moves out of Harwich, Sully dates Carol Gerber. Not long after he and Carol break up in 1966, Sully is shipped off to Vietnam to fight in the military.

During the war, Sully endures some particularly horrid things, as do so many soldiers in Vietnam. He witnesses the useless murder of an old woman by a soldier named Ronnie Malenfant, and the ghost of that old woman haunts him for the rest of his life. Also in Vietnam, Sully's life is saved by Willie Shearman, a guy from his own hometown.

Sully has a heart attack and dies while his car sits stuck in traffic one day. Impossibly, when he is found, he wears Bobby Garfield's baseball glove on his hand, a glove that had been stolen from Bobby when they were children, and that neither of them had seen since.

TED BRAUTIGAN: Ted is a mysterious figure. Little concrete knowledge is available in regard to him, including the era and even dimension to which he truly belongs. He enters Bobby Garfield's life in a year that, to Bobby, is 1960. But Ted is on the run, even then, from the agents of the Crimson King, a force for chaos in the infinite multiverse. Ted had been forced to work for the King as a "Breaker," someone who had the ability to psychically chip away at the bonds, or Beams, holding reality together. Ted is recaptured, but later escapes once more, as evidenced by the messages he sends to Bobby Garfield. His further adventures are detailed in *The Dark Tower* series.

LIZ GARFIELD: Bobby's mother, Liz is widowed young and, in trying to make ends meet, finds herself with an employer who turns out to be a sexual predator. Eventually she becomes a successful real estate agent in Danvers, Massachusetts. It is presumed that she still resides there.

PETE RILEY: As a student at the University of Maine at Orono (UMO) in 1966, Pete falls in love with Carol Gerber. Though he nearly flunks out of school due to an unending card game of Hearts in his dorm, he eventually gets back on track and graduates. During this time, partially due to his relationship with Carol, and also his exposure to people like Stokely Jones, he becomes a war protester. Pete Riley's current whereabouts are unknown.

SKIP KIRK: Stanley "Skip" Kirk is a good friend of Pete Riley's at UMO, and also nearly falls victim to the game of Hearts. Today he is an artist of note, residing in Palm Beach, Florida. He has had at least one heart attack.

NATE HOPPENSTAND: Nate is Pete Riley's quiet, almost prissy roommate at UMO, but he is also secretly a war protester, and helps to open Pete's and Skip's eyes to the horrors of Vietnam. He still exchanges Christmas cards with his old roommate.

STOKELY JONES: Crippled in an auto accident, Stoke Jones is forced to use metal crutches at all times. He is the first student to wear the peace sign at UMO, that fall of 1966. Despite his curmudgeonly persona, he inspires an interest in the crisis in Vietnam among many of his fellow students. He drops out of college to protest full-time, but later becomes an attorney, and is a constant presence on various TV network news and political programs.

RAYMOND FIEGLER: The mysterious leader of the group of war protesters that included Carol Gerber, he is supposedly killed in a fire in 1971. However, there is great reason to believe that Fiegler is actually the creature known as Randall Flagg.

WILLIE SHEARMAN: Willie grows up in Harwich, Connecticut, along with Bobby Garfield, Carol Gerber, and John Sullivan. Unlike them, he attends St. Gabe's, a local Catholic school. Though he doesn't really want to, Willie succumbs to peer pressure and becomes a local bully. In that role, he steals Bobby Garfield's baseball glove. He also helps his friends beat Carol Gerber very badly in the summer of 1960, and is haunted with guilt from that incident ever after.

In Vietnam, Willie saves the life of John Sullivan, who had been Carol's boyfriend for a time. Even that is not enough to relieve his self-torment, however. During the war, he is badly wounded, and left with an incredible handicap: for several hours each afternoon, Willie is blind. Otherwise, his eyesight is fine. Over the years, he develops a complex multiple personality system, all based upon his guilt and what he thinks of as penance, which includes begging for money on a New York City street corner, and giving some of that income to the church.

During that time, he uses Bobby's old baseball glove as one of the objects of his bizarre penance. Though in 1983 he is still working on his penance, it seems possible or even likely that some new fate befalls him in 1999, because that same baseball glove appears in the possession of the late John Sullivan.

THE CRIMSON KING: An enormously powerful entity serving chaos, the Crimson King is working to unravel the ties that bind the infinite multiverse together.

THE LOW MEN: The low men are supernatural creatures who are employees of and enforcers for the Crimson King.

HEARTS IN ATLANTIS: TRIVIA

- Stephen King attended the University of Maine at Orono during the same period (1966–1970) as Carol Gerber, Pete Riley, and the others, though the version of the campus in *Hearts in Atlantis* has been altered for the purposes of the story.

- The segment *Blind Willie* first appeared, in very different form, in the magazine *Antaeus* in 1994, and later, also in different form, in the small press collection of the author's work *Six Stories* (1997).

- Bobby saw a classic Western film called *The Regulators*, which King invented for the novel of the same name, written under his pseudonym, Richard Bachman. The fact that this fictional film exists in both Bachman's work and that of King further unifies their universes.

- Ted Brautigan is a big proponent of reading, but his choice of books to recommend to Bobby is interesting. William Golding's *Lord of the Flies* (1954) is a favorite of King's, and the source of the name of his fictional town Castle Rock. Another, Clifford D. Simak's *Ring Around the Sun* (1952), may well have influenced King's idea of a multiverse.

- At the same time that Carol Gerber and Pete Riley were attending the University of Maine at Orono, Bill Denbrough of the novel *It* was also on campus as a student.

- The red eye that indicates the low men's fealty to the Crimson King brings to mind the eye of the evil wizard Sauron of *The Lord of the Rings* fame.

12

THE STAND

(1978)

Though it almost exists as a separate universe unto itself, *The Stand*'s (1978) connections to the *Dark Tower* series, in particular the presence of Randall Flagg in that book and the series, are strong enough that the novel occupies a significant division of the Dark Tower universe.

The Stand is one in a long line of classic apocalyptic novels. Those that came before it include such seminal tales as Robert Merle's *Malevil* (1972), Nevil Shute's *On the Beach* (1957), and Richard Matheson's *I Am Legend* (1954). However, while *The Stand* is certainly not the first postapocalyptic novel, it is, without a doubt, the one that all subsequent works in that sub-genre will be measured by.

That is a literal statement. *The Stand*, one of King's most popular works, which was translated into a four-night miniseries on the ABC network in 1994, is also a novel whose shocking events are ingrained in the consciousness of readers around the world. Particularly, it should be noted, in America, where even those who have never read the book or seen its television counterpart are likely to be familiar with its basic concepts.

One of the things that sets *The Stand* apart, that makes it the touch-stone for such tales, is a King trademark: Americana. Both the original (published in 1978) and the revised, expanded version (published in 1989) are richly layered with pop culture references. But more than merely reaching readers on that level, the book tells an epic story of good and evil while communicating an intimate familiarity with American lives.

Frannie Goldsmith is a young woman pregnant by her unsupportive boyfriend. Harold Lauder is the bitter outcast whose love for her is spurned. Nick Andros is a deaf-mute whose handicap brings out both the best and worst in people. Stu Redman is the quiet man, the classic Western hero type. Larry Underwood is a drug-and-drink-ravaged rock artist whose shot at stardom falls short.

They're characters we understand. This is one of the elements that King does best. And it's a good deal of what makes this entry the ultimate postapocalyptic tale. That, and the horror, of course. The fear. The hope. The knowledge that in the end, we can choose to help or to hurt. It's all in our hands.

In addition to all of that, however, *The Stand* has a very vital place in the Stephen King Universe. It has its beginnings in a short story called "Night Surf," which was originally published in the men's magazine *Cavalier* in August 1974. This tale features the first references to a "superflu" in King's work, and actually uses the name "Captain Trips" for the illness, a nickname that recurs in *The Stand*. It isn't clear that the two exist in the same branch of King's universe—that they are in continuity with each other—but since there is no mention of a year in the short story, it isn't unreasonable to presume as much.

The novel is perhaps most important to the Stephen King Universe in that it introduces the demonic Randall Flagg for the first time. Flagg would later reappear in various forms in *Eyes of the Dragon* (1987) and *Hearts in Atlantis* (1999). In *Dark Tower IV: Wizard and Glass* (1997), the hero, Roland, and his friends cross over from their dimension into the reality in which the events of *The Stand* take place—or a world strikingly similar to it—while on their quest.

But let us reflect upon the novel for its own sake, rather than its relationship to the Stephen King Universe at large. The popularity of *The Stand* among the author's legions of fans cannot be overlooked. Many consider it the greatest of his early works. While there are likely many reasons for this, some of which have already been touched upon, another is this: the whole is greater than the sum of its parts, but the parts themselves are extraordinarily memorable. Some of the characters and scenes that linger in the mind include: Frannie dreaming about the coat hanger. Tom Cullen. Nick Andros. Mother Abagail. The Trashcan Man. Flagg and poor, deluded Nadine in the desert. The sacrifice of the story's heroes in the end. Lloyd in prison. And, oh, the Lincoln Tunnel, of course, one of the most harrowing bits of prose ever written.

Finally, any examination of *The Stand* would be incomplete without comment on its religious content. There are two things that seem certain about the Stephen King Universe upon the conclusion of this novel. First, that hope and faith and good will *can* triumph over evil. Second, and quite insidiously, that until the final battle is fought at the very end of all things, evil will always find its way back to test, tempt, and terrorize us again.

THE STAND: PRIMARY SUBJECTS

STUART REDMAN: One warm day in Arnette, Texas, Stu is standing around drinking beer and jawing with some of his close friends at Hapscomb's Texaco station when a car crashes into the station. The driver of the car, Charles Campion, is infected with the superflu, as were his wife and daughter, who have already died. Campion expires shortly thereafter, but not without passing "Captain Trips"—the nickname for the disease, likely taken from the nickname of Grateful Dead guitarist Jerry Garcia—on to those at the station. Stu turns out to be immune—as .6% of the population is—and after escaping from a plague center in Stovington, Vermont, he hits the road. He is inspired by dreams of an old woman named Mother Abagail, and frightened by nightmares about Flagg, "the walkin' dude."

Stu proves himself to be an easygoing yet heroic man. He becomes a leader among the survivors of the plague, and is among those who go to Las Vegas to confront Flagg and his followers. Stu is the only survivor of that trip. In the end, after Flagg's defeat, he and Frannie Goldsmith—another survivor of the plague who is now his wife—return to her native Maine with her son.

ACE HIGH: One of Flagg's most trusted men, he is part of the inner circle in Las Vegas, along with Lloyd Henreid. He dies in a nuclear explosion in the gaming capital.

RANDALL FLAG (a.k.a. Ahaz, Anubis, Astaroth, Ramsey Forrest, Richard Frye, Nyarlahotep, R'yelah, Russell

Faraday, Seti, "The walkin' dude"): Who can really say what Flagg is? A demon, or something quite like it, most certainly. He has been known by an infinite number of names, and sowed the seed of evil across multiple dimensions.

He is watching carefully as the world dies, as 99.4% of the human population is killed off by the superflu, and he does his best to take advantage. He manipulates the survivors and sends them dreams guiding them to him, and he gathers all those who would heed him and follow him in Las Vegas. There he hopes to start a new human race, a breed of people with darkness in their hearts, who will bow to him as he demands.

He is a tempter, a liar, a killer, and a maker of ultimate mischief. He is the rot of civilization. He is entropy itself, bringing all things to their eventual destruction. But he is not all-powerful. Like all evil, he believes too much in the extent of his own power, and can be tricked. And in the end, he must answer to a higher power, as he does in Las Vegas. He is about to execute Glen Bateman, Larry Underwood, and Ralph Brentner when the Trashcan Man arrives with a nuclear warhead scrounged from a nearby U.S. military site. The Hand of God reaches down from the sky and detonates the warhead.

Flagg is thwarted. But not destroyed, never that. Shortly thereafter, he finds himself on a beautiful, tropical shore, with a band of mystified natives whom he terrified into becoming his acolytes.

But that is just one tiny shard of Flagg's fascinating story.

NICK ANDROS: In his travels after the plague has begun, deaf-mute Nick Andros drifts into Shoyo, Arkansas. There he is beaten up by the locals and then befriended by the sheriff, a man named John Baker. When Baker and the rest of Shoyo are eliminated by the superflu, Nick moves on and eventually meets Tom Cullen, a retarded man who is also immune, and whose dreams of Mother Abagail are quite similar to Nick's own. When they finally meet, Nick quickly becomes a favorite of Mother Abagail's, but is killed by a bomb designed by the traitorous Harold Lauder. Later, however, Nick's ghost appears to Tom Cullen, guiding Tom in the proper care for the gravely ill Stu Redman. It is not known whether Nick's spirit is still able to manifest itself.

GLEN BATEMAN: A retirement-aged sociology professor from Woodsville Community College, Glen finds himself immune to the superflu. He adopts his dead neighbor's dog, which he rechristens Kojak, when it appears the canine is also a rare survivor of his species. Glen travels with Stu Redman for a while before they all end up in Boulder, Colorado. Along with Ralph Brentner and Larry Underwood, Glen is one of those whose perseverance and sacrifice helps to thwart Flagg's plans. Glen dies in a Las Vegas prison cell, shot to death by Lloyd Henreid.

RALPH BRENTNER: Like Stu Redman in many ways, Ralph is a good and simple man, with a quiet strength others seem to gravitate toward. After the flu epidemic hits, he drives his truck on a quest to find Mother Abagail, an elderly woman many of the survivors have been dreaming about. Eventually, he picks up Nick Andros and Tom Cullen. In the end, Ralph is among those chosen few whom Mother Abagail instructs to go to Las Vegas and face Flagg. He dies in the nuclear explosion that destroys the city. In Boulder, a large monumental rock is named in his honor.

CHARLES CAMPION: Campion works on the supersecret "Project Blue" at a top-secret U.S. biological testing site in California. When the superflu germ leaks from its containment unit, Campion and his family are the only ones to survive. However, they quickly fall ill. By the time Campion crashes his car at Hapscomb's Texaco station in Arnette, Texas, his wife and daughter are dead, and he lives only hours thereafter.

NADINE CROSS: A truly tragic figure, Nadine hooks up with Larry Underwood on the road, and likely because of her attraction to him, chooses Boulder—where Mother Abagail's followers have gathered—as a destination over Las Vegas, where Randall Flagg has set up shop. When her feelings for Larry are not reciprocated, Nadine, seduced by dreams of Flagg, conspires with Harold Lauder to plant a bomb meant to take out Boulder's leading citizens, then heads into the desert with him to become the dark man's "bride."

Although impregnated by Flagg, Nadine eventually rejects him, goading him into killing her by hurling her from the roof of his Las Vegas dwelling.

TOM CULLEN: A retarded man Nick Andros meets on the road, Tom eventually helps to save Stu Redman's life, aided by Nick's spirit.

Tom Cullen is presumed to still be residing in Boulder as part of the Free Zone.

TRASHCAN MAN: Donald Merwin Elbert, better known as the Trashcan Man, was taunted and beaten up as a child, and grew up to become a very twisted individual obsessed with setting fires. His dreams of the walkin' dude offer promises of fires beyond his imagination. While on his trek to Las Vegas, he travels for a time with "the Kid," a savage killer who is apparently the reincarnation of 1950s mass murderer Charles Starkweather. The Trashcan Man becomes progressively more insane, to the point where, believing Flagg would be grateful, he snatches a nuclear warhead from a military base and brings it back to Las Vegas, where it promptly explodes, eliminating everyone there (except Flagg, of course).

MOTHER ABAGAIL: Abagail Freemantle, the daughter of a slave, is more than a century old when the world as she's known it comes to an end. More than likely, she is the oldest woman alive when travelers who have been dreaming about her begin to appear on her doorstep in Hemingford Home, Nebraska. Mother Abagail herself has been gifted with special knowledge, certain prescience, both about the people who come to her and the evil they will face. As the focal point for good among the survivors of the world and Flagg's "opposite number," she becomes a reluctant leader until she dies peacefully.

FRANNIE GOLDSMITH: Frannie grew up in Ogunquit, Maine, an idyllic beach community. Her life, however, has been less than idyllic. Still a teenager, she finds herself pregnant by her boyfriend, who abandons her upon discovering her condition. Faced with the specter of a child she dares not tell her parents about or an abortion she doesn't want, she has the decision taken from her by the arrival of the superflu and the death of nearly everyone around her. It is a cruel irony that the only other survivor in Ogunquit is a neighbor of Frannie's named Harold Lauder, a malcontented misfit who has always lusted after her. The two set off together and end up traveling (against Harold's wishes) with Stu Redman, with whom Frannie falls in love. They later marry, and Stu becomes the stepfather to Fran's son. They settle in Maine after the final battle against Flagg has been won.

LLOYD HENREID: A two-bit criminal, Lloyd and his partner, Poke Freeman, hold up a grocery store not long before the superflu attacks. Poke is killed by the store owner, but Lloyd ends up in prison, where he is when the flu takes its toll. To survive, Lloyd is forced to eat not only rats, but bits of the corpse in the next cell. Flagg rescues him from that hellish existence and makes Lloyd one of his most trusted men. Lloyd is killed when Las Vegas goes nuclear.

HAROLD LAUDER: Harold grew up overweight, acne-stricken, sweaty, and lonely in Ogunquit, Maine. His whole life, he's had a crush on Fran Goldsmith. What luck for him, then, that she is the only other survivor of Captain Trips in his hometown. At least, that's what Harold thinks. However, when they begin to travel together and meet up with Stu Redman, Harold soon realizes that even if he *were* to be the last man on Earth, Frannie would never love him. He's always been a bit devious, but he becomes increasingly bitter and spiteful over time. Though Harold has never been trustworthy, Fran's love for Stu may well be the final straw for him. He constructs the bomb that kills Nick Andros, and then flees to join Flagg. On his way to Las Vegas, however, he falls prey to a distraction engineered by Flagg and crashes his motorcycle in a ravine. Badly injured in the accident, he eventually commits suicide rather than die a slow, painful death.

THE KID: In 1957, nineteen-year-old Charles Starkweather shot his fourteen-year-old girlfriend's parents and choked her baby sister to death. The two of them then escaped, with Starkweather stealing the car of a farmer whom he killed with a shotgun. Before he was done, ten people were murdered. The National Guard was called in, and eventually, after a high-speed chase, Starkweather was caught and later executed in the electric chair.

At some later date, Starkweather is reincarnated as "the Kid," a sadistically evil young man with a taste for classic cars and Elvis Presley. He meets the Trashcan Man on the road, but unlike so many others, the Kid has an evil that is not tainted by any trace of good. So dark is the Kid that he doesn't want to join Flagg, he wants Flagg's job. Which, of course, profoundly upsets the dark man. After the Kid tortures the Trashcan Man, Flagg sends a pack of wolves after him, and the Kid is eventually killed.

However, since he had been reincarnated once, it is not unreasonable to suspect that Starkweather may return to plague the world again.

LARRY UNDERWOOD: Larry has lived in the fast lane. Sex and drugs and rock 'n' roll nearly destroyed him. His one major hit as a musician, "Baby Can You Dig Your Man," is likely also to be his last. Reeling, and trying to stay off drugs, Larry returns to New York City to visit his mother. He is there when Captain Trips hit. In escaping the corpse-filled city, Larry undergoes a harrowing journey through a lightless Lincoln Tunnel. Though he has a very low opinion of his self-worth, Larry finds himself a very prominent citizen of the Free Zone, and is one of those who travels to Las Vegas to face Flagg, and dies in the nuclear explosion there.

THE FREE ZONE: The name Boulder, Colorado, and its surrounding environs is given by the survivors of the superflu who settle there.

HEMINGFORD HOME, NEBRASKA: The small town where Mother Abagail lived her entire life before the outbreak of Captain Trips.

CAPTAIN TRIPS: A nickname for the superflu created in an American military research facility and accidentally released into the general populace. It kills 99.4% of the world's population.

THE STAND: ADAPTATIONS

After years in which King went through draft after draft of screenplay versions of *The Stand*, the epic finally came to life on the small screen in an eight-hour ABC network miniseries (May 8, 9, 11, and 12, 1994). It was one of the most ambitious such miniseries projects ever attempted, with more than one hundred speaking parts and a reported budget of nearly thirty million dollars. Written by King and directed by Mick Garris (with whom the author has collaborated on several other occasions), the film boasted a stellar cast of veteran movie and television actors.

That cast included Gary Sinise as Stu Redman; Molly Ringwald as Fran Goldsmith; Jamey Sheridan as Randall Flagg; Laura San Giacomo as Nadine Cross; Ruby Dee as Mother Abagail; Ray Walston as Glen Bateman; Matt Frewer as the Trashcan Man; Rob Lowe as Nick Andros; and King himself in a small role as Teddy Weizak.

For years, King's fans had been hoping to see the novel adapted to the screen, and during an interview four years before the miniseries was finally made, executive producer Richard Rubinstein noted in an interview with the authors of this book that he had been taking an informal survey for some years of which scenes in the massive tome were absolutely indispensable to a film or television version. The number-one request on that list, the infamous "Lincoln Tunnel scene," was terrifying to view, but could not possibly duplicate the novel's intensity. This was mainly due to the fact that in the book, it takes place in total darkness.

Ratings were stellar and reviews generally positive, and King, of course, continues to have a very creative, productive, and profitable relationship with ABC.

THE STAND: TRIVIA

- In the uncut version of *The Stand*, Fran Goldsmith reads aloud from *Rimfire Christmas*, a Western novel by Bobbi Anderson—the main character of *The Tommyknockers* (1987)—which of course only exists within the Stephen King Universe.

- Real-life killer Charles Starkweather's deeds apparently haunt King. In addition to giving us "the Kid," a reincarnation of the killer (according to Douglas E. Winter's indispensable *Stephen King: The Art of Darkness*), King told *TV Guide* in 1994 that "[Randall] Flagg is like the archetype of everything that I know about real evil, going back all the way to Charles Starkweather in the '50s."

- Early on in the unexpurgated version of *The Stand*, King pays tribute to crime writer Ed McBain (a pseudonym for novelist Evan Hunter) by having a character, Lt. Edward Norris of the New York City Police Department, think about his colleague, Steve Carella of the 87th Precinct. Carella is an integral part of McBain's long-lived 87th Precinct series of novels. Set in Isola, a stand-in for New York City, the hard-hitting series premiered in 1956 with *Cop Hater*.

13

RELATED TALES

"Night Surf" (from 1978's Night Shift)

First published in the men's magazine *Cavalier* in 1974, the short story "Night Surf" was included in King's first short story collection, *Night Shift*. A precursor to *The Stand* (1978), this story introduces the idea of the superflu, nicknamed Captain Trips (an ironic reference to Grateful Dead guitarist Jerry Garcia, who shared the nickname), which kills most of the population of the world. The narrative focuses Bernie, Corey, Joan, Kelly, Susie, and Needles, a group of rural New England teenagers doing their best to survive in a postapocalyptic world.

The Little Sisters of Eluria (from 2002's Everything's Eventual)

Though Roland appears—or is at least referred to—in a number of other Stephen King works, his primary story has been confined to *The Dark Tower* series of novels. Until now. First published in 1998 in the massive *Legends*—a collection of fantasy novellas edited by Robert Silverberg—*The*

Little Sisters of Eluria reveals a previously untold story of Roland, and hints at connections we had only suspected before.

In this tale, early on in Roland's pursuit of the man in black that opens the first *Dark Tower* book (1982's *The Gunslinger*) but late enough in the epic storyline that he is already questing on his own, Roland finds himself in what amounts to a classic Western ghost town. There are echoes of "Children of the Corn" in that setup, of course, but it is a traditional fictional conceit. Of course, the town isn't completely deserted. There are "slow mutants" in the area. They are green-fleshed and horrid to look at, the victims or descendants of victims of radiation exposure from long ago.

Baseball field built by King, "The Field of Screams," Bangor   DAVID LOWELL

When Roland is attacked by a band of slow mutants, he is turned over to "the Little Sisters of Eluria." They appear, at first, to be a religious organization dedicated to nursing patients back to health. However, that is far from the truth. They turn out to be a special breed of vampire, and they have their sights set on Roland. Sister Mary, their mother superior, particularly dislikes him.

Roland is protected by a chain around his neck that he took from a dead boy, whose living brother he finds in the "hospital" with him. It isn't long before that young man succumbs to the vampires' charms. However, he is also protected by Sister Jenna, who appears to hold power over the others. She is, in some way, the chosen one among her kind, the inheritor of "the dark bells," ones that can call the black bugs called "the good doctors," insects that heal the sick.

But she misses her humanity and loves Roland, at least a little, so Sister Jenna eventually helps him to escape. Sister Mary is killed. When the sun comes up, however, Sister Jenna's fate is to be rendered into another form—transformed into an army of black bugs.

Clearly, these are not the vampires of *'Salem's Lot* (1975). But the two are related, one might suspect, given that Father Callahan—who encountered the vampires in that novel—eventually made his way into Roland's world.

In addition to presenting a new chapter in Roland's story, this novella also gives us both subtle and overt connections to other King works. The most obvious is that the boy in the bed next to Roland's is from the city of Delain, which is the setting of *The Eyes of the Dragon*.

Second, there is mention made of the witch, Rhea of the Coos, from *The Dark Tower* series, "and her sisters." Given that *The Eyes of the Dragon* mentions Rhiannon of the Coos, that is an additional connection.

Third, it's worth mentioning that Eluria is near the Desatoya Mountains, also the location of the China Pit mine in *Desperation*. Like the demon Tak, the little sisters also speak the language of the unformed.

Finally, a very small thing: Roland recalls that his friend Jamie DeCurry was fond of saying that Roland "could shoot blindfolded, because he had eyes in his fingers," likely a reference to the early King story "I Am the Doorway."

Everything's Eventual (from 2002's *Everything's Eventual*)

This story, about a young man gifted with a paranormal "wild talent" (King labels him a "tranny"), first appeared in the October/November 1997 issue of *The Magazine of Fantasy and Science Fiction* and later in the collection called *Everything's Eventual*. It represents the author's most recent return to the science fiction genre, and continues his fascination with otherwise ordinary individuals possessing incredible psychic abilities.

Dinky Earnshaw, the teenage narrator of this 20,000-word novella, tells of his ability to kill people merely by writing them letters, a talent he discovered when he dispatched a neighborhood dog simply by etching some runes and glyphs on an adjacent sidewalk. Dinky lives a pampered existence, his every need seen to by TransCorp, a private enterprise whose goals seem to parallel those of the secret research unit known as The Shop—all he has to do is write letters to people the corporation designates as targets. At first compliant, Dinky comes to loathe his job. Eventually he turns on his handler, the mysterious Mr. Sharpton, after receiving a message from a fellow "tranny" that causes him to question what he is doing.

Dinky later appears in the seventh volume of the *Dark Tower* series, alongside another Breaker, Ted Brautigan from *Hearts in Atlantis*.

(A brief aside: it's worth noting that one of Dinky's nemeses, Skipper Brannigan, was a friend of Henry Dean, gunslinger Eddie Dean's brother.)

SECTION TWO

The Prime Reality

In this and the following sections, we will discuss the most familiar Reality in the Stephen King Universe. We have called this section "The Prime Reality," only because it encompasses so much of the Universe, perhaps as much as 90 percent of King's canon. It should be noted, however, that as regards the overall struggle between good and evil, or the Random and the Purpose as King has sometimes referred to it, the Reality of the Dark Tower is more significant.

Yet there is no question—as you will undoubtedly find as you read the segments that follow—that this war is waged within the pages of nearly every one of Stephen King's works, and as such, nowhere with more frequency than in this, the Prime Reality.

For the sake of clarity and in order to make it a bit simpler for the reader to envision, we have broken down the Prime Reality into five parts: Derry, Castle Rock, King's Maine, Tales of the Shop, and Other Prime Reality Tales. Still, it must be reinforced that all of these parts combine to form the whole that is the Prime Reality. In addition to Prime, there are only three other Realities or Parallel Dimensions that are significant, those of *The Dark Tower*, *The Stand*, and of King's pseudonym, Richard Bachman (a complex division we will arrive at eventually). As you will have noted, we have already discussed the first two, and the latter we will cover a bit further on. For now: the Prime Reality.

THE PRIME REALITY, PART I: DERRY

Though perhaps not as "name-branded" for longtime King readers as Castle Rock, Derry has proved to be a key battleground in the cosmic struggle between good and evil that constantly rages within the Stephen King Universe.

While most of the settings King has invented for his Prime Reality (or most prominent parallel dimension), particularly those in Maine, have seen their share of skirmishes in this war, Derry's seem to have happened on a larger scale than others. It is, after all, the site of *It* and *Insomnia*, among others, both of which have evil antagonists who are undoubtedly more powerful and grander than their less all-encompassing counterparts in Castle Rock (e.g., Leland Gaunt) or Jerusalem's Lot (e.g., Kurt Barlow).

Derry has also proven to be one of the pivotal locations supporting our thesis that all of King's worlds and works are connected. While there are obvious links between Castle Rock, etc., to other locations and works within the Prime Reality, tales set in Derry, as you will see below, have provided some of the most significant links to the other Realities that together make up the substance of the Stephen King Universe.

Located near Bangor, Derry appears on its surface to be a typical New England town. Some unsettling statistics tell a different story, however:

- The murder rate in Derry is six times the murder rate of any other town of comparable size in New England.

- In Derry, children disappear unexplained and unfound at the rate of forty to sixty per year.

One would think that these statistics would alarm the populace, but, as Mike Hanlon commented in *It* (1986), "in Derry people have a way of looking the other way."

Apparently people have been looking the other way for quite some time—here are some significant events in the history of the town, many of which were gleaned from Mike Hanlon's unpublished book, *The Unauthorized History of Derry*. Hanlon, who along with many of his childhood friends faced the creature known as "It" twice in his life and survived, knows a great deal about the dark side of his hometown.

- 1741: the entire population of Derry township vanishes. Mike states, "The only case remotely like it in American history is the disappearance of the colonists on Roanoke Island, Virginia." This may create an interesting link between *It* and the sinister Andre Linoge, who, as we know from his appearance in the 1999 TV miniseries *The Storm of the Century*, was responsible for the disappearance of the colonists.

- 1851: John Markson kills his entire family with poison, then consumes a deadly "white nightshade" mushroom.

- 1879: A crew of lumberjacks find the remains of another crew that spent the winter snowed in at a camp in the Upper Kenduskeag, at the tip of the modern-day barrens. All nine had been hacked to pieces.

- 1906: On Easter Sunday, the Kitchener Ironworks explodes during an Easter egg hunt, resulting in 102 deaths.

- 1930: The Black Spot, a Negro social club, is burned to the ground by the Maine Legion of Decency. Dozens perish.

- 1958: One hundred and twenty-seven children, ranging in age from three to nineteen, were reported missing in Derry.

- 1985: Nine children are murdered; their killer is never apprehended. Also the year of the "Great Flood," which results in millions of dollars of damage to the town.

- 1994: Feminist Susan Day is killed when Derry resident Ed Deepneau—driven insane by an otherworldly being named Atropos—launches a kamikaze attack on the Derry Civic Center as Day addresses a capacity crowd.

Stephen King aficionados already know that many of these tragedies were caused by It, the creature who used the town as its own private killing ground for centuries (readers will recall that the events of 1958 and 1985 are chronicled in 1986's *It*, originally titled *Derry*). King used the town as a setting yet again in 1994's *Insomnia*, where Derry resident Ralph Roberts becomes embroiled in a battle between the cosmic forces King has named the Purpose and the Random (Order and Chaos, essentially), and in 1998's *Bag of Bones*, which presented a less cosmic view of the town.

Paul Bunyan statue in Bangor   VINTAGE POSTCARD

The fictional Derry is closely patterned on Bangor, Maine (its neighbor, according to King's invented geography of that state). In fact, a standard map of Bangor would prove useful in identifying many of the landmarks described in *It*, such as the Barrens, the Standpipe, the statue of Paul Bunyan, the Derry Public Library, and West Broadway, where the rich families of Derry make their homes (coincidentally, King lives on just such a street—it is even named West Broadway—in Bangor).

Like Castle Rock, another fictional town of King's creation, Derry also seems to have more than its fair share of writers (all also invented by King). For instance, 1990s midlist writer Mort Rainey, author of two novels and a short story collection, resided there with his wife until their divorce drove him mad (see "Secret Window, Secret Garden"). William Denbrough (*It*), famous for his fictions about "the Outsiders," also hails from Derry. Finally, there is bestselling author Mike Noonan (*Bag of Bones*), who, despite a successful career, seemingly abandoned writing in 1998.

Derry seems destined to play an important part in the saga of the Dark Tower. In *It*, King mentions the Turtle, which is also called one of the Guardians of the Tower in the *Dark Tower* series. The title monster itself, a creature from beyond our reality, is certainly one of the *can-tak*, the monsters of the multiverse, who serve chaos (or "the Random").

In *Insomnia*, the author introduced the Crimson King, whose appearances there and in subsequent works imply his status as a pivotal player in the cosmic chess game between order and chaos. In that novel, the Crimson King tells its main character, Ralph Roberts, that he has been working in Derry for centuries, and as *Insomnia* reveals, events in the town impact the life and existence of Roland the Gunslinger.

While the connections to the Reality of The Dark Tower are fairly obvious, the connections to other worlds and realities are sometimes a bit more subtle, but there nevertheless. *The Tommyknockers* (1987) is set in Haven, which is just above Derry in King's fictional Maine. In that novel, denizens of Haven see and hear It while traveling in Derry, even though the creature was supposedly destroyed a year before. The Tommyknocker connection is significant because it clearly links Derry to The Shop (see *"The Prime Reality: Tales of the Shop"*). It is also evoked in *Dreamcatcher* (2001), as, on a statue dedicated to the lost children of Derry, someone (or something) has spray-painted the words "Pennywise Lives."

Other connections to King's Maine exist. For instance, in *It*, Beverly Marsh is clearly aware of Frank (the Castle Rock Strangler) Dodd's infamous exploits as detailed in *The Dead Zone*. It is also clear that *Bag of Bones*'s Mike Noonan is familiar with the lives of Castle Rock natives Thad Beaumont and Alan Pangborn, whom readers met in *The Dark Half* (1989). Mike Noonan also owns a home at Dark Score Lake, the summer community where Jessie Burlingame of *Gerald's Game* (1992) was molested by her father.

Insomnia and *It* are also connected in other ways to the Prime Reality. One example is the picture of Susan Day that hangs in Anna Stevenson's office in *Rose Madder*. Another link from the pages of *Insomnia* is the fact that Atropos, a supernatural (or, perhaps more accurately supranatural) servant of the Random, has kept Gage Creed's (see *Pet Sematary*) sneaker as a macabre trophy. *It* is connected to *Misery* in that the latter novel's Paul Sheldon has personal knowledge of Eddie Kaspbrak of *It*.

Another, perhaps unintentional connection are the appearances of hotel and motel rooms numbered 217 in *The Shining, Apt Pupil,* and *It.* A final tie linking the realities is Dick Hallorann's presence in both *The Shining* (in the 1970s) and *It* (in the 1930s).

14

IT

(1986)

In size and scope, *It* is a monster of a book. At 1,138 pages, it is the second-longest novel King has published to date, bested only by the unexpurgated version of *The Stand*.

It constitutes King's final examination of themes he felt were covered exhaustively in his prior novels—i.e., kids and monsters. Kids, in that it deals with the rite of passage from child into adult, and the mythic power that childhood holds over our imagination. Monsters, in that It knows what scares people, and is willing to use that against them. It is an amorphous being from beyond the reality we know whose myriad forms are shaped by our own fears and imaginations. Thus, *It* is sort of a pop culture Monster Mash, with cameos from the Creature from the Black Lagoon, the Mummy, Dracula, Jaws, the Crawling Eye, Frankenstein, Rodan, and the Teenage Werewolf, among many others.

There's an intimacy about *It* that previous King books did not display, perhaps due to the fact that the members of the Losers Club, focal characters in this book, are contemporaries of their creator, who was born in 1947. They've experienced the same things King has lived through; one can imagine them sitting in the same dark movie theater King frequented in 1957 when the manager stopped the film to announce that the Russians had just launched *Sputnik*, an experience King would describe in *Danse*

Macabre (1981). Their coming together twenty-seven years later probably echoed King's experiences at high school reunions. The story of a group of friends getting together after the death of one of their number is not unlike the movie *The Big Chill* (1983), only with monsters added into the mix.

The publication of *It* marked the advent of a more socially conscious King. At the book's heart, *It* is an account of child abuse, about how isolated and vulnerable children are. *It* also deals with spousal battery, a theme King would develop further in subsequent writings. In addition, *It* is a veritable treatise on intolerance and prejudice, dealing with hatred of blacks and gays, virtually anyone who is different.

Inspired by the classic Norwegian fairy tale "The Three Billy Goats Gruff," *It* contains some of King's most harrowing turns—for example, George Denbrough's reluctant descent into his basement and his later death scene. *It* is also an interesting variation on King's oft-used theme of haunted houses. Here the concept is expanded, in that the town itself is permeated by It's sinister influence. Several times throughout the novel, It and Derry, the fictional Maine town where the novel takes place, are spoken of as if they were the same thing. Mike Hanlon, a member of the Losers Club, asks, "Can an entire city be haunted?" *It* also represents an interesting technical experiment with time, as King seamlessly melds the events of 1958 with those occurring in 1985.

In *It*, King provides a history of Derry, Maine, a town he had heretofore only mentioned in passing in stories such as "Mrs. Todd's Shortcut" (collected in 1985's *Skeleton Crew*). In fact, for reasons explained below, the original working title of *It* was *Derry*. Located to the south of the ill-fated Haven (see *The Tommyknockers*), Derry borders Bangor to the west. It is, in fact, almost a mirror image of Bangor, containing many similar landmarks. Like the author's home town, Derry has a series of canals and a unique standpipe/water tower; it, too, boasts an enormous statue of Paul Bunyan, no surprise given the influence of the lumber and paper industry on that region.

It represented the first, but not the last, time Derry was featured prominently in one of King's books. He's revisited the city several times since, most notably in his 1990 novella *Secret Window, Secret Garden* (the protagonist of that story, Mort Rainey, owned a house in Derry); in the novels *Insomnia* (1994) and *Bag of Bones* (1998); and in the 1999 short story "The Road Virus Heads North."

Based on the events related in *Insomnia*, it appears as if the city is a cosmic hot spot, a key location in regard to the tale of Roland, the protagonist of the author's the *Dark Tower* series. Although King doesn't specifically refer to that saga, the books contain many similar elements. The Losers could certainly be seen to have formed a *ka-tet*, similar to that described in the second Dark Tower installment, *The Drawing of the Three* (1987). King also uses circle imagery, images that pop up in The Dark Tower books; at one point, Mike Hanlon writes, "If the wheels of the universe are in true, then good always compensates for evil."

There may even be a connection between It and *Insomnia*'s villain, the Crimson King. At one juncture in *It*, Pennywise the Clown mocks Mike Hanlon, telling him, in an *Amos 'n' Andy* type voice, "I is de Kingfish in Derry, anyhow, and dat's de troof." Perhaps significantly, the Crimson King tells Ralph Roberts in *Insomnia* that he may refer to him as ". . . the Kingfish. You remember the Kingfish from the radio, don't you?" Another connection between the two is that in his trip into hyperreality, Ralph glimpses *deadlights*, a concept first mentioned in *It*.

Links to the Stephen King universe within *It* are wide and varied. Dick Hallorann of *The Shining* spent time in Derry as a cook for the Army Air Corps, and was present the night the Black Spot was torched. The Army Air Corps base stood on the spot that serves as Derry's airport today. Beverly, referring to Frank Dodd (*The Dead Zone*), mentions "that crazy cop who killed all those women in Castle Rock, Maine."

Voices emanating from a drain tell a frightened Derry resident, "Our name is legion," a biblical reference King used before and since in *The Stand* (Tom Cullen speaking about Flagg) and in the author's 1999 TV miniseries *Storm of the Century* (*Linoge* is an anagram for *legion*). Haven, the setting of *The Tommyknockers*, is mentioned, as is one of its residents, the unfortunate Rebecca Paulson. Henry Bower is picked up by a "1958 Plymouth Fury," conjuring up images of *Christine* (1983). Henry is a patient at Juniper Hill from 1958 through 1985; King has mentioned the asylum on numerous occasions in other novels (as he did, for example, in 1991's *Needful Things*). Finally, the adult Ben Hanscom, the architect who designed the Derry Civic Center attacked by Ed Deepneau in *Insomnia*, lives in Hemingford Home, Nebraska, birthplace of Mother Abagail from *The Stand*.

There's also the possibility that King may have been trying to integrate elements of the Lovecraft mythos into his own universe. Lovecraft fans may recall "The Dunwich Horror" (1929)—that tale featured a hideous creature named Yog Sothoth, described as "an octopus, centipede, spider kind of thing." *It*, like Yog Sothoth, is a manifestation from beyond, and appears to the Losers Club as a giant female spider (recalling the Queen Bitch from the *Alien* movies as well). Remember also that William Denbrough went on to create a similar mythos—readers learn in *Bag of Bones* that he writes about "Creatures from Beyond."

Despite It's apparent death at the end of the novel, characters in *The Tom-myknockers*, set a year later than *It*, see and hear It in visits to Derry, and Ralph Roberts, the hero of *Insomnia*, sees the ethereal "deadlights" discussed in *It* on his visit to hyperreality. In 2001's *Dreamcatcher*, readers learn that the words "Pennywise Lives" have been spray-painted on a statue dedicated to the lost children of Derry. This would seem to indicate that It is still out there, ready to oppose those who side with the forces of Order in the Stephen King Universe.

IT: PRIMARY SUBJECTS

THE TURTLE: It and the Turtle exist at "the end of Macroverse." Seemingly eternal, they have existed since the beginning of time, perhaps created by "the final other," the "author of all there was," who dwells in a void beyond the one where the Turtle resides. Bill Denbrough encounters the Turtle when he is propelled into the Macroverse. The Turtle, who claims to have made the universe, asks Bill not to blame him, as he had a bellyache that day (yes, our universe was apparently vomited from a Turtle's belly). The Turtle tells Bill that only the ritual of Chud can defeat It.

IT (a.k.a. Mr. Bob Gray, a.k.a. Pennywise the Clown): Apparently many centuries old, It, in the form of Pennywise the Clown, bears a chilling resemblance to serial killer John Wayne Gacy, a fiend who also preyed on children disguised as a clown. The origins of It are shrouded in mystery, though there are a few clues. Richie and Mike have a vision of It arriving on Earth inside a meteor, but this doesn't jibe with Bill's experiences in the Macroverse. According to Bill, It came from "the outside." When asked to elaborate, Bill said, "Outside everything," telling his friends that It had always been there.

Indeed, as far as Derry is concerned, It *has* always been there, perhaps waiting eons for the arrival of human inhabitants. From the early 1700s on, It treated Derry as its own private preserve. There are those who believe that It keeps Derry's people as if they were cattle, and those who posit that in some way, It *is* Derry. Speaking with the police after Adrian Mellon's murder, witness Don Hagerty tells of seeing Pennywise on the scene. When asked who it was, Don replied, "It was Derry. It was this town."

After being attacked by her father, Beverly thinks, "It's everywhere in Derry. It just fills the hollow places."

It exists "in a simple cycle of waking to eat and sleeping to dream," emerging from its home beneath Derry every twenty-seven years or so to feed. In 1958, It is confronted and defeated by a group of seven children calling themselves the Losers Club. Severely wounded, It retreats to its lair to heal and to plan the demise of its enemies. In 1985, its is apparently killed by the Losers Club, now adults. It may still be alive, however.

THE LOSERS CLUB: The name given by Richie Tozier to the seven friends (Bill Denbrough, Beverly Marsh, Richie Tozier, Stan Uris, Ben Hanscom, Mike Hanlon, and Eddie Kaspbrak) who battle It (and Henry Bower) in the summer of 1958.

GEORGE DENBROUGH: Bill's six-year-old brother, he falls victim to It in 1957 (his arm is ripped out of its socket as he reaches into a sewer in an attempt to retrieve his newspaper boat). Bill Denbrough, who made the boat for his brother, blames himself for George's death.

WILLIAM DENBROUGH: Seeking to avenge the death of his brother, Bill Denbrough, the acknowledged leader of the Losers Club, leads the group in its battle against It in the summer of 1958. Bill goes on to attend the University of Maine. Pursuing his dream of being a writer, Bill sends the manuscript of his first novel, *The Dark*, to Viking Press, mainly because he likes their logo. Surprisingly, Viking purchases the book, launching Bill's career. His second book, *The Black Rapids*, is filmed as *Pit of the Black Demon*; on the set, he meets actress Audra Phillips, who later becomes his wife.

Like the rest of the Losers Club, Bill receives a call from Mike Hanlon in the summer of 1985, reminding him of the promise they all made to return to Derry should It reappear. At first Bill can only recall bits and pieces of that summer; eventually he regains his memories, as well as the stutter that plagued him in his youth. After It attempts to scare him and the rest of his band away, Bill again leads the others (sans Stan Uris and the mortally wounded Mike Hanlon) back into Derry's labyrinthine sewer system to face It. The group triumphs once more, at the cost of Eddie Kaspbrak's life and Audra Denbrough's sanity.

Bill Denbrough is alive and well, but his present whereabouts are unknown. His career is still flourishing.

AUDRA DENBROUGH: William Denbrough's actress wife, she bears a striking resemblance to Beverly Marsh. Audra, worried about her husband, travels to Derry, where she is captured by It. Rendered comatose after staring into It's deadlights, Audra is rescued by the adult Losers. Bill Denbrough has reconciled himself to life with the mindless Audra when he spies his beloved bike Silver in Mike Hanlon's shed. Carrying Audra on its handlebars, he takes a wild ride through Derry. The harrowing bicycle ride snaps Audra out of her coma.

Audra Denbrough is presumed to be alive and well, still living with her husband, Bill.

MIKE HANLON: Mike differs from most of the Losers in that he has a positive relationship with his parents, especially his father. Due to his race (African-American), however, he learns the lessons prejudice and hate have to teach him early on. While the other members of the Losers Club leave Derry after It is vanquished, Mike stays, takes a job as a librarian at the Derry Public Library, and begins work on *The Unauthorized History of Derry*. As a result of his research, Mike knows more about the evil presence that suffuses the town than any other living being.

Because Mike stays, he, unlike his friends, never forgets the events of 1958. When Mike realizes that It has become active once again, he calls the members of the Losers Club back to Derry.

Mike acts as the group's historian, triggering the group's memories of the summer of 1958. He also points out the group's similarities—i.e., they are all very successful, and they are all childless. Although wounded by Henry Bowers, Mike survives his second encounter with It; this time, however, his memory is wiped clean of the events of 1958 and 1985.

Mike continues as the librarian in Derry to this day.

BEN HANSCOM: Ben has always been a builder—at the age of eleven, he designed the dam the Losers built in the Barrens in the summer of 1958, the dam that also cemented the bonds between the initial members of the Losers Club. Capitalizing on his inherent talent for design, Ben grows up to be a world-famous architect.

Ben survives his second encounter with It; in the process, he becomes romantically involved with Beverly Marsh, the only woman he has ever truly loved. Presumably, Ben returns to Hemingford Home, Nebraska, with Beverly after leaving Derry.

STAN URIS: The most reluctant member of the Losers Club, Stan's ultrarational mind was never fully able to accept the terror dwelling in Derry's sewers. When Mike Hanlon calls him twenty-seven years later, his mind snaps. Stan commits suicide in his bathtub, leaving the word "It" scrawled on his bathroom wall in his blood. It was Stan, however, who played an important role in forging the bond between the Losers that Mike exploited in 1985. After their first encounter with It, Stan and Bill were jointly responsible for having the group swear a blood oath to return to Derry if It should ever return. Stan broke a discarded Coke bottle and used a shard of glass to cut the palms of each of the Losers; Bill initiated the oath.

BEVERLY ROGAN (née MARSH): As a child, Beverly was abused by her father; as an adult, she is battered by her husband. Beverly is the only female member of the Losers Club. As tough as any of the others, she bears the group's weapon, a slingshot and silver slugs. During their first encounter with It, Beverly performed another ritual of sorts. By having sex with her male counterparts, she initiated their passage from childhood into adulthood.

Due to her second encounter with It, and to her budding relationship with Ben Hanscom, Beverly develops confidence she never had before, despite the fact that she grew up to be a world-famous fashion designer. She is presumed alive and well, most likely residing in Hemingford Home.

TOM ROGAN: Beverly's abusive husband, he recognized her as prey from the moment he first saw her. Tom forbids Beverly to leave after she receives Mike Hanlon's phone call; when she defies him, he attacks. Finally fighting back, Beverly fends him off, leaving her surprised husband battered and bruised. It draws Tom to Derry to do its bidding, using him to kidnap Audra Denbrough. Rogan delivers Audra to It's lair, but dies after staring into It's deadlights.

RICHIE TOZIER: Always a comedian, the young Richie is forever doing one of his voices. Richie grows up to be a radio personality, famous for his repertoire of outrageous characters. During their second encounter with It, Richie enters the Macroverse to bring Bill out.

EDDIE KASPBRAK: Dominated by his fearful mother, Eddie develops psychosomatic asthma (because of his fear of illness, It took the shape of a hideous leper when It confronted Eddie in 1958).

Eddie's aspirator plays an important role in the Losers' battles with It. In their first encounter, each member of the group ritualistically took a shot from the aspirator, further expressing their unity. Eddie, realizing that he, too, could exploit the nature of It's power, wounds It by spraying It with his aspirator. Eddie suffers a broken arm in both 1958 and 1985. He also guides the group to It both times.

Unfortunately, Eddie does not survive his second encounter with It.

HENRY BOWERS: As an adult, Ben Hanscom thought, "If there has ever been a genuinely evil kid strutting across the skin of the world, Henry Bowers was that kid." A bully who terrorized the Losers in the summer of 1958, Henry has been frustrated in most of his attempts to humiliate and injure the group. He does, however, manage to carve his initials into Ben's stomach and break Eddie's arm. Strangely enough, Henry is indirectly responsible for It's defeat—his constant harassment of those smaller or different from him resulted in the formation of the Losers Club.

Henry, whose hair turned white in 1958 after a personal encounter with It, was blamed for the crimes that occurred that summer. Found insane, he spent the next twenty-seven years as an inmate at Juniper Hill asylum. In 1985, It calls him back to Derry, where he severely wounds Mike Hanlon in the Derry Library. Henry then tries to murder Eddie, who kills him in self-defense.

THE OTHER: The otherworldly force that created both It and the Turtle; also the power behind the formation of the Losers Club.

THE RITUAL OF CHUD: The ritual the Losers Club perform to defeat It. As Bill Denbrough explains, it is the only way to subdue a glamour, or taelus, the closest description for It the boy finds in his research. The taelus sticks its tongue out, its challenger sticks his out, then the opponents bite into each other's tongues and don't let go until one is defeated. The essence of the ritual is that the Losers must look It in the eye to defeat It.

IT: ADAPTATIONS

The novel was adapted as a 1990 television miniseries called (surprise!) *Stephen King's It*. The production featured Richard Thomas (as Bill Denbrough), Harry Anderson (Richie Tozier), Dennis Christopher (Eddie Kaspbrak), Richard Masur (Stan Uris), Annette O'Toole (Beverly Marsh), Tim Reid (Mike Hanlon), and John Ritter (Ben Hanscom). A young Seth Green, later to gain fame playing the character of Oz on *Buffy the Vampire Slayer*, plays Richie Tozier as a youth.

Obviously not given a large budget for special effects (we see the Teenage Werewolf, but nothing else), this imaginative production makes effective use of low-tech scares (such as when one of the Losers is attacked in the boys' locker room when the shower heads come to life). The suspense mounts until It reveals its true visage to the Losers Club—a very weak special effect—then quickly dissipates, making for an unsatisfying conclusion. Although all the players do a good job, Tim Curry's portrayal of Pennywise the Clown stands out from the rest. Curry as Pennywise is genuinely frightening—his bravura performance has no doubt caused many a nightmare over the years.

IT: TRIVIA

- Bill Denbrough attended the University of Maine at Orono during the same period in the late sixties when Carol Gerber and Pete Riley of *Hearts in Atlantis* were there. It was also, of course, the same era when Stephen King was himself a student there.

15

INSOMNIA

(1994)

$\mathcal{C}$oming on the heels of *Gerald's Game* (1992) and *Dolores Claiborne* (1993), *Insomnia* provides further evidence that, following the destruction of Castle Rock in 1991's *Needful Things*, Stephen King had moved on to a new phase in his writing career. The evidence was certainly there: two character-driven novels in a row, with nary a supernatural element in sight, followed by a dark fantasy detailing the adventures of two senior citizens. Had the author made a conscious decision to avoid horror, the genre that had brought him his greatest fame to date?

King had used older characters before in his fiction, but none as elderly as Ralph Roberts and Lois Chasse, and none featured as prominently in a plot line. *Firestarter* (1980), *Pet Sematary* (1983), and *The Shining* (1977) featured Irv Manders, Judson Crandall, and Dick Hallorann, respectively, who either served as father figures to the particular male leads of those novels or as grandfather figures to younger characters. Glen Bateman, a secondary character in *The Stand* (1978), served a similar purpose there, also acting as mentor to the governing body of the Free Zone. King did showcase seniors in more expansive roles in the television miniseries *Golden Years* (1991), but only briefly. Its protagonist, Harlan Williams, ages backward after he is caught in a blast at a research lab. Of course, *The Stand* also highlights the brittle Mother Abagail, but she exists more as an icon than as a real human being.

Insomnia, however, takes two senior citizens and places them at the center of the action. During the 1994 novel's slow buildup, readers are told about the perils and mixed blessings of growing old; it isn't until the second half of the narrative that really wild things start to happen.

King zeroes in on the milieu of the elderly with laser-sharp focus—readers learn the details of insomniac Ralph's day-to-day existence, and suffer with him through the loss of a spouse and as his agonizing malady worsens. They see Ralph and the other "old crocks" struggle to live out their final days in dignity, something which society and even, in some cases, their own children, deny them. For example, prodded by his duplicitous spouse, Lois's son is unnecessarily considering putting her in a nursing home.

As Bill McGovern somberly reflects at one point in *Insomnia*, getting old is no job for sissies.

King may have been inspired to tackle the subject herein by Don Robertson's *The Ideal Genuine Man*, a book published by King's own Philtrum Press that deals with many of the same issues.

Insomnia is a unique hybrid, at once one of King's more down-to-earth and one of his more "cosmic" novels. Down-to-earth in that it stars Ralph Roberts and Lois Chasse, two senior citizens, who, up until the time the novel begins, have led a quiet, restrained existence. Cosmic in its consideration of human fate and destiny, and due to its explicit ties to King's *The Dark Tower* series, specifically mentioning the Tower of Existence and Roland, the tortured Gunslinger.

Insomnia is similar in a number of ways to King's 1993 short story "The Ten O'Clock People." There, too, the main character experiences a change in perception, due to his attempts to kick his smoking habit. As a result, he can see a race of "batmen" that nonsmokers cannot.

Insomnia also has ties to several other King novels. The story is set in Derry, the locale of *It* (1986). King here makes constant references to the events of that novel, like the Great Storm of 1985. Later, he mentions that things that fall into Derry's sewers have a nasty way of popping up again when you least expect it. Mike Hanlon, one of the heroes of *It*, appears briefly in *Insomnia* in his adult incarnation as the chief librarian at the Derry Public Library.

Within *Insomnia*, Ralph escapes the Court of the Crimson King and glimpses an unearthly glow of swirling colors, which he instinctively thinks of as "deadlights," a concept also used in *It*. Lois, meeting TV news personality Connie Chung, tells her she is "her number-one fan," perhaps a nod to the catchphrase first introduced in *Misery* (1987). A picture of *Insomnia* character Susan Day (not to be confused with actress Susan *Dey*) is noted in the pages of *Rose Madder* (1995). Atropos, who in the manner of a serial killer takes souvenirs from his kills, keeps Gage Creed's (*Pet Sematary*) lost sneaker in his lair. Ralph subsequently appears in 1998's *Bag of Bones*; he has a brief conversation with Mike Noonan, who comments that Ralph later died in a car accident.

Most explicit among all of these connections, however, are the links to King's Gunslinger books. Clothos and Lachesis tell Ralph and Lois about *ka*, the great wheel of being. Clothos and Lachesis also label their alliance a *ka-tet*, a concept introduced in *The Drawing of the Three* (1987).

We also learn that Patrick Danville, the young boy in *Insomnia*, dreams about *The Dark Tower* series' Roland. After his mother asks him about a picture he has drawn (featuring Roland squaring off against "the Red King" against the backdrop of the Tower), Patrick tells her that Roland is a king. Finally, after Patrick is saved, King cuts to a scene where "a man named Roland" turns over in his bedroll and "rests easily once again beneath the alien constellations." Patrick will later play an enormous role in combating the cosmic forces working against Roland's quest.

The book can also be seen as another contemplation of Fate and Destiny, topics first explored at great length in *The Dead Zone*. King obviously evokes that subject in *Insomnia*'s use of Clothos, Lachesis, and Atropos, the novel's three "little bald doctors" named for the three goddesses of Greek and Roman mythology who were thought to control human destiny. King suggests that we all have roles to play in this life, that we all are part of some cosmic plan.

In mapping out the forces at work in his Universe, Stephen King has his characters Clothos and Lachesis explain the Four Constants of existence—Life, Death, the Random, and the Purpose—and the hierarchy of short-timers (normal mortals), long-timers (enhanced mortals), and all-timers (immortals). But they also add that all are part of the same Tower of Existence (to Roland, the "Dark Tower"). Between the Random and the Purpose there is a kind of chess game being played, but still there is mystery aplenty in life. There is a plan, but that can be altered. In *Insomnia*, Atropos, an agent of the Random, tries to do just that, but is frustrated when Ralph and Lois intervene.

More of a dark fantasy than outright supernatural horror, *Insomnia* contains a number of literary references as well: to the Bible (Ed Deepneau mentions King Herod in the context of baby-killing), J. R. R. Tolkien's epic *The Lord of the Rings* (Ed's wedding ring plays an important part in the narrative, and Bilbo and Frodo Baggins are named), Greek mythology (the little bald doctors may have inspired the legends of Clothos, Lachesis, and Atropos), and Arthurian legend (Ralph is compared to King Arthur and Sir Lancelot several times).

With this book, King continues to show a willingness to deal with modern social issues as well. Pro-life versus right-to-choose groups clash in Derry, and the pro-lifers, such as Ed Deepneau, are depicted as madmen. The author also returns to the subject of spousal abuse, a grim topic he deals with in passing in books like *'Salem's Lot* (1975) and *Cujo* (1981), and later explores more graphically in *It*, *Gerald's Game*, and *Dolores Claiborne*. King would revisit this subject with a vengeance in his next novel, *Rose Madder*.

INSOMNIA: PRIMARY SUBJECTS

RALPH ROBERTS: After the tragic death of his wife, seventysomething Ralph begins to suffer from insomnia, waking three minutes earlier each night. The insomnia affects many aspects of his existence, and causes him to perceive reality in new ways. For instance, he begins to see people's auras, and can tell when they are about to die, due to the presence of black "death bags" that he perceives hanging over their heads.

Ralph's heightened perceptions allow him to observe two tiny, oddly dressed men whom no one else can see. For some reason, he immediately begins to think of them as "the little bald doctors." After he learns their function, Ralph gives them the names Clothos and Lachesis, after the Fates of Greek mythology who spin and measure the threads of human destiny.

Clothos and Lachesis work to promote the goals of "the Purpose." Another bald doctor opposes them. He is a hideous creature Ralph refers to as Atropos, after the Fate who severs the threads of destiny. Atropos serves "the Random" and, more directly, a fearsome entity known as the Crimson King. Using Ralph's neighbor Ed Deepneau as a pawn, Atropos sets events in motion that threaten the stability of the universe itself.

Ralph and his friend Lois Chasse have been cursed with insomnia to prepare them to act as human agents of the Purpose. In fact, they have become the "pivot point of great events and vast forces." Ralph and Lois are charged with stopping Ed Deepneau before he destroys the Derry Civic Center by means of a kamikaze attack. Ed, lost in the throes of madness due to Atropos's manipulations, believes he is attacking Susan Day, a pro-choice advocate who is speaking to a capacity crowd at the Civic Center. In reality, Atropos is using Ed to try to kill a small boy named Patrick Danville, attending the event with his mother. Patrick is important to the designs of the Purpose—per King's writings in *Insomnia*, eighteen years later Patrick is destined to save two men, one whose existence is also vital to the cause.

Eventually, Ralph squares off against Ed and the master manipulator, the Crimson King. He narrowly defeats them, averting disaster only by a thin margin. Patrick lives, hopefully to fulfill his destiny.

During an encounter with Atropos, the little bald doctor taunts Ralph with a vision of the future in which young Natalie Deepneau is struck and killed by an automobile. Ralph cuts a bargain with "the Purpose" to save Natalie: once he has fulfilled his own purpose, he will give his life in exchange for hers. As Ralph lays dying in the arms of Lois Chasse, now his wife, Clothos and Lachesis come to guide him to a new plane of existence.

CAROLYN ROBERTS: Ralph Roberts's first wife, Carolyn dies from brain cancer. She does, however, remain a presence in his life, in that he often "hears" her voice and sees her in his dreams.

BILL McGOVERN: A good friend to Ralph Roberts, Bill is also his tenant. Bill is gay, but not openly so. Atropos, who takes souvenirs from his future victims, steals one of Bill's hats and uses it to taunt Ralph. Bill McGovern dies after having his "lifeline" cut by Atropos.

LOIS CHASSE: Over time, Lois goes from being Ralph's friend and fellow insomniac to becoming his co-adventurer and his second wife. Lois also sees the special things Ralph sees. She, too, is chosen by "the Purpose" to battle the Crimson King. Lois is strong, independent, brave, intelligent, and loving, at once complementing and completing Ralph. Due to the intensity of their supernatural experiences, their mutual admiration for each other quickly deepens into love. Following the conclusion of their adventures, Lois, like Ralph, loses her memory of them. Her memories are reawakened, however, on the day Ralph dies.

It is presumed that Lois still resides in Derry.

ED DEEPNEAU: A research scientist at Hawking Labs, Ed becomes a pawn of Atropos. Atropos cuts Ed's "string," but Ed doesn't die. Instead, he is driven insane, and is programmed by Atropos to mount a kamikaze attack on the Derry Civic Center. Ed Deepneau dies in the assault on the Civic Center.

HELEN DEEPNEAU: Helen's marriage to Ed Deepneau is a nightmare. He beats her so savagely that she leaves him, fleeing to Woman Care, an organization associated with feminist activist Susan Day. Helen divorces Ed, and later adopts a lesbian lifestyle.

NATALIE DEEPNEAU: Ed and Helen's infant daughter. Years after the main events of *Insomnia*, Ralph sacrifices himself to save her life, frustrating Atropos' plans for vengeance.

DORRANCE MARSTELLAR: Ralph learns that "Old Dorr," though mostly regarded as the town oddball, is privy to the world and thinking of "long-timers" like Clothos, Lachesis, and their masters. Old Dorr (whom some King experts see as "*ka* personified") acts as the long-timers' liaison to Ralph and Lois, delivering cryptic messages to them at critical moments and providing guidance to the bewildered duo.

SUSAN DAY: A prominent women's rights activist, her proposed trip to Derry polarizes the pro-life and pro-choice factions there. She is decapitated in the aftermath of Ed Deepneau's attack on the Derry Civic Center.

THE CRIMSON KING: A mysterious and powerful figure of horrible evil, the Crimson King wants Patrick Danville dead. Raving to Ralph, Ed Deepneau likens the Crimson King to King Herod, going so far as to claim that Herod is merely one of the King's incarnations. Ed states that the Crimson King jumps from body to body and generation to generation, always looking for the Messiah.

During his struggles with Ed, Ralph actually meets the Crimson King in the King's Court. The King, apparently plucking memories from Ralph's mind, takes the form of Ralph's mother, then of an enormous red female catfish. Ralph, staring intently at the bizarre figure in front of him, begins to see a shape behind the shape, "a bright man, a red man, with cold eyes and a merciless mouth," an individual who in Ralph's eyes resembles Christ. The king tells Ralph he wants Ed to succeed ("I've worked very hard here in Derry") just before Ralph plunges the sharp point of one of Lois's earrings into the king's bulging eye and escapes.

THE GREEN MAN: This mysterious figure appears only briefly in the lives of Ralph Roberts and Lois Chasse, when he returns Lois's earrings, which had been stolen by Atropos. She, in turn, gives them to Ralph, who pockets them, and later uses them as a weapon in his escape from the court of the Crimson King. Apparently the Green Man is an enemy of the Crimson King's, but his nature has not been revealed further as of yet.

CLOTHOS, LACHESIS, AND ATROPOS: These creatures are mortal, but enhanced (long-timers), and certainly not human. Ralph Roberts calls them "the three little bald doctors." These otherworldly beings may have inspired the Greek myths of the Fates, who weave, measure, and cut the threads of human destiny. Clothos and Lachesis, who describe themselves as "physicians of the last resort," are agents of Death and of the Purpose. Atropos is a rogue, an agent of the Random.

Their current whereabouts are unknown.

PATRICK DANVILLE: Though only a boy when he comes into contact with Ralph Roberts and Lois Chasse, Patrick is vital to the designs of the Purpose. In the year 2012, Patrick is destined to sacrifice himself to save the lives of two men, one of whom is also important to the Purpose. Atropos is using Ed, who is in the service of the Random, to try to kill Patrick. His death would be disastrous to the Purpose. According to Clothos, Patrick is more important than Adolf Hitler, Winston Churchill, or Augustus Caesar. If he dies, "the Tower of all existence will fall."

Fortunately, Ralph and Lois save him from the Crimson King.

INSOMNIA: TRIVIA

- To promote *Insomnia*, King traveled to several independent bookstores across the United States on his Harley-Davidson. The ten-stop tour started in Vermont and ended in California. The trip also provided a great deal of inspiration for *Desperation* and *The Regulators* (both 1996).

16

BAG OF BONES

(1998)

Stephen King created quite a stir in 1997 when word spread through the publishing industry that he was allegedly unhappy with Viking, his New York–based publisher of close to two decades. The press reported that King was rankled by Viking's supposed refusal to meet his asking price for his latest novel; the full story is almost certainly more complex. A resolution was reached when the author signed a three-book deal with Simon and Schuster, entering into a unique partnership with the publisher—forgoing his usual large advance, he worked out an arrangement that reportedly gave him a higher percentage of the profits at the back end.

The first book King delivered to the publisher's prestigious Scribner imprint under this new deal was *Bag of Bones*. A marked departure from what the general public had come to expect from "America's best-loved boogeyman," the novel represents yet another step in the author's continuous challenge to himself to elevate the overall quality and emotional scope of his work. Equal parts ghost story, thriller, romance, mystery, and psychological suspense story, *Bag of Bones* demonstrates that King is as adept at evoking heartfelt emotion as he is at sending shivers up readers' spines. Critics who had previously dismissed the popular author as a mere "shock-meister" finally upgraded their opinions after experiencing this powerfully told, masterfully crafted roller coaster of a book.

Simply stated, it ranks among the four or five best novels the author has written in his entire career.

A love story with supernatural overtones, *Bag of Bones* consciously evokes Daphne du Maurier's *Rebecca* (1938). King, however, twists the premise of that classic romantic thriller to suit his own purposes. For instead of a wicked woman being mistaken for a good one, *Bag of Bones* features a good woman, Jo Noonan, whose recently revealed secret life causes her husband, bestselling author Mike Noonan, to doubt his previous complete trust of her. There are numerous other overt connections to du Maurier's novel—"I have dreamt again of Manderley" is a familiar refrain throughout—as well as more subtle ties, like evoking Max DeWinter by naming a character Max Devore. Other literary connections include Herman Melville's "Bartleby the Scrivener" (1856); the inclusion of Noonan's discussion of this short story earlier in the novel provides a poignancy to his words that close the book.

King's office   BETH GWINN

Finally, there is the quote that one of Mike's college professors attributes to nineteenth-century British novelist Thomas Hardy: "Compared to the dullest human being actually walking about on the face of the earth and casting his shadow there, the most brilliantly drawn character is nothing but a bag of bones." This quote resonates throughout the novel; it also has a more literal meaning in that a real *bag of bones* figures in the plot.

Besides its central focus as a "haunted love story" (as King himself succinctly describes it), *Bag of Bones* also provides insight into both the writing process and the publishing industry, deftly conveying Mike's (and presumably some of King's) insider's views on the interrelationship between business and art.

In addition to the references to du Maurier and Melville, *Bag of Bones* mentions several of Mike Noonan's companions on the bestseller lists, including Tom Clancy, Dean Koontz, Jean Auel, and Mary Higgins Clark. Noonan also talks about writing novels and purposely putting them aside for later publication, demanding editors and publishers, and publication dates influenced not by when the book is done, but by when it will be best positioned to sell out in the marketplace.

Although it downplays any element of the fantastic at first [Mike lives in Derry, Maine, the setting of *It* (1986) and *Insomnia* (1994), but has never spied a demonic clown poking his head out of a sewer], *Bag of Bones* is set squarely in the midst of the Stephen King Universe.

Residing in Derry, Mike interacts with residents of that town already familiar to King readers, such as druggist Joe Wyzer and Ralph Roberts. Although the novel begins in Derry, the action shifts to Dark Score Lake, where Jessie Burlingame (1992's *Gerald's Game*) was sexually molested by her father in 1963. Noonan refers to two writers from the King canon, William Denbrough (*It*) and Thad Beaumont (1989's *The Dark Half*). Denbrough and his "famous Creatures From Beyond" are favorites of Jo Noonan's. Thad Beaumont is mentioned in a less pleasant context: after learning that Thad broke up with his wife in *Needful Things* (1991), readers hear from Noonan that the troubled writer has committed suicide. Finally, Mike encounters Norris Ridgewick, formerly of the Castle Rock police (Mike inquires after Alan Pangborn and Polly Chalmers).

Bag of Bones marks a milestone of sorts in that, beyond its expected bestseller status, the author received extremely favorable reviews worldwide, even from the critics who had probably never read a ghost story—or a Stephen King novel—before.

BAG OF BONES: PRIMARY SUBJECTS

MIKE NOONAN: A successful writer who laughingly refers to himself as "V. C. Andrews with a prick," Mike is the author of several bestselling novels, including *Being Two*, *The Red Shirt Man*, and *All the Way from the Top*. Suffering from severe writer's block after the tragic death of his wife Jo (several weeks pregnant, she dies of an aneurysm), Mike resorts to publishing novels he had previously written and then purposely withheld from submitting to maintain the illusion that he is still creating new works.

Besides his writer's block, Mike experiences strange dreams centering on his vacation home at Dark Score Lake, Maine. Compelled by these dreams, hoping that the change in scenery will calm his anxieties and reignite his creativity, Mike moves back to Dark Score to his lakeside cabin, a large house known to locals as "Sara Laughs."

Shortly after arriving, he begins receiving messages from ghostly presences inhabiting his home. These spirits initially make their presence known in harmless ways—wailing in the night, sudden changes in room temperature, and refrigerator magnets that seem to move of their own accord—but their communications soon become more urgent, more insistent. Mike senses that one of the spirits might be Jo, but there are other, angrier and more dangerous presences haunting the environs of Sara Laughs as well.

Mike is troubled by his failure to understand these messages, and by new information he unearths that indicates his beloved Jo may have been having an extramarital affair before she died. He becomes distracted, however, by the plight of Mattie Devore, whom he meets after rescuing her young toddler, Kyra, from a busy local highway. An attractive twenty-year-old widow, Mattie is engaged in a bitter custody battle with her father-in-law, millionaire Max Devore, over Kyra. Sympathetic to her plight, and prompted by Jo's spirit messages, Mike offers his help.

Mattie's problems provide a much-needed diversion for Mike, who, for the first time since his wife died, actually feels useful. Buoyed by a budding romantic relationship with Mattie, Mike takes the battle directly to Devore, hiring savvy custody lawyer John Storrow to defend Mattie's interests. Max pushes back, first through flunkies like Sheriff George Footman and real estate broker Richard Osgood, and then more directly. Accompanied by his "personal assistant" Rogette Whitmore, Max takes Mike by surprise on the shore of Dark Score Lake and nearly kills him.

Mike obviously faces a powerful enemy in Max Devore, but has an even more formidable opponent in the vengeful spirit who haunts Sara Laughs. Following a trail initially blazed by his wife, Mike learns that Kyra's predicament has its roots in the town's past, specifically in the rape and murder of a vibrant blues singer named Sara Tidwell nearly a century ago. A black woman whose confident, forthright manner offended some of Dark Score's residents, Sara and her son Kito were killed by a group of local hooligans led by Max Devore's ancestor Jared. To conceal their perfidy, the killers stuffed the corpses in a burlap bag and buried it near the lake.

Sara takes her revenge on Dark Score from beyond the grave. Instigating the deaths of several children over the course of the next century, she has most recently turned to the progeny of her chief tormentor, Jared Devore, seeking the death of Kyra.

Knowing that Sara is the root cause of the evil he faces allows Mike to defy her power, no mean feat considering Sara has influenced otherwise loving parents to kill their own children. Mike breaks Sara's hold over the town by uncovering and destroying her remains, which had been laid to rest near the lake. Mike survives his supernatural encounter with the ghost of Sara, and, when last heard from, had initiated adoption proceedings to gain custody of Kyra. Meanwhile, shaken to the core by the tragic events related in *Bag of Bones*, Mike abandons his writing career.

JO NOONAN (née ARLEN): Mike's late wife, she died of a brain aneurysm in August 1994 at the age of thirty-four. Adding to the tragedy, Noonan discovers soon thereafter that she was pregnant with their first child. Mike also learns Jo was hiding something from him. Initially, Mike concludes it was an affair. Later, however, he finds out that she had uncovered the secret shame of Dark Score Lake (i.e., the rape and murder of Sara Tidwell). Jo had gathered these facts in secret, and was presumably waiting for the right moment to reveal them to Mike. Jo's spirit haunts Dark Score Lake, guiding, then actually aiding Mike in his supernatural fight against Sara Tidwell.

"SARA LAUGHS:" The name of the Noonans' summer residence at Dark Score Lake. The cabin is named after blues singer Sara Tidwell, a former resident. Sara was famous for (among other things) her raucous laugh.

MATTIE DEVORE: The widow of Lance Devore, mother of Kyra Devore, this young woman becomes involved in a tug of war with her father-in-law, Max Devore, over legal custody of Kyra. Although reluctant to do so, Mattie accepts Mike's emotional and financial support in her battle to keep her child, promising him she will someday pay him back. Despite their age difference (Mike is in his early forties; Mattie is only twenty), she is attracted to him, and makes her feelings very clear in this regard. Mike in turn struggles with his feelings for Mattie, eventually professing his love. Tragically, they never consummate their relationship, as George Footman fatally shoots Mattie.

LANCE DEVORE: The youngest son of millionaire Max Devore, Lance came to Dark Score Lake in 1994 to survey his father's holdings and instead fell in love with Mattie Stanfield, whom he met at a softball game. Three weeks later they were inseparable and Mattie was pregnant. They were married in September 1994, three months after they met. Mattie and Lance were married a little over three years when Lance died after falling off the roof of their trailer home in the midst of a lightning storm. During those years, Lance was estranged from his father, who disapproved of the marriage (and had, in fact, offered Mattie a considerable sum to abandon her husband and child). Lance attempts reconciliation with his father shortly before he dies, sending the old man a picture of his granddaughter. The picture arouses Max's interest in Kyra, and leads to his coming to Dark Score Lake a few weeks later.

KYRA DEVORE: The daughter of Lance and Mattie Devore, Kyra is a precocious three-year-old who steals Mike Noonan's heart seconds after he "rescues" her from the middle of a busy local highway. Mike feels a strong bond with Kyra, mainly because her name resembles one he and Jo had picked for their intended baby, and because she is the age his child would have been had Jo lived and given birth. Their bond grows stronger as Mike learns that the spirits who haunt Sara Laughs are also speaking to Kyra, and deepens after they share a dream in which they visit Dark Score Lake at the turn of the century. The focus of the custody battle between her mother and grandfather, Kyra is caught in the middle—she loves her mother, but also feels affection for her grandfather and her "White Nana," Rogette Whitmore. Kyra is suddenly orphaned when George Footman guns down her mother. After her mother's death, Mike begins proceedings to adopt her legally.

MAX DEVORE: The great-grandson of Jared Devore, the man who instigates the attack on Sara Tidwell. Said to be worth some $600 million, eightysomething Max Devore made his money in the advent of the modern computer revolution. Estranged from his son Lance, Max cut off all contact with him until Lance sent him a picture of his grandchild. After Lance's accidental death, Max returns to his childhood home of Dark Score Lake, currying favor with the locals by spreading his money around. Shortly thereafter, Max (no doubt "pushed" by the ghost of Sara Tidwell) seeks custody of his granddaughter Kyra. Due to the intervention of Mike Noonan, however, these efforts prove unsuccessful. Max dies shortly after he and Rogette Whitmore attack Mike at the Lake.

ROGETTE WHITMORE: Devore's "personal assistant," who is later revealed to be his daughter. Called "the White Nana" by her niece, Rogette lives for her father's approval, eagerly carrying out his every wish. Although Rogette has been ravaged by cancer (people automatically think of the horrific woman in artist Edvard Munch's painting "The Scream" when they see her), she seems to have an almost preternatural athletic ability. She demonstrates this skill when she starts hurling rocks at Mike after he flees her and Max Devore's roadside attack by diving into Dark Score Lake. Rogette's stone throws are amazingly strong and accurate; one hits Mike in the head, almost causing him to pass out.

After Max's death, Rogette schemes to kill Kyra, eventually sending her father's lackeys to shoot Mattie, Kyra, and their friends. When this attempt fails to destroy the little girl, Rogette kidnaps Kyra. When Kyra again escapes, Rogette perishes in her attempt to retrieve the little girl.

GEORGE FOOTMAN: The Castle County sheriff, he works for Max Devore on the side, threatening Mike in the early stages of his ongoing conflict with the multimillionaire. Footman is the gunman who opens fire on Mattie Devore's trailer, killing her and wounding three of her four guests. Footman is later captured by private investigator George Kennedy and Mike Noonan, and is eventually sent to nearby Shawshank State Prison for his crimes.

RICHARD OSGOOD: A local real estate agent who spies on Mattie Devore for her father-in-law, Osgood is driving the car from which George Footman shoots and kills Mattie Devore. Osgood dies horribly when George Kennedy's gunshots ignite the gas tank of the sedan he is driving; unable to free himself, he is burned alive.

JOHN STORROW: The lawyer Mike hires to protect Mattie's interests in her custody battle with Max Devore, Storrow successfully fends off of all Max Devore's legal feints. John, who has a crush on Mattie, is wounded in a hail of gunfire during Mattie's victory party to celebrate Max Devore's death.

SARA TIDWELL: A provocative turn-of-the-twentieth-century African-American blues singer, she and her family made their home on Dark Score Lake for a time, at least until prejudice brought them all tragedy. Sara makes the fatal mistake of humiliating Jared Devore in front of his cronies, Oren Peebles, Fred Dean, Harry Auster, and George Armbruster. The group strikes back, beating, raping, and finally killing her, but not before she witnesses her son's drowning at the hands of Harry Auster (who, unknown to Mike Noonan, is a distant relative of his). Sara's rage survives her death—over the ensuing decades, her vengeful spirit is responsible for the deaths of several children at Dark Score Lake, all descendants of the group that took her life. Nearly a hundred years later, Sara sets her murderous sights on Kyra Devore, but is ultimately frustrated by the efforts of Mike and Jo Noonan. Her spirit, anchored to Dark Score Lake by her mortal remains, vanishes when Mike destroys her skeleton in a final confrontation.

"THE RED TOPS": Sarah Tidwell's band, consisting of her family and friends. These performers and their families (approximately 40 individuals) tried to make a home at Dark Score Lake, settling in what came to be known as Tidwell's Meadow, where they built the home that was soon known as Sara Laughs. They are described condescendingly in ancient newspaper clippings Mike discovers as Castle County's "Southern Blackbirds" and "rhythmic darkies." Although most members of the white community had no objection to their presence, racism and prejudice eventually reared their ugly heads, resulting in the deaths of Sara and her son Kito. After that, the locals closed ranks against the survivors, most notably against

Sara's brother Reg Tidwell and his family. The Tidwells et al. abandoned Dark Score after Reg's son Junior died of blood poisoning—brought on by sustaining an injury in a bear trap set on a path he was known to frequent.

BAG OF BONES: ADAPTATIONS

A full-length audio version of *Bag of Bones*, read by the author, is available from Simon and Schuster audio. In many ways, King is the perfect reader for this novel. Because it is a regional novel, the author's natural Maine accent is perfectly suited to the material. Then, too, although King is more successful a novelist than his character of Mike, he still has a lot in common with his creation, lending verisimilitude to his reading. Finally, King is also in tune with what he refers to as the "temperature gradient" of the characters, meaning he knows precisely how much emotion to invest in any given scene. The audio version also includes a substantial interview with the author conducted by the tape's producer, Eve Beglarian, who is reportedly developing an operatic version of King's story "The Man in the Black Suit."

17

DREAMCATCHER

(2001)

We don't know the days that will change our lives." This sentiment, expressed by Gary Jones, a major character in *Dreamcatcher*, is the statement of a man who knows from painful experience just how true those words are. Gary, you see, is the recent victim of an automobile accident. Struck as he crossed a busy city street, Gary was nearly killed. As it was, he suffered serious damage to his hip and leg, leaving him with a pronounced limp.

Originally titled "Cancer," *Dreamcatcher* was King's first published novel after his near-fatal car accident in June 1999 (an event described in harrowing detail in 2000's nonfictional *On Writing: A Memoir of the Craft*). As such, it's not surprising that a car accident features prominently in the narrative. However, it's what King, the preeminent storyteller that he is, does with this incident that makes *Dreamcatcher* one of his most moving examinations of male friendship since his novella "The Body."

King describes how this novel, which author Colin Harrison described in his April 15, 2001, *New York Times* review as "a frenzied, multilayered, ever-accelerating nightmare," came to be in an author's note at the end of the book:

> I was never so grateful to be writing as during my time of work (November 16, 1999–May 29, 2000) on *Dreamcatcher*. I was in a lot of phys-

ical discomfort during those six and a half months, and the book took me away. The reader will see that pieces of the physical discomfort followed me into the story, but what I remember most is the sublime release we find in vivid dreams.

The plot is simple: four childhood friends from Derry, Maine, get together each November for a hunting trip. This year is especially important to them because it's the first time they've been together since one of their number was struck by a car some eight months prior. Their getaway is interrupted, however, by the crash landing of a spacecraft, bearing an alien life-form that spreads virally. The four find themselves embroiled in a battle to save the Earth from an alien takeover, caught between the aliens, who have possessed one of them, and a special military group intent on eradicating the aliens and every manifestation of the virus.

Perhaps because it was the first book King wrote after his accident, at a time when he wasn't sure if he'd ever write fiction again, it contains many familiar themes. Most prominent is the theme of a group combining to battle a great evil, featured in *The Dark Tower* series, and in novels like *It*. Gary (the memory), Henry (the brains), Joe (the drive), and Pete (the point man, the pathfinder) compose a *ka-tet*, much like Roland and his group, or the Losers. This *ka-tet* is unique, however, because it centers on a sickly man afflicted with Down Syndrome named Douglas Cavell. Duddits, as he refers to himself, is the human hub of the quintet, a telepath whose wild talents, like those of Carrie White and Dinky Earnshaw, make him, in King's parlance, a tranny.

The alien spaceship that crashed in the forest known as the Jefferson Tract (some 150 miles north of Derry) was not the first such craft to touch down in that neck of the woods—that honor belongs to the vehicle that bore the Tommyknockers to Earth, which came to rest near Haven. As in that eponymous novel, the aliens in *Dreamcatcher* can possess human hosts. Harkening back to one of the episodes of *Creepshow*, "The Lonesome Death of Jordy Verrill," the novel features a red-yellow fungus that quickly comes to cover everything it comes in contact with.

The snow and isolation recall such King works as *The Shining*, *Misery*, *Gerald's Game*, and *Storm of the Century*. One could even make the case that the unfortunate Richard McCarthy (obviously a reference to the main actor in the original film version of *Invasion of the Body Snatchers*) might have encountered the "god of the woods," featured so prominently in *The Girl Who Loved Tom Gordon*, in his trek through the forest.

Influences include movies like *Invasion of the Body Snatchers*, *The Evil*

Dead, Alien, and They Came from Within and novels like Joseph Conrad's *Heart of Darkness* (the name of the character Kurtz).

Major portions of *Dreamcatcher* take place in Derry, Maine. The four major characters grew up there in the 1970s, relatively unaware of the terror that lurked in the town's sewer system (Pennywise the Clown was still dormant during this time, licking wounds incurred in his battle with the Losers in 1958). Duddits, their friend, is a lifelong resident of the town.

Most importantly, the narrative references past history when Gary, possessed by the nefarious alien Mr. Gray, detours through the town, searching for a water supply that the alien hopes to infect with the virus his strange race uses to attack other species. It is at this point in King's narrative when his Constant Readers receive a not completely unexpected jolt. Coming upon the Derry Standpipe, Gary/Gray sees a monument at its base, a statue of two children, a boy and a girl "with their hands linked and their heads lowered, as if in prayer." In an obvious reference to *It*, a plaque attached to the statue reads:

To Those Lost in the Storm

May 31, 1985

And to the Children

All the Children

Love From Bill, Ben, Bev, Eddie, Richie, Stan, Mike

The Losers Club

The plaque is marred by graffiti, significant to those who know Derry's secret history—spray-painted over the inscription in "jagged red letters" are two words: "PENNYWISE LIVES!"

DREAMCATCHER: PRIMARY SUBJECTS

GARY JONES: Born in 1964, "Jonesy" grew up in Derry, Maine. There he made four lifelong friends in Henry Devlin, Joe Clarendon, Pete Moore, and Douglas "Duddits" Cavell. The quintet had many adventures together, the most important being the time they found a young girl, Josie Rinkenhauer, who had been the subject of a desperate search in town. Josie had fallen into a drainpipe and was trapped there until the boys, utilizing their strange bond, rescued her.

Gary grows up to be an associate professor of history at John Jay College in Boston. Although still a young man, Gary feels a void in his life, something his childhood friends are also feeling. On March 17, 2001, Gary is struck by a car as he crosses a busy street. Gary is severely injured (his heart stops twice), but is sufficiently recovered by November 2001 to make his annual pilgrimage with his boyhood friends (except for Douglas) to a cabin in the Maine woods that the group refers to as Hole in the Wall.

Alone at the cabin, Gary has the unfortunate pleasure of meeting Richard McCarthy, a hunter who has been infected by an alien virus. A manifestation of the virus possesses Gary, infecting him with the personality of an alien who dubs himself Mr. Gray (an anagram for Gary?). Mr. Gray is determined to spread his brethren throughout the human population via an infected dog, whose barely functioning body he wishes to drop in a major water supply.

In control of Gary's body, Mr. Gray travels to the Quabbin Reservoir in order to accomplish his goal. At the very last moment, Gary, who has maintained a foothold in his body by psychologically fleeing to a remote room of his mental "memory cathedral," gets the best of the alien, slaying him in mental combat, thus saving the world from disaster.

HENRY DEVLIN: As *Dreamcatcher* begins, Henry, now a psychiatrist, is struggling with depression and contemplating suicide. Although he and Pete Devlin are away from the cabin fetching supplies at Gosselin's Market when Richard McCarthy visits Hole in the Wall, Henry is not spared an encounter with the aliens, as the pair encounters an unfortunate woman who, like McCarthy, has become host to an entity King refers to as a "shit-weasel."

Henry later finds himself under quarantine in the camp of Blue Unit, facing extermination. Already used to psychic abilities from his exposure to the rest of the quintet, Henry uses the telepathic ability granted to all those touched by the virus to make contact with Owen Underhill, a leader of the unit who has doubts about the course of action the special unit is taking. He and Owen escape together, setting out to find Jonesy/Mr. Gray. Along the way, they travel through Derry to pick up Douglas Cavell, who aids them in their search. Although wounded in a car crash as they approach Quabbin reservoir, Henry survives. As *Dreamcatcher* ends, we see a more relaxed Henry hanging out with Jonesy and his family.

JOE CLARENDON: Nicknamed Beaver, Joe was a wisecracking, foul-mouthed kid who grew into a wisecracking, foul-mouthed adult. Beaver is a carpenter by trade, a drinker by habit, a man with few friends other than Jonesy, Henry, and Peter. He is killed by the shit-weasel that formerly inhabited Richard McCarthy.

PETE MOORE: Pete is described as a man for whom "hunting was a hobby, beer a religion." A car salesman, Pete has trouble connecting with others, perhaps because they sense a strangeness about him. The strangeness is caused by the telepathy he shares with his friends, and by Pete's ability to find "the line," which might best be described as the shortest path between two points. As a child, Pete followed the line to Josie Rinkenhauer. As an adult, he uses the power to find lost keys.

Pete single-handedly battles a shit-weasel, defeating it. Unfortunately, the injuries it inflicts upon him in battle prove fatal.

RICHARD McCARTHY: Part of an unfortunate hunting party, McCarthy wanders the Maine woods for hours after being infected by the "Ripley" virus. Taken in by Jonesy, he exhibits strange behavior, babbling incoherently; he also suffers from apparently uncontrollable flatulence. McCarthy dies on the toilet, depositing a shit-weasel in the bowl. The shit-weasel subsequently kills Beaver but is destroyed by Jonesy, who sets it and its eggs on fire, destroying Hole in the Wall.

DOUGLAS "DUDDITS" CAVELL: A child afflicted with Down Syndrome, Duddits is befriended by Jonesy, Henry, Joe, and Pete after they save him from a sadistic bully named Richie Grenedeau. As they spend more time together, the boys come to realize that they are now linked together telepathically through Duddits, who exhibits the wild talents of a tranny. As teenagers, the quintet uses these powers to locate the missing girl Josie Rinkenhauer. As adults, these powers come in handy in their struggles to subdue the Ripley virus.

In the end, it seems to Henry that Duddits had been waiting for the aliens to arrive, as he seems to have expected the arrival of his friend and Owen Underhill as they pursue Gary/Mr. Gray. Using the dying Duddits as a human bloodhound, Henry and Underhill are able to track Mr. Gray as he travels to the Quabbin reservoir. The experience proves too much for Dud-dits, the human dreamcatcher, who dies as they approach the reservoir.

THE DREAMCATCHER: An elaborate woven Indian charm meant to ward off nightmares. A dreamcatcher, which Beaver believes once caused all the boys to have the same dream at the same time, hangs from the ceil-ing at the cabin called Hole in the Wall. Duddits is the human dream-catcher who binds the group of five together.

MR. GRAY: A manifestation of the alien virus whose consciousness lit-erally takes over Jonesy's body, driving Jonesy's consciousness into a small room in his "memory cathedral." Having control over a human vessel gives the alien an opportunity to spread the alien virus more effectively. Tapping Jonesy's memory, Mr. Gray hits on a plan of dumping a virus-infected dog carcass into a major water supply. He thus embarks on a journey that leads him from Hole in the Wall to the Quabbin reservoir, where he is defeated by Jonesy before he can follow through with his plans.

ABRAHAM PETER KURTZ: Born Robert Coonts, this flamboyant soldier changed his name to purposely evoke the villain from Joseph Con-rad's memorable novella *Heart of Darkness*. Along with the members of his Blue Boy squad, retired Air Force officer Kurtz has grappled with the aliens for twenty-five years, always frustrating their invasion attempts because of his utter ruthlessness. Unfortunately, Kurtz has been driven mad by this struggle. Fearing a modern Typhoid Mary, Kurtz tracks Jonesy/Mr. Gray from the Jefferson Tract to the Quabbin Reservoir. Kurtz is killed by one of his own men shortly after fatally wounding Owen Underhill.

OWEN UNDERHILL: Second in command to Kurtz in the Jefferson Tract operation, Underhill (who bears the first name of one of King's sons and the last name of one of Peter Straub's more famous characters, Tim Underhill) begins to have doubts about Kurtz's sanity. Finding himself tele-pathically linked to Henry via the alien virus, he is persuaded by the psy-chiatrist to free him from quarantine. Together, they set off in pursuit of Jonesy/Mr. Gray.

Along the way, they stop in Derry to pick up Duddits, who aids them in their mission. Underhill is instrumental in frustrating the alien invasion, killing the shit-weasel Mr. Gray was trying to dump into the Quabbin reservoir with his rifle. Unfortunately, Underhill is gut-shot by the pursuing Kurtz. He subsequently begs a comrade to end his life; his buddy complies with Underhill's wishes.

THE RIPLEY VIRUS: The army's name for an alien virus, named for the Sigourney Weaver character in the various *Alien* movies, and for *Ripley's Believe It or Not*. Described as sort of an "interstellar kudzu," the virus takes several forms. The virus is carried by humanoid vessels the army refers to as "grays," alien beings resembling the little gray creatures featured in the classic movie *Close Encounters of the Third Kind*. These are essentially organic delivery systems. Humans infected by contact with a gray are said to be suffering from Ripley Prime. Under certain circumstances, Ripley Prime can cause a parasitic, egg-laying shit-weasel, a creature resembling a furry lamprey with a mouth containing "a nest of teeth," to gestate within its host. Another, less lethal manifestation of the virus is called "byrus." This manifestation takes the form a red-yellow growth that quickly spreads across everything it's exposed to.

The growth, or byrus, as the aliens refer to it, has proven successful in taking over other planets; it does not thrive as well on Earth, however, and seems susceptible to extreme cold. In all previous cases of alien attack, the threat has been eliminated by the military so quickly that the byrus has never had a chance to adapt or mutate. The aliens seek a better vessel to carry out their invasion. Gary Jones, who has somehow been forever changed by his car accident, proves to be that vessel.

DREAMCATCHER: ADAPTATIONS

Dreamcatcher was made into a film in 2003, directed by Lawrence Kasdan and based on a screenplay by veteran screenwriter William Goldman, who also did the screenwriting chores for the successful *Misery* and the less successful *Hearts in Atlantis* film adaptations. The movie is quite forgettable, despite the presence of the formidable Morgan Freeman, who plays military madman Col. Abraham Curtis (the name Kurtz was dropped to avoid the literary baggage of *Heart of Darkness*) in an off-putting, over-the-top manner. The four actors who play Gary, Henry, Joe, and Pete (Damian

Lewis, Thomas Jane, Jason Lee, and Timothy Oliphant, respectively) are largely interchangeable. Goldman remains faithful to his source material until the final moments, but the film never quite catches the camaraderie of the quartet, nor the deep affection they all feel for Duddits. The film's major departure from the book lies in transforming Duddits into an alien life form at the end of the movie—seems he was planted on Earth decades before should the deadly enemies of his spacefaring race ever appear on Earth. The final battle between the antagonistic aliens is silly at best.

DREAMCATCHER: TRIVIA

- As word of the military's presence in the Maine woods spreads, an excited radio DJ is heard to say: "Interstellar plague's on the loose, brothers and sisters, that's the word. Call it the Hot Zone, the Dead Zone, or the Twilight Zone, you want to cancel your trip up north."

18

RELATED TALES

"Autopsy Room Four" (from 1997's *Six Stories*)

Autopsy Room Four," a tale reminiscent of Edgar Allen Poe, details the travails of Howard Cotter, a golfer rendered unconscious by a snakebite while on Derry Municipal Golf Course. Howard awakens in an autopsy room just as the coroners are preparing to cut him from stem to stern. Able to see and hear, Howard is still paralyzed by the bite, and watches helplessly as the doctors prepare to go about their grim tasks. Fortunately for Howard, the autopsy is interrupted before he can be injured.

Going through his golf bag, paramedics are surprised to find an exotic snake. This is one instance where we won't reveal the ending—King's buildup, leading up to the story's last line, is outright hilarious.

"AUTOPSY ROOM FOUR": PRIMARY SUBJECTS

HOWARD COTRELL: Howard Cottrell is a golfer who is paralyzed by a snakebite and nearly autopsied as a result. He currently resides somewhere near Derry, Maine. He has, however, developed an interesting fetish as a result of his experiences in the autopsy room.

"The Road Virus Heads North" (from 2002's
Everything's Eventual)

This tale of the supernatural made its appearance in *999*, a massive anthology edited by Al Sarrantonio, published in 1999. King's contribution, entitled "The Road Virus Heads North," about a figure in a portrait that comes to life, recalls his 1990 novella *The Sun Dog* and his novel *Rose Madder* (1995), which featured similar elements.

Author Richard Kinnell is on his way back to Derry, Maine, after attending a writer's conference in Boston, when he decides to stop at a garage sale in Rosewood. Scanning the items for sale, he is taken with a vivid, framed watercolor. Purchasing the painting despite its bleak subject matter (a picture of a deranged, fanged driver in his Grand Am) and the fact that the artist recently committed suicide, Kinnell puts it in his trunk and proceeds on his journey, stopping at his Aunt Trudy's house along the way.

Kinnell shows the picture to his aunt, who is extremely disturbed by it. This bothers him, but not as much as the fact that the picture has changed since he bought it—the figure has moved, if only slightly. The next day, Kinnell tosses the painting into a ditch, only to find it waiting for him when he gets home. The watercolor has changed once again, this time showing a scene of carnage at the Rosewood home where he purchased it. Checking the news, Kinnell discovers that the woman who was running the garage sale is dead, brutally murdered by an unknown assailant.

Later he hears a car stopping outside, and realizes to his horror that the fanged man has come directly to his home.

SECTION THREE

The Prime Reality,
Part II:
Castle Rock

he small New England mill town of Castle Rock, Maine, was for many years, without a doubt, the geographical center of the Stephen King Universe. Located in southwestern Maine—ten miles south of Rumford and about thirty miles west of Augusta—the unusually tragedy-stricken town figures in several short stories (such as "Mrs. Todd's Shortcut," "Nona," "Uncle Otto's Truck," and "It Grows on You"), two novellas (*The Body* and *The Sun Dog*), and four novels (see below). Much more than a mere setting for King's tales of the strange and macabre, the site also effectively functioned as a scale model of contemporary American society.

King began experimenting with the idea of the small town as a "social and psychological microcosm" as far back as *Carrie* (1974) and became more ambitious with the concept in *'Salem's Lot* (1975). He did not hit his stride, however, until *The Dead Zone* (1979), his first novel to feature Castle Rock. There, psychic Johnny Smith is asked to lend a hand in tracking down the infamous Castle Rock Strangler. Smith reluctantly agrees, subsequently revealing the killer to be Frank Dodd, a popular local law enforcement officer. Dodd's crimes, and subsequent suicide, make national headlines, beginning what many locals consider to be nothing less than a curse on the town.

Clearly, King knows the town intimately. How intimately? Well, in the introduction to *The Sun Dog*, the author refers to his own wealth of unwritten knowledge about the town, noting examples including "how Sheriff George Bannerman lost his virginity in the back seat of his dead father's car."

As the years passed, the author "became more and more interested in—almost entranced by—the secret life of this town, by the hidden relationships which seemed to come clearer and clearer" to him. Castle Rock had become his town, the way "the mythical town of Isola is Ed McBain's town and the West Virginia village of Glory was Davis Grubb's town."

Unlike the town of Derry, or for that matter 'Salem's Lot, King has not revealed much of the Castle Rock's history before the turn of the 20th century. In fact, the most ancient history he's related has been in the short stories "The Man in the Black Suit" and "Uncle Otto's Truck." For all practical purposes, the history of Castle Rock as it relates to the Stephen King Universe began with the aforementioned *The Dead Zone*.

As previously mentioned, many residents believe Frank Dodd's actions cast a spell of evil on the town. The evidence? Since 1979, Castle Rock has certainly had more than its share of tragedy. In 1981, Joe Camber's two-hundred-pound St. Bernard, Cujo, went rabid and killed several people (see the chapter on *Cujo*). In 1989, famous writer Thad Beaumont was attacked by a madman claiming to be George Stark, a man who couldn't possibly exist (see the chapter on *The Dark Half*). Beaumont never fully recovered from the incident, first separating from his wife, then later committing suicide. And in 1990, Reginald "Pop" Merrill, a fixture of Castle Rock's business community, died in a fire of suspicious origin (see the chapter on "The Sun Dog").

The most disturbing incident, however, has to be the hysteria and madness that gripped the entire town in the fall of 1991, coincident with the grand opening of the store called Needful Things. Spouses killed one another, neighbor battled neighbor to the death, and rival churches fought tooth and nail in the streets. The town was nearly destroyed in the chaos, as several buildings were dynamited by known criminal Ace Merrill (see the chapter on *Needful Things*).

By 1990, King had decided to "close the book" on Castle Rock, the quirky little community where so many of his favorite characters had lived and died, triumphed and suffered. And close the book he did. As one can see from the events described above, Castle Rock went out, not with a whimper, but with a bang.

Although King had seemingly cut all ties to the town in *Needful Things* (which was boldly subtitled "The Last Castle Rock Story"), he is still drawn to its familiar environs every now and then. For instance, there is the putative epilogue to that book, a short story called "It Grows on You," which appeared in *Nightmares & Dreamscapes* (1993). The town was also mentioned in passing in 1996's tale "The Man in the Black Suit," and in 1999's *The Girl*

Who Loved Tom Gordon. Former townspeople have also appeared in subsequent stories, the most recent example being former Castle Rock deputy Norris Ridgewick's cameo at the conclusion of *Bag of Bones*.

Castle Rock, with its constant struggles between good and evil, seems to have been almost a microcosmic version of the much grander cosmic conflict going on in the Stephen King Universe as a whole. Though that certainly does not mean that the seemingly minor skirmishes in Castle Rock are not also a part of that larger struggle.

The town has served as a setting for King's ongoing examination of the eternal struggle between good and evil, detailing the conflicts between Johnny Smith and Frank Dodd, Donna Trenton and Cujo, and Thad Beaumont and George Stark. The battle described in *Needful Things*, however, provides the best example of this theme. Leland Gaunt is obviously of the same breed of monster as other evil denizens of King's Universe such as Randall Flagg *(The Stand, The Eyes of the Dragon)*, Andre Linoge *(Storm of the Century)*, Aredelia Lortz ("The Library Policeman"), and Kurt Barlow *('Salem's Lot)*, and the troubles he caused in the town a tiny reflection of the battle that rages between the Random and the Purpose mentioned in *Insomnia*.

One could even characterize the human combatants in *Needful Things*—Alan Pangborn, Polly Chalmers, and Norris Ridgewick—as a *ka-tet*, similar in structure to the one Roland leads. This drives home the point that although evil exists, it is always opposed by good.

Another recurring theme is that evil lingers, as proved by the legacy of Frank Dodd, which King detailed in *Cujo* and has mentioned several times since. Again, however, King points out that the forces of good are just as resilient, that a champion always arises in a time of need.

Perhaps the most telling physical evidence that Castle Rock is a key part of the Stephen King Universe is the map of Maine contained in the novels *Dolores Claiborne* and *Gerald's Game*. There, readers can easily see that Castle Rock is part of King's Maine, sitting as it does to the south of towns like Bangor, Derry, and Haven. Bolstering this evidence are the many references King makes to events in Castle Rock in other books (for instance, Frank Dodd's suicide made national news, and was mentioned in passing in *It*), and his frequent mentions of such fictional Maine landmarks as Shawshank Prison and the mental institution known as Juniper Hill.

Obviously very resilient, the people of Castle Rock have rebuilt their town and continue with their daily lives. Perhaps the conflagration that nearly destroyed the Rock has cleansed the town of evil, allowing its denizens to live out their days in peace. Perhaps, though, evil still lingers there, waiting for the proper moment to inflict additional horrors on the unsuspecting populace.

CASTLE ROCK: TRIVIA

• As noted in the Introduction, Castle Rock also figures in the fiction of King's wife, Tabitha King. One example of this appears in her 1993 novel *One on One*. There, Castle Rock is depicted as a sports rival of Greenspark Academy, the school that two of her main characters attend.

• Like Derry, Castle Rock has spawned more than its share of working authors. Besides the unfortunate Thad Beaumont, the town is also the birthplace of writer Gordon LaChance (an incident from Gordie's childhood is told in the 1982 novella *The Body*).

• King took the name Castle Rock from a favorite novel of his youth, William Golding's 1954 classic *Lord of the Flies*. The name in turn was used by Rob Reiner, director of *Stand by Me*, as the name of his production company.

19

THE DEAD ZONE
(1979)

Of the dozens of character-driven novels that Stephen King has published since 1974, *The Dead Zone* remains one of his most powerful, poignant, and emotionally involving. Tragic and terrifying, *The Dead Zone* was King's first novel to demonstrate that the acknowledged master of horror could also move readers to tears. Although not as overtly frightening as such previous bestsellers as *'Salem's Lot* (1975) and *The Shining* (1977), it is no less memorable.

A somber study of one man's strange and sad journey toward his unique destiny, *The Dead Zone* poses the question of whether one man's actions can change the fate of the entire world. The man in question is a New Hampshire high school teacher who goes by the nondescript name of Johnny Smith.

Johnny has a bright future stolen from him when, upon returning from a date with his sweetheart, Sarah Bracknell, he is involved in an automobile accident that renders him comatose for four and a half years. When he finally awakens from his long sleep, he learns from his parents that the world has gone on without him. The most shocking news, however, is that Sarah, with whom he was deeply in love and believed he would marry, has met and wed another man.

Meanwhile, in another part of the country, a sociopath named Greg

Stillson has decided to run for political office as a stepping-stone toward the presidency of the United States, though by rights he isn't fit to be a town's dogcatcher. Shrewd and cruel and totally amoral, Stillson wins that first race. Although it will be years before the two men eventually meet, their lives are intimately intertwined in ways they can't begin to imagine. Both are outsiders—but one is fated to heal people, the other is destined to destroy the world.

Johnny awakens from his coma with a special gift, a so-called "wild talent." He now possesses incredible psychic powers—mainly that of precognition—in which he can see the future of anyone he touches. However, due to what he refers to as "the dead zone" in his brain, Johnny is unable to see certain details of these future events. Nor can he "see" what his own future will be. And although the last thing Johnny wants is to be thought of as a "celebrity psychic," or some kind of sideshow freak, that, ultimately, is his destiny. His past life is over, and his future is a mystery. To complicate matters, he also has an inoperable brain tumor that is slowly but surely killing him.

After a long period of rehabilitation, Johnny reenters the world, trying to use his power to help those who need it most. His experiences, however, are more traumatic than rewarding. The worst is yet to come, though, as, attending a political rally for the fast rising politician Greg Stillson, Johnny shakes the candidate's hand. Upon contact, Johnny is stunned by a terrifying vision of the older Stillson as president, about to engage in an unprovoked act of nuclear aggression against the Soviet Union. Johnny realizes that this act—thankfully still off in the future—could signal the death knell for the entire world.

Johnny, now faced with an incredible moral dilemma, has to decide whether he has the right to intervene, to perhaps take the life of someone who—albeit only potentially—may indirectly murder billions. Johnny reluctantly accepts this responsibility, realizing it might cost him his own life.

The Dead Zone is remarkable not only for its intimate portrait of Johnny Smith (what better name to subtly represent Everyman?), but because King for the first time delves into the secrets of the small Maine town of Castle Rock. King, as he had already done with the fictional town of Jerusalem's Lot, and would later do with Derry, would eventually make Castle Rock stand out as vividly as any of his greatest characters. Although its primary focus is on Johnny Smith, *The Dead Zone* also zeroes in on the many secrets concealed by the pleasant façade that the town presents to the world.

King reminds us repeatedly in *The Dead Zone* how little control we ultimately have over our own destinies. Even if we were allowed glimpses into the future, there is very little chance that most of us would be able to substantially change our lot in life. It is not the psychic talent that Johnny Smith possesses that makes him special—it is that he has the courage to try to change fate despite the personal cost.

As the classic rock 'n' roll song by the Doors says, "No one here gets out alive," and in the Stephen King Universe, that is never more eloquently stated than in *The Dead Zone*. For here, King seems to be saying that, unfair though life may be, we must accept the cards fate has dealt us, and try to do the best we can. It's a profoundly sad lesson to absorb, to be sure, but a vitally important one.

THE DEAD ZONE: PRIMARY SUBJECTS

JOHNNY SMITH: An ordinary, likeable young man whose entire life is changed when he is involved in an automobile accident that leaves him in a coma for fifty-five months. Johnny awakens from that coma with the fully realized ability to see a person's future merely by touching them. Johnny initially does his best to assist all who ask for his help, but ultimately finds his psychic abilities more of a burden than a joy. After shaking corrupt politician Greg Stillson's hand, Johnny realizes that Stillson would someday destroy the world in a nuclear holocaust. Already slowly dying of a brain tumor, Johnny devotes the rest of his days to devising a way to eliminate the threat Stillson presents, ultimately concluding that he must kill the man. Although he dies in the attempt, Johnny knows that his sacrifice is not in vain— Stillson's cowardly response to Johnny's assassination attempt effectively squashes his political career, thus preventing the disaster Johnny foresaw.

SARAH BRACKNELL: Johnny's one true love, a fellow English teacher, she is Johnny's date on the night of his automobile accident. Not knowing if Johnny will ever emerge from his coma, Sarah meets and marries a man named Walter Hazlett and bears him two children. Although happy with Hazlett, she still considers Johnny Smith to be the greatest love of her life. She is believed to be still living in Castle Rock.

FRANK DODD: A Castle Rock police officer, one of the most respected men in the community, he harbors a terrible secret. Frank, you see, is also the serial rapist/killer known as the Castle Rock Strangler. When identified by Johnny Smith, Dodd cheats justice by slitting his own throat after composing a suicide note on the bathroom mirror with his mother's lipstick. The note reads, *"I confess."*

SHERIFF BANNERMAN: The likeable sheriff of Castle Rock, he is willing to give some credence to Johnny's paranormal powers until the psychic accuses his trusted deputy, Frank Dodd, of being the notorious Castle Rock Strangler. Much to his horror, he is proven wrong in his previous evaluation of Dodd. Bannerman continues on in Castle Rock in the role of sheriff until the fateful day Joe Camber's rabid dog, Cujo, kills him.

GREG STILLSON: Horribly abused as a child, he spends the rest of life getting back at the world that he believes, with the conviction of a paranoid zealot, that it is his destiny to rule. Given Stillson's blue-collar appeal, it seems that he may someday achieve that goal. A chance encounter with Johnny Smith at a political rally upsets his plans to gain the highest office in the land. As they exchange handshakes, Johnny experiences the insanity that Congressman Stillson is capable of, and dedicates his life to stopping him from rising any higher. Seeing no other way to bring him down, Johnny attempts to assassinate Stillson. Johnny is unsuccessful, as Stillson escapes serious injury. However, in an attempt to protect himself, Stillson plucks a child from the surrounding crowd, using the infant as a human shield. Although the child is unhurt, this cowardly act ends Stillson's political career forever.

DR. SAMUEL WEIZAK: A Polish refugee of the Nazi concentration camps of World War II, he is the physician who cares for Johnny after he awakens from his coma. Johnny is able to prove his unique "wild talent" to the doctor when he informs the elderly man that his mother, long believed to be a victim of the Holocaust, is still alive. A "small, roly-poly man," he is still believed to be on the staff at the local hospital, if he has not already retired.

RICHARD DEES: A brash reporter from *Inside View*, a sleazy supermarket tabloid. Dees's newspaper offers Johnny a job as a celebrity psychic to boost their circulation.

THE DEAD ZONE: ADAPTATIONS

The 103-minute screen version of *The Dead Zone*, released in 1983, remains one of the most faithful and effective adaptations of a Stephen King work ever executed. Although many of the events of the lengthy novel were modified or compressed, screenwriter Jeffrey Boam does a masterful job of retaining the fragile essence and somber tone of the original book. (Interestingly, at one point executive producer Dino De Laurentiis asked King himself to take a crack at adapting his own novel. After the author did so, De Laurentiis rejected the screenplay as being too "involved and convoluted.")

The director chosen for the R-rated project was Canadian David Cronenberg, who up until that point had never directed a movie not based on one of his own original screenplays. Cronenberg, already famous for such bizarre shockers as *They Came from Within* (1975), *The Brood* (1979), and *Videodrome* (1982), did an incredible job of capturing the Norman Rockwell "look" of Castle Rock and King's wintry New England. Reportedly, the author told Cronenberg that some of the changes the director and screenwriter Boam made to his novel improved and intensified the power of the narrative.

Equally fortuitous was the casting. Academy Award–winning actor Christopher Walken (*The Deer Hunter*) was featured in the starring role of Smith. Walken was, simply put, the best possible choice for playing the lonely, haunted, and forever "different" human being. As much as George C. Scott was Patton in the 1970 movie of the same name, so, too, is Walken the perfect realization of Johnny Smith. Walken portrays Smith as someone who may truly be one of the walking wounded, but who knows his innermost moral convictions are still intact.

In supporting roles, the choices in casting were equally appropriate: Brooke Adams as Sarah, Tom Skeritt as Sheriff Bannerman, Herbert Lom as Dr. Weizak, and Colleen Dewhurst as Henrietta Dodd are all tremendous. Martin Sheen, who portrays Greg Stillson, would be one of the few actors—such as Drew Barrymore and Kathy Bates—to ever appear in a second Stephen King movie adaptation. He would play another ruthless, amoral villain, Captain Hollister, in the following year's *Firestarter*.

The Dead Zone is that rare instance where a superb creative team joined together to make the most effective adaptation of a bestselling novel that could be done, while still remaining essentially true to its source material.

The Dead Zone's most recent incarnation is as a USA Network television series starring Anthony Michael Hall as Johnny Smith. An intriguing reinterpretation of King's novel and characters, the series is currently about to enter its fourth season.

THE DEAD ZONE TRIVIA

- *The Dead Zone* was the first book by the author to reach #1 on the *New York Times* bestseller list.

- The character Johnny Smith was born in 1947—the same year as the author. Like Johnny, King also was a teacher.

- In a 1998 interview, King stated that *The Dead Zone* remained one of his two or three favorite novels.

- The unflappable journalist Richard Dees would later appear again in the 1988 short story "The Night Flier."

- The film version of *Carrie* is mentioned when Johnny predicts the prom fire.

20

CUJO

(1981)

According to Douglas Winter's excellent and informative *Stephen King: The Art of Darkness* (NAL Books, 1984), Cujo, like so much of King's fiction, "had its origin in a real incident in King's life," springing from the author's encounter with a huge St. Bernard with the unlikely name of Gonzo. King emerged from that incident with the germ of the idea for a new novel, the story of a two-hundred-pound dog named Cujo that one day goes berserk, threatening the lives and safety of the people of Castle Rock, Maine.

The tragic tale of a good dog gone bad, Cujo also tells the story of two Castle Rock families, the Trentons and the Cambers. Vic and Donna Trenton have recently relocated to the town in an attempt to find a better quality of life for themselves and their four-year-old son, Tad. Joe and Charity Camber have lived in Castle Rock all their lives; Joe owns a garage in town, where his son, Brett, can often be seen playing with his dog, an amiable St. Bernard named Cujo.

Both families are under stress. The Trentons quickly discover that moving will not solve all their problems: Vic's New York advertising agency is on the verge of collapse, and he must devote all his time and energy to saving his last big account with the Sharp Cereal Company. Stressed by the move, Donna feels abandoned by her workaholic husband. More out of boredom than anything else, she drifts into a brief but destructive extramarital affair. Tad, meanwhile, suffers repeated nightmares about a terrible monster that dwells in the shadows of his bedroom closet.

The Cambers have more serious problems. Joe is an abusive alcoholic. Charity is weak-willed, more afraid of life without her man than she is of being beaten. Brett is content to hover below his parents' radar.

Both families are unhappy in their own way, oblivious to each other's pain. Their worlds are fated to collide, however. When the Cambers' dog is transformed into a mindless killing machine by the bite of a rabid bat, both quickly come to know absolute terror.

Despite being characterized as a "horror" novel, there is only the faintest trace of the supernatural in *Cujo*. The "monster in the closet" that terrifies Tad is only a ruse to distract readers from the real danger. In some ways, it would almost be more comforting if a boogeyman or the ghost of Frank Dodd *was* lurking in the closet. Instead, the horror springs from something more mundane, a family pet infected by a pernicious virus.

In *Cujo*, King focuses intently on the horrors of everyday life. Killers, both human and animal, can dwell among us. A single mistake can trash an entire career. Marriages can be bent or ruined. Spousal abuse and alcoholism can destroy families from within. King's point? Simply stated, misery, unhappiness, and shattered dreams know no age or social barriers. We live in a dangerous world, a world where even beloved pets can represent a threat to our well-being.

The novel can be seen as a sequel to *The Dead Zone* (1979) in that its opening pages remind readers of the tale of psychic Johnny Smith and serial killer Frank Dodd. Johnny, you will recall, used his paranormal talents to assist the Castle Rock police in tracking down the insane police officer, who ultimately escaped justice by committing suicide. In *Cujo*, however, neither the Trentons nor the Cambers have the ability to escape a series of unplanned and undesired events in their lives. Significantly, the Trentons have purchased Frank Dodd's former residence. King hints that the boogeyman in Tad's closet may in fact be the killer's ghost, and later suggests that it might have somehow possessed Cujo.

By invoking the legend of Castle Rock Strangler, King reminds readers that even though life does go on, so, too, do the monsters. We needn't be concerned with vampires or werewolves attacking us—the neighborhood wacko will suffice. And if the boogeyman need not be supernatural, it also need not be human. Before succumbing to madness, Cujo was one of the most likeable dogs in town. It took only an accidental encounter in a country field—a minor event in the endless progression of life—to turn the once-huggable animal into a vicious beast.

Tellingly, King begins the novel with the classic fairy tale opening, "*Once upon a time . . .*" as if encouraging readers to put their fears to rest at the very outset, reassuring them that nothing they are about to read is "true." And yet the bitter irony is that the novel presents nothing that is remotely dismissible on the level of a pleasant fairy tale. With the exception of the rare circumstance of a rabid dog on the loose, all the unpleasant, unsavory, and ultimately tragic events presented within could happen anywhere.

The author's repeated use of the catch phrase of one of Vic Trenton's creations, the Sharp Cereal Professor—"Nope, nothing wrong here"—reveals another facet of the irony that permeates the narrative. Despite reassurances provided by loved ones and authority figures, there often *is* something wrong here. King seems to be warning readers that terror may indeed lurk around the next bend, that life's ugly truths may be revealed to us at any moment. Cujo didn't choose to become rabid. Vic never intended to become a workaholic. Donna never meant to hurt her husband or child by engaging in a disastrous affair. Brett Camber isn't consciously growing into the crude and abusive mold of his father. Tad Trenton should never have died in such a violent and senseless manner.

But in the Stephen King Universe, fate often throws us a curve. The world is never as safe and peaceful as we wish. Forced to accept the cards that life has dealt us, we must play the game as best we can. Life isn't fair, King repeatedly reminds us, but whoever promised us that it would be?

CUJO: PRIMARY SUBJECTS

TAD TRENTON: The four-year-old son of Victor and Donna Trenton, Tad believes that there is a monster in his closet, recalling the classic King short story "The Boogeyman." Tad learns to fend off his invisible enemy by using a special chant his dad devises, but can't fend off the terror that's coming his way in the form of Cujo, a rabid St. Bernard. Sadly, Tad and his mother are trapped inside their stalled Ford Pinto by the dog, who seems hell-bent on attacking them. Suffering from heatstroke and dehydration, young Tad perishes after enduring a terrible two-day ordeal.

DONNA TRENTON: A good mother to her son, Tad, Donna is not quite as satisfactory a wife to her husband, Vic. Depressed and lonely, she feels empty whenever her husband or son are not around. Listless and bored, Donna drifts into an affair with a man named Steve Kemp, an action she quickly comes to regret. Donna is plagued by more mundane problems as well—for instance, her Pinto just isn't running right. Taking her car to Joe Camber's garage, Donna becomes involved in the fight of her life when Camber's rabid St. Bernard, Cujo, imprisons her and Tad in the stalled vehicle. Donna and Tad are trapped inside for two days, battling Cujo, the heat, and dehydration. Realizing her boy is close to death, Donna summons the courage to confront the dog, eventually bludgeoning him to death with a baseball bat. But Donna's heroics prove to be in vain—she's acted too late to save her son, and must carry that guilt with her for the rest of her life. Donna Trenton's present whereabouts are unknown.

VIC TRENTON: Tad's father and Donna's husband, Vic is a partner in the Ad Worx advertising agency. Vic finds his career in jeopardy when the firm's largest account, the Sharp Cereal Company, almost goes under due to some defective products. Vic loves his wife and son, but effectively abandons them as he throws himself into the fight to save Ad Worx. Choosing to devote his free time to keeping the agency afloat, Vic is not present when his family needs him the most. Vic Trenton's present whereabouts are unknown.

STEVE KEMP: A local furniture refinisher and self-described poet, he has a brief affair with Donna Trenton. When she breaks it off, he goes into a violent rage, and later breaks into her house when no one is home. Kemp trashes the Trentons' home after posting a letter to Vic informing him of Donna's extramarital activities. His current whereabouts are unknown.

JOE CAMBER: A lifelong Castle Rock resident, Joe operates the local garage. Joe is also the owner of Cujo. A thin yet surprisingly strong man, he regularly beats his wife and child. Joe is mauled, then killed by Cujo after the dog is infected with rabies.

CHARITY CAMBER: The oft-abused wife of Joe Camber, she believes she is doomed to a life of poverty and cruelty. But when she wins five thousand dollars in the state lottery, she finally sees a chance to escape. Charity tells Joe she's taking their son Brett to visit her sister in Connecticut. In reality, she's thinking about abandoning her husband and starting a new life. After Cujo killed her husband, Charity and Brett returned to Castle Rock, but it is not known whether they still reside there.

BRETT CAMBER: Joe and Charity Camber's ten-year-old son. Despite his fear of his abusive father, Brett exhibits more and more of Joe's worst personality traits with each passing year. After Cujo's death, he is given a new puppy to ease the pain of the loss of the beloved family dog; it's not clear if he is more upset at losing his father or his former pet.

SHERIFF BANNERMAN: The man who, with Johnny Smith, helped end the reign of terror of rapist-killer Frank Dodd (as told in 1979's *The Dead Zone*). Uncharacteristically ignoring proper police procedure in investigating the situation with Cujo, Sheriff Bannerman is brutally slain by the rabid canine. As he is being savaged, Bannerman imagines for one crazy moment that he sees the evil presence of killer Frank Dodd staring at him through Cujo's eyes.

FRANK DODD: The Castle Rock police officer responsible for a string of rape-murders several years before Cujo went rabid. His memory still haunts the town; for many, he has taken on the status of a mythical boogeyman.

CUJO: ADAPTATIONS

Released in the summer of 1983, the motion picture version of *Cujo* remains one of Stephen King's favorite adaptations. King's first choice to helm the picture was a young director named Lewis Teague, who had already made a few low-budget genre films (*The Lady in Red, Alligator*) that King greatly enjoyed. Although he did not receive screen credit, King supplied the initial draft of the screenplay, which was later heavily rewritten by the two credited screenwriters, Lauren Currier and Don Carlos Dunaway.

Regardless of who was responsible for the final script, the fact remains that *Cujo* was a fairly simple novel to adapt to the screen, a plus considering King had sold the screen rights to Taft Entertainment, a small, independent firm that couldn't afford a large-scale production or big-name stars. Luckily, there were few locations and a very compact cast of characters. In fact, the most challenging aspect of the entire production proved to be making audiences believe that a lovable St. Bernard could become a vicious killer. But the filmmakers succeeded on all accounts, and the last half of the ninety-one-minute feature—which primarily consists of an enormous dog attacking two people in a small car—contains some of the most suspenseful and harrowing moments ever put on screen.

Dee Wallace (best known as the mother in Steven Spielberg's *E.T.— The Extra-Terrestrial*) is the only name star, and she does a remarkable job of portraying Donna Trenton. King later stated that she should have been nominated for an Academy Award for her stirring performance.

Perhaps the primary reason King liked the production so much is because, like the adaptation of *The Dead Zone* that was released later that same year, the filmmakers captured the spirit and tone of his original novel, despite one crucial change from the original ending. Director Teague felt that it would be too much of a letdown for the audience for the boy to die after everything he and his mother had endured, and wished to alter King's ending. Realizing that most movies work on a much simpler and often far more direct emotional level than novels, King agreed to Teague's change. Thus, at least in the movie version, Tad Trenton was spared. Certainly an unusual instance in which, in their respective mediums, the radically different endings of *Cujo* both work.

CUJO: TRIVIA

- Cujo attacks Tad and Donna Trenton while they are in a Ford Pinto. At one time, Stephen King also was the owner of a Ford Pinto.

- Due to its mainstream sensibility and bleak ending, *Cujo* at one point was to be published as a Richard Bachman novel.

- In 1981, Mysterious Press released a signed limited edition of only 750 copies for $65.

- 250 custom-made guitars, dubbed "Cujo Guitars," were manufactured by Taylor Guitars using wood taken from a tree from the movie location. King signed each guitar; the initial price was $3,498.

- Cujo's ghost may have appeared in 1991's *Needful Things*. Burying a jar outside Joe Camber's old garage, Polly Chambers looks up and sees two red eyes peering at her from the dark recesses of the building. Needless to say, she leaves the vicinity as quickly as possible.

21

THE DARK HALF

(1989)

Like *'Salem's Lot* (1975), *The Shining* (1977), *Misery* (1987), and *The Tommyknockers* (1987), *The Dark Half* features a writer as one of the main protagonists. The plot of this novel revolves around a permutation of a question that King himself had to answer when his Richard Bachman persona was revealed to the world: *What if you kill off your pseudonym—and he refuses to stay dead?*

To hear him talk, you might think that King thinks of Richard Bachman as a real person, separate and distinct from himself (see the chapters on *Desperation* and *The Regulators* for more on this). As noted in the section on Richard Bachman, the author has often stated that "Richard Bachman is Stephen King on a cloudy day." In *The Dark Half*, King plays with this notion, examining it through the lens of his fiction. Thus, he asks, what if a pseudonym—essentially another part of an author's persona—came to life? How would he feel if his "creator" had tried to lay him to rest, to end his existence? King's answer to that question, played out in this novel, is that he'd probably become quite enraged and decide to turn the tables on his soulmate, to kill his creator before he, the creation, fades into nothingness.

This is the basic conceit behind *The Dark Half*: Thad Beaumont is a successful novelist—but only under the pseudonym of ultraviolent crime writer George Stark. Tiring of the charade, and hoping to devote himself to more serious work, Beaumont decides to publicly reveal his hidden identity and at the same time "kill" him off. The vehicle he chooses is a feature article in *People* magazine, replete with pictures of Beaumont standing over the "grave" of George Stark.

Although it's all done in a spirit of harmless fun, something goes seriously awry. Someone begins ruthlessly liquidating people in a manner eerily similar to that of Alexis Machine, a fictional hit man created by George Stark.

Incredibly, fingerprints lifted at the murder scenes seem to indicate that Beaumont is the killer, even though he has airtight alibis. Although it defies all logic, what has apparently occurred is that Beaumont's "dark half," a doppelganger of sorts, has somehow sprung into being, adopting the identity of Beaumont's cold-blooded alter ego, George Stark. And Stark, who writes so well about sadism and cruelty and death because they are at the core of his essential nature, is now hunting down Thad Beaumont, his wife, and his two infant children. He also hunts, then brutally dispatches, anyone remotely related to the *People* article, the one that so glibly "buried" him.

In the end, Thad Beaumont must literally face his "dark half" in a spectacular confrontation from which only one of them—Beaumont's Dr. Jekyll or Stark's Mr. Hyde—can emerge alive.

It is obvious that this novel was inspired by the real-life events in which King's Richard Bachman pseudonym was discovered and made public, ending many years of speculation. Indeed, in a droll author's note at the beginning of the book, King notes, "I'm indebted to the late Richard Bachman for his help and inspiration. This novel could not have been written without him."

The book allows King to comment on the trials and tribulations of being a bestselling author in the twentieth century. Like Ben Mears in *'Salem's Lot* and Paul Sheldon in *Misery*, Thad Beaumont is not struggling to find success in his chosen profession—he is more concerned with how to deal with his considerable fame. Like Sheldon with his romance saga of Misery Chastain, Beaumont is a writer who has attained the good life by giving the public what it wants—not necessarily what he truly desires to write. And, as he had done so wonderfully in *Misery*, King explores the fascinating mechanics of the creative process, most notably the idea that for horror and suspense writers to be truly successful, they must often look into the abyss of their creative "dark half"—knowing full well that the abyss is staring back at *them*.

One might be tempted to conclude that after completing *The Dark*

Half, King had said all he had to say about the writing profession. Indeed, at the time of the publication of *Four Past Midnight* (1990), King stated that the novella *Secret Window, Secret Garden* would be his last word on the profession of writers. In 1998, however, he would produce *Bag of Bones*, a novel whose main character is an acclaimed and successful . . . writer. Without a doubt, writing is an endlessly fascinating profession that remains very dear to some of the most intriguing inhabitants of the Stephen King Universe.

THE DARK HALF: PRIMARY SUBJECTS

THAD BEAUMONT: As a young boy, Thaddeus Beaumont suffered from unusually severe headaches during which he would hear the ghostly sound of thousands of sparrows in flight. An operation reveals that he has a benign brain tumor that was caused by a most unusual ailment—an unformed twin. At age eleven, he has the tumor removed and more or less forgets about the entire episode. A born writer, he continues writing all through his adolescence, and eventually becomes a published novelist.

Only moderately successful writing under his own name, Thad has published two novels which, while critically received, do not support him financially. He also teaches college courses, but his real financial success comes when he creates the pseudonym of "George Stark." It is Stark who writes the grisly crime novels that become international bestsellers, allowing Beaumont and his family to live comfortably.

Thad, who wants to be remembered for his serious work, decides to publicly retire his pseudonym, in effect killing George Stark. But the Stark persona takes on a life of its own, rising from the grave. Enraged, Stark stalks Beaumont, seeking revenge. Facing Stark man to man, Thad emerges the victor, having conquered his "dark half." For Beaumont's ultimate fate, please refer to the chapters on *Needful Things* and *Bag of Bones*.

GEORGE STARK: The homicidal "dark half" of Thad Beaumont, he is a pseudonym—a fictional alter ego—who literally springs to life. Born in New Hampshire, he grew up in Oxford, Mississippi. Also a writer, he would compose his fiction in longhand, using a particular brand of pencil (in "stark" contrast to Thad Beaumont, who prefers a typewriter or computer). When Stark is "buried" as part of an elaborate gag for *People* magazine, he rises from his grave and embarks on a blood-drenched journey in his black Toronado to find and slay anyone remotely connected to the publication of that article. His weapon of choice is a straight razor, as he enjoys inflicting pain on his victims.

After threatening Thad and his family, Stark is suddenly attacked by thousands of sparrows that pick him up and carry him away into the night sky. Asked by his wife whether his deadly alter ego was truly dead, Beaumont replies, "The book is closed on George Stark."

LIZ BEAUMONT: The loving wife of Thad Beaumont, Liz encouraged him to adopt the pseudonym of George Stark when he suffered from writer's block. She was equally supportive when Thad decided it was time to go public with the pseudonym before a man named Fred Clawson exposed the once well-guarded pen name to the public.

SHERIFF ALAN PANGBORN: The current sheriff of Castle Rock, he took over after the previous sheriff, George Bannerman, was done in by a rabid dog. Although never truly convinced by the fantastic idea of a writer's pseudonym coming to life, early on in the investigation he does become convinced that Thad Beaumont is innocent of the brutal murders that crime scene evidence seems to indicate he committed. Although he is taken prisoner by Stark, the sheriff survives the frightening misadventure. Pangborn's further adventures in the Stephen King Universe are chronicled in *Needful Things*.

FRED CLAWSON: The "creepazoid" (so nicknamed by Liz) who discovered that George Stark was Beaumont's pseudonym. He had been intending to reveal the truth to the public, hoping to blackmail Thad in the process for some of his wealth. But sometimes a little knowledge is a dangerous thing: Stark goes to Clawson's seedy apartment and mercilessly shreds him with his straight razor.

Note: it's possible that Fred Clawson also appeared in *The Dead Zone*. Near the end of that novel, Johnny meets "a real camera nut" named Mr. Clawson at the courthouse. Clawson was there to take a driver's test.

THE DARK HALF: ADAPTATIONS

The motion picture version of *The Dark Half* appeared in 1993, although it had actually been shot and completed a few years earlier (a series of financial problems involving the production company, Orion Pictures, kept the completed movie on the shelf). The R-rated picture was adapted and directed by George A. Romero, an outstanding director (*Night of the Living Dead, Martin, Bruiser*) who had been friends with the author for many years. Romero had already helmed King's screenplay for *Creepshow* (1982) and had adapted other King stories for *Creepshow 2* (1987).

Not surprisingly, Romero's 122-minute adaptation follows King's novel quite faithfully, effectively capturing the proper tone and essence of "a Stephen King novel," a rare achievement. Romero elicits fine performances from an outstanding cast: Timothy Hutton as Thad Beaumont/George Stark, Amy Madigan as Liz Beaumont, and Michael Rooker as the sheriff of Castle Rock, Alan Pangborn.

The Dark Half remains one of the best adaptations of a King work by one of the horror film genre's most influential directors.

THE DARK HALF: TRIVIA

- On the *Dark Half* movie posters, the character of Thad Beaumont (or is it supposed to be George Stark?) bears an uncanny resemblance to Stephen King.

- It's quite likely that King named Thad Beaumont in honor of Charles Beaumont (1929–1967), an author who is best remembered for writing some of the most chilling episodes of television's classic *The Twilight Zone*.

- Timothy Hutton also appears in another Stephen King movie thriller dealing with the dangers of the writing life, *Secret Window*, starring Johnny Depp.

22

NEEDFUL THINGS

(1991)

Stephen King, well known for creating an atmosphere of intimacy, takes it one step further in *Needful Things*. This 1991 novel was his farewell to Castle Rock, Maine, the small New England town that served as a backdrop for *The Dead Zone, Cujo,* and the memorable short story "The Body." The book, the last installment of a loose-knit trilogy begun in *The Dark Half* (where Castle Rock sheriff Alan Pangborn first appeared) and continued in the short novel *The Sun Dog* (the story of longtime resident "Pop" Merrill's demise), is the author's last visit to Castle Rock. The destruction of the town was reportedly an attempt on King's part to rejuvenate his writing, to move on to other things. As he explained, King "wanted to finish things, and do it with a bang."

King beckons readers into his world with a punchy prologue, captioned "You've Been Here Before . . . ," narrated by an unnamed Castle Rock gossip. The chatty narrator knows a little bit about everything, revealing secrets to an unidentified listener who stands in for the reader. The narrator sets the stage, dropping interesting tidbits about the denizens of Castle Rock, and about the new store that's about to open there, a curious operation called Needful Things.

Expertly articulating his thesis of the village as a microcosm of society, King takes us into the hearts and minds of a handful of the townspeople, simultaneously revealing the nobility and evil in each of us. He also explores small-town America in a way he hadn't done since *'Salem's Lot*, detailing the social structure and the unwritten rules of rural life. *Needful Things* is both drama and satire, a critique of American consumerism and greed, and of small-town life in general. King revisits themes from prior books, apparently trying to shake the dust of one style of storytelling off his feet before moving on to a new phase. It is at once one of his more cynical and one of his more hopeful books.

A store called Needful Things opens in Castle Rock during an unseasonably warm spell in October 1991. Eleven-year-old Brian Rusk is the first to meet the proprietor, a tall, kindly, strange old man wearing an old-fashioned smoking jacket. Introducing himself as Leland Gaunt from Akron, Ohio, the owner cuts the first of the many deals he will make with the denizens of Castle Rock—he sells Brian a 1956 Sandy Koufax baseball card worth $100 for cash (85 cents) and a seemingly harmless "deed." In Brian's case, it involves splattering a neighbor's clean sheets with mud. Over the next eight days, several other locals make similar bargains, and perform similar deeds.

Only Gaunt knows the ultimate purpose of these deeds. His strategy, honed over centuries, is to sow discontent, then reap a horrible bounty. Each deed acts to unleash a little of the rage simmering beneath the town's calm façade. The hatred and envy that exist between neighbors, the hatred of one religious group for another, the insecurities people conceal from the light of day—all these are grist for Mr. Gaunt's mill. Only Sheriff Alan Pangborn, distracted by the past, and by the increasingly violent and bizarre incidents occurring in his jurisdiction, has a prayer of stopping Gaunt before he achieves his goals.

The plot of *Needful Things*—a stranger comes to town, wreaking havoc for his own evil purposes—is certainly not unique. King himself used it before in *'Salem's Lot* (1976), and later in his 1999 teleplay *Storm of the Century*. The basic plot comes from a rich tradition in American literature for chronicling events in small towns, from Sherwood Anderson's *Winesberg, Ohio* to Thornton Wilder's *Our Town* to Don Robertson's *Paradise Falls*. The horror/suspense genre has similar entries, most notably Ray Bradbury's *Something Wicked This Way Comes*, Charles Beaumont's *The Intruder*, and Richard Matheson's short story "The Distributor."

In *Needful Things*, as in *Something Wicked This Way Comes*, evil, once confronted, flees. This harkens back to *The Stand*, where Flagg disappears, leaving only a pile of clothes. The comparison doesn't end there, however, because, like Flagg, Gaunt escapes to spread evil in a new locale.

The book showcases King's many strengths. He lovingly populates this novel with vivid, three-dimensional characters, and then sends them to their appointments with destiny. King's characterizations are brief but effective. Although the story hurtles from one situation to another, he never has to reestablish his characters, to remind readers who they are. Of course, he also expertly manipulates his readers' emotions, raising anxiety levels to new heights.

Gaunt is a fascinating character, not at all unlike Randall Flagg or Andre Linoge from *Storm of the Century*. He is an evil creature. If he was once human, he is certainly not human now. This self-styled "electrician of the human soul" delights in "cross-wiring" potential victims to achieve maximum chaos. Like Mr. Dark of *Something Wicked This Way Comes*, Gaunt travels the world, feeding off the misery of others. He does this through subtle manipulation and misdirection, exploiting human weakness and greed wherever he finds it.

Gaunt's background is vague. Echoing Bradbury's description of Cooger and Dark's Pandemonium Circus, and his own thumbnail sketch of Randall Flagg in *The Stand*, King tells us, "He had begun business many years ago—as a wandering peddler on the blind face of a distant land . . . a peddler who usually came at the fall of darkness and was always gone the next morning, leaving bloodshed, horror, and unhappiness behind him. Years later, in Europe, as the plague raged and the deadcarts rolled, he had gone from town to town and country to country in a wagon drawn by a slat-thin white horse with terrible burning eyes and a tongue as black as a killer's heart. He sold his wares from the back of the wagon . . . and was gone before his customers, who paid with small, ragged coins or even in barter, could discover what they had really bought."

Gaunt changes with the times, eventually coming to hawk his wares in a series of storefronts around the world. Where he belongs on the hierarchy of evil beings in the Stephen King Universe is unclear, though certainly he would place below Flagg. And yet they aren't that dissimilar. It could be, if they aren't one and the same, that all of these—Gaunt, Flagg, Linoge—are of the same species, brothers in a sense.

It seems that no matter how many times they're defeated, these evil creatures return to plague yet another beleaguered mortal hero, in this case Alan Pangborn. Pangborn exemplifies how tenuous happiness is in the Stephen King Universe. In the grand King tradition, he has lost a soul mate (like Ben Mears, Andy McGee, Stu Redman, Ralph Roberts, Mike Noonan, and Roland the Gunslinger before him) and his son (as do Louis Creed and Donna Trenton) in a car accident. Haunted by the memory (Alan can't fathom why his wife, normally careful about wearing seat belts, failed to buckle up that fateful day), and by the bizarre events he experienced in *The Dark Half*, Alan has tried to move on, losing himself in his job as Castle Rock's sheriff and in his relationship with Polly Chalmers. It is this example of humanity, with his vast array of human emotions, who turns out to be Gaunt's nemesis, not unlike so many before and after him, including many of those named above, as well as Mike Anderson from *Storm of the Century*, a tale that differs from *Needful Things* most particularly in the desires of its villain, and the severity of the secrets hidden by the townspeople.

Interestingly, the hero and the villain of the piece don't meet until the final pages of the novel, where, after shaking off Gaunt's last-ditch attempt to distract him, Pangborn sees through the mask the demonic salesman presents to the public. Echoing the end of *Something Wicked This Way Comes*, Alan uses white magic against Gaunt. First, he opens a "magic" can of snakes that once belonged to his son. The snakes, momentarily given life by Gaunt's belief in magic, attack him, causing him to reveal his true demonic form. Alan then produces a bouquet of paper flowers that generates an intense burst of white light. Finally, he uses his talent at creating hand shadows to invoke the ghosts that haunt the town (the sparrows from *The Dark Half*, and Joe Camber's dog *Cujo*).

On a final note, Brian Rusk is an interesting anomaly in the Stephen King Universe. Eleven years old, he's still young enough to maintain a child's sense of wonder, a trait that sometimes saves children from severe harm in King's world. Here, however, Brian's naiveté makes him the perfect dupe for Gaunt. By making him complicit in his evil, Gaunt strips Brian of his childhood, thrusting him without warning into the wicked adult world. Brian, unable to cope with his guilt, sees no way out but suicide.

NEEDFUL THINGS: PRIMARY SUBJECTS

LELAND GAUNT: A shadowy figure who turned out to be an ancient, evil creature, Gaunt arrives in Castle Rock to fill the void left by the late "Pop" Merrill, whose novelty store, the Emporium Galorium, had burned down a few months before. Gaunt's modus operandi is simple—he gives the people what they think they want (Pop, his mortal predecessor, called it "selling the worthless to the thoughtless"), secures promises to perform some dirty tricks, and then sits back and watches the ensuing mayhem. Then, at the crescendo of hysteria, he sells his customers the weapons they need to efficiently eliminate one another.

Over an eight-day period, Gaunt tightens his grip on the town, exacerbating existing feuds and suspicions between various citizens into violent conflict, and even triggering a battle royal between the local Baptist and Catholic congregations. To tie up loose ends, Gaunt flunkies Buster Keeton and Ace Merrill level the town with several tons of TNT.

On the verge of achieving his unsavory goals (he's been harvesting the souls of his victims, keeping them in a hyena-hide valise), Gaunt is finally confronted by a more formidable opponent in Sheriff Alan Pangborn, a man he has until that time studiously avoided. Pangborn simultaneously exposes Gaunt's true plan and demonic visage, and wrests the bag of souls he has stolen from his grasp. His plan thwarted, Gaunt flees Castle Rock, and proceeds to establish a new store called Answered Prayers in Junction City, Iowa. It would be foolhardy, however, to presume that he still resides there.

ALAN PANGBORN: The sheriff of Castle Rock, Alan Pangborn had lost his wife and son in a car accident. His life was haunted by the memory of the accident, and by a series of bizarre events he experienced in relation to a writer named Thad Beaumont. Alan tried to move on, losing himself in his work and in his relationship with Polly Chalmers.

Gaunt recognizes Pangborn as someone who could upset his plans. An amateur magician, and so able to appreciate the power of misdirection, Pangborn is the first to see the connection between the strange events in Castle Rock and Gaunt's store, Needful Things.

By instinct and intuition, Alan manages to access a kind of white magic, with which he drives Gaunt from Castle Rock. Later, he leaves the ruined town in the company of Polly Chalmers and Norris Ridgewick.

According to a statement made by Norris Ridgewick in *Bag of Bones*, Alan Pangborn moved to New Hampshire with Polly Chalmers.

POLLY CHALMERS: Polly, a Castle Rock native, left the town as a young woman when she became pregnant. Too proud and headstrong to accept her parents' assistance, she moved to San Francisco to have her child. There, tragedy struck—Polly's baby died in an apartment fire. The pain of this loss affected Polly as much as the pain of the arthritis that turned her hands into misshapen claws; the episode was so shattering to her that she never told anyone about it, not even her boyfriend, Sheriff Alan Pangborn.

Polly later returned to Castle Rock, where she eventually opened an establishment called You Sew and Sew, located across the street from Needful Things. Gaunt traps Polly by curing her arthritis—he gives her a locket called an Azka, which relieves her pain. In payment for the Azka, Polly plays a trick on Ace Merrill. Performing her errand out at the old Camber place, Polly hears growling coming from a barn. Looking that way, she sees "two sunken red circles of light peering out at her from the darkness." Afraid Joe Camber's fearsome St. Bernard has risen from the dead, she hurriedly completes her deed and flees.

Her happiness at escaping her arthritis blinds her to Gaunt's evil, and almost costs her her relationship with Alan—she questions Alan's love after she is manipulated by Gaunt into believing he had made inquiries into her past. Ultimately, Polly escapes from Gaunt's influence by literally embracing her sin, which takes the form of a huge fanged spider. Her triumph over Gaunt enables her to assist Alan in seeing through the old man's trickery, paving the way for his eventual defeat.

Polly left town with Alan and Norris Ridgewick. She currently resides in New Hampshire with Alan Pangborn.

BRIAN RUSK: This eleven-year-old is the first citizen of Castle Rock to shop at Needful Things. After showing Brian around the store, Gaunt asks Brian what he really wants. Brian, an avid baseball card collector, responds quickly—he wants a 1956 Sandy Koufax rookie card. Gaunt not only has the card, but, strangely, the card is autographed to someone named Brian. In exchange for the card, Gaunt takes eighty-five cents in cash, and secures Brian's promise to play a "prank" on Wilma Jerzcyk—he tells Brian to throw mud on Wilma's clean sheets drying on her clothesline. Later, after Gaunt tells him he's not done paying for the baseball card, he hurls rocks with notes tied to them through Wilma's windows, destroying her TV and microwave oven. Consumed by guilt over what he's done, Brian commits suicide with his father's rifle, after telling his younger brother, Sean, to never go into Needful Things.

NETTIE COBB: Nettie killed her abusive husband after he maliciously broke a piece of her precious carnival glass, and spent the next few years as a resident of Juniper Hill, a local mental institution. Later, sponsored by Polly Chalmers, she attempted to rejoin society. Her attempt is short-circuited by Gaunt's machinations as he sets her on a collision course with the volatile Wilma Jerzyck. When Hugh Priest kills her dog with a corkscrew, Nettie assumes Wilma did the deed. Grabbing a meat cleaver, the grief-stricken Nettie attacks the knife-wielding Wilma on a public street. Both women die in the grisly battle that ensues.

WILMA JERZYCK: Wilma is a hulking battle-axe who lives for a good fight. Primed by Brian Rusk's attacks on her property, she sees red and sets out in search of revenge against Nettie Cobb, whom she assumes was responsible. Both women die in the ensuing confrontation.

HUGH PRIEST: In return for a coveted fox's tail, Hugh kills Nettie Cobb's beloved dog, Raider. Hugh eventually squares off against bar owner Henry Beaufort in a gun battle that costs him his life.

ACE MERRILL: After doing time in Shawshank Prison, Ace is drawn back to Castle Rock to view the burned-out remains of his uncle's (Pop Merrill's) store, the Emporium Galorium. Once there, he is hired by Gaunt as an errand boy. In return for a treasure map ostensibly detailing where Pop buried his considerable fortune, Ace travels to Boston to pick up the weapons that Gaunt later sells to the citizens of Castle Rock. When not running Gaunt's errands, Ace engages in a personal treasure hunt for his uncle's money, but uncovers nothing more valuable than trading stamps and some rolls of steel pennies buried in Crisco tins. In one, he finds a letter planted by Polly Chalmers, supposedly written by Alan Pangborn. In the letter, Pangborn mocks Ace, telling him that he'd already recovered the money in the tin. Ace, primed by anger and Gaunt's special cocaine, vows to murder Alan, the man who put him in Shawshank for dealing cocaine. Ace is killed by Norris Ridgewick just as he is about to kill Alan.

POP MERRILL: Ace Merrill's uncle, Pop died when his store and living quarters, the Emporium Galorium, burned down just prior to Gaunt's arrival.

NORRIS RIDGEWICK: Alan Pangborn's deputy, he is lured into Gaunt's circle by a bazun fishing rod, which brings back pleasant memories of lazy days spent with his father. Later Norris, on the verge of suicide, suddenly sees through Gaunt's trickery, and vows revenge. Although he does not achieve it directly, he saves Alan and Polly from Ace Merrill. Norris leaves town with Alan and Polly. Norris subsequently makes a brief appearance in *Bag of Bones*.

NEEDFUL THINGS: ADAPTATIONS

In this 1993 adaptation released by Columbia Pictures, Max Von Sydow is well cast as the demonic Gaunt. At once charming and sinister, he assays the character as well as time allows. Ed Harris and Bonnie Bedelia are also well cast as Alan Pangborn and Polly Chalmers, but neither is given the chance to fully explore their roles. Unfortunately, the movie cannot take advantage of a leisurely buildup that King exploits in his novel.

The movie also makes subtle changes to certain events, compressing and embellishing them. Thus, all but the major subplots are eliminated. Also, several of the "needful things" are changed—Brian Rusk's Sandy Koufax card becomes a Mickey Mantle card; Nettie Cobb's carnival glass becomes a Hummel statuette; and Hugh Priest's fox's tail becomes a more convincing varsity football jacket. Ace Merrill is entirely eliminated from the story line. The producers, possibly constrained by a small special effects budget, even rewrote the ending. Instead of working his magic, Alan is reduced to delivering a Capraesque speech about evil, which Gaunt dismisses with a few pointed quips.

NEEDFUL THINGS: TRIVIA

- King himself does a masterful job in his full-length reading of the book for the audio version. Especially interesting is the thick Maine accent he adopts to read the prologue, "You've Been Here Before."

- Ace Merrill, of course, was one of the bullies in *The Body*, which became the film *Stand by Me*. Also, he spent some time in Shawshank Prison, the locale of the story *Rita Hayworth and Shawshank Redemption*.

23

RELATED TALES

As mentioned in the preface to this section, King has also used Castle Rock as a backdrop for several short stories. Here, in no special order, are brief summaries of those tales.

The Body (from 1982's *Different Seasons*)

There are a great many things that Stephen King does well. Some of them he accomplishes as well as, and arguably better than, anyone else writing popular fiction today. In *The Body*, as in *'Salem's Lot* and *It* (1986), among others, King seems to send his imagination back in time to his own youth. Though only a novella, *The Body* is so steeped in nostalgia and Americana, and thick with real emotion and fondness and primal fear, that it is a fully realized exploration of what it meant to the author to be a boy growing up in Maine in 1960. There are those who have equated King with Mark Twain. That comparison is never more accurate than here.

The Body relates the story of four friends who undertake a quest—without their parents' knowledge, of course, and in peril of severe punishment—to see the corpse of a boy who has disappeared, but whom they discover has been hit by a train.

As a coming-of-age-in-America story, it can rightly be termed a masterpiece.

"I never had any friends later on like I had when I was twelve," King—as narrator Gordon LaChance—tells us. "Jesus, does anyone?"

The Body also provides a solid foundation for King's fictional town of Castle Rock, which would appear as the background to so many subsequent works. The realism of this tale helps to build a sense of authenticity and history around Castle Rock itself.

In the narrative, the four friends trek through rain and slug-filled ponds and run across a train bridge just ahead of the locomotive, all to find the corpse of Ray Brower. When their goal is reached, after a day and a half of hard travel, they feel a sense of proprietorship over the dead boy. However, they are challenged by a gang of local toughs that includes the older brothers of two of the youths. Though they drive the older boys off, they are eventually beaten soundly for their affront.

There are so many elements that make this fiction much more than a mere coming-of-age story. Gordie, the main character, is the smart one. He wants to be a writer. Though his best friend, Chris, is intelligent, he is from a poor family with a reputation for making trouble. The other two, Vern and Teddy, are not very bright and seem destined for a dead-end future.

We learn that later Chris triumphs over the expectations placed on him. He goes to law school, even, and becomes an attorney. And then he dies, senselessly, trying to break up a fight. Just as Teddy and Vern both die senselessly, later on. As the entire story seems to predict, Gordie is the only one who survives and succeeds. And yet, save for Chris, their deaths are revealed with the distance of age and the passage of time, so that it seems more sad than tragic. For we only know them as the children they were, instead of the men they became.

For all the promise and hope we had for Chris Chambers, however, his death is the real tragedy.

THE BODY: PRIMARY SUBJECTS

GORDIE LaCHANCE: Gordon is twelve in 1960, when he and three of his friends go on an adventure to find the corpse of a missing local boy. Though they find the body, the experience changes them all, forcing them to grow up in a way that none of them could be prepared for. They drift apart after that, except for Gordon and Chris Chambers. Gordon LaChance becomes a successful novelist.

CHRIS CHAMBERS: Along with his best friends, Chris embarks on a mission to find the corpse of a missing local boy. Though he is from a family with a bad reputation, he makes good and eventually becomes an attorney. Sadly, Chris is killed while trying to break up an altercation in a restaurant in Portland, Maine.

TEDDY DUCHAMP: One of the four who set out on a trek to locate a missing local boy, Teddy has never been quite right in the head. He dies in a car accident in late 1971 or early 1972.

VERN TESSIO: Vern overhears his brother telling a friend about the body of Ray Brower, a bit of knowledge that leads to the quest for the missing boy's corpse. Vern dies in a house fire in Lewiston, Maine, in 1966.

ACE MERRILL: The leader of the gang of hoods who try to claim the body of Ray Brower after Gordie and his friends found it, Ace is a sadistic bully. He will die many years later when a mysterious man named Leland Gaunt opens a store called Needful Things in Castle Rock.

RAY BROWER: It is never clear if Ray Brower had run away from home or merely gotten lost. Either way, he finds himself on the train tracks at the wrong time, is struck by a train, and dies. Though a handful of kids in Castle Rock know where his body is, it is some time before it is finally discovered by the authorities, thanks to an anonymous tip to the police.

THE BODY: ADAPTATIONS

Of the four tales collected in *Different Seasons*, three have been made into films. The first of these, *Stand by Me* (based on *The Body*), was released by

Columbia Pictures in 1986. The motion picture adaptation, apparently
among King's favorites, was directed by former television actor turned director Rob Reiner *(When Harry Met Sally, The Story of Us)*, and featured a
plethora of young talent among the cast.

Star Trek: The Next Generation's Wil Wheaton portrayed Gordie
LaChance (with Richard Dreyfuss appearing and narrating as the character
as an adult). The late River Phoenix costarred as tough kid Chris Chambers.
Omnipresent 1980s child star Corey Feldman was Teddy Duchamp, and
Jerry O'Connell, who would later go on to fame in film *(Scream 2)* and
television *(Sliders)*, was chubby enough back then to play Vern Tessio.

Stand by Me also included performances by Kiefer Sutherland as Ace
Merrill and John Cusack as Denny LaChance, Gordie's older brother.

Reiner's direction of this coming-of-age story is flawless. Much of
King's narrative remains as voice-over by Dreyfuss, and despite moving
Castle Rock from Maine to Oregon, there is a universal quality to the
representation of the time period here, and a timelessness to the relationships between the kids, that makes this picture speak to the entire audience.

It may be that *Stand by Me* is the closest a director has ever come to
replicating the texture that King has put down on the page. Ironically, the
film that is its only real competition is also based on a story in this collection.

THE BODY: TRIVIA

- Although the town of Derry was not prominent in King's fictional
  landscape at the time, it is mentioned in *The Body*, as are Jerusalem's
  Lot and Shawshank penitentiary.

- *The Body* features many references to Constable Bannerman, who
  would, in such later works as *The Dead Zone* (1979) and *Cujo* (1981),
  become Sheriff Bannerman.

- Gordie LaChance, the narrator of *The Body*, refers to the events of
  Cujo.

"Nona" (from 1985's *Skeleton Crew*)

A story that recalls Charlie Starkweather's murderous rampage in the late 1950s, and prefigured such films as Oliver Stone's *Natural Born Killers* (1994), "Nona" tells of a murder spree that concludes in King's fictional town of Castle Rock, Maine. Says Nona: "We're going to Castle Rock. It's a small town just south and west of Lewiston-Ashburn." It turns out that the narrator has had a run-in with Castle Rock's most famous juvenile delinquent, Ace Merrill. Ace's presence links the story to the 1982 novella *The Body*, as does a mention of the GS & WM railroad trestle.

"NONA": PRIMARY SUBJECTS

THE NARRATOR/THE PRISONER: Nona's narrator is unnamed; we only know he has just been released from prison. Entering Joe's Good Eats one evening, he meets a woman named Nona. After he gets into a fight with one of the patrons, they leave the diner together, embarking on a long, strange trip to the narrator's hometown of Castle Rock. On the way, he kills a Good Samaritan who foolishly picks him up near an off-ramp and steals the victim's car. The man also murders a policeman who pulls him over, and two power company employees who are out fixing a downed line. The narrator eventually ends up in the crypt of a former girlfriend, where he is found the next day. The narrator is arrested, and is presumably spending his days in safely locked away again in prison. It is up to the reader to decide whether Nona actually existed—or was merely a creation of the narrator's twisted mind.

"Uncle Otto's Truck" (from 1985's *Skeleton Crew*)

Another story of Castle Rock (Billy Dodd, father of "Crazy" Frank Dodd who figures so prominently in *The Dead Zone*, is mentioned at one point), this one is about a haunted truck that, despite its decrepitude, drags itself across a field, moving toward the house of the man who once used it as a murder weapon in the killing of his business partner. Like 1985's "Beachworld," this is King in an EC Comics/*Creepshow* frame of mind.

Otto enters into a partnership with George McCutcheon in order to obtain a choice piece of land from the New England Paper Company. Their association makes both men rich, but when they have their inevitable falling-out, Otto kills George by dropping an old Cresswell truck on him. Now able to live anywhere he chooses, Otto spends his days in a house he built across the road. His corpse is found one Wednesday evening by his nephew (Quentin Schenk, the narrator of the story), oil spewing from a mouth that also contains a 1920s vintage spark plug that almost certainly came from the Creswell. The coroner's verdict, however, is that Otto committed suicide by swallowing the oil.

"Gramma" (from 1985's *Skeleton Crew*)

A tale of a young boy left home alone with his invalid grandmother, this offering, which contains elements King later used in *Dolores Claiborne* (1993), had its roots in the author's childhood. King's grandmother lived in their home during her last illness, nearly driving daughter Ruth crazy with her constant nagging. Apparently King was home alone with his grandmother the day she died. Another tale set in Castle Rock, the story features cameos from Henrietta Dodd and Joe Camber, owner of the dog featured in the novel *Cujo* (1981).

Like any eleven-year-old, the young protagonist of this story, George, thinks he's a great deal more capable than he really is. Therefore he is not fazed when his mother asks him to stay alone in the house with his spooky old gram. George doesn't know what he's in for, however—just when it looks like his Gramma has died, he turns around and discovers she has shambled into the kitchen. It develops that Gramma is actually a witch, who covets George's youth. It's not clear at the end of the story whether George has been totally possessed by the spirit of the woman, or has merely absorbed his grandmother's powers for his own use.

"Gramma" was adapted for television by famed fantasist Harlan Ellison. This 1986 adaptation appeared as part of CBS television's anthology series *The New Twilight Zone*.

The Sun Dog (from 1990's *Four Past Midnight*)

Bracketed by 1989's *The Dark Half* and 1991's *Needful Things*, *The Sun Dog* was the second installment of what King has called the Castle Rock trilogy. *The Sun Dog* tells the story of Kevin Delevan, and the strange camera he receives on his fifteenth birthday. As it is set in Castle Rock, the

Constant Reader hears the names of many of the locals, some of whom are destined to play significant roles in *Needful Things*. Ace Merrill, Norris Ridgewick, Buster Keaton, Alan Pangborn, and Polly Chalmers are all mentioned or make brief cameos.

THE SUN DOG: PRIMARY SUBJECTS

KEVIN DELEVAN: On his fifteenth birthday, Kevin receives a Polaroid 660 Instant Camera. Something is wrong with the camera, however—no matter what he points it at, the camera produces pictures of what appear to be a dog in front of a picket fence. Kevin is fascinated by the camera and continues to use it, despite the flaw.

Laying the pictures out in the order in which he took them, Kevin makes a startling discovery—the dog is moving *closer* to the foreground in every shot. Frightened, he seeks out his dad, who suggests they take the camera to Pop Merrill, a cagey old gent for whom John Delevan has a grudging respect.

Intrigued by the mysterious camera, and sensing a quick score, Pop rooks the pair out of their possession. After experimenting with it, Pop tries to unload the camera on one of his "Mad Hatters," but is unsuccessful. Falling under the camera's spell, he continues to snap shot after shot, bringing the dog closer and closer from that other dimension to this one. Kevin, realizing that Pop has tricked him, confronts the old man just as the last picture is snapped. Fortunately, Kevin has come prepared—using another Polaroid, he captures the Sun Dog just as it enters this world. The camera then implodes, seemingly ending the threat.

Kevin emerges unscathed, but soon realizes his business with the Sun Dog is not finished. On his sixteenth birthday, he receives a WordStar personal computer. Booting up the PC, he types *"The quick brown fox jumped over the lazy sleeping dog"* and hits the print button. He's shaken to the core by what comes out of the printer: *"The dog is loose again, and it is not sleeping. It is not lazy. It's coming for you, Kevin. It's very hungry. And it's very angry."*

JOHN DELEVAN: Kevin's father, who, seeking to connect with his troubled son, reveals his secret shame to his offspring. Early on in his marriage, John made and lost an extravagant bet, threatening the young couple's financial stability. Desperate to hide this from his wife, John borrowed money from Pop Merrill to cover the wager. It took many years of hard work to pay off, given the high rate of interest Pop charged. After relating this story, John convinces Kevin to take the camera to Pop, a man who's seen much in his long and varied life.

REGINALD MARION "POP" MERRILL: Knowing that they have a unique item, John and Kevin Delevan bring the camera to the shrewdest man in town, Pop Merrill. Pop is a character right out of Charles Dickens, larger than life and twice as cunning. He runs a shop called the Emporium Galorium, becoming wealthy by making usurious loans and by "selling the worthless to the useless." Pop takes just one look at the camera and dollar signs instantly spring up in his eyes. Unable to purchase the camera from its owner, Pop quickly conceives and implements a plan to steal it from Kevin. Pop tries to sell the camera (see next entry), but is unsuccessful.

Unknown to Pop, the camera has been exerting its unnatural influence on him, forcing him to take pictures. Unable to control himself, Pop repeatedly uses the camera until the Sun Dog actually emerges from the last photo. As the Sun Dog draws closer to this reality, the camera grows so hot it eventually bursts into flame. Pop dies in the subsequent fire that guts his store.

"THE MAD HATTERS": Pop Merrill's name for a unique group of customers fascinated by the occult. One mad hatter buys a "spirit trumpet" from Pop for $90; another claims to engage in twice-weekly conversations with Adolf Hitler. Pop offers the Polaroid Sun 660 to four mad hatters—Cedric McCarty, the "Pus" Sisters (identical twins Miss Eleusippus Deere and Mrs. Meleusippus Verrill), and Emory Chafe—but is unable to close a sale with any of them.

"It Grows on You"
(from 1993's *Nightmares & Dreamscapes*)

This tale is an epilogue of sorts to *Needful Things* (1991), featuring a handful of elderly survivors of the debacle caused by Leland Gaunt, a demonic evil force who had destroyed most of the town. Focusing on a strange house that is modified and enlarged whenever someone in town dies, it recalls H. P. Lovecraft's 1929 classic "The Dunwich Horror."

"IT GROWS ON YOU": PRIMARY SUBJECTS

THE NEWALL HOUSE: An old house situated out on Town Road #3, overlooking the section of Castle Rock known as the Bend. The unpainted house has a look of evil to it that one could sense immediately upon entering.

JOE NEWALL: The owner of the Newall House, Joe is constantly adding rooms, then entire wings, to the edifice, arousing curiosity among the surviving residents of Castle Rock. His life is marred by tragedy—his daughter, born misshapen and malformed, died shortly after birth; his wife, Cora, died after falling down a flight of stairs.

GARY PAULSON: An eighty-four-year-old resident of the Bend, he's an ailing widower who has, over the years, lost all three of his sons (two in wars and one in a car accident). He suspects there's some kind of unholy connection between the way local people die and the continued construction of the Newell House. When Paulson passes away in his sleep, his friends are not surprised to see a new cupola being added onto a new wing of the Newell House.

Bridge between Lisbon Falls and Durham   VINTAGE POSTCARD

"The Man in the Black Suit" (from 1997's *Six Stories*)

This story of the devil won both the 1994 World Fantasy Award for Best Short Fiction and the 1994 O. Henry Award for Best American Short Story. It's a neat little tale of innocence confronted by evil, perhaps best described as King à la Ray Bradbury. King has written that the entry comes out of "a long New England tradition of stories which dealt with meeting the devil in the woods . . . he always comes out of the woods—the uncharted regions—to test the human soul."

"THE MAN IN THE BLACK SUIT": PRIMARY SUBJECTS

GARY: In 1914, fishing off the banks of Castle Stream, Gary falls asleep and wakes to discover that he is not alone—a sinister man wearing a black suit has entered the glen, a man the boy quickly realizes is not human. The stranger taunts the boy, telling him that his mother is dead, the victim of a bee sting. Terrified because his younger brother Dan died the same way a year before, the youngster stands there paralyzed. The man approaches, telling Gary he is going to kill him, tear him open, and eat his guts. The threat galvanizes the boy, who takes a fish from his basket and stuffs it in the man's mouth, then runs home. There he finds his mother alive and well.

Gary is old now, and currently resides in a nursing home. He has, however, lived his entire life in fear that the man in the black suit will one day reappear.

SECTION FOUR

The Prime Reality,
Part III:
Jerusalem's Lot and
King's Maine

aine is the setting of so many of King's stories. We have already discussed several key sites in the state, most importantly the fictional towns of Castle Rock and Derry, and in the section on The Shop we will discuss Haven. But those towns represent only a small part of Stephen King's Maine—one must also consider such locales as 'Salem's Lot, Little Tall Island, Dark Score Lake, and other rural Maine communities that have figured so prominently in King's fiction over the years.

The people who inhabit this reality are tough, down-to-earth, stoic types who, given a choice, keep themselves to themselves. They are an intriguing mix of good and evil—for every Jud Crandall *(Pet Sematary)*, Mark Petrie *('Salem's Lot)*, Johnny Smith *(The Dead Zone)*, Dolores Claiborne, or Mike Anderson *(The Storm of the Century)*, there are flawed, troubled, sometimes inhuman types such as Louis Creed, Father Donald Callahan, Frank Dodd, Joe St. George, and Robbie Beals (from the same stories, respectively).

How do these tales of a more rural Maine connect to the rest of the Prime Reality, and to the other realities in the Stephen King Universe? It is obvious from one look at the maps contained in both *Dolores Claiborne* and *Gerald's Game* that the reality that includes Little Tall Island *(Dolores Claiborne, Storm of the Century)*, Dark Score Lake *(Gerald's Game* and *Bag of Bones)* and Lake Kashwakamak *(Gerald's Game)* is the Prime Reality, the one that includes Derry, Haven, and Bangor. But these locales represent only a small part of Stephen King's Maine. Obviously, there are other locales that figure in his stories.

Consider *Rita Hayworth and Shawshank Redemption*, set at everyone's favorite penal institution, the oft-mentioned Shawshank Prison (in *Needful Things* and *Bag of Bones*, for example). The GS & WM train line, which runs through Castle Rock, also winds through Tarker's Mills, Maine, the setting of *Cycle of the Werewolf*. Louis Creed, the chief protagonist of *Pet Sematary*, lives in Ludlow, near the University of Maine at Orono, where he works as the head of health services. Goat Island (from "The Reach") could very well be a sister island to Little Tall Island. Finally, *The Girl Who Loved Tom Gordon* is set in Maine, as its heroine wanders the woods in the southern part of the state, and hallucinates the presence of her hero, Boston Red Sox pitching sensation Tom Gordon.

Are the characters in these stories aware of the rest of the Stephen King Universe? It certainly seems so. For instance, *Pet Sematary's* Jud Crandall makes reference to the events that occurred in *Cujo*, and Rachel Creed reads the name of the town Jerusalem's Lot off an ancient road sign. As mentioned above, Louis Creed works at the University of Maine at Orono, which is prominently featured in *Hearts in Atlantis* and "Riding the Bullet" (it is also King's alma mater). Finally, Trisha McFarland of *The Girl Who Loved Tom Gordon* picks up a Castle Rock radio station while listening to her Walkman in the Maine Woods. Serial killer Andrew Ray Joubert, who figures in the events described in *Gerald's Game*, is mentioned in passing in *Insomnia*. Perhaps the best example of the cross-pollination within the Maine locales in the Prime Reality is offered by King's novella *The Body*— besides a reference to Derry, Castle Rock sheriff Bannerman, and a dog named Cujo, it also mentions 'Salem's Lot and Shawshank Prison.

There is one locale we haven't mentioned yet, but with ample reason. One of the more important towns in the Stephen King Universe, it was effectively reduced to a ghost town over a quarter of a century ago, when it succumbed to a great evil.

You see, long before the words "Castle Rock, Maine" first graced the printed page in *The Dead Zone* (1979), Stephen King had created and destroyed another fully realized fictional community. Jerusalem's Lot—or "'Salem's Lot" to the locals—became Maine's answer to Roanoke, Virginia.

England attempted to colonize that now-notorious island several times, only to find—first in 1587 with one group, and again with a second in 1590—that the respective Roanoke colonies had disappeared without a trace.

King has shown an interest in Roanoke, most recently in 1999's TV miniseries *The Storm of the Century*, but in the Stephen King Universe, nothing is so reminiscent of the seemingly cursed Roanoke Island as

Jerusalem's Lot. It has been occupied and abandoned several times, and now, after a vampire plague fell upon the town, is a veritable Flying Dutchman of burned-out homes and stores and offices.

While Stephen King has created many parallel universes in his work, perhaps the three that are primary are the world of the ongoing *Dark Tower* series, that of *The Stand* (1978), and, finally, what we'll call the Prime Universe—that being the one that includes all of the stories that have taken place in his carefully crafted fictional towns: Castle Rock, Derry, Haven, and Jerusalem's Lot.

But of the several fictional towns King has created, restructuring the map of Maine to suit his own needs, Jerusalem's Lot was the first. In the novel *'Salem's Lot* (1975) and the short stories "One for the Road" and "Jerusalem's Lot"—both of which appear in the 1978 short story collection *Night Shift*—King meticulously crafts the birth, life, and awful death of a small American town, a town imbued with evil from its very inception.

In the creation of this town in "Jerusalem's Lot," King has taken a classic horror conceit and made it his own, echoing works by some of horror's earliest masters, in which a house or even an entire town have been forever tainted by evil. As early as the 1765 publication in England of the first gothic novel—*The Castle of Otranto* by Horace Walpole (1717–1797), which concerned haunting events in a medieval castle—the lingering of evil has been a major theme in horror literature. The story "Jerusalem's Lot" seems a descendant of Walpole's novel, as well as the work of Edgar Allan Poe (1809–1849) in such tales as "The Fall of the House of Usher" (1839), in its use of the mysterious old house that holds dark and unspeakable secrets.

However, in many ways *'Salem's Lot* and its atmosphere of lurking evil, terror, and the erosion of the natural world are most reminiscent of the work of H. P. Lovecraft (1890–1937), who is also known to have had quite an influence on King. "The Shadow Over Innsmouth" (1936) is just one example of a Lovecraft tale about a cursed small town or village that holds within its confines a dark, deadly secret. The same author's "The Dunwich Horror" (1929) also features townspeople coming to grips with an evil that lurks among them. Thus Lovecraft had taken the gothic old, dark house tale and moved it out into the larger setting of an entire town.

In the 1960s, television series such as Rod Serling's *The Twilight Zone* and the classic horror films from England's Hammer Studios contributed to the expansion of the "old dark house" mythos to include, as in Lovecraft's work, an entire town. The work of Richard Matheson (1926–), who wrote for *The Twilight Zone* in addition to his many novels and short stories, also heavily influenced King. Matheson often demonstrated evil as being present in the most contemporary and mundane surroundings. In other words, a vampire could just as well be found lurking in a meat locker in a local supermarket as it could be in an old European castle crypt.

What King has done in the creation of Jerusalem's Lot, and in particular the novel *'Salem's Lot*, is to bring that kind of paranoia-inducing fear into a very familiar, contemporary setting, draped in pop culture. The more familiar elements King introduces into the story, the more we identify with the characters, the more terrifying the story becomes.

The classic structure of such a story—as shown in many period horror films from Hammer (*Horror of Dracula*, *Curse of Frankenstein*) and other studios, as well as in various episodes of *The Twilight Zone*, and even the 1981 horror-comedy classic *An American Werewolf in London*—usually went something like this: our protagonists are innocent outsiders who pass through the spooky town in the night and are put off by the odd behavior of its secretive residents, who cower in fear of the evil that lives all too nearby.

While in many ways the story "Jerusalem's Lot" follows that standard structure *'Salem's Lot* and "One for the Road" most certainly do not. The protagonists of these tales are the people who actually live in the town, who then discover that lurking evil, and who must somehow work as a team to combat and finally destroy it. These people *know* that there are monsters among us, and that they must do something to stop the evil from spreading.

In this deceptively simple manner, with an ancient evil arriving in the average Joe's proverbial own backyard, King lays the bedrock for the essential horror tale of the final quarter of the twentieth century. It would have been merely a new take on an age-old conceit, yet before long, virtually dozens of writers—including such bestsellers as Dean R. Koontz and Robert R. McCammon—would build entire careers around it during the horror boom of the 1980s.

It is important to note, then, that *'Salem's Lot* was not merely the continuation of a growing trend toward "mainstream horror" stories, but truly its vital beginning in contemporary literature.

Incorporated in 1765, Jerusalem's Lot was named almost by accident. Jerusalem was the name of a particularly large and nasty pig owned by Charles Belknap Tanner, a local farmer. When Jerusalem broke out of her pen, she entered the nearby woods and stormed about angrily, prompting Tanner to warn children in the vicinity to stay out of "Jerusalem's Lot."

But long before that, sinister forces had already drawn together in 'Salem's Lot, establishing a pattern that would leave the town empty and tainted by evil not once, but twice in its history, and eventually lead to its destruction.

Upon examining the texts of the short story "Jerusalem's Lot" and the novel *'Salem's Lot*, it is possible to put together a more specific timeline, one that is haunting in the way in which evil is drawn to the town time after time.

- In 1710, a splinter group from the original Puritan settlers of that region of southern Maine—led by a man named James Boon—founded the town of Jerusalem's Lot. A preacher, Boon worships a horrid, demonic creature known only as "the worm," and leads his followers to do the same. He is a fanatical leader, and breeds with many of the cult's women.

- An adjoining hamlet, once called Preacher's Rest and later Preacher's Corners, is founded in 1741.

- In 1765, Jerusalem's Lot is officially incorporated as a township.

- Boon's descendants (Robert and Philip Boone, their surname inexplicably altered) build a house called Chapelwaite in the Lot in 1782, not far from Preacher's Corners. They are unaware at the time that James Boon was their ancestor.

- On October 27, 1789, after Philip Boone has become involved with the cult that still exists in 'Salem's Lot, Robert Boone follows his brother to the church where James Boon and his cult first worshipped the worm. Whatever happens that night between the Boone brothers, the cult, and the worm, Jerusalem's Lot is completely deserted the next day, with no sign of life at all.

- In 1850, Robert's grandson Charles moves into Chapelwaite, his family estate, and happens upon documents that reveal part of his family's history. Also, the attitudes of the people of Preacher's Corners make him realize some of the horror related to his ancestors. On October 27 of that year, Charles faces the worm and the rotted zombielike form of James Boon, both of which still live beneath the abandoned church in 'Salem's Lot.

- By 1896, the evil that has suffused the Lot's history has been all but forgotten, or only whispered about, and the ghost town is settled anew. In that year, the main street, formerly the Portland Post Road, is renamed Jointner Avenue after a local politician.

- In 1928, Hubert Marsten, president of a sizable New England trucking company (and secretly a Mafia assassin), retires to 'Salem's Lot with his wife, Birdie. Of course, Hubie is still in touch with the "family."

- In summer 1939, Marsten inexplicably shoots his wife to death and then hangs himself. It later becomes clear that he had been in touch with a mysterious stranger who was residing in Hitler's Third Reich Germany, a stranger who turns out to be the vampire Kurt Barlow.

- On a childhood dare in 1951, a young boy named Ben Mears enters the reputedly haunted Marsten House and, in the attic, sees what he believes to be the ghost of Hubie Marsten. It haunts him for the rest of his life.

- In October 1971, James Robert Boone, the final descendant of that family, takes up residence in Chapelwaite. Though indications seem to point toward the ancestral home being haunted, there are no subsequent references to the worm or the living corpse of James Boon, or the evil lurking beneath 'Salem's Lot. However, it is also logical to presume that should a Boone ever venture near the spot where that old church had once stood, with the right frame of mind and the right book, that evil would rise again.

- On September 5, 1975, Ben Mears, who had lived in the Lot as a boy, returns to town only to discover that the Marsten House has been purchased by two mysterious European gentlemen.

- By mid-fall 1975, the vampire Barlow has killed or transformed or driven out nearly all of the townspeople before finally being killed by Ben Mears and Mark Petrie. Ben and Mark destroy as many vampires as they can, and then flee the empty township.

- In late 1976 or early 1977, Ben Mears and Mark Petrie return to 'Salem's Lot—prompted by newspaper reports of suspicious disappearances that they link to Barlow's remaining vampiric offspring—and burn the town to the ground.

- On January 10, 1978, the Lumley family of New Jersey are taken by the vampires who still hunt the area around the burned-out town. Two men from a neighboring town, Herb Tooklander and his friend Booth, barely escape the same fate.

Though more than two decades have passed as of this writing, the pattern of dark events indicates that something evil still lurks in the remains of 'Salem's Lot.

Located east of Cumberland, some twenty miles north of Portland, Maine, the fictional 'Salem's Lot boasted a population of 1,300 prior to the vampire holocaust that decimated its populace. For the most part, the town was made up of "a lot of old folks, quite a few poor folks, and a lot of young folks who leave the area with their diplomas under their arms, never to return again."

In order to reach 'Salem's Lot, it would be simplest to take Interstate 95 (a.k.a. the Maine Turnpike) to the exit sign that reads ROUTE 12, JERUSALEM'S LOT, CUMBERLAND, CUMBERLAND CENTER. The off-ramp from the highway leads down onto Route 12, which, if one were to follow it, would turn into Jointner Avenue before too long. Jointner runs straight through the heart of 'Salem's Lot.

The town itself looks much like the crosshairs in a rifle sight. It is nearly round, with Brock Street and Jointner Avenue intersecting at the center of 'Salem's Lot. The northwest corner of town, also called North Jerusalem, consisted mainly of heavily wooded hills. On the hill nearest the center of town stood the Marsten House before it burned.

On the west side, where the town borders Cumberland, one might arrive via the Burns Road and then, more than likely, turn onto Brooks Road, which passes right by Harmony Hill Cemetery. South of there, the poorest of the Lot's residents lived in an area called the Bend, which consisted mainly of dilapidated trailers and shacks.

Much of the northeast section of town consisted of open fields, with the exception of the shimmering Royal River, which once provided a perfect destination for locals who enjoyed fishing now and again.

The southeast section of 'Salem's Lot was dominated by the Griffen Dairy Farm, which stretched along both sides of Griffen Road, and by Schoolyard Hill. Electrical towers for Central Maine Power still carry power lines on a straight course from southeast to northwest, cutting through forest and field.

The town itself was governed by a town meeting, rather than a town

council, and 'Salem's Lot had three selectmen, a constable, a town clerk, a
school commissioner, and a volunteer fire department.

Of course, by the time of the fire that destroyed the town in 1976 or
1977, the volunteer firefighters had either run away, been killed, or, worse
still, been transformed into something terrifying that still hunts by night.

There were a great many landmarks once upon a time. Schools and
businesses and churches and homes.

But they're all gone now.

Subsequent to the slaughter of so many of the town's residents and the
abandonment of the town, 'Salem's Lot developed a widespread reputation
as a local ghost town, not unlike Roanoke Island in Virginia. Rumors about
what had happened to cause so many people to disappear or simply up and
leave raged like small wildfires. Some believed a group of young devil-
worshippers had caused the whole problem. Other stories varied widely in
plausibility but were all equally mysterious and unpleasant.

Still, over the following months several enterprising people attempt to
buy houses or businesses in "the Lot" only to disappear or to madly flee the
town just as their predecessors had. Local legends are far more specific as to
their probable fate. Continued whispers about the undead indicate that the
vampire problem may not be over, and that those who have disappeared may
have fallen prey to the creatures. Despite the efforts of Ben Mears and Mark
Petrie, who burned the town to the ground, some vampires reportedly still
stalk the surrounding communities. The stories about vampires keep those
from the surrounding towns from going anywhere near Jerusalem's Lot.

For the most part.

Since no one has yet to follow up on the saga of the accursed little
township of Jerusalem's Lot, it must be assumed that those few undead citizens are still there. It appears that Ben Mears and Mark Petrie left the job
unfinished. Someday it may fall to others to complete that job.

Only time will tell.

Time and blood.

For whatever reason, the battle between good and evil, between the Purpose
and the Random, is being fought on many fronts. Without question, the
Maine of King's Prime Reality is perhaps the most common battlefield of all
in this war. Whether it be monumental, such as Mike Anderson's struggle with
Andre Linoge, or more mundane (but equally horrible), as in Dolores Claiborne's struggle to prevent her husband from molesting their daughter, a great
many of these individual battles are likely significant to that cosmic struggle.

24

CARRIE

(1974)

King's dedication to his first published novel, *Carrie*, reads as follows:

> This is for Tabby, who go me into it—and then bailed me out of it.

The story behind this dedication is one that King has told many times, but one that bears repeating, primarily because of the pivotal role the book played in making King into a household name. As King relates the tale in 2000's *On Writing*, he was having problems with completing a story he had begun about a high school loser named Carrie White, so many that he threw the manuscript in the trash. King writes:

> The next night, when I came home from school, Tabby had the pages. She'd spied them while emptying my wastebasket, had shaken the cigarette ashes off the crumpled balls of paper, smoothed them out, and sat down to read them. She wanted me to go on with it, she said. She wanted to know the rest of the story. I told her I didn't know jackshit about high school girls. She said she'd help me with that part. She had her chin tilted down and was smiling in that cute way of hers. "You've got something here," she said. "I really think you do."

Constant readers know the rest. King sent the completed manuscript to his editor, Bill Thompson, who bought the book for Doubleday for the princely sum of $2,500. The real shock came when Thompson called King a few months later to tell him that Signet had bought the paperback rights for $400,000. Stunned, all King could think to do was to buy his wife a hair dryer to celebrate their sudden good fortune. To paraphrase Thompson's telegram announcing *Carrie*'s initial sale, their future lay ahead.

Although *Carrie* was King's first published novel, it was not by any means his first attempt at a novel-length work, as the author had been working with that form since high school, beginning his first Bachman offering, *Rage*, as a teenager, and going on to craft novels such as *The Long Walk* and *The Running Man* in the interim.

Written by King in his early twenties, *Carrie* reflects the interests and concerns of someone not far removed from a high school setting. It's not surprising that King would feel an affinity for this subject matter, given his high school teaching experience and his admiration of John Farris's *Harrison High* novels of the late 1950s and early 1960s.

The themes presented in the novel often recur in King's subsequent work, in novels as diverse as *Firestarter* and *Christine*, the first about another young woman with wild talents, the second about another high school outcast, who, through the intervention of the supernatural, is able to take revenge on his tormentors. The book is also significant in that it would be the first of many novels in which a much-put-upon protagonist would be a strong, willful female—rather than traditionally male—character.

To ground his fantastic tale in a more mundane reality, King intersperses his narrative with a series of reports, official documents, and eyewitness testimony. Apparently Carrie White's telekinetic attack on her schoolmates spawned several books and scholarly articles, from which King "quotes" over the course of the novel. Among them are *The Shadow Exploded: Documented Facts and Specific Conclusions from the Case of Carrieta White* by David R. Congress (Tulane University Press, 1981), and *My Name Is Susan Snell* by Susan Snell (Simon & Schuster, 1986). Her rampage also led to the formation of a special commission to study the incident, similar to the Warren Commission, formed a little over a decade before to determine the facts behind the Kennedy assassination.

Even with his first published novel, King was already adding to the landscape of the Pine Tree State. In Carrie, he establishes that the fictional Chamberlain is near the real Lewiston, Maine's second-largest city (Portland is the first). King refers to Lewiston in several subsequent works, most recently *The Dark Tower VII* and *Kingdom Hospital*. He also mentions, for the first time, the Blue Ribbon Laundry, as the place where Mrs. White is employed. Sharp-eyed readers will note that this is the same company that employed Bart Dawes, the tragic protagonist of Richard Bachman's *Roadwork*.

Another, perhaps more tenuous connection to other aspects of the Stephen King Universe is the mention of the demonic figure that Mrs. White refers to as "the Black Man." Featured in a portrait that hangs in the closet where Carrie is often sent as punishment, the Black Man appears to be the very embodiment of evil. One might assume he's the devil, but it's interesting to note he's never referred to as Satan, or Beelzebub, or Old Scratch, only as the Black Man, recalling an alias of the one and only Randall Flagg. This is not to say that he's one and the same as Flagg, Roland's Man in Black, but perhaps that the author was already unconsciously weaving this villain into his universe.

Rather than a simple tale of gruesome supernatural horror, *Carrie* more accurately involves readers on the subliminal level of the classic Grimms' fairy tale "Cinderella," featuring contemporary versions of the cruel stepmother (Margaret White), the fairy godmother (Susan Snell), the wicked stepsisters (the female students who taunt Carrie), and even Prince Charming (in this case Tommy Ross), who escorts Carrie to the ball. Unlike the whitewashed Disney versions of classic fairy tales, however, there is no happy ending for Carrie. As happens so often in the Stephen King Universe, the good perish as frequently and haphazardly as the bad. As in Cinderella, the bad are punished. But in *Carrie*, the good also suffer; those who don't perish must deal with the aftermath of the tragedy for the rest of their lives.

In the real world, King reminds us, sometimes Cinderella herself doesn't survive the ball.

CARRIE: PRIMARY SUBJECTS

CARRIE WHITE: The only child of Ralph and Margaret White, the teenage Carrie is a classic wallflower, destined to serve as a doormat for the other, more popular, students. Friendless, Carrie only has her demented mother to instruct her in the ways of the world.

Carrie, however, turns out to be a little bit different from the other misfits targeted for harassment by the in crowd, having inherited a rare genetic trait for telekinesis from her late father. The gene, which allows her to move objects with the power of her mind, fully manifests itself shortly after she has her first period, during her senior year in high school.

Unfortunately, Carrie first menstruates while in the shower at school. Unaware that this is totally natural for women, she panics, believing that she is bleeding to death, exposing herself to even more abuse from her cruel classmates.

Trying to make up for joining in with her classmates as they taunted Carrie, Susan Snell asks her boyfriend, Tommy Ross, to ask Carrie to the prom. Tommy agrees to ask, and Carrie accepts.

At the prom, Carrie falls victim to an elaborate and cruel practical joke orchestrated by Chris Hargensen in which she is doused in pig's blood shortly after being voted queen of the prom. This is the last straw for Carrie, who, enraged, uses the telekinetic powers she's been secretly honing to slaughter the majority of her fellow promgoers.

Carrie eventually dies from a knife wound inflicted by her mother later that night, but not before laying waste to most of the town and killing many of those who had so callously wronged her along the way.

MARGARET WHITE: Carrie's fanatical, ultrareligious mother, she has spent the majority of her adult life atoning for one night of passion, the result of which was the birth of her only child, Carrie.

Mrs. White has turned her small house into a sad sanctuary of religious icons and paintings. She believes that sex, even within marriage, is evil, and that God has punished her by giving her a child to serve as a daily reminder of her unspeakable sin of lust.

Her idea of "educating" Carrie about menstruation is to lock her in a closet filled with religious symbols and demand that she pray for forgiveness. When Margaret's madness ultimately overwhelms her on the night of the prom, she wounds her daughter with a knife. Enraged, Carrie uses her telekinetic ability to stop Margaret's heart.

SUSAN SNELL: A usually decent sort who uncharacteristically took part in ridiculing Carrie in the girls' shower room, Susan later comes to regret her actions, and attempts to atone for them by convincing her boyfriend, Tommy Ross, to ask Carrie to the prom. One of the few survivors of the ensuing night of destruction and death, she wrote a book about her role in the tragedy entitled *My Name Is Susan Snell*.

TOMMY ROSS: Susan Snell's affable boyfriend. Although he agrees to take Carrie to the prom strictly out of respect for his girlfriend's wishes, he gradually comes to like Carrie on her own merits. Attending the dance, he and Carrie are voted king and queen of the prom. When a falling bucket of pig's blood apparently kills Tommy, Carrie unleashes her terrible power, turning the high school gym into a killing zone. Tommy ultimately dies in a fire triggered by Carrie's attack on her classmates.

CHRIS HARGENSEN: The classic town slut, Chris is the chief instigator in the "hazing" Carrie receives in the girls' shower room. Punished for their involvement, Chris and several other girls seek revenge against Carrie, creating an elaborate plan to humiliate her at the prom. Chris's orchestrations ultimately result in Carrie being doused with pig's blood seconds after being voted queen of the prom. Although her plan works like a charm, Chris doesn't reckon on Carrie's vengeful rampage—she dies later that night as Carrie, departing the gym, proceeds to lay waste to the town.

BILLY NOLAN: Chris Hargensen's delinquent boyfriend, Billy is every father's worst nightmare, at least when it comes to the young men their daughters date. Not very bright, Billy provides the brawn Chris requires to obtain the pig's blood and rig the buckets over the stage. Billy dies alongside Chris when he tries to run Carrie down with his car. Carrie telekinetically deflects the oncoming vehicle, sending it careening into the side of a roadhouse. Billy and Chris are killed in the resulting explosion.

RITA DESJARDEN: Rita is the sympathetic gym teacher who stops her class from taunting Carrie in the girls' shower. One of the few people ever to show kindness toward Carrie, Rita is unfortunately slain in the burning gymnasium when the gym is suddenly transformed into a slaughterhouse.

CARRIE: ADAPTATIONS

Carrie was made into a highly successful motion picture in 1976, directed by Brian De Palma from a screenplay by Lawrence D. Cohen. Although the production had a paltry budget of $1.8 million, it was one of the top-grossing films of the year, earning more than $30 million dollars in domestic receipts.

The ninety-seven-minute thriller was notable as a showcase for many young actors who would later become major stars, including Amy Irving, William Katt, Nancy Allen, and John Travolta. Sissy Spacek and Piper Laurie, who played Carrie and Margaret White, respectively, were both nominated for Academy Awards as Best Actress and Best Supporting Actress.

Director De Palma and screenwriter Cohen had to restructure the story for the screen, but due to the quality of the young cast and the sincerity with which everyone played their parts, the R-rated movie remains a truly moving and frightening experience. Unlike so many adaptations of King's works to come, the movie was faithful in spirit to the novel, if not always to the literal translation of the original story.

King loved the movie, reportedly attributing his ascension to the bestseller lists to the success of the picture and the subsequent success of the movie tie-in edition of *Carrie*.

In early 1999, *The Rage: Carrie 2* was released as a motion picture. The story shamelessly repeated many of the plot elements of the original: a lonely teenage girl discovers she has telekinetic powers, which she uses against her tormenters in high school. The movie starred Emily Bergl in the role of Rachel, and also featured Amy Irving as the sole surviving character from the original film of two decades earlier. Directed by Katt Shea and written by Rafael Moreu, *The Rage: Carrie 2* died a quick death at the box office. King had no involvement whatsoever with the production.

Following the tradition of *The Shining*, *Carrie* was subsequently remade for television. Appearing on NBC, the 2002 miniseries attracted little attention. Starring Angela Bettis as Carrie, it featured Patricia Clarkson as Margaret White, Rena Sofer as Rita Desjarden, and David Keith as a police investigator, a character unique to this version.

CARRIE: THE MUSICAL

In contrast to the original movie adaptation, *Carrie: The Musical* was not quite as successful. Later touted as "the biggest flop in Broadway history," the musical, budgeted at nearly $8 million dollars, opened on Broadway on May 12, 1988, and closed after a run of only five performances. The best-known actress in the production was Betty Buckley, who coincidentally had also portrayed the friendly gym teacher, Miss Collins, in the film version.

Here, however, she was cast as Mrs. Margaret White. An unknown named Linzi Hateley played Carrie.

The New York critics utterly loathed the stage production, and the bad publicity that followed quickly insured its almost overnight demise. That the theatrical production followed the story line of the blood-soaked and body-strewn movie and book fairly faithfully indicates the perhaps insurmountable challenge the naive producers of a musical version were up against.

CARRIE: TRIVIA

- Carrie White's seventh-grade English teacher was a Mr. Edwin King. King's middle name is Edwin.

- As part of an unusual marketing ploy, the cover of the first paperback edition of the novel did not feature King's name.

- Carrie White's birthday is September 21, 1963. King's birthday also falls on September 21.

- Per an excerpt of a letter at the novel's end dated May 3, 1988, other people with telekinetic powers exist. The letter, from Amelia Jenks of Royal Knob, Tennessee, to her sister, Sandra Jenks of Macon, Georgia, describes an incident where Amelia's young daughter, Annie, makes her brothers' marbles move about without touching them. Yet another example of a young woman with similar powers is another girl named Annie, Annie Wheaton of *Rose Red* fame.

- John Swithen is a minor character in Carrie. King later published his story "The Fifth Quarter" under this name.

25

'SALEM'S LOT

(1975)

Though longer than *Carrie* (1974), in comparison to many of King's later epic novels, *'Salem's Lot* is quite succinct. As he had in his previous novel, the author paints a canvas that is gloriously and unabashedly American, for better or worse, or in this case, both. He weaves a tapestry of small-town life that is startlingly true and familiar and, perhaps most importantly, safe. And from the sanctuary of this familiar setting, with all its colorful characters and nostalgia—nostalgia reinforced time and again by the memories of the central character—King breeds his horror.

This isn't an epic novel. But it isn't meant to be.

Instead, it's a story about a town so far off the map that it can wither and die and, quite simply, nobody cares. Here, Stephen King takes the Bavarian village from the classic horror films of his own youth and turns it into a tiny hamlet in Maine, right next door to all the small towns of our collective youthful memories.

This element of the narrative is what made *'Salem's Lot* so special, and such a milestone. In several tangible ways, it changed horror fiction and, in so doing, altered the state of American publishing for years to come. Traditionally, horror previous to *'Salem's Lot* was found in arcane tomes and ancient locales. With this small-town vampire tale, King set off an entire generation's worth of horror stories set in the proverbial backyard of the American reading public.

Strange, perhaps, that it would be King's second book that would have that impact, but the reason is quite clear. *Carrie* isn't really a horror novel, but actually more of a precursor to the kind of female-driven thrillers King would write much later in his career. *'Salem's Lot*, by comparison, could not possibly be called anything else. It is unashamedly a vampire novel, perhaps the most important such work of this century. What King has done here, in a way others would try to mimic for decades after the publication of *'Salem's Lot*, is take the traditional horrors of the scary books, monster comic books, and B-movies he had enjoyed as a boy, and transport them to small-town, mainstream America. (sort of Peyton Place meets Dracula).

'Salem's Lot is also important because it represents the beginning of King's real effort to create a fictional counterpart of his home state of Maine. The town is slipped right into the existing geography of this part of New England, and described in such exhaustive and loving detail that one is almost disappointed to realize it has no real place on the map. With repeated references to surrounding Maine communities, and to landmarks like the Androscoggin and Royal rivers (the Royal would also be used later in other tales), he offers a sense of place that would become a touchstone of modern horror fiction.

In the Stephen King Universe, Jerusalem's Lot is the archetypical ghost town, the Flying Dutchman, and the Bermuda Triangle rolled into one. The novel introduces the concept that evil begets more of the same, that it attracts itself with magnetic force, and that it can linger long after its perpetrator has gone to his damnation.

Even more to the point, King brings to the forefront the concept that supernatural horror is not necessarily something that can only occur in a Gothic castle in Transylvania, but that the undead can exist in the house down the street. Or in our own attics or basements or neighbors' backyards.

As King will show repeatedly in his novels and short stories, home can well be where the horror is.

'SALEM'S LOT: PRIMARY SUBJECTS

JERUSALEM'S LOT: If you drive north on Interstate 95 in Maine, not far north of Portland you'll cross the Royal River and come to an exit sign that reads, ROUTE 12, JERUSALEM'S LOT, CUMBERLAND, CUMBERLAND CTR. As you crest the hill of the ramp and look down along Route 12 toward town, you may just be able to spot the burned ruins of the enormous manse that once stood sentinel over the town, the old Marsten House.

Methodist church next to King's house   DAVID LOWELL

Before the vampire, Kurt Barlow, came to town, the Lot was a thriving little New England community. Now it's a ghost town. Or perhaps something worse, given the horrors that occurred there.

Jerusalem's Lot was incorporated in 1765, taking its name from the proprietary behavior of a particularly large pig (named Jerusalem, of course) owned by one Charles Belknap Tanner.

THE MARSTEN HOUSE: The home of Hubert Marsten up until the time he murdered his wife and took his own life. By the time Ben Mears comes to live in the Lot as a boy, the Marsten House has become the ultimate haunted manse. Even the bravest of local children are afraid to enter the moldy interior, which sits atop Marsten Hill, almost as though it is watching over the town—albeit more as evil tyrant than vigilant sentinel.

As a boy, Ben enters the house on a dare, and later reveals that he believes he has seen the ghost of Hubie Marsten there. Though the Lot's residents never discover this connection, it seems that the late Marsten had been in frequent correspondence with the vampire Kurt Barlow, who would later bring his evil to the Lot, inspired by Marsten.

The Marsten House is eventually burned to the ground. However, Ben Mears believes that the house itself has somehow retained Marsten's evil, and that this evil has acted as a kind of beacon for other horrors. If so, it is possible that the burned-out remains of the house, and its very foundation, still retain some of that evil essence.

BEN MEARS: Though born on Long Island in New York, Ben Mears is raised by his aunt, Cynthia Stowens, in 'Salem's Lot. Haunted by a terrifying experience he had in the Lot as a child, and by the tragic death of his wife, Miranda, in a motorcycle accident, Mears returns to 'Salem's Lot many years later to write a new novel. His previous books include *Conway's Daughter*, *Air Dance*, and *Billy Said Keep Going*.

Ben's memories of the Lot are both fond and melancholy. Though very little has changed, the town has certainly forgotten him. He, however, has never forgotten 'Salem's Lot. He dreams quite regularly of that horrific childhood experience—upon a dare he had entered the spooky mansion called the Marsten House and come upon a frightening specter of the late owner of the home, a suicidal Mafia hit man named Hubie Marsten. But the dreams were nightmares.

Little does Ben know that Hubie Marsten's evil has lingered, and drawn another sinister force to the town.

Despite his nostalgia, Ben makes no attempt to contact those few men with whom he played as a boy in the Lot. Instead, he makes new friends in Susan Norton, a younger woman with whom he falls in love; her father, Bill Norton; and an aging teacher named Matthew Burke.

It isn't long after his return on September 5, 1975, that Ben realizes something is horribly wrong in the Lot. Though the vampire, Barlow, and his manservant, the preternaturally strong Straker, have actually been murdering the townspeople or transforming them into vampires, as an outsider Ben is an early suspect. Later, of course, he becomes one of the few who realizes the truth of what is happening in the Lot, and takes action.

Along with a local boy named Mark Petrie and a doctor named Jimmy Cody, Ben and those closest to him attempt to permanently rid the town of

Barlow and his vampires. They manage to burn down the Marsten House, and later kill Barlow (like Father Callahan, Ben briefly shines with a preternatural white light while opposing the vampires), but there are too many vampires. Ben suffers another loss when his lover, Susan Norton, is transformed into one of the undead.

In the end, the only survivors, Ben and Mark, leave 'Salem's Lot and travel as far away as they are able. Attempting to start a new life, they eventually settle in the small Mexican village of Los Zapatas. Only when they come across a press clipping that indicates the vampires are active again in the Lot do they acknowledge they must return to finish the job.

Together, they go back to the Lot for the last time, and set fire to the entire town.

According to the story Father Callahan tells in *Wolves of the Calla*, he "went todash" to Los Zapatas and witnessed Ben's funeral.

SUSAN NORTON: A young woman who has lived all her life in the Lot and dreams of one day moving to the city, Susan is dating Floyd Tibbits before Ben comes into her life. They meet in the park on a sunny September afternoon, and Susan is instantly charmed by him, partially because she is reading one of his books at the very moment at which she first spots him.

Susan lives at home with her parents, Bill and Ann Norton. She is a painter who is just beginning to have some success. Sadly, when she investigates Ben's wild claims about the Marsten House—and Barlow and Straker—she is captured by Straker and later turned into a vampire by Barlow. Eventually Ben is forced to drive a stake through her heart, ending her undead existence. Her soul is now free to make its final journey.

MATTHEW BURKE: As an English teacher at the Lot's Consolidated High School, Matt Burke has earned a great deal of respect from former students, but not many accolades from those who operate the facility. It is Matt who first realizes what is truly happening in 'Salem's Lot. He encounters a former student, Mike Ryerson, at a bar and, concerned by Ryerson's apparent illness, invites him to stay at his home. During the night, Ryerson is attacked and killed by a vampire. When Ryerson later returns, now a vampire, Matt suffers a massive heart attack.

Though the seizure keeps him from the physical struggle, Burke becomes the thinker for those attempting to thwart the vampire Barlow's plans. Sadly, Matt dies of a second heart attack in the hospital, never to learn the fate of his town and his friends.

MARK PETRIE: Though he grew up in Kittery, Maine, Mark Petrie has the bad luck to have moved to 'Salem's Lot with his parents just before the vampires come to town. He was twelve years old at the time. Tall for his age, but slightly built and bespectacled, Mark is forced to fight the school bully soon after his arrival in the Lot, and makes a fool of him. He is an intelligent boy who can take care of himself.

Mark also has a great fondness for monster movies and Aurora monster model kits. It is on the way to Mark's house to see these models that Danny and Ralphie Glick are attacked. Danny later appears to Mark as a vampire and attempts to get Mark to invite him inside. Mark, however, uses a plastic cross from his Dracula model to frighten away the vampire.

After being captured himself by Straker, Mark escapes, and it is he who takes Straker's life. Barlow later murders Mark's parents in retribution. Eventually, Mark and Ben Mears terminate Barlow and leave 'Salem's Lot. They wander the country, eventually living in a Mexican village called Los Zapatas. However, they begin to suspect the vampires are back in Maine. They return to set fire to the entire town.

Mark Petrie's current whereabouts are unknown.

KURT BARLOW: A horrid, ancient vampire, Barlow thrived in Nazi Germany until he found it necessary to remove himself from that part of the world. He began a correspondence with Hubert Marsten, a Mafia soldier who resided in 'Salem's Lot and gave Barlow a good deal of information about the town. At one point Straker, Barlow's servant, refers to Marsten as Barlow's "benefactor" in America.

Years pass and Marsten hangs himself after murdering his wife. Eventually Barlow determines to come to the United States, and 'Salem's Lot is his chosen target, a town where he can "feed" indiscriminately and not be discovered. In a shady real estate deal, he purchases the Marsten House as well as a storefront in the town. There his servant, Straker, opens an expensive antique shop to throw off the townspeople's usual suspicions of strangers.

When Barlow realizes that there are some in the town who know the truth, he moves from the Marsten place into the basement of Eva Miller's boardinghouse. It is here that he is eventually killed by Ben Mears and Mark Petrie.

There are those who say Barlow's vampiric offspring continue to roam the area around 'Salem's Lot.

RICHARD THROCKETT STRAKER: Straker is Barlow's servant, his human agent. For his master, Straker performs many tasks, from propitiation of demons to abduction and murder of children. His incredible strength and enduring youth make it obvious that Straker is not entirely human, thanks to Barlow's influence. However, he is certainly not a vampire.

Straker arranges a deal with local realtor Larry Crockett to buy the Marsten House and the storefront in town, and perpetuates the charade of the shop itself.

When Susan Norton and Mark Petrie break into the Marsten House, it is Straker who discovers them. When Mark attempts to escape, Straker tries to kill the boy, but in the struggle is himself killed by Petrie. Imagine, a monster killed by a twelve-year-old boy!

FATHER DONALD CALLAHAN: As the pastor at St. Andrew's Church in the Lot, Father Callahan is responsible for the spiritual well-being of the town's Catholics. As an alcoholic, however, he has a great deal of trouble even caring for his own soul. Even before the horrible events occur in the Lot, Callahan doubts his faith. When the truth is revealed to him, for a time his faith is restored. Surely, he reasons, the presence of such evil indicates the existence of God as an opposing force.

After Barlow murders Mark Petrie's parents, Callahan saves Mark from the vampire. Standing up to Barlow, Callahan is briefly imbued with an otherwordly power, manifesting itself as white light. The light ebbs, however, when Barlow challenges Callahan's shaky faith. In the end, his faith is not strong enough, and Barlow takes some of Callahan's blood, enslaving him. In the only act of defiance left to him, Callahan flees 'Salem's Lot forever, leaving his parishioners and the town to suffer in Barlow's evil grasp.

Father Donald Callahan eventually spends years battling the vampires elsewhere in the world . . . and beyond.

HUBERT MARSTEN: An eccentric and evil man, Hubie Marsten was a hit man for the Mafia whose house looked down on 'Salem's Lot. In his later days, he taped all of his money to the insides of magazines. He corresponded with Barlow the vampire when Barlow still resided in Europe.

Later, Marsten murders his wife and then hangs himself in the attic of the old mansion. It seems possible, even likely, that his spirit somehow remains tied to the house, for when young Ben Mears visits the house on a dare, he sees a ghastly vision of what might be Hubie Marsten's ghost.

THE GLICK FAMILY: Nine-year-old Ralphie Glick is taken by Straker as a sacrifice for Barlow while he and his older brother, Danny, are on their way to Mark Petrie's house. In time, the entire Glick family falls victim to the vampires.

THE NORTON FAMILY: Bill and Ann Norton and their daughter Susan all become victims of the vampires.

THE PETRIE FAMILY: Though the son, Mark, survives the evil that destroyed 'Salem's Lot, his parents do not.

MIKE RYERSON: A local blue-collar worker and former student of Matt Burke's, Mike is filling in Danny Glick's grave in Harmony Hill Cemetery when Danny comes back to life as a vampire. Danny attacks him, and soon Mike is also one of the undead. After his own resurrection, Mike attempts to kill Matt Burke but is unsuccessful.

'SALEM'S LOT: ADAPTATIONS

In November 1979, CBS broadcast a two-part miniseries based on *'Salem's Lot*. The groundbreaking event featured David Soul *(Starsky & Hutch)* as Ben Mears, respected British actor James Mason *(Heaven Can Wait)* as Straker, and Bonnie Bedelia (who would later be best known for playing Bruce Willis's wife in the *Die Hard* thrillers) as Susan Norton. At the time, the four-million-dollar budget (a million an hour!) was considered an enormous expenditure. Under the able direction of Tobe Hooper, who had previously helmed *The Texas Chainsaw Massacre* (1974) and would later direct *Poltergeist* (1982) and *Lifeforce* (1985), the miniseries turned out to be a highly effective mood piece, though the horror was heavily diluted by network censors.

While the miniseries diverged significantly in some aspects of plot (specifically, the relocation of Barlow to Eva Miller's boardinghouse late in the story), for the most part it was a very faithful adaptation by Paul Monash, who previously had produced the film version of *Carrie*. King himself was reportedly very satisfied with the production, given the restrictions of the medium, though he disagreed with Barlow looking more like the ghastly creature from the 1922 silent classic *Nosferatu* than the way he had actually been portrayed in his novel.

A theatrical version specifically for European distribution was reedited from the miniseries and called *'Salem's Lot: The Movie*. While it was more graphic in terms of visual elements of violence and shock, its running time (112 minutes versus the original 210 minutes) also unfortunately ensured that much of the careful character development that had been integral to the original miniseries would be lost. (Curiously enough, in 1987 writer-director Larry Cohen would be the main creative force behind a direct-to-video sequel authorized by Warner Bros. called *A Return to 'Salem's Lot*. Starring Michael Moriarty and Andrew Duggan, it bore only a passing resemblance to the characters and situations from the original novel. Even so, King was given a screen credit as "creative consultant.")

Like *The Shining* and *Carrie* before it, *Salem's Lot* was filmed a second time for television, twenty-five years after Tobe Hooper shot the first version. Premiering on TNT in June 2004, it featured Rob Lowe as Ben Mears, James Cromwell as Father Donald Callahan, and Andre Braugher as Matt Burke (!). Although superior in some ways to the original film version, this incarnation was summarily dismissed by many critics as not living up to its source material. One bright spot was the inspired casting of Rutger Hauer and Donald Sutherland as Barlow and Straker; the duo had previously appeared together in the roles of the vampire Lothos and watcher Merrick in the 1992 film version of *Buffy the Vampire Slayer*.

'SALEM'S LOT: TRIVIA

- King's original title for *'Salem's Lot* was *Second Coming*.

- As a marketing technique by his paperback publishers, the first edition of the novel in paperback did not have King's name anywhere on the cover.

- Trying to distract himself from Danny Glick's hypnotic power, Mark Petrie whispers, "The rain in Spain falls mainly on the plain. In vain he thrusts his fists against the posts and still insists he sees the ghosts." The latter phrase is one that young Bill Denbrough of *It* fame uses as a vocal exercise to hinder his stuttering. Bill also uses the phrase to calm himself when he encounters the Turtle in the Void.

- For a time, King considered writing a sequel to *'Salem's Lot* that would chronicle the travels of Father Callahan after he left the town. Instead, Callahan shows up in the final three volumes of the *Dark Tower* series, in which we learn of his trials and tribulations and his war against the vampires.

- In 2004, Centipede Press released a limited edition of *'Salem's Lot* that featured over fifty pages of material deleted from the original book prior to publication, included at the back as "deleted scenes" (i.e., not reincorporated into the text as was done with the unexpurgated version of *The Stand*). Viking published a trade edition in the fall of 2005.

26

PET SEMATARY

(1983)

Although it may be rightfully argued that such Richard Bachman titles as *Rage* (1977) and *Roadwork* (1981) constitute Stephen King's darkest
visions, it has to be said that the novel that the writer himself considers his
bleakest and most pessimistic is *Pet Sematary*.

Originally written in the spring of 1979, this is the book that for several years had the reputation of being known as the "story so horrifying that
he was for a time unwilling to finish it." (So states the dust jacket copy of
the hardcover first edition.) A further indication of how long King struggled with it comes from the author's notation on the last page stating the
composition of the novel occurred from "February 1979–December 1982."

What is generally not known is that King actually did complete the
novel in the summer of 1979, but found it so grim that he decided not to
publish it. Even his wife, Tabitha, whom King has always used as the first
reader for all his work, agreed with him that he had finally written a story
that should be permanently put away in a drawer. And so it was. The fact
that it was eventually published in 1983 had far more to do with a dispute
with a past publisher, Doubleday & Co., than it did with a desire to squash
the rumors that he had once authored a novel he himself found "too nasty"
to have published.

Like so many of his early novels, *Pet Sematary* focuses on the lives of a single, small family unit residing in Maine. A young doctor, Louis Creed, moves from Chicago to set up residence in the small town of Ludlow. His family consists of his lovely wife, Rachel, and two small children, five-year-old Ellie and two-year-old Gage. On the surface, life is good—Louis is to be the new head of health services for the University of Maine at nearby Orono. But the comfortable old house in which they live is set near a busy road, one often used by truckers driving their massive eighteen-wheelers. And one day Ellie's beloved cat, Church (derived from "Winston Churchill"), is run over and killed by a speeding vehicle.

Ellie is grief-stricken, and Louis, who has never been particularly strong in discussing or practicing matters of religion or faith, is at a loss to satisfactorily comfort her in her loss. From an elderly neighbor, Jud Crandall, the doctor learns an incredible secret known only to the locals. Nearby is a "pet sematary" (as it reads on a crude sign misspelled by children) that was once an ancient Indian burial ground. It has existed there for untold centuries, and is supposedly haunted by the legendary creature known as the Wendigo. The amazing secret of the cemetery is that anything buried there does not stay dead. Whatever is buried is soon revived to some semblance of life. Louis buries the cat there, and incredibly, the pet *does* return—although it is a mean, zombielike incarnation of its former self.

In a situation similar to one expressed in the classic 1902 tale by W. W. Jacobs, "The Monkey's Paw," Louis Creed finds himself in the extraordinary circumstance of having the power—through the use of the pet cemetery—to be granted three wishes. His first is to have his daughter's beloved pet returned to her, and it is. It is not normal, it is not friendly, but at least it is *back*.

Then a far greater tragedy occurs—young Gage later runs out into the same busy road and is struck and killed by a truck. Now it is the parents who cannot be consoled in their overwhelming grief. Rachel's sister had died a lingering death from spinal meningitis when she was quite young, and she cannot bear the tragic and sudden death of her boy. Too many painful wounds have reopened, and she is nearly insane from the senseless loss of their younger child.

Half mad himself, Louis digs up the body of his dead son from the local cemetery and reburies him in the dreaded pet burial ground, hoping against hope that he can bring his son back to life. He doesn't care what price has to be paid for the boy's return; he only knows that he will do anything to make his family whole again. And so his second grisly wish is granted through the unholy power of the Micmac Indian burial ground.

But what returns from the pet sematary is his son in appearance only.

Gage is actually an undead, soulless monster, cursed with murderous instincts of pure evil. Using one of his father's scalpels, the boy first brutally murders Jud Crandall, and then butchers and mutilates his own mother. Louis in turn has to destroy the loathsome creature that was once his son. (Ellie has gone to stay with her mother's family in Chicago and is spared the entire ordeal. However, through her psychiclike nightmares she is aware of the horror befalling the rest of her family.)

But Louis has not learned from his terrible experience. Although he dimly realizes what unnatural horror had befallen his son, he insanely reasons that if he can just bury his recently deceased wife in the pet sematary quickly enough, then she will be revived more or less "normal." However, Louis's third and final wish doesn't come true in quite the way he desires. In the novel's devastating last sentence, his loving wife does return to him after being revived by the supernatural powers of the pet sematary: " 'Darling,' it said."

Fade out to total darkness.

Pet Sematary shares many themes prevalent in the darkest corners of the Stephen King Universe. Chief among them is that no one is truly the master of his destiny, that anyone and anything we love can be taken away from us at a moment's notice. The only force we can depend upon in our life is the love we share with our families, and even that can be stolen away at any point. King has repeatedly stated in interviews that for him, the greatest horror one can experience in life is the sudden and tragic loss of a child.

In the early novels *Carrie* (1974), *Rage (1977)*, *The Long Walk* (1979), and especially *Cujo* (1981), teenagers and children die violent and senseless deaths. Yet in each of them there is some faint ray of sun on the horizon that King leaves to comfort the reader. However, in *Pet Sematary* there is no sense of any happy ending, even though young Ellie apparently will survive to see another day. The father, mother, and son, however, remain dead—or undead. It is only mere chance that the daughter is allowed to live, and it's extremely unlikely the remainder of her existence will be a happy or fulfilling one.

The author is also dealing here with the question of one's faith and religion. Louis is a man who believes, as a doctor, that he is somehow above the laws of God and nature, that he can circumvent the natural order of life and death simply because he is well-educated and supremely rational. But within the Stephen King Universe, death can come at any time to anyone—for any reason. Most importantly, death can visit any of us—good or bad, young or old, beloved or stranger—for no logical reason whatsoever. Even so, life is not always worth holding onto at any cost.

Indeed, as an unheeding Louis Creed is warned by Jud Crandall, "Sometimes, dead is better."

PET SEMATARY: PRIMARY SUBJECTS

LOUIS CREED: A thirty-five-year-old doctor, he has brought his family to Maine to better his career and their lives. A pragmatic man, the fact that he holds no strong religious beliefs enables him to find a rational meaning behind every mystery. But when he brings his daughter's cat and then his young son back from the dead, he realizes to his everlasting misfortune that there are some mysteries that should never be explored. When he restores his murdered wife back to life, it can only be presumed that she, in turn, destroys him.

RACHEL CREED: The loving wife of Louis Creed, she is a devoted mother to her young son and daughter. She has been emotionally scarred since childhood by the experience of her sister Zelda dying a lingering death from spinal meningitis. At age eight, Rachel witnessed her sister's agonizing demise, and has never forgotten the horror of that experience. Rachel is later slain at the hand of her own undead son, wielding the bloody scalpel he has stolen from his father's doctor's bag. Her husband refuses to accept her untimely passing, and brings her back using the supernatural powers of the pet cemetery. But she comes back to his forgiving arms as an "it," *not* a "she."

GAGE CREED: The toddler who is killed by a speeding truck and is then only temporarily laid to rest by his grieving family. After sending his wife and daughter to stay with her parents, Louis Creed digs up his corpse and reburies him in the dreaded pet cemetery. Gage returns from the dead as an evil thing who then butchers Jud Crandall and later his own mother. Gage is then killed a second time, this time with lethal injections administered by his own father, now gone insane.

ELLIE CREED: The five-year-old older sister of Gage Creed, she escapes the fate of her parents when she is placed in the care of her mother's parents in Chicago. Like her father, she is cursed with psychic visions of the dead. Her current whereabouts are unknown.

VICTOR PASCOW: A young man who has the misfortune to be fatally hit by a speeding car on the first day that Louis Creed starts work at the university's health center. He is brought to the facility near death, but before he expires he supernaturally warns Louis about the awful consequences to be reckoned with should he ever use the cursed power of the pet cemetery. Ghostly visions of him continue to haunt Louis—and later his daughter, Ellie—but to no avail in preventing further tragedy to the Creed family.

JUD CRANDALL: The elderly neighbor, born in 1900, who lives closest to the Creed home. He becomes fast friends with the Creed family, especially with Louis, who regards Jud as the wise father he had never known. (Louis's father had died when the boy was only three.) A native of Maine who enjoys a good long beer and a good long talk, he is the man who reveals to Louis the terrible secret of the pet cemetery so that Ellie could have Church returned to her. After Gage's death, he rightly suspects that Louis will try and bring his only son back to life, but his warning goes unheeded. Ultimately Jud pays for his sharing that forbidden knowledge at the murderous hands of little Gage.

PET SEMATARY: ADAPTATIONS

By the time King decided he would sell the film rights to *Pet Sematary*, his career had advanced to such a stage that he could demand in his contract that the production be shot in Maine or not be made at all. He also had the power to dictate that only his own screenplay adaptation be used. (This was the first of his novels that he would be openly credited with having adapted to the screen.) In both cases, his stipulations were carried out, and King had the further pleasure of seeing the motion picture become a moderate success at the box office when it was released in 1989.

Although directed by Mary Lambert, who had only helmed one feature previously (entitled *Siesta*, it was not in the horror genre), *Pet Sematary* remained faithful to King's close adaptation of his original novel. (His old friend George Romero was originally slated to direct, but scheduling conflicts forced him to bow out.) Starring Dale Midkiff as Louis Creed and Denise Crosby as his wife, Rachel, the most notable bit of casting was Fred Gwynne in the role of Jud. Gwynne delivers a wonderful performance that

captures the essence of a Stephen King character better than almost anyone who has come before or since. Unflinchingly gory and shocking, the
102-minute picture is in many ways as dark and bleak as its source material. Unlike the radical change in ending he had allowed in the movie version of *Cujo* in 1983, King knew that his growing legion of fans could deal
now with a totally downbeat ending.

The success of *Pet Sematary* at the box office led to a totally unneces-
sary sequel being released in 1992. Not too surprisingly, it was called *Pet
Sematary 2* and starred Edward Furlong and Anthony Edwards. (It is a standard clause in the purchasing of motion picture rights for a story or a novel
that the producers also retain the rights to any possible sequel. This explains how, without King's desire or participation, there have also been
screen sequels—often direct to video—to *'Salem's Lot*, and multiple low-
budget follow-ups to the features based on the stories *Sometimes They
Come Back* and *Children of the Corn*.) Although capably directed by the
same director as the original, Mary Lambert, there is unfortunately little to
recommend here, even for King completists.

PET SEMATARY: TRIVIA

- Jud Crandall mentions in passing a tale of a Maine tragedy in which
  four people were savagely killed by a rabid dog. That story was, of
  course, fully related in *Cujo*.

- At one point, driving through southern Maine to try to return home,
  Rachel Creed reads a group of road signs. Several towns are listed,
  including one named Jerusalem's Lot. She thinks to herself that it is not
  a pleasant name, although she has no idea of the legends surrounding
  the accursed town as related in *'Salem's Lot*.

- In the movie adaptation, Stephen King has a cameo role as a minister.

- In the television adaptation of *The Shining*, Stephen King appears in a
  cameo as band leader Gage Creed.

- In *Insomnia*, readers are told that the little bald doctor Atropos keeps
  one of Gage Creed's sneakers in his lair as a trophy.

27

CYCLE OF THE WEREWOLF

(1983)

One of Stephen King's quirkier projects, *Cycle of the Werewolf* began as an idea for a calendar. The concept was to create a story that would be told in quick bits in each month on the calendar, and what better monster for such a concept than one that appeared only once (with a rare exception) every month—the night of the full moon.

The story grew, and soon became too unwieldy for a calendar, but the structure remained, so that the 113-page book is divided into twelve chapters, each named for a month. First released in a very limited edition by specialty publisher Land of Enchantment, *Cycle of the Werewolf* was later rereleased in two different 1985 trade paperback editions, one of which tied into the published screenplay of the film version—retitled *Silver Bullet*—and is no longer available.

Cycle of the Werewolf, despite its brevity, is classic King. A werewolf begins to prey on the people of Tarker's Mills, Maine, in January. Six victims are taken, one a month. Then, in July, the werewolf attempts to kill young Marty Coslaw, a ten-year-old boy who is confined to a wheelchair. Marty's Uncle Al had given him fireworks, and he fires them at the creature, blasting out one of its eyes and forcing it to flee.

Marty is sent away to stay with relatives, but when he returns, he searches the citizens of Tarker's Mills for someone with a damaged eye. It isn't until Halloween night, when he sees the Baptist minister Reverend Lowe with an eyepatch, that Marty realizes who the wolf actually is. He sends the reverend notes, urging him to turn himself in or to kill himself. But the reverend has not only become aware of his dual nature, but embraces it.

On New Year's Eve, after Marty has purposely revealed his identity to the reverend, he waits in his own living room with Uncle Al, who has had a pair of silver bullets made for Marty. Though Al doesn't really believe his nephew's claims about the werewolf, he doesn't dare disbelieve, considering the possible consequences. Of course, the wolf comes and attacks, and despite his being confined to his wheelchair, Marty kills it, with Uncle Al and his father as witnesses.

One-room schoolhouse King attended, Durham   DAVID LOWELL

Marty is a classic King character, a boy not unlike so many of his others, Mark Petrie in *'Salem's Lot* (1975) and the young cast of *It* (1986) in particular. He has always written young people with a sureness that reveals how well he must recall or imagine his own youth. But with Marty and Mark Petrie and the youngsters from *It* (who even call themselves "the losers"), there is an additional element. They're the odd kids, out of the mainstream, whose usual playground is within their own minds. They also become the only ones among their families (and neighbors and teachers, etc.) to see that the monster is real and must be stopped. In spite of their status as "different" from other kids, they find the strength to combat the monster and triumph.

Marty is physically disabled, which makes him even more of an outcast, and more heroic. It is no coincidence that of the characters in *It*, Bill Denbrough (who suffers from a severe stutter) is the one to really do the monster in at the end, triumphing over his impediment. Confined to his wheelchair, Marty faces a werewolf down in his living room, making him perhaps the bravest of them all.

CYCLE OF THE WEREWOLF: PRIMARY SUBJECTS

MARTY COSLAW: A ten-year-old boy confined to a wheelchair, Marty is the only one of the werewolf's intended victims to survive. When it first attacks, in July, he fends it off with fireworks, destroying one of its eyes. When he realizes that it is Reverend Lowe, he taunts the clergyman into attacking him again. This time, he is ready with silver bullets his uncle has brought him. It is presumed that Marty still resides in Tarker's Mills.

REVEREND LESTER LOWE: The minister at the local Baptist church, Reverend Lowe is a werewolf. He does not realize his dual nature for some time, but eventually he discovers and embraces it. When he learns that Marty Coslaw might reveal his secret, he tries again to kill the boy, but Marty shoots him dead with silver bullets.

AL: Marty's uncle (his mother's brother), Al doesn't really believe Marty's claims about the reverend's true nature, but the boy is convincing enough to get him to have a pair of silver bullets made for New Year's Eve. Al is with Marty when the werewolf attacks again, and Marty kills the beast. It is presumed that Al still lives in Maine, and visits his sister's family often.

CYCLE OF THE WEREWOLF: ADAPTATIONS

Perhaps the only movie ever to be made from an idea for a monthly calendar, *Stephen King's Silver Bullet* was released by Paramount Pictures in the fall of 1985. It was the *fourth* King movie project produced by Dino De Laurentiis, who clearly wanted a hand in any motion picture that King would participate in in any way. Scripted by King, and helmed by first-time director Daniel Attias, the seven-million-dollar picture is perhaps most notable for its variation of a classic monster theme and its lack of big-name actors. The star, of course, is the werewolf (actually there are a number of variations on the main werewolf), which was created by Italian creature maker Carlo Rambaldi. His human counterpart was played by the wonderful Everett McGill (*Dune, Twin Peaks*). King, De Laurentiis, and Attias reportedly never could completely agree on the right "look" for the monster, and so audiences saw a creature that appeared as much as a weredog or werebear as it did a traditional werewolf.

Nineteen-eighties kid-movie stalwart Corey Haim (*The Goonies, Lost Boys*) played young Marty Coslaw, while Gary Busey (*Lethal Weapon, The Buddy Holly Story*) portrayed Marty's uncle, now called "Red" instead of Al. Although Academy Award nominee Busey is always enjoyable to watch, what is perhaps most extraordinary about the ninety-five-minute feature is how stunningly ordinary it is. There is truly nothing in *Silver Bullet* that anyone with a passing knowledge of werewolf movies hadn't seen before. Had it not been written by the Master of Horror, it's highly unlikely that such a project would ever have gotten out of the special effects makeup room.

CYCLE OF THE WEREWOLF: TRIVIA

- The novella is connected to King's other work in perhaps the most natural of ways—by railroad. The GS&WM train line, noted in King's novella *The Body* (1982), apparently runs through both *that* story's fictional town, Castle Rock, and *Cycle of the Werewolf*'s setting, Tarker's Mills.

28

GERALD'S GAME

(1992)

Just as *Needful Things* (1991) marked the end of one phase of Stephen King's career (basically the "Castle Rock" era), *Gerald's Game* signaled the beginning of another. Over the course of his next four novels, beginning with *Gerald's Game* and ending with *Rose Madder*, King focused much more intensely on character development. He had already written his end-of-the-world novel, *The Stand* (1978), and published what he considered his ultimate statement on supernatural horror in *It* (1986). Perhaps he felt it was time to further investigate the two-legged monsters and maniacs who live just down the street or reside in the adjoining room.

Although the supernatural remained an important element of his fiction, King began a shift to a more realistic style of storytelling, realistic in the mode of books like *Cujo* (1981), *Misery* (1987), and, more recently, *The Girl Who Loved Tom Gordon* (1999). Like those books, *Gerald's Game* features a single character's struggle for survival against overwhelming odds. The novel is an example of the challenges King frequently imposes on himself to keep his creative juices flowing. Here he limits himself to a single character in a single setting to further test his resourcefulness and powers of observation as a writer. It's a tribute to King's talent that he meets these self-imposed challenges so well.

Dedicated to "six good women" (Margaret Spruce Morehouse, Anne

Spruce Labree, Catherine Spruce Graves, Tabitha Spruce King, Stephanie Spruce Leonard, and Marcella Spruce) who have favorably impacted on his life in one way or the other, *Gerald's Game* also signaled the emergence of a more "feminist" King. This may have been perhaps in response to critics who asserted that the most convincing females King was capable of creating were either teenagers or small children.

Beginning with *Gerald's Game*, the theme of "men as monsters" (previously explored briefly in books like *Cujo*, and more explicitly in *It*) emerges again and again in King's work. Gerald Burlingame, the soon-to-die husband of Jessie Burlingame, is the first in a depressingly long line of loathsome males, child-molesting fathers, and wife-beaters King would introduce over the next three to four years.

Originally intended to be one half of a single volume entitled *In the Path of the Eclipse*, *Gerald's Game* is a companion piece to King's next novel, *Dolores Claiborne* (1993). The total eclipse of the sun on July 20, 1963, plays an important part in both novels. During that solar event, twelve-year-old Jessie is molested by her father, while many miles and an entire novel away, Dolores Claiborne slays her abusive husband, Joe St. George. Both characters briefly have visions of the other later in that fateful day. Their strange bond persists some thirty years later. On the day her employer, Vera Donovan, passes away, Dolores thinks of Jessie, and somehow knows "she's in terrible trouble." The eclipse acts as a powerful metaphor in both novels, expressing the notion of secrets once hidden in the dark, eventually emerging into the light of day.

Gerald's Game, *Dolores Claiborne*, and *Rose Madder* all showcase women who, over the course of these novels, learn how to exert control over their lives. *Gerald's Game* is perhaps the most intense and immediate, relating Jessie's life-and-death struggle to free herself from physical and mental bonds.

GERALD'S GAME: PRIMARY SUBJECTS

JESSIE BURLINGAME: Though she is always reluctant to do so, Jessie participates in mild bondage games that her husband finds sexually arousing. Over time, she becomes more and more disturbed by these games, but when he pleads with her, Jessie allows Gerald to handcuff her to a bed at their cabin at Lake Kashwakamak, Maine. Finally having had enough, Jessie demands to be freed from her bonds. Pretending not to understand, Gerald ignores her pleas. Enraged, Jessie lashes out at her husband, kicking him solidly in the chest. The blow triggers a heart attack, and Gerald slumps to the floor, dead. Jessie finds herself alone, almost naked, and handcuffed to the bed, in a cabin on a remote dirt road.

Thus begins a twenty-eight-hour ordeal that results in both injury and healing—and changes the woman forever.

The bedroom becomes Jessie's entire world—her major concerns lay in how to reach a glass of water on the shelf behind her, and the handcuff keys on the bureau in front of her. Her attempts to free herself became increasingly gruesome, building to the point where she uses her own blood as a lubricant to slip off one of the cuffs.

Wracked by pain and dehydration, Jessie begins to hallucinate. She engages in imaginary conversations with friends and family, and with her mental alter ego, the demure "Goodwife Burlingame." What Jessie doesn't realize is that her mind is attempting to tell her something, trying to get her to confront a horrible incident she has spent her whole life trying to forget. Alternating between the rational and delusional, Jessie eventually uncovers the buried memory of what had unfortunately become the central event of her life: the day of the eclipse, July 20, 1963, when her father molested her. Her father's abuse has since ruined her life, perhaps even causing her poor decisions that have led to her present predicament.

Due to the cabin's utter isolation, it is unlikely someone will find her before she starves to death. Things are complicated by the appearance of Prince the dog, a hungry stray who feasts on Gerald's corpse. Finally, there is "the dead cowboy . . . the specter of love," a hideous creature who shows up at the cabin and simply stares at her. In her delirium, she mistakes the hazy figure for her father, returned from the dead. Later, she realizes that the figure was real. Shortly after she escapes her bonds, the figure reappears, bent on doing her harm. Summoning all her remaining strength, Jessie escapes and flees in her Mercedes.

Although Jessie achieves closure of sorts regarding her molestation, the experience leaves her physically and mentally traumatized. For months after, she lives as a virtual recluse, shutting herself off from the world. It is only when she reads in the newspaper about the ghoulish Andrew Ray Joubert that she begins to emerge from her self-imposed isolation. Jessie realizes that Joubert is the spectral figure who haunted her during her strange imprisonment. Traveling to the court where Joubert is being tried for various perverted sex crimes, she confronts him and, when he laughs at her, spits in his face. This act of defiance is, hopefully, an indication that Jessie may be on the road to a full recovery.

GERALD BURLINGAME:

A lawyer by trade, Gerald hopes to revitalize his listless marriage by cajoling his wife into participating in bondage games. Jessie goes along out of love and a desire to keep the peace, but is enraged one day when her husband willfully ignores her repeated requests to open the handcuffs that chain her to the bed in their remote cabin. Gerald's brutish behavior angers Jessie, who kicks him in the chest, triggering a fatal heart attack. His corpse is later partially consumed by a stray dog. Fortunately for Jessie, Gerald had purchased significant amounts of life insurance—at his death, she receives several large checks, allowing her to live comfortably for the remainder of her life.

ANDREW RAY JOUBERT:

Joubert, who suffers from acromegaly (a progressive enlargement of the hands, feet, and face that causes his forehead to bulge and his arms to dangle all the way down to his knees), began to indulge his perverted sexual desires first by vandalizing graves, then escalated into looting crypts and mausoleums. From these grisly activities, he graduates to taking body parts—noses, arms, feet, hands—and having sex with male corpses. Although the police investigation lasts over seven years, it is kept very quiet, and is not reported in the press until he is apprehended in the act. Searching Joubert's van, police discover a variety of body parts and cutting tools. On the front seat is a sandwich—a human tongue on Wonder Bread, slathered with yellow mustard.

Before his arrest, Joubert comes upon the captive Jessie in the cabin at Lake Kashwakamak. She thinks he is a hallucination, but only when she is free, and realizes he was real, does he try to attack her. Later, Jessie appears at his arraignment, and spits in his face.

GERALD'S GAME: TRIVIA

- Joubert is later mentioned briefly in *Insomnia* (1994) by a stranger who is involved in a car accident with Ed Deepneau.

29

DOLORES CLAIBORNE

(1993)

In the 1990s, Stephen King spent a great deal of creative time broadening his approach to horror by exploring the psyche, and concentrating less on the supernatural, in a number of books including *Gerald's Game* (1992), *Insomnia* (1994), and *Rose Madder* (1995). Primary among these is *Dolores Claiborne*, in which the author created one of his most complex and memorable characters.

A novel executed in the form of a monologue, *Dolores Claiborne* is a well-conceived, marvelously executed work of art that also functions as a distorted mirror for the events of *Gerald's Game*. The book explores themes similar to those explored in King's previous novel, this time from the perspective of an older woman. In *Gerald's Game*, a father molested a daughter, but the girl's mother never knows, attributing her child's subsequent odd behavior to a contrary personality. In contrast, Dolores discovers a similar problem and takes brutal action to stamp it out. In each case, the molestation has severe consequences some thirty years later. Both women are forced to confront their past, Jessie because of her perilous situation, Dolores because she has been accused of killing her long-time employer, the formidable Vera Donovan.

The relationship between Dolores and Vera echoes situations in King's own past, events about which he wrote in his memorable 1984 short story

"Gramma." There, as in *Dolores Claiborne*, an elderly, bedridden woman terrorizes a household.

In "Gramma," the title character turns out to be a witch who steals her grandson's soul and takes over his body. In *Dolores Claiborne*, the character Vera Donovan fills a similar role, in a decidedly nonsupernatural manner. These plot elements may be a reflection of the uneasy relationship between King's mother, Ruth, and his invalid maternal grandmother. Ruth King cared for her mother for many years, enduring her many demands and abusive tongue.

Readers sympathize with Dolores, both because of the skillful way King builds her characterization and because of the totally unsympathetic way he renders her husband, the sniveling Joe St. George. As in *Gerald's Game*, men are portrayed as the enemy, both for their actions and their complicity. Dolores's father beats her mother, and Joe St. George beats Dolores. Dolores knows it's a male-dominated world, but is nonetheless stunned when reminded, as when she confronts the bank manager who let Joe close out their joint accounts without even advising her. By adding on the injustices done to Dolores, the author deftly switches the expected sympathies on his readers—we quickly move from "Did she do it?" to "Why didn't she do it sooner?"

Although this book downplays the horror and the supernatural elements that his readers have come to expect in the majority of his work, there are discomforting glimmers of both in the narrative. One obvious supernatural touch is the strange link between Dolores and Jessie Burlingame (see the chapter on *Gerald's Game*). King also betrays his lifelong fondness for EC Comics–type touches—Joe's plaintive wails of "Duh-lorrr-iss" issuing from the well bring to mind the mutterings of the assorted reanimated corpses who rise up to torment their killers in those gleefully ghastly comic book stories.

Dolores Claiborne is also a remarkable example of King as a regional writer, an aspect previously revealed in shorter works like "Mrs. Todd's Shortcut" (1984), *The Sun Dog* (1990), and the prologue to *Needful Things* (1991). Dolores is clearly a product of her environment, from her practical, pragmatic morality to her thick Maine accent. Her home, Little Tall Island, is a microcosm for her rural state, revealing both its glory and its blemishes.

DOLORES CLAIBORNE: PRIMARY SUBJECTS

DOLORES CLAIBORNE: Suspected of murdering Vera Donovan, the ancient, rich, "off-island" woman who employs her first as a maid and then as a caregiver/companion, sixty-six-year-old Dolores Claiborne insists she is innocent. Even though the foul-mouthed, hardheaded, outspoken islander denies that crime, she readily admits to the police, by way of explaining more recent events, that she killed her reprobate husband, Joe St. George, some thirty years before.

As Dolores tells it, Joe was a mean, ill-tempered, dishonest alcoholic who, after physically abusing her, was likely to brag about it to his low-life friends. One night, Joe hits her in the back with a piece of firewood, hurting her very badly. When she is finally able to stand again, Dolores takes swift action, smashing Joe in the side of the head with a cream pitcher, then holding him off with a hatchet.

Dolores promises Joe that if he ever hits her again she would bury the hatchet in his head. Joe, agreeing to end the abuse, finds he is no longer able to perform sexually in bed. Flaunting his behavior, he begins abusing their daughter Selena, first by playing on her sympathies, then by demanding sexual favors. This, together with his mistreatment of their sons, proves too much for Dolores, who decides to leave Joe and move to the mainland with her children.

However, when Dolores seeks to withdraw the money from the local bank she had been saving to send the children to college, she discovers that Joe had secretly transferred her savings to his own account. Later, the frustrated Dolores breaks down in front of her long-time employer, widow Vera Donovan, who, comforting her, told her that sometimes an accident can be a woman's best friend. She cited herself as an example, pointing out that she inherited her husband's estate when he passed away. Vera gives Dolores the impression that she may have been instrumental in her spouse's demise.

Inspired by Vera's example, and desperate to save herself and her children from further abuse, Dolores devises a plan to dispatch her husband. On July 20, 1963, the day of a total eclipse of the sun, Dolores gets Joe drunk, then tricks him into running over the rotted wood covering of an abandoned well she'd discovered near their home. He falls through the flimsy covering over that well, a tumble that proves fatal.

The widowed Dolores raises her children and sends them out into the world. She continues working for Vera Donovan, evolving from maid into primary caregiver. Over the years, Vera deteriorates mentally and physically, and lives in irrational fear of the "dust bunnies" under her bed, afraid they will kill her. One morning, she becomes so frightened by them that she flees her bedroom and in a panic throws herself down a staircase. Near death, she pleads with Dolores to kill her. Dolores reluctantly agrees, but is saved from performing this grisly duty when Vera expires. The police, however, suspect foul play. At the police station, Dolores reveals her involvement in Joe's death.

Eventually cleared of a possible "wrongful death" in the demise of Vera Donovan, it is presumed that Dolores Claiborne still resides on Little Tall Island.

VERA DONOVAN: Vera Donovan is a wealthy widow who lives on Little Tall Island, Maine, and who employs Dolores Claiborne as a maid and later general caregiver for over thirty years. During that time, in a strange way, Vera and Dolores became best friends. The two women understand and respect each other, accepting abuse from one another they simply would not tolerate from anyone else. It is Vera, who very likely murdered her own abusive husband, who gives Dolores the idea to kill Joe St. George. Vera becomes quite mentally unstable in her later years, terrified of the "dust bunnies" living under her bed. One day she flees her bedroom in abject terror and leaps down a flight of stairs, an irrational act that causes her death.

JOE ST. GEORGE: Joe is a chronically unemployed, drunken coward, a despicable man who sees nothing wrong with physically, sexually, and emotionally abusing his wife and children. Joe, a classic ne'er-do-well, is manipulated by his wife, Dolores Claiborne, into falling into an abandoned well. Although injured, he climbs out, only to have Dolores push him back down. He dies when struck by a large rock Dolores shoved down the well.

SELENA ST. GEORGE: Dolores's daughter and eldest child, Selena is another victim of Joe St. George, who abused her mentally and sexually. Selena escapes further mistreatment at the hands of her father only because her mother killed him. Selena grows up to be a successful but troubled journalist in Manhattan. It is presumed that she still resides in New York City.

DR. JOHN MCAULIFFE: The medical examiner who investigates Joe St. George's death, McAuliffe suspects that something was amiss. He questions Dolores closely about her activities on the day Joe died, but is unable to shake her story. McAuliffe reluctantly renders a finding of "death by misadventure" regarding Joe's demise.

LITTLE TALL ISLAND: A tiny island off the coast of central Maine, Little Tall is the home of Dolores Claiborne and Vera Donovan.

DOLORES CLAIBORNE: ADAPTATIONS

Released in 1995, the R-rated film version of *Dolores Claiborne* starred Kathy Bates in the title role and was directed by Taylor Hackford. Bates, of course, won an Oscar for her portrayal of another King character, the demented Annie Wilkes in *Misery*. The movie also starred Jennifer Jason Leigh as Selena St. George and Christopher Plummer as Lt. John Mackey (Dr. John McAuliffe in the novel).

The 131-minute feature is a compelling yet strange reflection of the book—Tony Gilory's screenplay focuses far more on Selena and Mackey/McAuliffe than does King's novel. Selena returns to Little Tall Island to be at her mother's side after Dolores is accused of murdering Vera Donovan. The estranged daughter has repressed the memory of her father's abuse, but her ugly memories soon resurface due to her mother's current problems.

Mackey, convinced that Dolores escaped justice thirty years before, returns, seeking vengeance. In the movie, Dolores does not confess to Joe's murder; the viewer learns the facts via a series of flashbacks. Mackey brings Dolores up on charges, but Selena is able to convince the presiding magistrate of her mother's innocence.

Kathy Bates brings Dolores to life, dominating the screen when allowed, and some key scenes from the novel—Vera's death, the night Dolores stands up to Joe, the afternoon Dolores learns her spouse stole her savings, and Selena's recounting of Joe's molestation—are faithfully and powerfully rendered. Jennifer Jason Leigh gives yet another outstanding performance as a emotionally scarred survivor of her dysfunctional childhood. The script, however, focuses entirely too much on Selena and Mackey, diminishing the intense, powerful woman whom readers come to know so intimately in King's book. The fact that Dolores, an outspoken, proud woman if there ever was one, does not speak in her own defense at her hearing is a perfect example of the movie's conceptual flaws.

DOLORES CLAIBORNE: TRIVIA

- Little Tall Island, where *Dolores Claiborne* is set, is also the setting for the 1999 television miniseries *Storm of the Century*.

- The actress Frances Sternhagen, who appeared in such King film and television projects as *Misery* (1990) and *Golden Years* (1991), was the reader on the *Dolores Claiborne* audiobook, on which she gave a truly memorable performance.

- Atropos, a figure from Greek mythology mentioned in *Dolores Claiborne*, is also a character in *Insomnia* (1994).

30

STORM OF THE CENTURY
(1999)

Promoted widely as Stephen King's first "novel for television," *Storm of the Century* was broadcast by ABC during the February sweeps period in 1999, and its massive screenplay was simultaneously published in trade paperback by Pocket Books. In a lengthy introduction, King relates the genesis of the story and provides fascinating background notes to the production. Former *Wings* TV sitcom star Tim Daly has the lead role as Mike Anderson, while Debrah Farentino plays his wife, Molly. Casey Siemaszko plays Mike's able deputy, Alton "Hatch" Hatcher, and Jeffrey DeMunn (who also appears in the feature film version of *The Green Mile*, released later that same year) adds a lot of color as Robbie Beals. In the pivotal role of Linoge is Colm Feore.

As he had done so often in recent productions, King hand-picked the director for the massive, 35-million-dollar production that ran for six hours over three nights. He was Craig R. Baxley, a relatively unknown filmmaker of such exploitation movies as *The Twilight Man* (1996) and *I Come in Peace* (1990), starring Dolph Lundgren.

As we have with *Golden Years* (1991), *Sleepwalkers* (1992), and others, we must consider the TV miniseries as much a part of the Stephen King Universe as any work of prose. Indeed, it is a vital part of the universe and a very worthy addition to the canon of King's work.

Storm of the Century is a story about community, no doubt about that. But it's a disturbing tale of community, almost perverse in the pleasure it takes in depicting a group of people who come together to make an impossible decision. It also plays on a subject that became very familiar and dear to King in the 1990s: secrecy.

In his introduction to the published screenplay, King discusses the milieu of the narrative by drawing comparisons and contrasts between the self-sufficiency and isolation of small-town people in general, and island people in particular. There are similarities, of course. King grew up in a small town in Maine, so when he created 'Salem's Lot, Castle Rock, and Derry, he knew what he was writing about.

But when he devised Little Tall Island, the setting for this story and for *Dolores Claiborne* (1993), he admits he was writing as "an outsider." You'd never know it. What King has observed here is that, as insular and familial as small towns can be, they are positively cosmopolitan in comparison to island communities. The people of Little Tall Island are, as a group, descended from half a dozen families who first settled there. Thanks to matrimony and reproduction, it can be extrapolated that, in one sense or another, they are nearly all family to one another in some way.

Like a family, they keep each other's secrets, no matter how great. They maintain this silence with the mainland world, certainly, but also with each other. Just as many families do not discuss the dark truths they have kept hidden, the entire community of Little Tall Island keeps their own counsel. They may know that one of their number, Peter Godsoe, imports marijuana, but they'll never speak of it. They may be aware of who has slept with whom, and which local deaths might not have been accidental. However, they'll not share that knowledge. Even in the company of others who are aware of them, such grave matters are not discussed.

Like the secret of *Dolores Claiborne*, some years previous to the events of *Storm of the Century*. And the truth about what really happened to those who "disappeared" in the storm.

There is an interesting parallel that can be drawn between this chronicle and another King creation, *Needful Things* (1991), which was billed as "the last Castle Rock story." Comparing the two illustrates what King is expressing about island communities.

Like *Storm*, *Needful Things* relates the account of a community with horrible secrets; in both, an evil stranger comes to town with intimate knowledge of those guarded secrets and uses it to tear the town apart. Like *Storm*, at the center of the plotline is the town's top lawman. But while the structure of the two narratives may seem quite similar at first, the differences set *Storm of the Century* apart as not merely its own entity, but one with a far more insidious nature.

In *Needful Things*, as in *'Salem's Lot* (1975), and on a much larger scale, *The Stand* (1978), there is a crisis that shatters the society, pitting residents against one another. The island village self-destructs, until an individual or individuals with the necessary moral strength makes a stand against the evil that has poisoned the populace and, to greater or lesser degrees depending on which story you examine . . . wins.

Good triumphs over evil and, particularly, over chaos.

But in *Storm of the Century*, the island community is not splintered. It is too tightly woven to be torn asunder so simply. Instead, the neighborhood is drawn together to face the crisis, and to make a terrible decision: to face probable death at the hands of a profoundly evil creature, or to willingly give one of their children to that same demonic force. Any parent worthy of the job knows the only real decision.

But that isn't really practical, is it? When the entire town must decide, and their lives are in jeopardy as well, how can we expect them to choose the life of someone else's child over their own safety? Apparently we can't, for the people of Little Tall Island vote, in a relatively orderly and traditional fashion, to give the demonic sorcerer Andre Linoge one of their children.

The chosen child? The son of our hero, Mike Anderson, the island's constable. Linoge takes little Ralphie Anderson away to corrupt and raise as his own and transform into a being just like Linoge himself, and the town breathes a sigh of relief that it is done. Except for Mike and Molly Anderson, whose lives are destroyed by what their community has decided.

But just like the rest of the people on Little Tall, they keep the secret.

STORM OF THE CENTURY: PRIMARY SUBJECTS

MIKE ANDERSON: The constable of Little Tall Island and the owner of Anderson's, the community's general store, Mike has lived there all his life. When Andre Linoge comes to town and murders Martha Clarendon, Mike and his deputy, Alton "Hatch" Hatcher, are the ones who arrest him. Anderson is also one of the first to suspect that Linoge is not precisely human.

When Linoge has suitably terrified the town, caused the murder of several of its inhabitants, and stolen the minds of its children, it quickly becomes apparent that the monstrous being regards Mike as his main opposition. Finally, when Linoge presents the locals with his ultimatum—give up one of their children willingly to be trained by him and become what he is, in order to save all their lives—Mike is the sole opposing voice.

The fact that Molly Anderson, Mike's wife, is willing to make a deal with Linoge, at the possible expense of their son, Ralphie, destroys the marriage in an instant. In due course, the worst happens, and Ralphie is indeed chosen. Linoge takes the boy away, and when Mike goes to stop him, the townspeople prevent him from doing so, in order to save themselves.

Not long thereafter, Mike leaves Molly and Little Tall Island forever. He takes to the road for a while, and ends up in San Francisco. There he goes back to school, and eventually becomes a federal marshal. It is on the streets of San Francisco that he sees Linoge and Ralphie again. Years have passed. His son is now a teenager, and doesn't recognize his father.

In response to Mike's approach, Ralphie hisses, revealing fangs just like Linoge's. He has become something horrendous, something evil. Linoge has won. However, Mike Anderson isn't a quitter. Now that he has seen Ralphie again, he knows his son is out there and that Linoge still lives, and as long as both are true, there is always the possibility that Mike will try to track them down.

ANDRE LINOGE: "I've lived a long time—thousands of years—but I'm not a god, nor am I one of the immortals." Those are the words of Andre Linoge when he finally identifies himself and his desires to the people of Little Tall Island.

What he is, however, is not much clearer than that. It seems likely that he is related to creatures such as Randall Flagg of *The Stand* (1978), *The Dark Tower* series (1982–present), and *The Eyes of the Dragon* (1987). Linoge has a great many extraordinary abilities. To see the truth in the darkest corners of people's thoughts, to control minds, to whisk people away to another dimension slightly out of sync with our own, to move objects with his mind, to change his appearance and mingle with the shadows: those are only a sampling of Linoge's talents.

But powerful as he is, Linoge will die eventually. Since his mortality became apparent to him, he has attempted to find a human child he can transform and teach and make his own, a youngster he can mold to become what he is. At least once before he came to Little Tall—namely, on Roanoke Island, Virginia, in 1587—Linoge attempted to force a community of humans to provide him the heir he requires. It didn't work then, and in retaliation he destroyed the entire population.

It should be noted that the word "Croaton," which may be the name of an ancient city or something completely different, is associated with Linoge's visits to any given place.

RALPH "RALPHIE" ANDERSON: The son of Mike and Molly Anderson, Ralphie seems, from the very beginning, to be afforded special attention by Linoge. When Ralphie is chosen to be handed over to the stranger, it does not seem an accident or whim. Years later, when he encounters his father again, Ralphie does not seem to recognize Mike. By then, Ralph Anderson has already begun to transform into whatever manner of being Andre Linoge is.

MOLLY ANDERSON: The town's day-care provider, Molly is the wife of Mike Anderson and the mother of Ralph. When the question is put to her, rather than standing with her husband in defiance of Linoge, Molly agrees with the townspeople to risk a single child's life to save them all. After Ralph is taken away by Linoge and Mike leaves her, Molly undergoes therapy and eventually marries Hatch. It is believed Molly still lives on Little Tall.

ROBBIE BEALS: The town manager, Robbie clashes with Mike Anderson a great deal over the initial treatment of the situation with Andre Linoge. Hated by his wife, Sandra, and father to bratty Don Beals, Robbie is not a very likeable man. He is tormented by Linoge's knowledge that when Robbie's mother was ailing, he put her in a disgusting rest home, and he was with a whore on the mainland when she died. According to Linoge, Robbie's mother has become a cannibal now that she's in hell, and she plans to eat him when he gets down there, over and over again, because that's what hell is about: "repetition."

Sandra Beals drowns herself seven years after the storm, though she leaves the word "Croaton" written on the boat she has taken out into the water. Apparently she was still haunted by Linoge or at least his memory.

It is presumed that Robbie and his son, Don, still live on Little Tall.

MARTHA CLARENDON: An innocent old woman, Martha Clarendon is Linoge's first victim on Little Tall. He clubs her to death with his silver wolf's-head cane. Her body is found by Davey Hopewell.

CAT WITHERS: An employee at Anderson's General Store, Cat is impregnated by Billy Soames and doesn't tell a soul, even Billy (because she knows he is cheating on her). Instead, she has the baby aborted on the mainland. Cat is eventually mesmerized by Linoge and his wolf's-head cane and is influenced into beating Billy to death with the cane.

It is presumed that Cat still lives on Little Tall.

ALTON "HATCH" HATCHER: Mike Anderson's deputy, Hatch and his wife, Melinda, have a daughter, Pippa, who is in Molly Anderson's day care. Melinda works at Anderson's. A year after the storm, Melinda dies of a heart attack, and eventually Hatch marries Molly Anderson. It is presumed that Hatch, Molly, and Pippa still live on Little Tall.

LITTLE TALL ISLAND: Located just across the reach from Machias on the coast of Maine, Little Tall Island is, nevertheless, a world away. The people there are descended from its original settlers, and the community knows how to keep secrets.

THE WOLF'S-HEAD CANE: Linoge's cane seems to be either the source of his power or a significant outlet for it. The stick can appear and disappear at will, moves of its own accord, and mesmerizes humans, and its wolf's-head both moves and hisses.

ROANOKE (1587): In 1587 the entire population of Roanoke Island, Virginia, disappeared. Their fate is a mystery, but according to Andre Linoge, he forced them all to take their own lives after they refused to provide him with an appropriate heir.

MACHIAS: A mainland town just across the water from Little Tall Island.

STORM OF THE CENTURY: TRIVIA

- In *Storm of the Century*, Robbie Beals makes specific reference to Dolores Claiborne, and the secrets the islanders have kept about her for years before the events of this story. This is another link solidifying the Stephen King Universe.

- Stephen King, in a cameo role, appears on Martha Clarendon's television set while Andre Linoge sits and waits to be arrested.

- Though no mention of it is made in the dialogue, in the published script of *Storm of the Century*, King notes in passing that Catrina Withers is reading to the children from *The Little Puppy*, a book that the author notes was "a great favorite of Danny Torrance's, once upon a time." Danny Torrance, of course, is the little boy in *The Shining* (1977).

31

THE GIRL WHO LOVED TOM GORDON

(1999)

*T*he world had teeth and it could bite you with them anytime it wanted. *Trisha McFarland discovered this when she was nine years old."*

So begins *The Girl Who Loved Tom Gordon,* a novel that, despite its relatively average size (it's a mere slip of a book for King, weighing in at only 224 pages), manages to touch on many of Stephen King's favorite themes: spirituality, baseball, children in jeopardy, and the uneasy feeling that something bad is always lurking just over the horizon.

The book came as a total surprise to everyone—his fans, his publisher, and, in fact, to the author himself. (In a note to reviewers accompanying promotional copies of this novel, King said, "If books were babies, I'd call *The Girl Who Loved Tom Gordon* the result of an unplanned pregnancy.") King's idea, conceived during a baseball game at Boston's Fenway Park, was to write a variation on "Hansel and Gretel," only without Hansel. The end result was a modern fairy tale divided into nine "innings" rather than chapters, a thoughtful reflection on the nature of God with echoes of Jack London's classic story "To Light a Fire" thrown in for good measure.

King has been writing about God—the possibility of God, and the ramifications of His existence—for over two decades now, in books as diverse as *The Stand* (1978) and *Desperation* (1996). Lost in the woods, young Trisha McFarland, the central character in *The Girl Who Loved Tom*

Gordon, finds herself contemplating this subject as well; praying, she reflects on a conversation she had with her father a month before. During that talk, she asked him if he believed in God. Her bemused dad said he didn't have faith in a God that marks the death "of every bird in Australia or every bug in India." But he does believe there has to be *something;* he refers to this "insensate force for the good" as the "Subaudible," reflecting his belief in a benevolent deity who doesn't necessarily involve himself in humanity's day-to-day activities.

The author walks a fine line between these two concepts, never quite committing to either one. This being a Stephen King novel, however, there is a countervailing force, a malevolent entity that Trisha comes to think of as "the God of the Lost." This god feeds on her fear, waiting for the proper moment to strike.

Utterly realistic, this *bildungsroman*, or coming-of-age fiction, nevertheless contains numerous references to the Stephen King Universe. For example, listening to her Walkman, Trisha picks up radio station WCAS in Castle Rock, a town she remembers passing through once on her way to the Appalachian Trail. The town has apparently recovered from the massive wounds Leland Gaunt inflicted on it—in delivering the local news, the announcer mentions that folks in the Rock are up in arms about a bar that is featuring topless dancers, and that Castle Rock Speedway is supposed to reopen on the Fourth of July.

THE GIRL WHO LOVED TOM GORDON: PRIMARY SUBJECTS

TRISHA McFARLAND: Nine years old, but "big for her age," Trisha McFarland finds herself in an uncomfortable position after her parents' divorce. Although favoring her father, Trisha is placed in her mother's custody, along with her older brother, Pete. Life with her mother is okay, but Trisha feels that her whiny brother gets all the attention. Coerced into participating in a six-mile hike (part of her mother's forced program of family togetherness), Trisha wanders off the trail to relieve herself and to escape her mother and brother's constant bickering. Mistakenly believing that she is only a few yards from the trail, Trisha loses her bearings. But because she keeps moving, she quickly places herself beyond the reach of even the most diligent search party.

Trisha spends nine days wandering in the forest, searching for a way out. She proves quite resourceful, surviving due to bits and pieces of forest lore she has managed to store up over her young life. Desperate for food, and nearly dehydrated, Trisha begins to hallucinate, imagining that she is being accompanied by her hero, Boston Red Sox relief pitcher Tom Gordon. At first merely a silent, reassuring presence, Gordon eventually begins to talk to her, revealing his philosophy on being a good closer in the game. Trisha takes this advice to heart; it proves invaluable when she is forced to confront the God of the Lost, a malevolent presence that has been stalking her since she entered the forest.

Trisha survives her ordeal. When last seen, she was recuperating from pneumonia in a hospital bed.

TOM GORDON: Lost in the woods, Trisha finds herself imagining that her favorite Boston Red Sox player, relief pitcher Tom Gordon, is with her. She fantasizes that he is keeping her company and providing guidance on how to tough out the terrible situation in which she finds herself. Tom's presence keeps her sane; his advice helps her stay alive. Tom tells Trisha that, like a relief pitcher, it's God's nature to come on in the bottom of the ninth. He also advises her that the secret of being a good closer is establishing who is better—you can let your opponent beat you, but you must not beat yourself.

These are the thoughts that cascade through Trisha's mind when the God of the Lost confronts her near the end of her journey. The God, having taken the form of a bear, looms over the girl, ready to maul her. Trisha faces the deadly animal, pelting it between the eyes with her Walkman, delivering a pitch her hero would surely appreciate.

(It should be noted for non-sports fans that professional baseball player Tom Gordon, #36, actually exists. In 1998, he saved forty-four games for King's beloved Red Sox. Gordon is famous for what one character in *The Girl Who Loved Tom Gordon* refers to as "that pointin' thing"—after each successful save, he points briefly to the sky, acknowledging God's presence.)

LARRY McFARLAND: Trisha's dad, a folksy man given to saying things like, "I believe it's beer o'clock." Larry and his daughter are quite close, bonding during the many happy hours they spend together watching and discussing their favorite team, the Boston Red Sox. Larry introduces Trisha to the idea of the "Subaudible." Although Larry takes comfort in his wife's bed during their ordeal, it seems apparent that they will not reconcile.

QUILLA ANDERSON: Trisha's mother, she does the best she can as a single parent of two children. Forced to minister to her whiny son, Pete, Quilla virtually ignores her daughter, Trisha. This benign neglect contributes to Trisha's exasperation with her mother and brother, an emotion that leads her to abandon the trail and become lost in the Maine woods.

THE SUBAUDIBLE: Larry McFarland's name for the force "that keeps drunken teenagers—most drunken teenagers—from crashing their cars when they're coming home from the senior prom or their first big rock concert. That keeps most planes from crashing even when something goes wrong." Larry believes that the very fact that no country has used a nuclear weapon on living people since 1945 suggests that *something* must be looking out for the human race. He calls that something the Subaudible.

THE THREE ROBED FIGURES: Trisha hallucinates this trio, who represent the various gods Trisha has been thinking about during her trek. Two of them are in white garb, one wears black. The first, who resembles Mr. Bork, Trisha's science teacher at Sanford Elementary School, is clothed in white. He tells Trisha he represents the God of Tom Gordon, the "one he points up to when he gets the save." He also informs her that Tom's God can't help, being busy with other things: "As a rule he doesn't intervene in human affairs, anyway, although I must admit he is a sports fan. Not necessarily a Red Sox fan, however."

The second figure is also outfitted in white. He resembles Trisha's father, Larry McFarland. When Trisha asks him if he comes from the Subaudible, he tells her he *is* the Subaudible. Stating that he is "quite weak," the figure tells her that he, too, cannot help her. The third figure, draped in black, lifts its claws to its hood, pushing it back to reveal a misshapen head made of wasps. "I come from the thing in the woods," he tells her. "I come from the God of the Lost. It has been watching you. It has been waiting for you. It is your miracle, and you are its."

THE GOD OF THE WOODS: Also known as the God of the Lost. Shortly into her odyssey, Trisha realizes she is not entirely alone—something subhuman, purely evil, is stalking her, waiting for an opportunity to strike. Trisha knows instinctively that it can take her anytime it wants, but is merely waiting for her to "ripen." The God of the Woods confronts Trisha at the end of the novel, taking the form of a bear.

TRAVIS HERRICK: A poacher, Travis is hunting for an out-of-season deer when he comes upon a little girl facing off against a bear. The youngster is Trisha, the bear is the God of the Lost. Herrick shoots the bear's ear off seconds before Trisha hits him in the head with her thrown Walkman. Shaken, the bear lumbers off into the woods. Rather than a fine, Travis instead becomes a hero, receiving a float in Grafton Notch's 1998 Fourth of July parade.

THE GIRL WHO LOVED TOM GORDON:
TRIVIA

- Actress Anne Heche narrated an unabridged audio version.

- At 224 pages in the hardcover edition, *The Girl Who Loved Tom Gordon* is King's second-shortest published novel to date, after *Carrie*.

- In 2004, a pop-up version of *Girl* aimed at a younger audience was published by Little Simon, a division of Simon and Schuster. King's novel was adapted by suspense writer Peter Abrahams. The book featured illustrations by Alan Dingman and paper engineering by Kees Moerbeek.

32

KINGDOM HOSPITAL

(2004)

T his fifteen-hour novel for television was inspired by a 1994 Dutch miniseries, *Riget* (a.k.a. *The Kingdom*), by film director Lars von Trier. That series, which proved popular enough to spawn a sequel, was about a haunted hospital whose quirky staff is too busy engaging in petty bureaucratic squabbles to take notice of the supernatural mayhem occurring all around them.

King became aware of *The Kingdom* while on location in Estes, Colorado, for the filming of the 1997 remake of *The Shining*, where he rented and viewed a VHS tape of the miniseries. Feeling an affinity for the material, he secured the necessary rights to adapt Trier's material for an American audience. King put his own spin on the story by adding a subplot about a famous artist who is admitted to the hospital after being struck by a car (sound familiar?).

To bring the series to the screen, King (himself an executive producer) once again allied himself with director Craig R. Baxley and executive producer Mark Carliner. The series was scored by Gary Chang, who had also performed that task on *Rose Red* and *Storm of the Century*.

A cross between *Twin Peaks* and *E.R.*, or *E.R.* and King's own *The Shining*, *Kingdom Hospital*'s premiere garnered significant ratings, but failed to keep its audience, losing significant chunks of its viewership as the series progressed. ABC seemed to lose faith in the series, and began shuffling its airdates, further reducing any potential audience by making it difficult to find (according to King, the show "went from initial ratings of 5.5 to 3.7 to 2.3, finally bottoming out at something like a 1.0, which is basically the ratings equivalent of the black death"). Musing about why the show failed in a column in *Entertainment Weekly* titled "A Kingdom That Didn't Come," King theorized that the show required its viewers to do a lot of "heavy lifting" in the first few episodes, work they apparently weren't willing to do.

Although a bit over the top at times, *Kingdom Hospital* did have its moments. Two episodes, the ninth and tenth in the series, were especially noteworthy. Episode 9, entitled "Butterfingers," featured a Bill Buckneresque character named Earl "Error" Candleton, whose untimely error cost his team, the Robins, the 1987 World Series title. Through the intervention of Peter and Mary, Earl travels back in time, makes the play, and avoids fifteen years of heartbreak. The episode was an odd foreshadowing of the Boston Red Sox's journey to baseball redemption later in 2004 (it also heralded Roland's loop back in time to when he made the mistake of failing to pick up the horn of Eld at Jericho Hill). Episode 10, "The Passion of Reverend Jimmy," was a touching retelling of the story of the life and death of Jesus Christ, giving the series its second uplifting episode in as many weeks.

Following the lead of King's previous miniseries, *Rose Red*, *Kingdom Hospital* spawned a companion diary, entitled *The Journals of Eleanor Druse: My Investigation of the Kingdom Hospital Incident*. Purporting to be Mrs. Druse's personal account of her investigations into the psychic phenomena at Kingdom Hospital, it chronicles a period beginning in December 2002 and ending in November 2003, a few months before the miniseries begins. The book, written by King's collaborator on the series, Richard Dooling (who wrote episodes 6, 7, and 8 and cowrote 5), enjoyed modest commercial success.

KINGDOM HOSPITAL: PRIMARY SUBJECTS

PETER RICKMAN: A gifted artist, Peter Rickman functions as King's alter ego in the miniseries. Rickman (perhaps named after British horror writer Phil Rickman) finds himself in Kingdom Hospital after he is struck by a vehicle driven by the stoned David Hooman. Initially in a coma, the badly injured Rickman awakens with telepathic powers, coming into contact with several supernatural creatures, including Antubis, Mary Jensen, and the teenage boy Paul. Peter, who witnesses many wonders while a patient in Kingdom Hospital, is instrumental in solving the mystery that haunts the cursed institution.

NATALIE RICKMAN: Peter Rickman's wife, she stays by his side during his ordeal. To pass the time, she reads the book *Misery,* by an author named Stephen King.

OTTO: A visually impaired security guard at Kingdom Hospital, he is always accompanied by Blondi, a German shepherd, who helps him get around. Otto's eye problems are miraculously cured in the episode entitled "The Passion of Reverend Jimmy."

DR. HOOK: The brilliant, eccentric Hook is considered a maverick by the more conservative members of the Kingdom Hospital staff. The fortysomething neurosurgeon has spent his time at Kingdom Hospital amassing evidence against doctors he considers incompetent, which he stores in his apartment located in the depths of the hospital. Hook is drawn into the middle of the supernatural phenomena occurring in the hospital by virtue of being Peter Rickman's physician and surgeon, and by his association with Eleanor Druse.

ELEANOR SARAH "SALLY" DRUSE: A psychic with a strong connection to the world beyond, Eleanor feels personally obligated to solve the mystery of Kingdom Hospital. Concocting false illnesses as a way to remain inside its walls, she conducts her private investigation into the hospital's past.

DR. STEGMAN: The head neurosurgeon at Kingdom Hospital, "Steg" is arrogant, pompous, overbearing, and, sadly, incompetent. Forced by his incompetency to leave a prestigious Boston hospital, Stegman spends much of his time making his colleagues at Kingdom Hospital miserable. Taking advantage of Stegman's instability, the evil forces at the hospital attempt to use him as a weapon against the likes of Hook and Eleanor Druse.

DAVID HOOMAN: The hit-and-run driver of the minivan that hits Peter Rickman, he later falls off the roof of his house, sustaining fatal injuries.

ROLF PEDERSON: The hospitalized killer whom the evil forces of Kingdom Hospital influence to do their bidding.

GATES FALLS MILL: A Dickensian textile mill that burned to the ground on All Souls' Day in 1869, claiming the lives of dozens of innocent children working on-site at the time. The fire was set by the mill's owners, desirous of the insurance money the tragedy would generate.

EBENEZER GOTTREICH: Owner of the Gates Falls Mill. In 1869, he conspires with the mill's foreman, Hagarty, to burn it down for the insurance money.

HAGARTY: The foreman of the Gates Falls Mill, he helps Ebenezer Gottreich to burn down the facility.

DR. KLAUS GOTTREICH: Ebenezer's sadistic brother, he runs an on-site clinic to care for the sick and injured employees of the mill. The clinic, however, is merely a front for his horrid experiments into the nature of pain. Gottreich, whose spirit haunts Kingdom Hospital, was responsible for the death of young Mary Jensen.

KINGDOM HOSPITAL: Located in Lewiston, Maine, the hospital was built on the site of the former Gates Falls Mill. It is actually the second hospital to be built on that site; the first, Gottreich Hospital, burned down at the end of the 1930s, again on All Souls' Day. The hospital is haunted by the spirits of several children who tragically died in the first fire. The hospital is subject to several unexplained phenomena, including minor, localized earthquakes.

ANTUBIS: To all appearances an oversized anteater or aardvark, Antubis (the name seems to be a combination of anteater and Anubis, the jackal-headed Egyptian god who conducted the dead to judgment) physically enters Peter Rickman's life on the day of his accident (Peter had painted the beast prior to encountering it in the flesh). He tells Peter he saved him from sure death because he needs the artist to do him "a solid."

ABEL and CHRISTA: Two twentysomething hospital workers with Down Syndrome, this happy pair seems acutely in tune with all goings-on at the hospital, both natural and supernatural.

MARY JENSEN: The nine-year-old Mary worked at the Gates Falls Mill as a timekeeper. Mary's tortured spirit is trapped within the walls of Kingdom Hospital. Through the efforts of Sally Druse, Dr. Hook, and Peter Rickman, her spirit is freed from its prison.

PAUL: Like Mary, a spirit that haunts Kingdom Hospital. Unlike Mary, he labors on behalf of the dark forces present in the complex. He implores Rolf Pederson to kill Peter Rickman and Sally Druse, then tries to work through Earl Candleton, a deceased ex-major league baseball player. Finally, he turns his attention to the already unstable Dr. Stegman.

JOHNNY B. GOODE: The mysterious maintenance man of Kingdom Hospital, he doesn't appear in the flesh until the last episode. Johnny is played by none other than Stephen King.

KINGDOM HOSPITAL: TRIVIA

- When Dr. Stegman makes a call to Maintenance, Johnny B. Goode's fill-in Hawk is reading the Stephen King book *Bag of Bones*.

- Castle Rock is mentioned in episode 4.

- The series includes a now seemingly de rigueur Hitchcock-style cameo from its creator, as King appears in the last episode as the elusive maintenance man, Johnny B. Goode. King also did voice work in episode 6.

- While Rickman lays bleeding, a Nozz-A-La soda truck passes by the scene of the accident. Nozz-A-La is a brand of soda mentioned in several volumes of the *Dark Tower* series.

- When jogging, Rickman is wearing a "Little Tall" T-shirt, referencing the island setting of *Storm of the Century* and *Dolores Claiborne*.

- The Gates Falls Mill is in Lewiston, Maine . . . but King once wrote about another mill located in a town called Gates Falls—in the short story "Graveyard Shift."

- In the series finale, Peter Rickman, traveling back in time, uses a mysterious piece of chalk to draw a fire extinguisher that he uses to douse the flames that threaten to consume the Gates Falls Mill, exhibiting abilities similar to those displayed by Patrick Danville in *The Dark Tower VII*.

33

RELATED TALES

"Jerusalem's Lot" (from 1974's *Night Shift*)

A Lovecraftian-style tale that introduces a dark prehistory for the novel *'Salem's Lot*. Other than the southern Maine setting, the two stories seem to have nothing in common, but the story is still valuable for its fleshing out of a location vital to the Stephen King Universe. It concerns the resurgence of an old horror where it had been thought vanquished, and the connection that malignant presence seems to have to one family in particular.

"JERUSALEM'S LOT": PRIMARY SUBJECTS

CHARLES BOONE: In 1850, Charles had inherited his family home, called Chapelwaite, which was located in or around Jerusalem's Lot. He moved there with his companion, Calvin McCann, and later discovered a horrible evil dwelling beneath the town. Apparently it had initially been called there by a cult led by his ancestor, James Boon.

JAMES BOON: An ancestor of Charles Boone's. According to this tale, he founded Jerusalem's Lot in 1710. However, this is in contradiction to another local belief among the townspeople, which sets forth that the town was founded by a farmer named Charles Belknap Tanner. James Boon was apparently a religious leader who worshipped old, dark powers, until those forces claimed him.

JAMES ROBERT BOONE: The last survivor of the Boone family line. In 1971, he moves into Chapelwaite, and the horrors Charles Boone confronted twelve decades earlier begin to resurface. The fate of James Robert Boone is unknown.

CALVIN MCCANN: Charles Boone's friend and companion, who is killed by the worm.

THE WORM: An ancient, demonic creature, it was apparently worshipped by James Boon and his followers in the eighteenth century. Later, when its existence is threatened by Charles Boone and Calvin McCann, it rises again to attack them, killing McCann in the process.

DEMON DWELLINGS (by Degoudge): A book of horrid, arcane knowledge used by James Boon in the religious guidance offered to the cult that sprang up around him in Jerusalem's Lot.

MYSTERIES OF THE WORM: Another book of terrible magic and ritual, used in connection with worship of the demonic worm. Only five copies were known to exist as of 1850, and one of those was burned by Charles Boone.

"Graveyard Shift" (from 1974's *Night Shift*)

A particularly gruesome narrative, "Graveyard Shift" concerns a drifter named Hall who has lately come to work at a mill in Gates Falls, Maine. Over the Fourth of July holiday, he agrees to help with a cleanup that is many years overdue. During the job, he and the cleanup crew encounter giant, mutated rat-creatures in a sub-subbasement.

"GRAVEYARD SHIFT": PRIMARY SUBJECTS

HALL: A worker at the mill; it is Hall's hatred of Warwick, the foreman, that causes him to insist—almost in the form of a challenge—that they descend into the sub-subbasement and clean the rats out. Hall is devoured by the monster rodents.

WARWICK: The mill's tyrannical foreman, he is consumed by the huge, blind queen of the rats.

HARRY WISCONSKY: One of Hall's coworkers, he has the misfortune to join Hall and Warwick on their descent into the hellish sub-subbasement, but turns and runs, saving his own life. Harry Wisconsky's current whereabouts are unknown.

"One for the Road" (from 1974's *Night Shift*)

While *Night Shift*'s initial offering, "Jerusalem's Lot," is a prequel to the novel *'Salem's Lot* (1975), "One for the Road" is the novel's coda. The story establishes a long-term legend that will surround the town for generations. During a massive blizzard in Maine, a pair of old-timers try to save a family from the vampires that still haunt 'Salem's Lot.

"ONE FOR THE ROAD": PRIMARY SUBJECTS

BOOTH: During the blizzard, Booth is at Tookey's, his favorite watering hole, when a tourist from New York stumbles in covered with frostbite. When Booth learns that the man had gotten his car stuck while trying to take the unplowed road through 'Salem's Lot—and left his wife and daughter in the car while he went for help—Booth is a lot more concerned about marauding vampires than the idea that the tourist's wife and daughter might freeze to death. He, Tookey, and the tourist head out to try to rescue them, only to find that they have already been turned into vampires. He is almost the victim of the little girl, now a vampire, but Tookey saves him. Booth's current whereabouts are unknown.

HERB TOOKLANDER: The owner of Tookey's Bar, he closes for the night to try to save the tourist family. During the evening, he has a heart attack, but still manages to save Booth by throwing a bible at the little girl vampire. Tookey dies two years later, peacefully, during the night.

GERARD LUMLEY: A tourist from New York who foolishly tries to drive on an unplowed stretch of highway in the middle of a blizzard. The car becomes snowbound, and while he goes for help, his family is turned into vampires. Later, when he returns with help, Lumley is either killed or turned into a vampire.

FRANCIE LUMLEY: Lumley's wife. She becomes a vampire.

JANEY LUMLEY: Lumley's daughter. She is also turned into a vampire, and would have fed off Booth if Tookey hadn't stopped her.

TOOKEY'S BAR: It's still there, but is now owned by a couple from Waterville, Maine. They keep it pretty much the same.

Rita Hayworth and Shawshank Redemption
(from 1982's Different Seasons)

Though the novella is narrated in the second person by a convict named Red, this wonderful tale is the story of Andy Dufresne. Falsely accused and later convicted of the murder of his wife and her lover, Andy is a banker and lawyer who puts his education to work for him behind bars at Maine's Shawshank Prison. But that education would be nothing without the single-mindedness with which he goes about arranging his escape—over the course of many, many years—digging a hole in the wall of his cell and hiding it behind a succession of posters, which begins with one featuring Rita Hayworth.

Andy does successfully break out of the prison, and later, when Red is paroled, he sets off to join his friend.

The first thing that comes to mind when reading this account is how convincing King's representation of life inside a prison is. It does not feel like the typical genre story. There is a kind of monotony here against which the colorful story of Andy Dufresne is all the more fascinating. To anyone who had doubted that King had the ability to write mainstream fiction, this first novella in *Different Seasons* erased all such concerns. Of course, King would return to a prison setting much later with the incredibly successful serialized novel, *The Green Mile* (1996).

One is tempted, upon examining this novella, to study King's other nonhorror, nonfantasy work for parallels. *Rita Hayworth* is, after all, a story about triumph over adversity. A man is wrongly imprisoned, and even those who know the truth conspire to keep him down. And yet he works tirelessly over an almost inhuman span of time, on a scale that would drive most people insane, until he finally achieves his freedom.

With that as the story's outline, however, it isn't King's mainstream work that most echoes this tale. Rather, it is *The Eyes of the Dragon*. Strangely enough, that fantasy novel, written for his daughter, rife with castles and wizards and dragons and kings, has a fundamental structure that is quite similar to *Rita Hayworth*. There, also, a person wrongly accused of murder spends years and years to achieve his escape, right in front of his captors.

RITA HAYWORTH AND SHAWSHANK REDEMPTION: PRIMARY SUBJECTS

ANDY DUFRESNE: Wrongly imprisoned for the murder of his wife and her boyfriend, banker Andy Dufresne spends a large part of his life in prison, planning a way out. Though he finds a way to prove his innocence, his efforts are met with resistance. Not only does Andy manage to manipulate the prison system so that he has his own cell, but under the noses of his captors, he tunnels out of his confinement, and escapes.

He now lives in Zihautanejo, Mexico, under the assumed name Peter Stevens.

LINDA DUFRESNE: Andy's late wife. She is murdered by a man named Elwood Blatch, and Andy is falsely imprisoned for the crime.

GLENN QUENTIN: A golf pro who was Linda Dufresne's lover, he is murdered by Elwood Blatch, and Andy is wrongly convicted of the homicide.

RED: An inmate at Shawshank, Red has a life sentence for the murder of his wife, a neighbor woman, and the neighbor's infant. He had only meant to do away with his spouse and he never denied that, though he grieves for the other deaths he caused. In prison, Red is the one who can get things for other inmates, making him a prime black marketeer. Red becomes friendly with Andy Dufresne in prison, and supplies Andy with the things he needs to escape—though Red never realizes it until after Andy breaks out.

Red is paroled from Shawshank in 1976, and the next year, he breaks parole and follows Andy to Zihautanejo, Mexico. It is presumed that both are alive and well and still living there today.

ELWOOD BLATCH: He kills Andy Dufresne's wife and her boyfriend. Though he eventually goes to prison on other charges, Blatch is never charged with the murders that Andy went to prison for.

RITA HAYWORTH AND SHAWSHANK REDEMPTION: ADAPTATION

The Shawshank Redemption, the screen adaptation of King's longer-titled novella, was adapted and directed by Frank Darabont (who would later do the same for 1999's *The Green Mile*). Made by Castle Rock Entertainment (no small irony there, as the company was formed by Rob Reiner and named after King's fictional town of the same name) and released in 1994 by Columbia Pictures, the prison drama starred Morgan Freeman as Red and Tim Robbins as Andy Dufresne. It received seven Oscar nominations, including Best Picture, Best Actor (Freeman), and Best Adapted Screenplay.

While *Shawshank* is a slow-moving feature, reflecting the passage of time in prison, it is also a triumphant one. Though not a financial success in theaters, it has nevertheless gained in reputation over time, to the point where a certain contingent of the audience consider it among the best American movies ever made. Its popularity on video and DVD, as noted in magazines such as *Entertainment Weekly* and online at such Web sites as reel.com, is testament to that.

RITA HAYWORTH AND SHAWSHANK REDEMPTION: TRIVIA

- Frank Darabont, writer/director of the film adaptations of *Rita Hayworth and Shawshank Redemption* and *The Green Mile*, had done an earlier King adaptation as well—a student film version of King's short story "The Woman in the Room," for which King gave him permission.

- It seems quite possible that Peter Stevens, the assumed name Andy Dufresne uses in *Rita Hayworth and Shawshank Redemption*, is a combination of the names of the author and his good friend, novelist Peter Straub.

"Mrs. Todd's Shortcut" (from 1985's *Skeleton Crew*)

A trip through King's version of Maine, this tale tells of a cosmic road trip that begins in Castle Rock, winds its way through towns like Haven and Derry, and ends in King's own hometown of Bangor. In his Note on this story, King reveals that his wife, always seeking the shortest distance between two points in terms of her local treks, is the inspiration for Mrs. Todd.

"MRS. TODD'S SHORTCUT": PRIMARY SUBJECTS

OPHELIA TODD: The first wife of Worth Todd, Ophelia was obsessed with finding the quickest route to her destination. Ophelia disappeared in 1973.

HOMER BUCKLAND: Employed as a caretaker by the Todd family, he tells the story of Mrs. Todd's shortcut to Dave Owens. Going to Bangor with Ophelia Todd in her Mercedes, he travels through a hole in reality (a thinny, perhaps?) and visits a surreal landscape.

"The Reach" (from 1985's *Skeleton Crew*)

One of King's most poignant tales, it was originally published as "Do the Dead Sing?" in *Yankee* magazine in 1981. Stella Flanders is the oldest resident of Goat Island. Well into her nineties, she has never been off island. When she begins seeing specters from her past, however, she knows it is time for her to leave. One cold January night, Stella rises from her sickbed and sets out to cross the Reach (the name the locals have given to the water between the island and the mainland), which is frozen for the first time in over forty years. Stella's spirit is reunited with her husband and friends; her frozen corpse is found later on the mainland, seated in a natural chair of rock.

Secret Window, Secret Garden (from 1990's *Four Past Midnight*)

Secret Window, Secret Garden is another of King's metafictions, a disturbing morality play that can stand proudly next to other works of this nature, such as *Misery* (1987) and *The Dark Half* (1989). Written between drafts of *The Dark Half*, the narrative is King's effort to convey the powerful hold fiction can achieve over a writer. King calls this his "last story about writers and writing and the strange no man's land which exists between what's real and what's make believe." If that is indeed the case, he goes out with a bang, delivering a roundhouse punch of a story about how the sins of the past can catch up with you when you least expect it.

SECRET WINDOW, SECRET GARDEN: PRIMARY SUBJECTS

MORT RAINEY: In *Bag of Bones* (1998), author Mike Noonan says, "A writer is a man who has taught his mind to misbehave." Mort Rainey, author of *The Delacourte Family, The Organ Grinder's Boy*, and the short story collection *Everybody Drops the Dime*, can attest to that—his mind misbehaves in a manner that ultimately proves fatal. One day, a stranger appears at his door, clutching a manuscript called "Secret Window, Secret Garden." The man, who introduces himself as John Shooter, tells Rainey, "You stole my story. You stole my story and something's got to be done about it."

At first skeptical of Shooter's claim, Rainey later realizes the story is a dead ringer for one he published many years before called "Sowing Season." The stories, each about a man who murders his wife and buries her in a garden, are eerily similar in terms of grammar and syntax.

Shooter doesn't go away, even when Rainey claims Shooter's story was written after his own. Shooter wants tangible evidence, in the form of the magazine where the story was first published. Rainey promises to show him his file copy, which is stored at his ex-wife's house in Derry. Before he can retrieve it, however, his house burns down under mysterious circumstances. An increasingly frantic Rainey requests a copy from the publisher, but the issue arrives sans his story—someone has removed it with a razor.

Rainey tells his story to various people on the lake, but anyone who can confirm his encounters with Shooter is later found dead. Under extreme pressure, Rainey's mental state deteriorates; he has a flashback to an incident in his past, a time when he, in a moment of desperation, claimed another writer's story as his own, one he renamed "Sowing Season." It turns out that Rainey has carried the guilt of this crime with him ever since. Wanting to punish himself, he convinces himself of Shooter's existence when it was actually *he* who burned his house down, mutilated the magazine, and murdered the people who threatened to expose his charade.

Driven insane by this realization, Mort surrenders control to his John Shooter personality, allowing it to take over for good. He attacks his ex-wife, Carolyn. However, before he can seriously harm her, he is shot and killed.

SECRET WINDOW, SECRET GARDEN: ADAPTATION

In 2004, Johnny Depp starred as Mort Rainey in *Secret Window*; John Turturro essayed the role of his alter ego, John Shooter. Ever the "actor's actor," Depp manages to imbue Rainey with plenty of quirks and ticks. Writer-director David Koepp *(Stir of Echoes)* does his best to flesh out King's story, but the movie's twist is telegraphed early on. The climactic scenes are particularly grisly, but a Philip Glass score makes the whole thing tolerable. Ultimately, though, *Secret Window* proved a disappointment for King fans.

"Suffer the Little Children"
(from 1993's *Nightmares & Dreamscapes*)

King calls this a "ghastly sick-joke with no redeeming social merit whatever." He adds, "I like that in a story." Reminiscent of the early, more sinister work of Ray Bradbury, in the theme of all children being natural-born monsters or some form of alien, "Suffer the Little Children" is an effective chiller.

"SUFFER THE LITTLE CHILDREN": PRIMARY SUBJECTS

MISS SIDLEY: Veteran grade school teacher Miss Sidley sees something out of the corner of her eye one morning that shakes her—the face of one of her students seems to change for a moment, altering into something monstrous. That student, Robert, adds to her disquiet, telling her that "there's quite a few of us." Miss Sidley becomes more and more paranoid, increasingly sure her class is full of monsters hiding behind human masks. Taking matters into her own hands, Miss Sidley invites Robert to accompany her to the mimeograph room; once there, she kills him. She eliminates eleven more students before she is interrupted. There is no trial. Miss Sidley is committed to the asylum known as Juniper Hill, located in Augusta, Maine, where she eventually kills herself.

Stephen King—"Teen Anger"   SUSANNE MOSS

"The Night Flier" (from 1993's *Nightmares & Dreamscapes*)

This modern vampire tale originally appeared in the popular 1988 anthology *Prime Evil: New Stories by the Masters of Modern Horror*, edited by noted King scholar and biographer Douglas E. Winter. Among its other qualities, the story is notable for bringing back to the limelight reporter Richard Dees, who was first seen in *The Dead Zone* (1979).

"THE NIGHT FLIER": PRIMARY SUBJECTS

THE NIGHT FLIER: A vampire pilot who travels from airport to airport in his Cessna Skymaster in search of prey. The nameless vampire, who sleeps in the plane's cargo hold, is more amused than annoyed with his pursuer, Richard Dees; instead of ripping his throat out, he lets him go with a warning to keep his distance. The Night Flier evidences a wry sense of humor, using the name of Dwight Renfield to identify himself to various airport officials. (Horror aficionados know this is a play on the name Dwight Frye; a character actor, Frye appeared in a handful of classic horror movies, among them Tod Browning's 1931 *Dracula*, where he played the part of the madman Renfield.)

RICHARD DEES: A tabloid reporter/photographer who once hounded Johnny Smith for his unusual life story, as detailed in *The Dead Zone*. Pursuing the facts of the Night Flier killings for his tabloid newspaper, *Inside View*, Dees picks up on the mysterious Dwight Renfield's trail, eventually meeting the vampire face to face in an airport men's room. The completely terrified Dees escapes with his life, but is not allowed to keep the photos he took of the Night Flier in action.

"Popsy" (from 1993's *Nightmares & Dreamscapes*)

Another contemporary vampire tale, written in much the same vein (ahem) of "The Night Flier."

"POPSY": PRIMARY SUBJECTS

SHERIDAN: A gambler who has fallen on hard times, Sheridan kidnaps small children and sells them to an unsavory character named "the

Turk." One day, he makes the mistake of snatching a small child whose grandfather turns out to be a vampire. The grandparent eventually catches up with Sheridan, beats him, and then feeds him to his grandson.

POPSY: The boy's grandfather, who just happens to be a vampire. In his commentary on the story, King asks, "Is this little boy's grandfather the same creature that demands Richard Dees open his camera and expose his film at the end of 'The Night Flier'? You know, I rather think he is."

"Rainy Season" (from 1993's *Nightmares & Dreamscapes*)

The second "peculiar town" story in this collection, this one recalls Shirley Jackson's 1948 classic tale of ritual sacrifice, "The Lottery" (a story that has always been a personal favorite of King's). It's never explained why these deadly toads rain from the sky every seven years on the rural Maine hamlet of Willow; what matters is that somebody—anybody—has to be sacrificed to make it stop.

"RAINY SEASON": PRIMARY SUBJECTS

ELISE and JOHN GRAHAM: A vacationing couple visiting the small Maine town on the eve of what the locals call the rainy season, Elise and John ignore the warnings to beware an imminent rain of toads from the sky. They are both eaten alive when they encounter the hideous rain of killer toads that hits Willow every seven years on June 17. The only way the bizarre rain of razor-toothed toads can be stopped is to sacrifice two out-siders to appease whatever dark gods have cursed this otherwise idyllic town. The snobbish Grahams serve that purpose well.

"Riding the Bullet" (from 2002's *Everything's Eventual*)

This short story, only available online and in a read-only format, created quite a stir when King published it early in the year 2000. Web sites offer-ing the tale were inundated with requests; it is estimated that more than four hundred thousand customers downloaded it.

This story of college student Alan Parker's unfortunate encounter with the supernatural echoes such tales as "Mrs. Todd's Shortcut" and "The Road Virus Heads North" in what is essentially a travelogue through King's Maine. Informed that his mother has just suffered a stroke, the carless Parker decides to hitchhike from the University of Maine at Orono to his hometown in Lewiston, some 120 miles south. Along the way, he is picked up by one George Staub, who Parker knows died in a car accident almost three decades prior. Staub, whose body is apparently held together by stitches, tells the frightened Parker that he must choose between his life and his mother's. Panicked, Parker chooses his own, and is released from the car. Mrs. Parker lives for a few years after her stroke, but Alan is always tortured by his cowardice.

Describing his ordeal early in the story, Parker says something that many denizens of the Stephen King Universe might agree with:

> The way I looked at the world changed that night, changed quite a lot. I came to understand that there are things underneath, you see—underneath—and no book can explain what they are. I think that sometimes it's best to just forget those things are there. If you can, that is.

"RIDING THE BULLET": *ADAPTATIONS*

King favorite Mick Garris adapted this property for the screen. Jonathan Jackson is appropriately troubled in the role of Alan Parker, but the movie is pretty much stolen by the quirky David Arquette, who essays the role of the undead George Staub. Barbara Hershey and Erika Christensen also appear, but their performances are wasted. Released to little fanfare in 2004, it has recently become available on DVD.

SECTION FIVE

The Prime Reality,
Part IV:
Tales of The Shop

It is a familiar theme by now, particularly in the post–*X-Files* generation: Within the American government there exists a covert organization dedicated to the study of the paranormal. In the Stephen King universe, that organization is known only as "The Shop."

As noted in the chapter entries below, The Shop investigates such phenomena, but it also *instigates*. As in *Firestarter*, they have been known to fund experiments in the paranormal. Further, however, like all great, ominous covert groups (mostly fictional, we hope), they are willing to go to any lengths, including assassination, to achieve their goals and keep their secrets.

The tales surrounding or tangentially touching upon The Shop very clearly exist within the Prime Reality of the Stephen King Universe. One must only read *The Tommyknockers*, which includes Shop agents as supporting characters, to know that. For in that novel, there are connections to a great many other King works set in the Prime Reality (see below).

Though The Shop does not play any obvious role in the grand cosmic struggle between the Purpose and the Random, it does seem logical to think that they may have served either side unwittingly over the years. Further, though there is no immediately visible link between The Shop and any of the other realities, two observations can be made. First, though operating in the Prime Reality, they seem to share certain facets with the "Low Men in Yellow Coats" from Roland's Reality *(Hearts in Atlantis)*. Second, it stands to reason that if there are thinnies between the Prime Reality and any of the others, The Shop is almost certainly aware of them.

34

FIRESTARTER

(1980)

Considering its similar protagonist—a young girl with terrifying paranormal powers—*Firestarter* is an interesting counterpoint to *Carrie* (1974). Where the latter is, without question, a tale of great tragedy and loss, *Firestarter* is, more than anything, an uplifting if relentless thriller. In part, it is the account of two innocent college students, Andy McGee and Vicky Tomlinson, who take part in a secret government experiment intended to jump-start paranormal abilities in test subjects. In the case of Andy and Vicky, the experiment succeeds—and more successfully than anyone could have ever imagined. Partially as a result of this shared experience, they fall in love, marry, and have a daughter.

This girl, Charlie McGee, is actually the central character of *Firestarter*. In fact, the title takes its name from her ability to start fires simply with her mind: pyrokinesis. And that's only one of Charlie's amazing paranormal abilities.

The novel is a masterwork of paranoia that preceded TV's *The X-Files* (1993–2002) by well over a decade. And yet, without question, this is exactly the type of case that series' Scully and Mulder would get involved with—though hopefully they would not be as merciless as the government agents from The Shop. In the late 1960s, Andy and Vicky participated in an experiment run by the Department of Scientific Intelligence, which portrays itself as a benevolent research organization. However, it is actually The Shop, a top-secret government agency doing whatever it takes—including parascientific research—to create fantastic new weapons for America's arsenal. (The Shop would receive mention in later works by King, but none of the principal characters of *Firestarter* have made appearances in other works. Not yet, anyway.)

As noted, *Carrie* is also the chronicle of a young woman born with paranormal abilities. But the two could not be more different. Whereas Carrie is subject to emotional and physical abuse by her mother, Charlie McGee is purely a victim of circumstance and greed by ruthless adults. Her dad loves her more than life itself, and ultimately proves it. Where Carrie is finally destroyed by her "wild talent," Charlie is tempered by it, like steel in the forge. She emerges only more powerful—and wiser—after the tragedy of her tale.

The evil King presents here is not Charlie's fantastic talent, but the fact that government agents would purposely use human beings in immoral experiments simply to better develop secret weapons. The killers here are people in the U.S. government—salaries for whom the public pays without even being aware of it.

Firestarter is among a small handful of King's novels that, like *'Salem's Lot* (1975), absolutely demands a sequel. The story of Charlie McGee can hardly be considered over after she walks into the offices of *Rolling Stone* magazine to tell a reporter all that has happened to her thus far in her amazing life.

To return once again to the counterpoint of *Carrie*, *Firestarter* proves itself to be a book about hope and affirmation, not destruction and loss. Whereas *Carrie* concerns itself mostly with the despair and tragic life of its central female character, the heroine of *Firestarter* is just that—a hero. And a survivor against incredible odds. Charlie McGee overcomes the gravest injustices and immoral actions a nation can heap on one of its own citizens, and manages to triumph over that adversity, to stand proud and shout her defiance to the world.

But lest we forget, those still working for The Shop remain deeply concerned that a girl with Charlie's power might one day, as she matures, gain the awesome power to split the world itself in two with merely a concentrated thought.

And Charlie and others just like her are still out there, in the Stephen King Universe.

FIRESTARTER: PRIMARY SUBJECTS

CHARLIE McGEE: From birth, Charlene "Charlie" Roberta McGee has shown herself to be gifted—or cursed—with a number of remarkable psychic abilities. These have included limited telekinesis, a kind of instinctive clairvoyance, and, most powerful of all, pyrokinesis.

As college students, Charlie's parents, Andy McGee and Vicky Tomlinson McGee, were experimented upon by a shadowy government agency called The Shop. While most of the subjects in that test died or committed suicide, Andy and Vicky both gained certain psychic abilities, and later married.

Not long after Charlie's birth, the infant begins to set fires with her mind. Her crib and other areas need to be fireproofed, and Andy and Vicky have to fire-train her, in a manner similar to the way in which parents potty-train their children. Charlie's memory of the burning of her beloved teddy bear stays with her to this day.

Her father tells her that starting fires is a very bad thing. So Charlie, even as a very small girl, determines never to do it again.

But then her mother is murdered by The Shop, and its agents set out on a horrible quest to bring Andy and Charlie in for scrutiny. Eventually, they succeed. Under the direction of Cap Hollister, and with the influence of the assassin known as John Rainbird, Charlie is convinced not only to light fires again, but to practice doing so, to learn to control it better.

When her father reveals to her the depth of The Shop's deceptions, and their intention to kill them both when she outlives her usefulness, Charlie uses her power to burn The Shop compound to the ground.

Charlie McGee's current whereabouts are unknown.

ANDY McGEE: In 1969, in order to earn two hundred dollars he desperately needed, Andy McGee participated in an experiment held on his college campus. The testing, conducted by Dr. Joseph Wanless for The Shop, involved a drug known as Lot Six. Lot Six was supposed to draw out of the dormant parts of the human brain certain paranormal abilities that would otherwise never manifest themselves.

In Andy McGee, it is something he calls "the push." With a bit of a mental push, Andy can suggest very strongly to someone that they do a particular thing, and they will comply instantly. He can also convince people that they are seeing something they are not.

Eventually, Andy marries Vicky Tomlinson, who was also part of the Lot Six experiment, and together they produce a child, Charlie.

Over time, Andy's "push" ability diminishes. He begins to suspect that using the power causes him minor brain damage each time, and that the ill effects are growing worse. He tries not to use the power anymore, but is later forced to employ it quite frequently. Meanwhile, Vicky is murdered by The Shop, and Andy and Charlie have to go on the run.

After their eventual capture, Andy spends months in a drug-induced haze. However, after that time, he is able to recover the "push" ability, and uses it to arrange for his and Charlie's escape. During their flight, Andy goes up against the assassin, John Rainbird, and is killed.

VICKY TOMLINSON McGEE: As a young woman, Vicky Tomlinson had been sexually assaulted. It is only through the special mental contact that she and Andy McGee share during the Lot Six experiment that she is able to overcome the fears of intimacy that had been with her since that assault.

She and Andy marry, and she later gives birth to Charlie. For many years, she has a low-grade telekinetic ability that seems to come and go. Her use of it is instinctive, and sometimes she doesn't even realize she is employing it. Apparently the limited scope of her gift made her very expendable. When The Shop determines to take Charlie and Andy into custody, Vicky is tortured and murdered.

JOHN RAINBIRD: A Native American assassin for The Shop, John Rainbird is obsessed with death. He enjoys looking into the eyes of the people whose lives he claims, trying desperately to determine what happens to their life force when they die, searching for some sign of an afterlife, of passage to another world.

Rainbird is assigned the execution of Dr. Joseph Wanless, the scientist behind the Lot Six experiment. He is also responsible for the eventual capture of Andy and Charlie McGee. Later, Rainbird uses knowledge of The Shop's operations and the personal life of its director, Captain Hollister, to force Cap into allowing him certain "freedoms" with young Charlie.

In order for The Shop to study her, and so that Rainbird can observe her, the assassin poses as an orderly at The Shop installation where Charlie is a prisoner and cleans her rooms every day for months. One night, during a blackout, he finally gains the girl's confidence by fabricating a story about his Vietnam War service, playing on the sympathy she feels for him because of the horrible scars on his face and the loss of one of his eyes.

It is Rainbird who convinces Charlie to start setting fires again, to cooperate with The Shop. It is also Rainbird who gets everything The Shop wants from her. He does all of this in return for a guarantee from Cap Hollister that when it comes time for Charlie to be executed, the job will be his. She is, in Rainbird's estimation, an extraordinary and powerful young girl. As such, he wants to watch her eyes while he slowly kills her.

When Rainbird discovers that Andy McGee has his special power back, he foils the man's escape plan and kills Andy, only to be then burned to death by Charlie.

CAP HOLLISTER: As director of the Department of Scientific Intelligence (The Shop), Captain James Hollister is in charge of all operations relating to the fallout from the late 1960s Lot Six experiments. This includes the pursuit and capture of, and later experimentation upon, Charlie and Andy McGee.

Cap Hollister also orders John Rainbird to execute Dr. Wanless. In addition, he arranges for Rainbird to work with Charlie McGee, and is later psychically coopted by Andy McGee into planning Andy and Charlie's escape. In the ensuing chaos, he is burned to death by Charlie McGee.

DR. JOSEPH WANLESS: The scientist who supervised the trial experiments on a chemical compound called Lot Six. Wanless later has a stroke and becomes a vocal supporter of execution for all participants in that experiment. That idea extends to Charlie McGee, the offspring of two of those participants.

When Cap Hollister decides that Wanless has become a nuisance and a potential danger to him politically, he orders John Rainbird to execute the man.

THE SHOP: Also known as the Department of Scientific Intelligence, The Shop is a Virginia-based agency of the American government that participates in what are generally referred to as "black ops." Loosely defined, these are operations that are not officially sanctioned by Congress and whose budgets are blacked out or buried as part of other operations. The Shop's specialty is researching scientific avenues for potential use in warfare.

LOT SIX: A chemical compound, created by The Shop, that forces latent paranormal powers to manifest in certain test subjects, and that causes madness in others.

DR. HOCKSTETTER: Patrick Hockstetter (who, coincidentally, bears the same name as one of the victims in *It*) is the scientist in charge of testing Charlie McGee while she is held captive by The Shop. Hockstetter apparently survives the conflagration that destroys the Shop compound in Longmont, Virginia.

His current whereabouts are unknown.

ORVILLE JAMIESON: Also known as O. J. or Juice, Orv Jamieson is a Shop agent. He is one of the very few to survive the fire that Charlie McGee visits upon the Longmont compound.

Orv Jamieson's current whereabouts are unknown.

IRV and NORMA MANDERS: When Andy and Charlie McGee are on the run and hitchhiking, a farmer named Irv Manders picks them up. He and his wife, Norma, show the McGees every hospitality, right up until several carloads of Shop agents come looking for the fugitives. Even then, Irv tries to protect his guests and his property with a shotgun—enraged that an American citizen's rights could be so heinously violated—and is shot for his trouble.

As a result of the battle on the Manders' farm, Charlie lets her power loose on a large scale for the first time, and the Manders' house is burned to the ground. Irv later recovers from the gunshot wound.

After the destruction of the Shop compound, Charlie finds her way back to the Manderses on her own. They lovingly help her to recover from the recent horrors she has been through, and set her on the path to bringing the truth to light about The Shop, the way her father would have wanted.

It is assumed that Irv and Norma Manders still live on Bailings Road in Hastings Glen, New York.

TASHMORE POND: The Vermont retreat where Granther McGee, Andy's grandfather, used to take him and his family when he was a boy.

This cabin in the woods is also where Andy and Charlie hide out from The Shop for an entire winter. Unfortunately, it is also where they are captured by John Rainbird and other Shop agents.

FIRESTARTER: ADAPTATIONS

In October 1984, just in time for Halloween, Universal Pictures released the film version of *Firestarter*. Though quite faithfully adapted by screenwriter Stanley Mann, it was, in a curious and detrimental way, *too* faithful. Due mainly to the fact that each scene is fit together with very little in the way of texture or characterization but rather with an eye to expediency—in order to fit in all of the novel, one might imagine—the resulting film comes off as very flat and lifeless. Every major character and scene from the original novel is there, but King himself would comment that the whole of the movie was somehow less than the sum of all its parts.

This might well be the fault of director Mark L. Lester, whose only real claim to fame is the cult favorite *Class of 1984* (1982). His other films include such "classics" as *Truck Stop Women* (1974), *Bobbie Jo and the Outlaw* (1976), and the early Arnold Schwarzenegger vehicle *Commando* (1986). Clearly Lester knew how to blow things up and set people on fire, but whenever it came to drawing more than rudimentary performances from his powerhouse cast, the director seemed out of his element.

The film benefits greatly from its lead actor, the always underappreciated David Keith *(An Officer and a Gentleman)*, as Andy McGee, and the presence of Martin Sheen as Cap Hollister. (Sheen had already appeared in 1983's *The Dead Zone*.) Young Drew Barrymore, the only real choice in 1984 to play the lead as Charlie McGee, was widely considered the finest young natural actress working in Hollywood. Spielberg loved her when he put her in *E.T. The Extra-Terrestrial* (1982). So did King, who would later see that she was cast again in *Cat's Eye*. Unfortunately, like so many others in the cast, here Barrymore delivers a rather flat performance, though her undeniable charm does rise above that level frequently enough.

Art Carney and Louise Fletcher, two of the most well-respected character actors in Hollywood, have small yet worthy roles as Irv and Norma Manders, and their presence lends a certain amount of venerability and humanity to the screen project.

Ironically, however, the opposite is true of the presence of another Academy Award–winning actor, George C. Scott. A legendary talent, Scott does only an adequate job of portraying the terrifying Native American assassin, John Rainbird. But no matter how Scott glowers on camera, no matter what makeup effects are used to make his face appear scarred, he is simply *not* John Rainbird. In one of the few times in his career, here he's just an actor cashing a paycheck.

Still, on a fifteen-million-dollar budget, *Firestarter* is competently executed and fast-paced. It must be applauded for its faithfulness to the original novel, a point of view rarely taken by any Hollywood production of a bestselling book.

A sequel to this film, *Firestarter 2: Rekindled*, premiered on the Sci Fi channel in 2002. Featuring Margueritte Moreau as a teenage Charlie, the film blithely ignores much of the original's continuity, resurrecting John Rainbird, played by Malcolm McDowell, as the leader of a small army of children with wild talents. Overlong and heavily reliant on special effects, this version is for only the most rabid of King fans.

FIRESTARTER: TRIVIA

- Pay close attention while watching the movie version of *Firestarter*. She isn't in it long, but there, in the role of the doomed Vicky McGee, is nighttime soap diva Heather Locklear, leading lady of *Spin City*, *Melrose Place*, *Dallas*, and *T. J. Hooker*.

- The Shop later appears in *The Tommyknockers* (1987). There, the mysterious agency dispatches agents to investigate the odd happenings in Haven, Maine.

- *Firestarter* was one of the first novels to be issued as a signed, limited edition. It appeared in 1980 from Phantasia Press in an edition of 725 copies at $35 each. Even more "fireproof" was a tiny run of only 26 copies that were specially bound in asbestos cloth.

35

THE TOMMYKNOCKERS

(1987)

*T*he *Tommyknockers* is Stephen King's bittersweet look at runaway science, pointing out how unchecked technology for its own sake is not necessarily progress. Here, King examines the ramifications of "dumb evolution," looking at a community so enraptured by what it *can* do that it never stops to wonder if it is doing what it *should*. This book is extremely relevant to our times, in which new technology becomes obsolete almost immediately after it is introduced. Like the Tommyknockers, the town's nickname for a race of highly advanced aliens, we love our gadgets—even if we have no idea how they work, or if they ultimately cause more harm than good.

Stories like "The Word Processor of the Gods" aside, King has always evidenced a healthy mistrust of technology and science. Examples abound in his fiction: Captain Tripps, the superflu that killed most of the world's population in *The Stand* (1978), was most likely created as part of a secret military project. Likewise, *The Mist*, which may have had its origins in the military's fabled "Arrowhead Project." In *Firestarter* (1980), The Shop meddles with human DNA, producing mutants with the experimental chemical solution code-named Lot Six. Then there's machinery in and of itself. Who could forget "The Mangler," which featured the evil Model-6 Speed Ironer and Folder, or the malign vehicles depicted in "Trucks" and *Christine* (1983). King even casts a wary eye at the scientific method, in *'Salem's Lot*

(1975), when rationalism allows the vampire epidemic to spread through the entire town.

The adults in *The Tommyknockers* also convey the fears King must have felt as a child who grew up during the Cold War. As a product of the 1950s, King evinces both a healthy fear of radiation from the Bomb, and the loss of individuality so feared by Americans in terms of the threat of Communism. Whatever radiates from the uncovered Tommyknocker ship, its effects mimic radiation poisoning, while the Tommyknockers' takeover of Haven, Maine, brings to mind classic cinematic parables of paranoia like *Invasion of the Body Snatchers* (1956) and *Invaders from Mars* (1953).

Purposely reminiscent of H. P. Lovecraft's classic 1927 tale "The Colour Out of Space," *The Tommyknockers* also contains several explicit connections to the rest of the Stephen King Universe. Desperate to reveal the strange doings in Haven, local Ev Hillman speaks with David Bright, a journalist who reported on the events chronicled in *The Dead Zone* (1979). In Derry attending to the needs of his comatose grandson, Ev hears "chuckling sounds" emanating from a sewer. Another Haven resident thinks he saw a clown "grinning up at him from an open sewer manhole" on Wentworth Street while passing through Derry. As *The Tommyknockers* is clearly set in 1987, this would indicate that the main evil known simply as "It," a.k.a. Pennywise the Clown from *It* (1986), may still be alive at the time of the curious events occurring in Haven.

The surviving Haven Tommyknockers are brought to a government installation in Virginia. In an obvious reference to the events detailed in *Firestarter*, King tells readers, "This installation, which had once been burned to the ground by a child, was the Shop." Finally, King indirectly references himself, as when Ev Hillman briefly thinks about smutty books, "like that fellow up in Bangor wrote."

THE TOMMYKNOCKERS:
PRIMARY SUBJECTS

ROBERTA "BOBBI" ANDERSON: While walking in the woods one day, Bobbi trips over a piece of metal partially buried in the earth. Curious, she tries to dig it out, only to realize that it is part of something much bigger. For reasons she cannot yet fathom, she feels compelled to free the object from its earthen tomb; forgoing her writing (Bobbi is a bestselling author of several Westerns), she works on her dig day and night. Although she doesn't know it yet, Bobbi has fallen under the influence of the Tommyknockers, a race of highly advanced intergalactic gypsies. Her contact with the ship yields varied results. On the positive side, she is able to improve her water heater's efficiency several times over, modify her tractor (the gearshift now has a setting that reads "UP"), and invent a typewriter that reads her subconscious mind so she can write in her sleep. On the negative side, she seems to be suffering the effects of long-term radiation poisoning (e.g., Bobbi's general health deteriorates, and her teeth begin to fall out.).

Being the first to start "becoming" (a process by which human beings are transformed into Tommyknockers), Bobbi becomes the de facto leader of the townsfolk in Haven who fall under the Tommyknockers' influence. Although she's quickly shedding her humanity, Bobbi does retain some human traits—her love for Jim Gardener, for instance. Despite repeated demands from her compatriots that she dispose of Jim, Bobbi uses her influence to keep him alive. This proves to be a bad mistake—shortly after they explore the alien vehicle for the first time together, Gardener suddenly turns on his former lover. Their brief scuffle in Bobbi's kitchen ends in her accidental death.

PETER: Bobbi's aged beagle, Peter is invigorated by his exposure to the Tommyknocker ship. Forgetting her humanity, Bobbi coldly turns the animal into a sort of "living battery." Keeping him in the shed adjacent to her home, the former pet is later joined there by Ev Hillman and Anne Anderson.

JIM GARDENER: Bobbi's friend and lover, Jim is a poet and an alcoholic. He is not with Bobbi when she first finds the spaceship carrying the Tommyknockers—he's traveling New England as part of a caravan of poets, doing readings and attending parties. At one of these parties, Jim gets drunk in spectacular fashion: enraged by the statements of a proponent of nuclear power, antinuclear activist Jim delivers a spirited lecture, then proceeds to completely disrupt the party.

Jim continues drinking, waking up several days later on a beach in New Hampshire. Frightened by his relapse, he returns home to beg Bobbi's forgiveness. Seeing the woman for the first time in weeks, Gardener is frightened by her unhealthy appearance and odd behavior. After agreeing to help with her excavation project, Jim spends the next few weeks digging during the day and drinking himself into a stupor at night. Although Jim is not immune to the effects of the Tommyknocker ship, the process is hindered by the presence of a metal plate in his skull, a souvenir of a youthful ski accident. The plate also keeps the telepathic Tommyknockers in town from reading his thoughts.

Although he helps Bobbi, Jim certainly doesn't condone her bizarre behavior. Discovering that Bobbi has turned Peter, Ev Hillman, and her sister Anne into living batteries, he decides he must stop her. After exploring the Tommyknocker ship for the first time, Jim decides to act, and attempts to shoot Bobbi. The gun misfires, and they scuffle. Bobbi is killed, electrocuted when a radio falls into a puddle of liquid she's standing in.

Jim then enters the Tommyknocker ship for a second time, assuming control of its simplistic navigation system. At his command, the ship rises from the woods and takes off into space. The effort proves fatal; when last we see him, the dying Jim is lying on the transparent floor of the ship's control room in a widening pool of his own blood.

RUTH McCAUSLAND: Haven's no-nonsense police chief, Ruth is referred to as the heart and conscience of the town. When the Tommyknockers begin taking over various residents, Ruth resists becoming mentally enslaved, knowing it's not right. The rest of the town, however, does not agree with her, and as a result cruelly shuns her. Realizing she won't be able to resist the Tommyknockers much longer, Ruth sacrifices her life in an attempt to warn the outside world, blowing up the town hall clock tower in hopes that it will attract the attention of the authorities of neighboring townships. The sacrifice is in vain, as the Tommyknockers produce a convincing hologram of the tower that manages to fool the eyes of the investigating Maine state troopers.

HILLY BROWN: Under the influence of the Tommyknockers, aspiring magician Hilly invents a device that actually makes things disappear. Unfortunately, ten-year-old Hilly uses his younger brother David as a "volunteer" from the audience for his magic show. Hilly makes David disappear—to Altair-4—but can't bring him back. Sick with guilt, Hilly worries himself into a coma. He escapes the influence of the Tommyknockers when his grandfather takes him to the hospital in Derry.

DAVID BROWN: Hilly's younger brother, David is whisked to a world the Tommyknockers refer to as Altair-4. David spends several uncomfortable days there, but survives the experience, due to the combined efforts of his grandfather and Jim Gardener. David was last seen alive and well in the Derry hospital.

EV HILLMAN: If Ruth McCausland is the heart and conscience of Haven, Ev Hillman could be thought of as its memory. Realizing early on that something is very wrong in Haven, Ev spirits his remaining grandson, Hilly Brown, out of town before anything else can happen to him. While in Derry, Ev tries to raise an alarm; his tale is too wild for the local newspapers to publish, but he does convince Derry policeman Butch Dugan to investigate. Unfortunately, Ev and Butch are captured while investigating the woods near Bobbi Anderson's home. Butch is programmed by the Tommyknockers to commit suicide, while Ev is taken to Bobbi's shed and used as a human battery.

BIG INJUN WOODS: Also known as Burning Woods, this piece of land borders Bobbi Anderson's property. The site of many an odd occurrence over the years, it is also the resting place of the Tommyknocker ship.

THE SHOP: When the secret government agency, first introduced in *Firestarter*, learns of the strange goings-on in the town, it descends on Haven only hours after Jim Gardener has piloted the Tommyknocker craft into deep space. The Shop studies the devices left behind by the Tommyknockers; they also examine Haven's survivors, all well on their way to becoming a form of Tommyknockers themselves. How much The Shop is able to learn from their studies is not known—all the survivors die within two months.

THE TOMMYKNOCKERS: As King states in a prefatory note to the book, *Webster's Unabridged* states that Tommyknockers are either 1) tunneling ogres, or 2) ghosts that haunt deserted mines or caves. The author received his original inspiration from a verse he had heard as a child:

Late last night and the night before,
Tommyknockers, Tommyknockers,
knocking at the door.
I want to go out, don't know if I can,
'cause I'm so afraid
of the Tommyknocker man.

—Traditional

Rather than fantasy ogres or horrific ghosts, here the Tommyknockers are the alien inhabitants of the ship Bobbi Anderson finds buried in the earth. Judging by its depth, the enormous craft has been there for centuries. When Jim boards the vehicle, he notes that its occupants have six-fingered hands, taloned feet, and what looks like a dog's head on top of a large frame. Described as "interstellar gypsies with no king," this belligerent race (they were apparently fighting among themselves when their ship crashed) creates technology that they themselves don't fully understand.

Besides the aliens themselves, there are the citizens of Haven who are in the process of "becoming" Tommyknockers—toward the end of the novel, King begins to refer to both groups by that name. The fantastic process by which humans become Tommyknockers is never made clear, but has something to do with repeated exposure to the Tommyknocker ship, and to treatments given to Havenites within the confines of Bobbi Anderson's shed. The process is long and slow, and requires a change in atmosphere—the newly minted Tommyknockers create a bubble over Haven, filling it with rarified "Tommyknocker" air. Outsiders entering Haven become ill; Haven residents who leave the town risk death.

THE TOMMYKNOCKERS: ADAPTATIONS

Stephen King's The Tommyknockers: This four-hour ABC miniseries, adapted by Lawrence D. Cohen and directed by John Power, first aired in May 1993. Starring Jimmy Smits (*L.A. Law*) and Marg Helgenberger (*CSI*) as Jim Gardener and Bobbi Anderson, the miniseries also features *Creepshow* alumnus E. G. Marshall as Ev Hillman and former adult film star Traci Lords as Nancy Voss. The two-hundred-minute production was shot entirely in New Zealand—even though of course the story is set in Maine.

The well-produced miniseries remains fairly faithful to the novel, but differs noticeably by providing a happier ending for Bobbi Anderson (here she survives and reverts back to human form, her body and movements conveying none of the trauma the "becoming" a Tommyknocker must have put her through).

There are other changes to the story elements, but most add to, rather than detract from, the overall narrative. Examples include an eerie scene where Ruth McCausland (Joanna Cassidy) is attacked by her doll collection, and a scene where Rebecca Paulsen (Allyce Beasley) is informed of her husband's extramarital escapades by a chatty television game show host. The special effects are uniformly excellent—the producers obviously took the effort to make the Tommyknockers look just right. Writer Lawrence D. Cohen, who had previously done the screenplay for *Carrie* (1976) and cowrote the adaptation for the miniseries *It* (1990), clearly has a strong affinity for the work of Stephen King.

36

STEPHEN KING'S GOLDEN YEARS
(1991)

Without a doubt, *Stephen King's Golden Years* is a singular oddity in the Stephen King canon. It aired in 1991 as a summer replacement series on CBS and lasted for seven one-hour episodes, ending in a cliffhanger. Of course, the hope at the time was that the network would pick up the series, which would then continue where the original segments left off. When that did not happen, the series' producers released a videotape version of *Golden Years* that brought the story to a still-somewhat-mysterious conclusion. In order to do so, however, they also changed several scenes leading up to the ending.

This book focuses on the televised version of *Golden Years*, with the exception of the changes made and new additions included in the videotape release.

The series starred Keith Szarbajka as Harlan Williams, with Frances Sternhagen (*Misery*) as his wife, Gina. Others in the cast included Felicity Huffman (*Desperate Housewives*) as Terry Spann and Ed Lauter as General Louis Crewes. The seven episodes boasted a variety of directors, most notably Michael Gornick, who had directed the feature *Creepshow 2* in 1987.

The main character of the show is Harlan Williams, an elderly janitor working at a top-secret military installation, where supposedly agricultural testing takes place. Not that anyone actually believes that, especially given the high-voltage electric fence that surrounds the Falco Plains facility.

In truth, the bizarre Dr. Richard Todhunter (Bill Raymond) is doing research on cellular regeneration. His negligence leads to an accidental explosion. Harlan is caught in the explosion, and exposed to an experimental energy form called K-R3 that causes him to grow younger.

One of the federal agents sent to investigate the accident, Jude Andrews (R. D. Call), turns out to be working for the insidious covert government agency called The Shop. The installation's security director, Terry Spann, had once been employed by The Shop as well. Appalled by Jude's depravity, she quit, and eventually ended up at Falco Plains.

With Jude searching for Harlan, Terry realizes that the "old" man will

Old Durham town hall   DAVID LOWELL

STEPHEN KING'S GOLDEN YEARS

suffer a horrible fate if she cannot save him. Eventually, she receives help from the facility's director, General Crewes.

The Shop, of course, first appears in the Stephen King Universe as the antagonists of *Firestarter*. Not only do they perform assassinations and any other nasty little jobs that no other government agency could be called upon for, but they have been involved in just the kind of experimentation that Todhunter was conducting. It seems only natural, then, for The Shop to take an interest in Harlan Williams.

Jude Andrews has his orders—bring Williams in as a test subject, no matter what. If that means he has to murder Harlan's wife, Gina, it isn't something he's going to lose any sleep over. In fact, Jude Andrews is such a cold-blooded SOB that he is considered to be the "best" assassin The Shop has ever had, better, even, than the legendary John Rainbird (who is, of course, one of the major characters of *Firestarter*, 1980).

The Shop also plays a role in both *Tommyknockers* (1987) and *The Langoliers*, a novella from *Four Past Midnight* (1990).

Golden Years is yet another work where King delves into the concept of a government experiment gone horribly wrong. The theme is repeated in *Firestarter*, *The Stand* (1978), *The Mist* (collected in *Skeleton Crew*, 1985), and various King short stories.

The theme of aging—in this case, the defiance of age—is also, quite obviously, a major part of this television excursion. Earlier in his career, King had touched on this subject primarily in short stories such as "The Reach," but subsequently it became a major theme in both *The Green Mile* (1996) and—more prominently—*Insomnia* (1994).

Golden Years is also quite notable for the inconclusive nature of its ending. It had been previously implied that Harlan's power was growing exponentially, in a fashion greatly similar to The Shop's predictions about Charlie McGee's eventual power level in *Firestarter*. Harlan could cause earthquakes, speed up time, and cause mechanical things to go haywire. In the end, he created a force field of energy that protected himself and his still-elderly wife, Gina, from attack by Jude Andrews. Then, in a burst of similar energy, they both disappeared.

To where?

It is possible that Harlan is able to actually teleport them elsewhere. It is also conceivable (and somewhat implied by an earlier scene) that he regresses them both backward in age to before their births, effectively erasing their existence, but that hardly seems in character for Harlan.

So what happened to Harlan and Gina Williams?

Time will tell.

GOLDEN YEARS: PRIMARY SUBJECTS

HARLAN WILLIAMS: A janitor at the Falco Plains military research installation, Harlan is caught in an accidental explosion and exposed to an experimental form of energy that causes him to begin an age regression. As a result, he is pursued both by the military and by the insidious government agency known as The Shop. During the final confrontation with Jude Andrews, a Shop agent, Harlan disappears in a flash of green energy. His fate and/or whereabouts are unknown.

TERRY SPANN: A former Shop agent, Terry becomes head of security at Falco Plains and enters into a relationship with the commanding officer of the facility, General Louis Crewes. The relationship suffers when she chooses to protect Harlan Williams from Jude Andrews, her former partner from The Shop. To save Harlan, Terry kills Andrews, but by then Crewes has come around to her way of thinking, and the two depart together. Her current whereabouts are unknown.

GINA WILLIAMS: The wife of Harlan Williams, Gina is the first to notice that he is growing younger. Her life is put in jeopardy when Jude Andrews threatens to kill her if Harlan doesn't turn himself in. In the end, she disappears with her husband in a flash of green energy. Her fate and/or whereabouts are unknown.

FRANCESCA WILLIAMS: The blind daughter of Harlan and Gina Williams, Francesca does her best to keep her parents out of danger. First she takes them to a kind of "hippie" commune where she once lived, hoping they will be safe there. Later she visits a friend who creates false identities for her parents, hoping to aid them in starting a new life. However, while she is gone, her parents have their final confrontation with Jude Andrews, and then disappear. It is presumed that she still resides in Chicago.

DR. TODHUNTER: A scientist working at Falco Plains, the mentally imbalanced Todhunter is doing research into cellular regeneration for the U.S. government. During an experiment, a malfunction occurs, but Todhunter ignores the warnings of his staff, and an explosion follows. He lies his way out of trouble, and it is presumed that he is still conducting research at Falco Plains.

GENERAL CREWES: Louis Crewes is the commanding officer in charge of the military research installation at Falco Plains at the time of the incident that changes Harlan Williams. At first he obeys orders to put Williams under surveillance, but when he discovers that The Shop is involved, he joins with Terry Spann, with whom he is romantically involved, to protect Harlan. After Terry murders Jude Andrews, Crewes goes off with her. His current whereabouts are unknown.

JUDE ANDREWS: Andrews is an agent for The Shop, a covert government agency. He is also reputed to be the best assassin they have ever employed. He is assigned to bring Harlan Williams in for study, but is eventually killed by his former partner, Terry Spann.

CAPTAIN TRIPS: A resident at the commune where Francesca Williams takes her parents, the man called Captain Trips is actually a Shop infiltrator. He tells The Shop where to find the Williamses, and is later killed by Shop agent Jude Andrews.

GOLDEN YEARS: TRIVIA

- In the original televised version of *Golden Years*, the Gina Williams character dies. However, in the videotape version, she is left alive through the miracle of editing.

- "Captain Trips" is not merely the name of The Shop informant in this television drama, but the nickname of the horrible plague in *The Stand*.

- Of the seven episode scripts that were completed, King wrote the first five; the last two were penned by Josef Anderson based on King's outlines.

- Stephen King has a cameo role in the fourth episode as a bus driver.

37

RELATED TALES

The Langoliers (from 1990's *Four Past Midnight*)

"Submitted for your approval: Captain Brian Engle, a pilot with American Pride Airlines. Captain Engle is a sturdy soul, but he's just been shaken to the core by an in-flight pressurization problem that almost caused the explosive decompression of the aircraft he was piloting. He managed to land that craft safely in Los Angeles, and is now walking toward the terminal, where he'll receive tragic news about his ex-wife. Forgoing rest, Engle will board American Pride Flight 29, a flight that is heading toward a date with destiny. Although scheduled to land in Boston, Flight 29 will be forced to make a detour, a change in flight plan that will take it directly into the heart of . . . the Twilight Zone."

While *The Langoliers* never appeared on *The Twilight Zone*, it certainly *feels* like a lost episode of that classic show. Dedicated to "Joe, another white knuckle flier," this story had its origins in a bizarre image that flashed through King's mind of a woman pressing her hand over a crack in the wall of a commercial jetliner. The plot is simple—ten passengers taking a flight from Los Angeles to Boston wake up in midflight to find the crew and the majority of their cabinmates gone (one additional passenger is present, but asleep). Luckily, one of their number can pilot the craft, and takes command. Unable to contact anyone on the ground (no one responds to his calls, and major cities below are blacked out), Captain Brian Engle makes an executive decision to land the plane at Bangor International Airport. There they discover they are the only living things in the immediate vicinity. Nothing feels right to them; even the air smells different. Then they hear sounds in the distance, crunching sounds, as if someone is literally chewing up the landscape. Before the day is through, these unlucky souls discover where all our yesterdays go.

This unique tale of time travel contains several links to the Stephen King Universe. Debating what has occurred, one passenger mentions similar events in history, mainly the disappearance of the entire crew of the *Mary Celeste*, and of the colonists at Roanoke Island, Virginia, two historical events that have fascinated the author for years. The same passenger wonders if he and his fellow travelers may be guinea pigs of an experiment conducted by a top-secret outfit like The Shop (a ruthless "black ops" government agency, first introduced in *Firestarter*). Finally, most of the action of the story takes place at the Bangor International Airport, located in King's hometown in Maine.

THE LANGOLIERS: PRIMARY SUBJECTS

THE LANGOLIERS: According to Craig Toomey's father, the Langoliers are horrid monsters who prey on lazy, time-wasting children. The passengers of Flight 29 adopt Toomey's name for the creatures he's convinced are coming to destroy them. They are described as black balls that contract and then expand again. According to the narrative, "They shimmered and twitched and wavered like faces made of glowing swamp gas. The eyes were only rudimentary indentations, but the mouths were huge: semicircular caves lined with gnashing, whirring teeth." The Langoliers use those teeth to literally chew up the scenery of the world—they are reality's scavengers, complete consumers of yesterday.

CAPTAIN BRIAN ENGLE: Brian Engle is proof that bad luck does come in threes. As the tale begins, Engle has just safely landed a plane that almost suffered an explosive decompression. Arriving at the airport, he is informed that his ex-wife has been killed in a fire. Last, and most important to the story, he boards American Pride Flight 29 for the trip back to Boston to deal with his wife's remains. Exhausted, Engle falls asleep the minute he sits in his seat on the plane. Awakened by Dinah Bellman's screams, he realizes that the crew and most of his fellow passengers are no longer aboard. After breaking down the door to the cockpit with the help of Nick Hopewell, he assumes control of the plane and, indirectly, of the group. Engle survives the incredible events of the Langoliers—he's among those who wink back into existence before the eyes of a startled little girl at the end of the journey.

DINAH BELLMAN: A blind girl with telepathic powers (she can see through others' eyes, and speak to them via telepathy across great distances), Dinah is on Flight 29 with her Aunt Vicky, traveling to Boston to have an operation that might restore her sight. The first to stir after the plane literally crosses over into yesterday, she awakens the remaining passengers with her frightened screams. Dinah demonstrates her powers when she views the other passengers through Craig Toomey's eyes (he sees them as monsters). Frightened by this vision, she clings to Laurel Stevenson during the rest of the ordeal. Despite being stabbed by the paranoid Toomey, the little girl plays an important part in the group's eventual escape, mentally luring the near-dead Toomey to reveal himself to the ravenous Langoliers. The creatures then veer toward him, giving those on the plane valuable time to take off. Mortally injured, Dinah passes away before the aircraft safely crosses back across the border between yesterday and today.

ALBERT KLAUSNER: An exceedingly bright young man who, along with Robert Jenkins, represents the brains of the beleaguered group. It is Albert who realizes that, coming from the future, they and their craft are far more real than their present surroundings at Bangor Airport. Applying his theory, the group refuels their plane with the flat (other-dimensional) mixture contained in the fuel tanks at the airport. Once inside Flight 29's fuel tanks, the fuel becomes more real, allowing them to take off at the approach of the Langoliers. Albert also survives the Langoliers. He is presumed alive and well, perhaps pursuing a romantic relationship with Bethany Sims.

LAUREL STEVENSON: A schoolteacher, Laurel is taking the flight to Massachusetts to meet with a man she only knows through letters. During her adventures in the world of the Langoliers, she and Nick Hopewell fall in love. Before Nick sacrifices himself to save the rest of the group, he asks Laurel to pass a message on to his estranged father. She agrees.

NICK HOPEWELL: An operative of the British government, Nick describes himself as Her Majesty's Mechanic. On his way to Boston to assassinate the paramour of an outspoken supporter of the IRA, Nick instead becomes involved in the adventure of a lifetime. He becomes the *de facto* leader of the group once Captain Engle lands the plane. His sure manner and quick thinking make him a good leader; his no-nonsense attitude keeps human time bomb Craig Toomey in line long enough for Engle to safely touch down. Attempting to return home the way they came, the group realizes that they need to be asleep to cross the barrier safely. Nick, knowing it could mean his death, offers to remain awake and see the craft through the temporary portal safely. Nick is gone when his fellow passengers emerge from their brief sleep and is presumed dead.

DON GAFFNEY: Don takes charge of Craig Toomey after Nick calms his initial outburst (Hopewell grabs Toomey by the nose, threatening to break it if he doesn't back off). Toomey later kills Don with a letter opener.

CRAIG TOOMEY: In introducing this character, King references certain fish that live near the ocean floor, thriving despite the tremendous pressure. Bring these fish up to the surface, however, and they explode: "Craig Toomey had been raised in his own dark trench, had lived in his own atmosphere of high pressure." Raised by a domineering father and castrating mother, Toomey has grown into a paranoid, insecure, Type A adult. An employee of Desert Sun Banking Corporation, the self-destructive Toomey has made a disastrous investment, costing the company millions.

Waking up on board the nearly empty plane, Toomey begins his final descent into madness. Utterly panicked, he starts bullying his fellow passengers until Nick Hopewell forcibly convinces him to back off. His paranoia reaches epic proportions; he attacks the group at the Bangor Airport. First he shoots Albert point-blank in the chest, an attempt that fails because the bullet, subject to the laws of this reality, is not propelled with enough force to hurt the boy. He later stabs Dinah with a letter opener, giving her the wound that eventually kills her; he uses the same weapon to dispatch Don Gaffney shortly thereafter.

Toomey then tries to kill Albert but fails, taking a heavy beating in the process. Albert leaves him in the airport, but a dying Dinah rouses Craig telepathically, forcing him to rise and walk out to the airfield. Once there, he is then attacked and devoured by the Langoliers.

ROBERT JENKINS: Introducing himself to Albert (who eventually comes to play Dr. Watson to Jenkins's Sherlock Holmes), Jenkins says, "I write mysteries for a living. Deduction is my bread and butter, you might say." Jenkins is thrilled by the intellectual challenge his predicament provides—his theories are usually right on the money, helping the others to remain calm and to survive in their strange new environs. Jenkins saves the day late in the game when he realizes that he and his fellow passengers must be asleep to safely cross the divide. Jenkins is presumably alive and well, still writing mystery novels.

BETHANY SIMS: Bethany's mom is sending her to visit her Aunt Shawna, who would most likely have placed her in a rehab center to dry out. Bethany forms a romantic bond with Albert Klausner, who becomes her knight in shining armor. Bethany is presumably alive and well, perhaps pursuing a romantic relationship with Albert.

RUDY WARWICK: A.k.a. "the bald man," Rudy's main preoccupation is eating. At the Bangor Airport, he finds to his horror that the food is tasteless and all but inedible. One of the six people who survive the trauma of the journey to the land of the Langoliers, Rudy is presumed to be alive and well.

THE LANGOLIERS: ADAPTATIONS

Stephen King's The Langoliers was made into a four-hour TV miniseries in 1995. Directed by Tom Holland (who also helmed the lackluster feature version of *Thinner* a year later), this ABC production is faithful to its source material, but comes off as an overly long episode of *The Twilight Zone*. The acting is competent, but surprisingly wooden for the most part. There are bright spots, however: David Morse and Dean Stockwell turn in convincing performances as Captain Engle and Bob Jenkins, and Bronson Pinchot is downright brilliant as Toomey. Like the 1990 television miniseries version of *It*, however, *The Langoliers* is diminished by cheap special effects—all the carefully wrought tension evaporates when the Langoliers, strange hybrids of Pac Men and Tasmanian Devils, appear.

Look closely for Stephen King's cameo as Tom Holby, senior vice president of Desert Sun Banking; the author appears in a fantasy sequence which occurs near the end of the show.

SECTION SIX

Other Prime Reality Tales

he Prime Reality can be seen as the backbone of the Universe, or perhaps the main stage on which most of King's fictional dramas are played out. Items in Other Prime Reality Tales end up there because they cannot be clearly classified as part of any of the other sections of the Prime Reality we've discussed. That is why, for instance, we have chosen to discuss the bulk of King's shorter fiction in this section.

As pointed out in the Introduction to the *Dark Tower* section, King himself only recently came to understand that Roland's world did indeed contain all the others of his making. What remains to be seen, however, is just HOW all the worlds are connected. Some connections are obvious, while others are not, and only King himself can create the connective tissue that pulls all his works together into a cohesive whole. To venture forth, however, it seems reasonable to connect all of the material in this section to the rest of the Prime Reality. In doing so, we can then logically presume, based on other examples, that they are likewise connected beyond the Prime to the Realities of *The Dark Tower, The Stand*, and Richard Bachman.

That said, we can examine some of the works within this section in a little more detail, and mention briefly how they fit in. Some connections are explicit, some are a little more tenuous, but valid nonetheless. Some are not readily apparent, but someday might be made clear.

The first entry deals with *The Shining*, a book about a boy with a wild talent. It certainly must be evident to most at this point that King's Universe contains numerous examples of people with similar talents, described in such novels as *Carrie, The Dead Zone, Firestarter,* and another book described in this section, *The Green Mile.* A more explicit connection lies in one of the book's main characters, Dick Hallorann, who briefly lived in Derry during his military service in World War II.

Dick, of course, is instrumental in helping Danny Torrance defeat the evil that permeates the Overlook Hotel, an evil very reminiscent of that which saturates another famous King edifice, *'Salem's Lot's* Marsten House. Dick and Danny's battle could very well be another, although lesser, skirmish in the eternal war between good and evil, which, as we know, is the overarching theme and plot in the Stephen King Universe. This case could also be made for the events detailed in *The Green Mile,* which features the miracle worker John Coffey, surely a soldier for good in the never-ending war between the Random and the Purpose.

Rose Madder is another example of the connections. As you will read, the title character of that novel visits a world within a painting, a world that, because of references a resident of that world makes to the City of Lud, we strongly suspect is Roland's. This is not the first or the last time that realities have spilled over into one another, as demonstrated by Randall Flagg's reality-hopping, or by Roland's brief foray into the world of *The Stand,* chronicled in *The Dark Tower IV: Wizard and Glass.*

Further connections within the Prime Reality itself spring from Paul Sheldon, bestselling author and protagonist of the novel *Misery.* Sheldon's books are mentioned in both *Rose Madder* and *Desperation.* Thus, since *Rose Madder* is connected to the Reality of the *Dark Tower,* then by virtue of the Paul Sheldon connection, so is *Misery.* A similar argument can be made to connect the Prime Reality to the Reality of King's pseudonymous Richard Bachman novels. The Prime Reality's *Desperation* chronicled events that parallel similar goings-on in the Bachman Reality novel *The Regulators.* There is also an explicit connection between Paul Sheldon and Eddie Kaspbrak from *It,* mentioned in *Misery.*

As mentioned above, this reality also contains most of King's shorter work, which tends to be more eclectic and quirky than his novels. Thus, we consider King's numerous short story collections in this section (though some stories have been removed and reassigned to their proper Realities, where possible). *Night Shift,* for instance, features two stories, "Jerusalem's Lot" and "One for the Road," that can be taken respectively as prologue and epilogue to the novel *'Salem's Lot. Nightmares & Dreamscapes* also features "The Night Flier," a story starring Richard Dees, who figured prominently in *The Dead Zone.*

King playing with the Rock Bottom Remainders   SUSANNE MOSS

Six Stories also contains "Blind Willie," a precursor to a story that appeared in *Hearts in Atlantis*, linking that volume to the Reality of *The Dark Tower* via *Hearts'* novella *Low Men in Yellow Coats*. *Four Past Midnight* contains references to The Shop (a casual comment from one of the passengers in *The Langoliers*), Castle Rock (*The Sun Dog* is set there), and Derry (the unfortunate soul at the center of "Secret Window, Secret Garden" used to live there before his divorce). There is also a link between *Four Past Midnight* and *Needful Things*, as readers are informed at the end of the latter that Leland Gaunt has set up shop in the Junction City, Iowa, building that once housed Sam Peebles's (from "The Library Policeman") insurance office.

Finally, *Everything's Eventual* contains both the title story, featuring Dinky Earnshaw (who would later show up in the *Dark Tower* series), and the *Dark Tower* novella *Little Sisters of Eluria*. "Autopsy Room Four" takes place in Derry.

With all the connections that exist between the books, and King's own declaration that his works are connected, it seems evident that the cosmic war for the fate of the multiverse, the battle between the Random and the Purpose, will go on. We can hypothesize, then, that though certain stories will seem distantly removed from that cosmic struggle, all of the works are connected. The battle goes on, and nowhere on a more individual level than the Prime Reality of the Stephen King Universe, in Castle Rock, Derry, and King's Maine as a whole, all around the world in this parallel dimension where the author has spent the lion's share of his time and energy.

Here, then, are Other Prime Reality Tales.

38

THE SHINING

(1977)

If *'Salem's Lot* (1975) can be rightly judged as one of the finest contemporary treatments of the vampire legend ever written, Stephen King once again hit the bull's-eye only two years later with *The Shining*, which many critics regard as one of the greatest contemporary ghost stories in the history of the genre. Yet even if the supernatural element were completely removed—and this is where King's often overlooked strengths as a mainstream writer quickly become evident—the story would be no less powerful or tragic . . . and no less terrifying.

The Shining, on the surface, concerns the old Overlook Hotel, situated high in the Colorado Rockies. In spite of its national ranking, the massive resort has had a violent history and is rumored to be haunted by a sinister presence. Because of the severe winters cutting off the only access road to the summit, it is closed for several months of the year. A caretaker is hired annually to maintain the facility until it reopens in the spring. The caretaker's family is required to stay with that person, as the solitude in the high mountains can sometimes make a person go a little bit off the deep end with an extreme case of "cabin fever."

The new family hired for this winter are the Torrances: Jack, his wife, Wendy, and their son, five-year-old Danny. Jack, currently in between careers, is appointed by a sympathetic friend to oversee the Overlook Hotel with his family. None of them have any interest in legends of the supernatural or ghosts. Unfortunately, this small family is already haunted by various emotional and psychological problems that make them perfect potential victims for whatever diabolism is hovering about the Overlook.

Jack Torrance is a former (i.e., fired) teacher at the Stovington Preparatory Academy who believes that the months of isolation will only aid him to write a Pulitzer Prize–winning play. But an always supportive Wendy is well aware that privately her husband is deeply troubled. He has such monumental doubts about himself as a man, a husband, and a father that he tends to drink to excess. And when he does so, he tends to lose control of his inner rages and become both verbally and physically abusive toward his wife and son. But since there is no alcohol kept in the Overlook during the winter off-season, Wendy has convinced herself that Jack can find the peace of mind to both write and become close once again to her and their troubled youngster.

Little Danny has his own nearly overwhelming concerns. He has disturbing visions, which cannot be rationally explained. In fact, the child has an amazing psychic gift, which, he is told by the Overlook's friendly cook, Dick Hallorann, is called "the shining." The elderly Hallorann admits he has never seen anyone have such a powerful grasp of the power at such a young age. But it's a dark gift, even though it allows Danny to see glimpses of the future. However, the grisly sights he witnesses often deal with episodes of the utmost violence and horror.

On top of everything, there is a powerful, evil presence waiting patiently for those who overstay their welcome at the Overlook. It craves young Danny most of all, hoping to harness his tremendous psychic powers. Yet the presence realizes that because the boy's father is so weak at heart, it is easier to possess Jack first to more swiftly destroy this already highly fragile family unit.

For it's the accelerating destruction of the family that is of the greatest concern to King in *The Shining*. Indeed, in much of the Stephen King Universe, families are often shown as being broken or dysfunctional in some manner. In *Carrie* (1974) and *'Salem's Lot* (1975), for example, young people are often portrayed as growing up without caring parents, or if they have a mother or a father, they are perhaps better off without them. Monsters can come in many forms and guises—they can sometimes be the people we are supposed to love.

Throughout this work, King depicts young Danny as being in as much danger from his own mentally unbalanced father as he would be from his recurring supernatural visions. It is by making the mundane horrors of child abuse, alcoholism, mental illness, and spousal abuse so terribly plausible that the author is effectively able to take us one step further over the edge to where the reader will readily accept that *anything* can happen to the Torrances. And if bad things can befall good people like them, why couldn't they occur to any one of us?

Just on a level of inducing palpable fear into the reader, *The Shining* may be considered King's masterpiece of horror to date. Many critics feel it is truly one of the most frightening novels ever published. Simply stated, anyone who reads of Danny's awful encounter with the dead woman in Room 217 will never forget it. As King has stated in interviews, "I create people you care about—and then I turn the monsters loose."

From a geographical viewpoint, *The Shining* is unusual in its placement in the Stephen King Universe primarily because it is *not* set in Maine. (Though if King had not chosen to base the Overlook on a real hotel in Colorado that he once visited, it most certainly could have been situated somewhere in rural northern New England.) Yet, because so much of the action takes place within a single isolated setting, for once it does not really matter in which state the novel is set. Even so, it would be unusual in future works for King to stray very far afield from the geographical locations in Maine that he knew so well.

On the other hand, this would not be the last time that King's protagonist would be a writer. (Ben Mears of *'Salem's Lot* was a moderately successful author.) In such future works as *Misery* (1987), *The Dark Half* (1987), and *Bag of Bones* (1998), the main character would also be an author, although each would be a far more successful wordsmith than the doomed Jack Torrance is here. Again, the unique trials and tribulations of a working writer are all part of an occupation that King is highly qualified to explore.

THE SHINING: PRIMARY SUBJECTS

DANNY TORRANCE: A shy five-year-old boy who is gifted—or cursed—with the precognitive power called "the shining." Like his parents, he is trapped for the winter in the Overlook Hotel with an unseen evil presence. When the hotel blows up, killing his possessed father in the process, Danny escapes with his mother and the hotel cook. He is last seen recovering from the terrifying experience at a lodge in western Maine.

TONY: Danny's imaginary friend, Tony warns Danny when something bad is about to happen. In times of stress, he often murmurs the dire word "redrum." (Spell it backward.) It should be noted that Danny Torrance's middle name is Anthony.

JACK TORRANCE: A failed teacher, a recovering drunk, an unsuccessful writer, a desperate husband, and an occasionally abusive father, Jack views coming to the Overlook as his last chance to straighten out his life and prove his worth to himself, his wife, and their son. Regrettably, the loathsome presence of the Overlook knows all too well that Jack will make a perfect vessel through which to obtain the raw psychic power that exists within his son. Jack tries to fight off the demons within him and around him, but ultimately is taken over by the horrific presence. After trying to kill Wendy and Danny—and Dick Hallorann—Jack dies in the explosion that destroys the hotel.

WENDY TORRANCE: Jack's submissive wife and Danny's overly protective mothers, she must do battle against the growing madness of her husband and the horrors of the Overlook. In the end she survives with her son, but loses her husband to the demons who had possessed him and the Overlook.

DICK HALLORANN: The head cook of the Overlook, he also has "the shining" and instructs Danny on how to use the power and what its limitations are. A tall, middle-aged African-American, he rescues Danny and his mother, Wendy, at the Overlook resort when the boy "calls" to him, using his psychic powers. Hallorann survives the attack by a possessed Jack Torrance and the destruction of the cursed hotel. Later, he settles in as a cook at the Red Arrow Lodge in Maine.

DELBERT GRADY: A previous caretaker of the Overlook. The spectres in the hotel eventually drove him mad, and he murdered his two young daughters with an ax and did in his wife with a shotgun. After blowing his brains out with the same weapon, he becomes a ghost himself—a permanent guest—at the Overlook.

MRS. MASSEY: A sixty-year-old guest of the hotel who killed herself when her seventeen-year-old lover deserted her. Her lonely, still lustful spirit haunts Room 217, waiting in the bathtub for her beau to return, until the hotel's destruction.

THE OVERLOOK HOTEL: A massive structure with 110 rooms, situated high in the Colorado mountains. Constructed between 1907 and 1909, it is one of the most beautiful resort hotels ever built; it is also, unfortunately, the most evil. When Jack Torrance fails to properly maintain the boilers, the entire facility explodes and goes up in flames. It is still unclear if the evil presence, which existed in every room and board and nail of the hotel, was completely and forever destroyed in the resulting devastation.

THE SHINING: ADAPTATIONS

In 1980, legendary filmmaker Stanley Kubrick brought his vision to the screen of what many critics believed was a powerful and extremely visual interpretation of the novel. Although King was at first extremely flattered that the great director would be adapting his novel for the movies, the author was dissatisfied ultimately with the final results. (For one thing, Kubrick rejected the screenplay offered to him by King and adapted it himself with another screenwriter.)

Although the production boasted impressive performances from stars Jack Nicholson, Shelley Duvall, Scatman Crothers, and newcomer Danny Lloyd as Danny Torrance, it was evident that Kubrick's ideas about how to effectively portray cinematic horror were not the same as King's. Kubrick also had no hesitation in changing characterizations or crucial elements of the novel to better suit his own needs as a visual stylist, such as the totally unwarranted plot twist of slaying Hallorann. King also believed that star Jack Nicholson never portrayed Torrance other than as a man already half insane when we first see him, thus giving the audience an unpleasant character few could remotely care about.

King has often stated that the R-rated film reminded him of a big, expensive-looking car—but one that had no engine to make it go. The author also believed that the director was to some degree "above" making a genre horror movie—that it would somehow be beneath his talents if he truly tried to frighten the audience. The pace of the movie also didn't help—originally released at 146 minutes, the filmmaker cut it by four minutes for general release. In spite of King's increasing fame over the years, the movie would forever be known—for good reasons and bad—as "Stanley Kubrick's *The Shining.*"

Over the years, King became less and less a fan of the 1980 motion picture, and as noted never had any hesitation in letting his feelings be known to the public. In 1996, King convinced the ABC television network that the novel's author was the best judge in terms of who should write and produce a definitive version of the modern classic of horror. King worked with one of his favorite directors, Mick Garris, to create a six-hour miniseries that initially aired in three parts (April 27, April 28, and May 1, 1997). King now firmly believed the television miniseries format—which had worked so well with *The Stand* (1994)—was the best way to present his vision of *The Shining.*

By this point, in the late 1990s, King had far more clout than he had had when Stanley Kubrick had first optioned the film rights to *The Shining.* The network reportedly offered him a blank check to executive produce his next miniseries (ultimately about $23 million) and the choice of any of his works to adapt. King had always wanted to remake *The Shining,* but to do so had to strike a bargain with Stanley Kubrick that he would no longer publicly comment upon or criticize Kubrick's earlier version of his novel.

Yet even King took liberties in adapting his story to the miniseries format, and to a noticeable degree focused strongly on Jack Torrance's drinking problem as an integral part of the plot line. And rather than use well-known movie stars like Jack Nicholson, King purposely chose actors familiar to television viewers, such as Steven Weber (from the series *Wings*) as Jack and actress Rebecca De Mornay to play Wendy. Under the capable direction of Garris (who had also helmed *Sleepwalkers* and *The Stand*), there finally came to be a version that will forever be known—for both good reasons and bad—as "Stephen King's *The Shining.*"

THE SHINING: TRIVIA

- The original title of the novel was *The Shine.* King changed it, as he thought it might be somehow misconstrued as a racial slur.

- The novel was originally constructed in the format of a five-act play. To keep it from becoming too long, King dropped both the Prologue and the Epilogue. However, a reworked version of the prologue titled "Before the Play" appeared in 1982 in *Whispers* magazine and later in the April 26, 1997, issue of *TV Guide* that featured articles on his miniseries *The Shining*. The epilogue has apparently been completely lost.

- Stephen King has a cameo role in the television miniseries portraying a ghostly bandleader. The name of his orchestra? "The Gage Creed Band."

39

NIGHT SHIFT

(1978)

After only three novels in print under his own name, King published this, his first volume of short stories. Most of the tales within this collection first appeared in men's magazines during the early to mid-1970s. At the time, publications such as *Penthouse*, *Cavalier*, and *Gallery* were a booming market for horror fiction. The exceptions include "One for the Road," which was a coda of sorts to his *'Salem's Lot* (1975), and appeared in *Maine* magazine. The other, "I Know What You Need," was first published in *Cosmopolitan* in 1976.

Within this collection we have some of King's very earliest work. Some of the material predates *Carrie* (1974) significantly. In addition, a good number of the stories herein have a familiar flavor to them, a tone reminiscent of the kinds of classic science fiction and horror that King had weaned himself on. The first entry, "Jerusalem's Lot," is a traditional horror tale in the mold of genre grandmaster H. P. Lovecraft, author of such bizarre short classics as "The Dunwich Horror" and "The Shadow over Innsmouth." Rising beyond the nod—or even homage—to Lovecraft, King's own voice, familiar and confident, is clear. Throughout the rest of the volume, King establishes without question that his is the only voice in this book. Each of these stories is spun from the webbing of his unmistakable imagination.

It's as simple as the first line of his foreword to *Night Shift*. "Let's talk, you and I," the author says, seductively. "Let's talk about fear."

And he does—magnificently.

"I Am the Doorway"

A former astronaut is afflicted with a terrible curse: an alien intelligence has infiltrated his body and begins to take it over; using his body, it murders those who might threaten it.

"I AM THE DOORWAY": PRIMARY SUBJECTS

ARTHUR: The astronaut who, while on a mission code-named Project: Zeus—whose purpose is to find intelligent life in outer space—is infected or infiltrated by an alien presence that then begins to grow in his body. First it shows up as golden eyes on his fingers and palms. Later, after he has burned his hands off, the eyes return to grow again on his chest, attempting to control his every action. Arthur's fate is unknown, though he was last known to be contemplating suicide.

RICHARD: A friend of Arthur's, murdered by the creature inhabiting Arthur's body when the alien decides Richard might jeopardize its presence on Earth.

LEDERER: An astronaut whose failed mission leaves him trapped in a spaceship that will orbit the sun until he dies.

PROJECT: ZEUS: The mission that Arthur was participating in when he first came into contact with the alien species that somehow entered his body and began to take possession of it.

"The Mangler"

A horrifying series of accidents at an industrial laundry leads a police officer to realize that an incredible set of coincidences has allowed a powerful demon to possess a commercial laundry ironer and folder.

"THE MANGLER": PRIMARY SUBJECTS

JOHN HUNTON: As a police officer, his investigation of the death of Adelle Frawley in "The Mangler" leads him to eventually consider the possibility of demonic possession. When he and his friend Mark Jackson attempt to exorcise the demon, the giant laundry machine roars to life and attacks them. It is not known if John Hunton survived his final confrontation with the Mangler.

MARK JACKSON: It is partially due to Mark Jackson's influence that Hunton begins to consider possession as a possibility. Jackson's research allows them to confirm that suspicion. It is not known if Mark Jackson survived his final confrontation with the Mangler.

SHERRY OUELETTE: Due to the fact that she is a virgin, Sherry's blood is a vital ingredient in the purely unintentional ritual that invests a demonic spirit into the Mangler.

BLUE RIBBON LAUNDRY: The industrial laundry—in an unnamed American city—where the Mangler comes to life.

THE POSSESSED REFRIGERATOR: A safety inspector tells Hunton the tale of a refrigerator that had been moved to a dump, only to apparently prey on anything that came near it, including birds and a young boy whose parents believed he knew better than to crawl inside a discarded refrigerator. (Recall that young Patrick Hockstetter of *It* met his demise in a discarded refrigerator.)

THE MANGLER: A Hadley-Watson Model 6 Speed Ironer and Dryer, it becomes known as "the Mangler," due to several accidents that took place with the machine. Eventually, it becomes possessed by a demon and later, to protect itself, literally comes to life, tears its way out of the Blue Ribbon Laundry, and goes after those who would destroy it. It is not known if the Mangler survived the final confrontation with its enemies.

"The Boogeyman"

Over the course of several years, Lester Billings's three children die mysteriously in their cribs. Lester reveals to his new psychiatrist, Dr. Harper, that in hindsight, the behavior of his children immediately previous to their deaths led him to the eventual conclusion that they were murdered by a creature called "the Boogeyman."

"THE BOOGEYMAN": PRIMARY SUBJECTS

LESTER BILLINGS: All three of his children supposedly died at the hands of the Boogeyman.

DR. HARPER: Lester's psychiatrist. It is unclear, but it seems that either the Boogeyman murdered Harper and disguised himself as the psychiatrist in order to continue terrorizing Billings, or that Harper has always been the Boogeyman.

THE BOOGEYMAN: A legendary monster who is supposed to lurk in the closets of children, attacking when they are made vulnerable by their parents' disbelief in such mythical creatures.

"Gray Matter"

A group of older men hanging out at a package store called Henry's Nite-Owl are surprised one night by a visit from Timmy Grenadine. The boy claims that a bacteria-infected beer has transformed his father into a gelatinous monster who eats dead, putrefying animals and perhaps even worse. The group of men investigate the boy's story.

"GRAY MATTER": PRIMARY SUBJECTS

RICHIE GRENADINE: His unemployment leads him to even heavier drinking than usual. One day, a "skunked" beer, containing a kind of bacteria or virus, infects him, and he begins to change into something monstrous—a huge, gelatinous creature with a hunger for flesh, living or dead. The result of his confrontation with Henry Parmalee is unknown.

TIMMY GRENADINE: Richie's son, who tells Henry Parmalee and the other regulars at the Nite-Owl what has been happening to his father. His current whereabouts are unknown.

HENRY PARMALEE: Owner of the Nite-Owl, he is horrified enough by Timmy Grenadine's story—and convinced enough by the boy's tale—to go out in a snowstorm to check it out. Though he is armed with a gun, the outcome of his battle with Richie Grenadine remains unknown.

"Battleground"

A hit man assassinates the owner of a toy company, only to have the victim's mother send him a box of toy soldiers who are somehow—likely through supernatural means—alive, and determined to murder him.

"BATTLEGROUND": PRIMARY SUBJECTS

JOHN RENSHAW: A professional assassin in the employ of a syndicate of organized crime figures, his career is cut short when the mother of his most recent target decides to retaliate. Renshaw is murdered by the living toy soldiers sent by Mrs. Morris.

HANS MORRIS: Owner of the Morris Toy Company, he is assassinated by John Renshaw.

MRS. MORRIS: Hans Morris's mother, she sends living toys to take revenge upon her son's killer.

TOY SOLDIERS: While the soldiers' sentience is never explained, it seems there are two possibilities. Either they are finely manufactured, artificially intelligent, tiny robots . . . or they are invested with supernatural life and intelligence.

"Sometimes They Come Back"

A high school English teacher is terrified to discover that the teenagers who murdered his brother when they were kids all later died violently. They have now returned as demonic yet incarnate spirits to dispose of him.

"SOMETIMES THEY COME BACK": PRIMARY SUBJECTS

JIM NORMAN: In 1957, when Jim was nine and his older brother, Wayne, was twelve, they were cornered by a group of older bullies. During the ensuing struggle, Wayne Norman was murdered even as he screamed at Jim to flee the scene. Decades later, and now a schoolteacher, Jim suffers from recurring nightmares. After he begins teaching at Davis High, some of his students die mysteriously, and the new students who fill the school's vacant seats turn out to be the demonic spirits of the boys who killed his brother years earlier. He is forced to call up the spirit of his deceased sibling to defend him once again. Jim Norman's current whereabouts are unknown.

WAYNE NORMAN: Jim's older brother, he was murdered at the age of twelve.

VINNIE COREY, DAVID GARCIA, and BOBBY LAWSON:
Three teenage thugs. In 1957, they murdered Wayne Norman. Later, they each die a violent death, and eventually return as spirits to torment and attempt to kill Jim Norman. Their spirits are destroyed or returned to their rightful rest.

RAISING DEMONS: A book used by Jim Norman to find the spell that he then uses to raise the spirit of his brother Wayne.

"Strawberry Spring"

A man tells the story of a series of murders that took place on the campus of New Sharon Teachers' College—located in an unnamed American city—while he was a student there. He then relates a series of recent murders that seem to be the work of the same killer, whom the authorities dub "Springheel Jack."

"STRAWBERRY SPRING": PRIMARY SUBJECTS

SPRINGHEEL JACK: A vicious serial murderer who is also the storyteller. His current whereabouts are unknown.

"The Lawnmower Man"

A man reluctant to mow his own lawn hires a lawn care service and gets more than he bargains for when a mysterious, barely human figure with a sentient lawnmower arrives to do the job.

"THE LAWNMOWER MAN": PRIMARY SUBJECTS

HAROLD PARKETTE: He doesn't want to mow his own lawn, and hires the lawnmower man. Eventually, the lawnmower man orders his supernaturally intelligent mower to kill Harold, and the lawnmower mulches him.

THE LAWNMOWER MAN: A cloven-hoofed worshipper of the god Pan, he follows his mower around naked and eats all the grass clippings. He later murders Harold Parkette for being an unbeliever and threatening to call the police.

"I Know What You Need"

A young woman discovers that the man she has been dating has been obsessed with her since childhood, and has used voodoo to force her to fall in love with him.

"I KNOW WHAT YOU NEED": PRIMARY SUBJECTS

LIZ HOGAN: A college student whose boyfriend, Ed Hamner, has been magically manipulating her, and has also committed murder. She manages to break free of his manipulations, but is left with a great deal of self-doubt. Her current whereabouts are unknown.

ED HAMNER: Since boyhood, he has had special mental powers that allow him to read the minds and needs of those around him, and to simply know things otherwise impossible for him to know. Not only does he cause the deaths of his parents, but also that of Liz Hogan's previous boyfriend. His current whereabouts are unknown.

"Children of the Corn"

A young couple on a cross-country trip come upon a town where the children have slaughtered all the adults at the behest of a demonic presence that lives in the cornfields of Gatlin, Nebraska.

"CHILDREN OF THE CORN": PRIMARY SUBJECTS

BURT ROBESON: When a dead boy is thrown in front of his car on a Nebraska highway, Burt insists that he and his wife go to the nearest town in the middle of nowhere. There they are captured by the children of the corn, and sacrificed to their dark god.

VICKY ROBESON: When the Robesons run over a dead boy on the highway, Vicky wants to backtrack to the last major town they had passed through, and leave the body there. Burt insists they go on. Like her husband, Vicky is crucified by the children of the corn and offered up as a sacrifice.

HE WHO WALKS BEHIND THE ROWS: The demonic presence worshipped by the children of the corn. It is presumed that he *still* walks behind the rows.

"The Last Rung on the Ladder"

Upon discovering that his sister, Kitty (Katrina), has killed herself, a man named Larry recalls the day, back during their childhood, when he saved his sister's life. Now he feels a great deal of guilt for not having been there for her in the end.

"The Man Who Loved Flowers"

A serial murderer who uses a hammer as his weapon of choice buys flowers for a long-lost love and confuses his victims with that old flame. He presents the flowers to his victim before the murder. It is presumed he is still at large.

"The Woman in the Room"

A man assists in the suicide of his disease-ravaged mother in the Central Maine Hospital in Lewiston.

[NOTE: The short stories "Jerusalem's Lot," "Graveyard Shift," and "One for the Road" are discussed in the section on Jerusalem's Lot and King's Maine. "The Ledge" and "Quitters, Inc." are discussed in the section entitled The World of Richard Bachman. The story "Night Surf" is addressed in the section entitled The Worlds of The Dark Tower *and* The Stand.*]*

NIGHT SHIFT: ADAPTATIONS

Night Shift has the distinction of having spawned more film and television projects than any other King collection to date.

In 1983, Granite Entertainment produced a direct-to-video release containing two short films based on King's work: "The Boogeyman" and "The Woman in the Room." The video, entitled *Stephen King's Night Shift Collection*, is perhaps most notable for the fact that the latter tale was adapted and directed by Frank Darabont, who would go on to adapt and direct both *The Shawshank Redemption* (1994) and *The Green Mile* (1999).

In 1984, actor Peter Horton (*Thirtysomething*) and *Terminator* star Linda Hamilton co-starred in the screen version of *Children of the Corn*, which has spawned countless (and increasingly only vaguely related) sequels.

The 1985 feature film *Cat's Eye*, directed by Lewis Teague, incorporated two tales from this collection: "Quitters, Inc.," starring James Woods and Alan King, and "The Ledge," featuring *Airplane* actor Robert Hays. (See the separate entry on this film, which was written by King.)

The following year saw the release of *Maximum Overdrive*, thus far the only movie written and directed by Stephen King. He adapted the screenplay from his short story "Trucks." The R-rated thriller featured Emilio Estevez, Pat Hingle (*Batman*'s Commissioner Gordon), and Yeardley Smith (the voice of Lisa Simpson on *The Simpsons*), and is not to be confused with the 1997 cable television version of *Trucks*, which headlined Timothy Busfield (*Thirtysomething*).

In 1990, Paramount Pictures released *Stephen King's "Graveyard Shift,"* based on the wild story of the same name and starring popular character actor Brad Dourif.

The year 1991 brought the made-for-television version of *Sometimes They Come Back*, starring Tim Matheson and Brooke Adams. The release led to several direct-to-video sequels.

And, lest we forget, the 1992 film *The Lawnmower Man* was named after—and purported to be based on—King's short story of the same name. However, the sci-fi thriller shared so little with the original story that King successfully sued to have his name removed from the project. (Which still didn't stop the producers from making a sequel, even without an official King connection to exploit.)

NIGHT SHIFT: TRIVIA

- At the opening of the film version of *Children of the Corn*, the main characters are driving along a deserted road in Nebraska. On the dashboard of their car is a copy of the paperback of *Night Shift*.

- The powers of Ed Hamner in "I Know What You Need" are quite similar to those of the main character of a classic *The Twilight Zone* TV series episode that might have inspired King. Its title? "What You Need."

- "The Woman in the Room" was likely influenced, and certainly informed, by King's own deeply personal and traumatic experience: his mother died of cancer.

- *Night Shift* is the only book by King that carries no dedication.

- "The Lawnmower Man" was adapted to comic form by King and Walt Simonson in 1981, for the black-and-white Marvel Comics magazine *Bizarre Adventures*. Save for the stories in *Creepshow*—which was published in a comic version to tie into the film's 1982 release—it stands with "Popsy"—adapted for Innovation Comics' horror anthology *Masques*—as the only such adaptation of King's work.

40

CREEPSHOW

(1982)

*C*reepshow isn't a novel, nor is it exactly a short story collection. Its two incarnations are as a motion picture and as a comic book graphic novel. But its origins are in the fevered mind of Stephen King himself, of course.

The film version consists of five segments, plus a sort of prologue and epilogue featuring a character called the Creep, whose resemblance to the Cryptkeeper only solidifies the relationship the film and the stories therein have to such classic early comics series as *Tales from the Crypt, The Haunt of Fear,* and *The Vault of Horror.* Thus it is only fitting that the published version of *Creepshow* is presented in comic book form, with art by legendary horror comics master Berni Wrightson (who provided the illustrations for *Cycle of the Werewolf*).

Two of the stories in the film have their origins in text form. "The Lonesome Death of Jordy Verrill" began life in the mid-1970s as a short story published in a pair of men's magazines, *Cavalier* and *Nugget,* both of which were repositories of many early King stories. The other tale, "The Crate," first appeared in *Gallery* magazine. Both have the kind of structure and twist ending that were typical of the comics stories King read and loved as a young man.

Creepshow was created as a kind of living version of those horror anthology comics of the 1950s. In addition to creating the Creep, King added three brand-new stories to the script, narratives that had never appeared in purely text form. Those were "Father's Day," "Something to Tide You Over," and "They're Creeping up on You." King also somewhat altered the two older stories used in the picture.

Most notably, particularly for our purposes, King moved Jordy Verrill's small town from New Hampshire to Maine, only several miles away from Castle Rock, itself a major component of the King Universe.

It should be noted that in the case of the two already published stories, we have adhered here to the later (film/comic book) versions in our own discussion, just as we have adhered to the unabridged version of *The Stand*. Since the *Creepshow* screenplay was written by King, we consider his update in the form of the film's script to be the official continuity.

"Father's Day"

A savagely cruel old man, murdered by his much-beleaguered daughter, returns from the grave seven years later to take vengeance upon her, and the rest of his cold-hearted family.

"FATHER'S DAY": PRIMARY SUBJECTS

BEDELIA GRANTHAM: After caring for her cruel, ungrateful father for thirty years, Bedelia is finally driven over the edge when her dad arranges the murder of her fiancé. On Father's Day, Bedelia crushes her parent's skull with a glass ashtray. Each subsequent year, she returns on that day to dine with her family and visit her father's grave. Seven years after she killed him, Bedelia's father, Nathan Grantham, returns from the grave to kill his daughter and the rest of the family.

NATHAN GRANTHAM: A sadistic old man, murdered by his daughter after arranging the "accidental" death of her fiancé. He comes back from the grave seven years later to murder her, as well as numerous other family members. The current status of the resurrected corpse that was Nathan Grantham is unknown.

PETER YARBRO: An unfortunate man, Peter Yarbro makes the mistake of becoming engaged to Bedelia Grantham. Unwilling to be parted from the daughter he treated as a slave, Bedelia's father, Nathan, has Peter Yarbro murdered.

"The Lonesome Death of Jordy Verrill"

In this story (a.k.a. "Weeds") a slow-witted farmer discovers a meteor on his property. He believes at first that he will be able to sell it for a great deal of money. However, when he attempts to retrieve it from the hole it made on his farm, he burns himself. Worse, the meteor infects him with a spore or virus of some kind that causes green weeds to grow wildly over everything, including his own flesh.

"THE LONESOME DEATH OF JORDY VERILL": PRIMARY SUBJECTS

JORDY VERRILL: Jordy is the doomed and none-too-bright farmer. He has what he calls "Verrill luck," which is all bad. After being infected by the "meteor shit," Jordy commits suicide by blowing off his head with a shotgun.

THE METEOR SHIT: Whatever it is that comes out of the meteor continues growing all over Jordy Verrill's farm, five miles from Castle Rock. If this is the same Castle Rock seen in other stories, and not some alternate dimension, we must presume that the spread of the infection was somehow interrupted. However, the manner of that interruption and its permanence are unknown at this time.

"The Crate"

In June 1834, an explorer named Julia Carpenter sent a large crate from the Arctic to Horlicks University. Misplaced, the crate remains under a stairwell in Amberson Hall for more than a century and a half, until it is discovered by a janitor. The janitor, curious, informs Professor Dexter Stanley, who hurries to Amberson Hall to open the crate with the janitor. Inside there is a vicious monster, who promptly eats the janitor upon the opening of the crate, and later devours a student as well.

"THE CRATE": PRIMARY SUBJECTS

HENRY NORTHRUP: This much-put-upon professor, upon being told of a monster in a crate, leads his wife into a trap, causing her to be eaten by the beast. His current whereabouts are unknown.

WILMA NORTHRUP: Insists upon being called Billie, right up until the time her husband—whom she has tormented and sneered at for years—traps her with the evil thing. Billie is consumed by the creature.

DEXTER STANLEY: Professor Stanley is the one who actually opens the crate, an action that immediately results in the deaths of two people. Distraught, he tells Henry Northrup about it. Henry drugs him so that he will have time to dispose of his wife and the monster in the crate. Later, Northrup and Stanley make a pact of mutual silence. His current whereabouts are unknown.

THE MONSTER IN THE CRATE: After eating three people, including Billie Northrup, it is chained again in the crate by Henry Northrup, and then the box is dumped into Ryder's Quarry. However, Henry does not do a very good job. It seems likely that the monster has escaped, but its current whereabouts are unknown.

"Something to Tide You Over"

In a homicidal rage, Richard Vickers murders his wife and her lover by burying them up to their necks at the shore, and then letting the tide come in. When he returns to find the bodies, however, they appear to have been swept out to sea. Instead, they show up as undead creatures ready to do him in in the same fashion.

"SOMETHING TO TIDE YOU OVER": PRIMARY SUBJECTS

HARRY WENTWORTH: Harry is murdered by the enraged husband of his lover, Becky Vickers. After their deaths, the lovers return from their watery grave to take vengeance.

BECKY VICKERS: Killed for her infidelity, Becky comes back from the dead to get even with her husband.

RICHARD VICKERS: After eliminating his cheating wife and her lover by burying them up to their necks on the beach and waiting for the tide to come in, Richard is done in via the same manner by his resurrected victims.

"They're Creeping Up on You"

A fabulously rich recluse, Upson Pratt is a soulless businessman who destroys lives without remorse. He is also obsessed with his environment, keeping his home perfectly white, very neat, and almost completely sterile. So when the cockroaches show up in force during a blackout, it drives him over the edge.

"THEY'RE CREEPING UP ON YOU": PRIMARY SUBJECTS

UPSON PRATT: Unhealthily obsessed with hygiene, Pratt particularly hates bugs. Especially cockroaches, which begin to proliferate in his seemingly sterile apartment. Perhaps it is some kind of cosmic payback for his life of cruelty that Pratt is set upon by thousands of cockroaches, who enter his body and take up residence in his hollowed-out corpse.

CREEPSHOW: ADAPTATIONS

In October 1982, Warner Bros. released *Creepshow*, written by King and directed by horror veteran (and personal friend) George A. Romero. The producer was Richard Rubinstein, whose Laurel Entertainment would later produce, among a great many other things, *Tales from the Darkside*. The film has special effects by another horror vet, Tom Savini. (Savini also appears as a garbage man in a cameo at the end of this movie.)

The five stories in the picture are bookended by a brief framing sequence in which a young boy is seen reading *Creepshow*, the comic book, only to have it taken away by his mother.

The 120-minute feature is dotted by an array of stellar talent in brief appearances. "Father's Day" features Viveca Lindfors as Aunt Bedelia and Ed Harris as Hank Blaine. "Something to Tide You Over" showcases Leslie Nielsen as Richard Vickers and Ted Danson as Harry Wentworth. "The Crate" has Hal Holbrook as Harry Northrup, Adrienne Barbeau as Billie, and Fritz Weaver as Dexter Stanley. Finally, "They're Creeping up on You" stars veteran actor E. G. Marshall as Upson Pratt.

And, lest we forget, King himself is seen as the title character in "The Lonesome Death of Jordy Verrill."

While the R-rated release was by no means a blockbuster at the box office, it did well enough to spawn a sequel. The aptly titled *Creepshow 2* (1987) was written by the first film's director, George Romero (who did not direct this follow-up), "based on stories by Stephen King." The credit itself is suspect, however, when only "The Raft" segment is based on a published King story. The other two installments in the film ("Old Chief Wood'nhead" and "The Hitchhiker") are apparently stories initially developed by King and later scripted by Romero.

Plans for a *Creepshow 3* never reached the production stage.

CREEPSHOW: TRIVIA

- Billy, the boy in the bookend segments of the 1982 feature, was played by Joe King, son of the author.

- In addition to his starring role in a segment of the first *Creepshow*, Stephen King had a cameo as a truck driver in the sequel, as did his long-time assistant, Shirley Sonderegger, who played Mrs. Cavenaugh.

41

DIFFERENT SEASONS

(1982)

Though he has since seen several similar books published, *Different Seasons* was a milestone for King in at least two significant ways. First, it was a collection of novellas—or short novels—a form of prose writing not generally considered very marketable. Short stories are a quick read, of course, and novels are the accepted format for prose fiction. Novellas fall somewhere in between. This entry helped slightly to lighten the stigma of the novella.

In addition, *Different Seasons* represented a major change for King. Of the four novellas in this collection, three of them are very specifically *not* horror stories, though one of those three, *Apt Pupil*, is certainly disturbingly horrific. Given that King had been crowned the "king" of horror and was expected to do nothing else, writing such mainstream work—and in novella form—was indeed a risk. Fortunately, it was a gamble that was eagerly embraced by the public.

In some ways, the entries included here are the best loved of King's writing to date. That might, at first, seem hard to accept. Fans love *The Stand* (1978) and *The Shining* (1977), among others. But with the films *The Shawshank Redemption* (1994), *Apt Pupil* (1998), and particularly *Stand by Me* (1986) all originating from this material, it seems less of a stretch to conclude that, collectively, *Different Seasons* has reached one of the broadest audiences and received perhaps the best response (both *Shawshank* and *Stand by Me* were Oscar nominees) of any of King's work.

It also contains a body of work that is considered among his best.

Apt Pupil

Without a doubt, *Apt Pupil* is the dark heart of this remarkable collection, and is among the grimmest pieces King has ever written. Just as he has subverted so many long-accepted conventions of Americana over the years, here King takes a small-town conceit and relationship worthy of Norman Rockwell and inverts it, turning the innocence of that *Saturday Evening Post* image of America into a perversely insightful study of evil.

Apt Pupil tells of Todd Bowden, a practical, above-average student with a sense of humor and natural athletic ability. He's every parent's dream child. Except that Todd has found himself with a weird, unwholesome fascination for all things related to Nazi Germany and the Holocaust of World War II. When he recognizes an old man on the local bus as the former commander of a Nazi death camp, living in hiding in rural California (where the novella is set), Todd's response is not at all that of a normal teen.

He doesn't confide in his friends. He doesn't tell his parents. He doesn't inform the police. Instead, he is thrilled by his secret. Since his private hobby and obsession is the Holocaust, he uses his extensive knowledge to blackmail the Nazi, Kurt Dussander, into sharing with him the horrible stories of those years, complete with every nasty detail. Like a hideous Peeping Tom, Todd gets a thrill from all of this illicit activity.

Meanwhile, his optimistic, conventional parents see only the Norman Rockwell side of things. From their point of view, Todd is a good kid, spending time reading to an elderly man who is losing his sight. What could be more a part of the American myth? They see only what they want to. Meanwhile, when Todd's academic career falls apart, he dares not allow his parents to discover the truth, and can confide in and rely on only one person: Kurt Dussander.

What begins as a weird obsession and a blackmail scheme begins to evolve. Spurred on by the hideously evil nature of what they share, Todd and Dussander each turn to murder, and eventually trap one another in a web of lies. Because of their shared guilt, neither can inform upon the other. In the end, Dussander has a heart attack and is recognized by a man who had been incarcerated at the death camp where he was commandant. After this truth about Dussander hits the news, Todd is visited by the school counselor Dussander helped him fool. Todd kills the man before re-treating to a tree above a nearby highway, where he fires upon cars passing below for hours before police sharpshooters take him down.

Like *Rage* (1977), one of the half-dozen novels King wrote under the Richard Bachman pseudonym, *Apt Pupil* depicts harrowing behavior by a high school student. In a time today when such events have become all too common in real life, we are greatly sensitized to such things. It would be easy to allow those depictions—though in the case of *Apt Pupil*, the story is far more complex than the acts of violence themselves—to overshadow the stories that King is telling, and the themes that lie therein. There is rage in many young people. But what causes them to turn to violence, even mur-der? There is no single answer.

In the case of *Apt Pupil*, it seems clear that Todd Bowden is genuinely a bad seed, a mind ripe for twisting. It may be that evil lurks in him the way it lingers in the Marsten House in *'Salem's Lot* (1975). In any case, however, he is evil, not merely misguided or disturbed or misunderstood, as it ap-pears he may be at the outset. It is unusual in a King book for a mere hu-man being to be so unrepentantly sinister, but that is the exploratory nature of this narrative.

APT PUPIL: PRIMARY SUBJECTS

TODD BOWDEN: A high school student in California, Todd discov-ers that Nazi death camp commander Kurt Dussander is living in his home-town under an assumed name. Already obsessed with the Holocaust, Todd blackmails Dussander into sharing his horrifying memories, and the two enter into a symbiotic relationship that leads them each to commit murder. After Dussander's death, Todd takes a rifle up into a tree overlooking the highway and fires at cars passing below. He is killed by police sharpshoot-ers.

ARTHUR DENKER (a.k.a. KURT DUSSANDER): Under the Denker alias, Kurt Dussander has created a new life for himself in America after having spent years as a death camp commander in Nazi Germany. When Todd Bowden discovers his identity, Dussander must confront a past he has tried to escape. In doing so, he finds himself almost compelled to commit more atrocities. After a heart attack, he is hospitalized and shares a room with a survivor of the camp, who recognizes him and turns him in. Dussander commits suicide in the hospital.

EDWARD FRENCH: As Todd Bowden's guidance counselor, Mr. French is taken in by a ruse played out by Todd and Dussander. When Todd's grades are falling, Dussander pretends to be Todd's grandfather and speaks to French on Todd's behalf. When Dussander dies, French realizes the deception, and would have revealed the truth if Todd had not murdered him first.

MORRIS HEISEL: A survivor of the Nazi death camps, he recognizes his one-time tormentor Dussander when he sees him in the hospital.

Morris Heisel's current whereabouts are unknown.

The Breathing Method

It is appropriate that *The Breathing Method* is dedicated to Peter Straub and his wife, Susan, since the fundamental conceit owes so much to Straub. Like the Chowder Society in Straub's masterpiece, *Ghost Story* (1979), King introduces here a men's club dedicated to the telling of tales. On the wall is a plaque: IT IS THE TALE, NOT HE WHO TELLS IT.

However, King has put his own imprint on this premise. In the club's library, there are volumes of masterful prose and poetry on the shelves by writers the narrator has never heard of, published by houses that don't exist. The building itself, an old brownstone located at 249B East Thirty-fourth Street, seems to have endless rooms in which people have been known to become lost forever. And the butler, the de facto host of the club, is named Stevens, perhaps after King himself.

Are those rooms pathways into other dimensions? Perhaps. Is each door a "thinny," as the term is introduced in the *Dark Tower* series (1982–2004)? That seems likely. Suffice it to say that the club itself is a setting in which King could set a great many of his own tales. In addition to *The Breathing Method*, there is at least one other tale in which King did just that, called "The Man Who Would Not Shake Hands."

Here, however, we are introduced to a man named David Adley, who has achieved moderate success in his firm, but feels he will rise no further. When his boss invites him to the club, he thinks it may be a step up. On that count, he is disappointed. Instead, however, Adley is drawn into the enigmatic group of men who gather at the club to tell stories around the fire. Though at Christmas there is always a "weird tale," the stories are not usually sinister, or even supernatural.

On the other hand, there is the tale related by Dr. Emlyn McCarron: the narrative of Sandra Stansfield and "the Breathing Method." It is telling to note that thus far this is the one piece in this collection that has not been filmed. Nor is it likely to be, given the hideousness of the conclusion, in which a woman who has been decapitated continues to breathe for many minutes in order to give birth to her child.

It seems likely that King will revisit the club in the future. As Stevens says, "There are always more tales."

THE BREATHING METHOD: PRIMARY SUBJECTS

DAVID ADLEY: Adley is a moderately successful lawyer who becomes a member of the club after being invited there by a senior partner at his firm. The club has been an endless source of fascination for Adley in the years since he first passed through its doors.

EMLYN McCARRON: A doctor and member of the club. One night, he relates his experiences with Sandra Stansfield, a young, single woman who had become pregnant, and whom he had taught "the Breathing Method," a practice that was much maligned in its time, but that Dr. McCarron heartily endorsed.

Though retired, it is presumed that Dr. McCarron is still a member of the club.

SANDRA STANSFIELD: A young, single woman, she becomes pregnant by a man who deserts her, and seeks Dr. McCarron's help in delivering her child. When she comes to term and is about to deliver, she rushes to the hospital in a taxi. The cab is involved in a car accident, and Sandra is decapitated. Somehow she continues to breathe through her severed windpipe for the duration of time it takes Dr. McCarron to safely deliver her child, and then she dies.

STEVENS: The butler at the club. It is presumed that he still holds that position; he may, in fact, hold it forever.

[NOTE: *The novellas* Rita Hayworth and Shawshank Redemption *and* The Body *are discussed in the sections on Jerusalem's Lot and King's Maine, and Castle Rock, respectively.*]

Outside King's high school   DAVID LOWELL

DIFFERENT SEASONS: ADAPTATIONS

Of the four tales collected in *Different Seasons*, three have been made into films. The first of these, *Stand by Me* (based on *The Body*), was released by Columbia Pictures in 1986. (See The Prime Reality, Part Two: Castle Rock.)

The Shawshank Redemption, which dropped off the *Rita Hayworth and . . .* part of its literary title for the screen adaptation, was adapted and directed by Frank Darabont (who would later do the same for 1999's *The Green Mile*). (See The Prime Reality, Part Three: Jerusalem's Lot and King's Maine.)

Finally, there's the dark one. If *Stand by Me* is about hope, and *The Shawshank Redemption* is about the triumph of the spirit, then *Apt Pupil* is the antithesis of both films. A TriStar picture, starring Ian McKellen as Dussander and Brad Renfro as Todd Bowden, this 1998 drama was directed by Bryan Singer (*The Usual Suspects*). Though there are a number of major differences between the text and the screen adaptation (primarily in the number of murders committed by each character), the essence of it remains the same.

A notable exception is its ending. Rather than send Todd up into a tree to shoot at passing cars until he himself is shot down, director Singer shows Todd mentally intimidating the one man who can reveal his secret, threatening to destroy him with rumor and innuendo. As depicted on screen, Todd is much more consciously evil, in his way, than in the book. This switch, while making the ending less brutal, perhaps, achieves the impossible: it also makes the ending even darker.

It may be that the critical success of these three films has lent itself to the growing perception—as noted earlier—of *Different Seasons* as a seminal work in King's career.

DIFFERENT SEASONS: TRIVIA

- Kurt Dussander, in his Arthur Denker identity, had made quite a bit of money from a stock portfolio set up for him by Andy Dufresne.

- In *Apt Pupil*, Ed French goes to a conference and stays at a Holiday Inn, in Room 217. That's the number of the room where the ghost of an old woman tries to kill Danny Torrance at the Overlook Hotel in *The Shining*.

- Although the town of Derry was not prominent in King's fictional landscape at the time, it is mentioned in *The Body*, as are Jerusalem's Lot and Shawshank penitentiary.

- *The Body* features many references to Constable Bannerman, who would, in such later works as *The Dead Zone* (1979) and *Cujo* (1981), become Sheriff Bannerman.

- The narrator of *The Body* refers to the events of *Cujo*.

- Before the 1998 screen version, an earlier adaptation of *Apt Pupil* was planned and even began filming, with *NYPD Blue*'s Rick Schroder as Todd Bowden, and *Excalibur*'s Nicol Williamson as Dussander. The film was abandoned partway through, due to a collapse in funding.

- Frank Darabont, writer/director of the film adaptations of *Rita Hayworth and Shawshank Redemption* and *The Green Mile*, had done an earlier King adaptation as well—a student film version of King's short story "The Woman in the Room," for which King gave him permission.

- It seems quite possible that Peter Stevens, the assumed name Andy DuFresne uses in *Rita Hayworth and Shawshank Redemption*, is a combination of the names of the author and his good friend, novelist Peter Straub.

- The brownstone where men gather to tell stories in *The Breathing Method* is also the setting for the short story "The Man Who Would Not Shake Hands," which was included in King's collection *Skeleton Crew*.

42

CHRISTINE

(1983)

The classic love affair, we all know, is boy meets girl, boy gets girl, and so often, boy loses girl. But in America, and in today's popular culture, there's a common variation on that theme: Boy sees car, boy buys car, boy falls in love with car, and they live happily ever after to a rock 'n' roll soundtrack. Oddly enough, in the mythology of twentieth-century America, men can rely far more on their automobiles than they can on true love with a living, breathing human being.

In *Christine*, King takes that bizarre notion and twists it to the heights of perversity. Published in 1983, it is a novel of obsessions and hauntings, of teenage lust and high school angst. If this storyline were pitched in Hollywood, it would be *Carrie* meets *The Shining* . . . with cars.

Cars are everywhere in the book. To nearly everyone in this story—save for its protagonist and narrator, Dennis Guilder—cars are vitally important. It's a wonder that the plot line is set in the Pittsburgh suburb of Libertyville, instead of somewhere outside of Detroit.

King grew up in New England in the late 1950s and early 1960s. A flashy car was everything to a teenage boy then. It still is, though other things have since become almost as crucial. So there's no surprise that the status symbol all the guys in the story—teenagers and their elders alike—covet most is a fine automobile.

The exception, as noted, is Dennis Guilder. He is sufficiently mature to look askance at this kind of posturing. Unfortunately, his best friend, Arnie Cunningham, not only partakes of this, but embraces it. Arnie becomes a contorted funhouse-mirror image of what the average American male's obsession with cars looks like to someone who doesn't share that passion.

On the other hand, it isn't really Arnie's fault. He's a lonely, pimply-faced kid, lusting after the smart, pretty girl in school who he thinks barely notices him. His best friend is a handsome jock, and he's just the forlorn sidekick.

Until he meets Christine, a 1958 red Plymouth Fury. In reality, she's a pile of junk, but she calls out to him, seduces him in a sense. He can see in her a vision of what she should be, and buys her in order to restore that beauty. Arnie believes, in his secret heart, that he also has that beauty and specialness within himself, and he sees restoring Christine as a way to bring it out.

Well, we know where that leads.

Christine isn't your average automobile. She's possessed by the corrupt spirit of her first owner, Roland LeBay. He's a vicious SOB, and he plays Arnie wonderfully, manipulating him until his insecurities have made him so desperate and cruel that he almost becomes evil himself. Fortunately, Arnie is eventually redeemed. Sadly, it comes too late.

Cars. Can't live with 'em, can't live without 'em.

Christine is also, perhaps more than any other of King's works, the author's paean to rock music. As a musician and radio station owner himself, there's no doubt that music is important to him. Here, King puts it in perspective as part of the high school experience. Each chapter begins with a quote from a classic rock song. More than that, however, when Christine (or, more accurately, the ghost of Roland LeBay) goes out on the prowl to punish those who've wronged Arnie, the music pouring from the car's speakers is the music of the period in which the auto was built.

That element of the story is also present in King's masterpiece of a haunting, *The Shining* (1977). Like the malevolent auto in *Christine,* the Overlook Hotel of *The Shining* (and, let us not forget, the Marsten House of 1975's *'Salem's Lot*) is not only inhabited by the spirits of the damned, but in a real, tangible way, possessed by some other, greater, more distinct evil. In *Christine,* it is never truly elaborated on. In *The Shining,* however, we actually see the evil rising in the fire cloud above the exploding hotel.

All three King novels present their malignancy as a collaboration between seemingly ancient, preternatural evil and simple human cruelty and corruption. The lingering malignancy is created, in all three cases, by that collaboration of ethereal malevolence, human weakness, and, interestingly, the creations of humanity: a car, a house, a hotel. This combination recurs frequently within King's work, where events conspire to make an object the focus of both mortal and immortal evil.

Further, in all three cases, the human weakness on display generally plays itself out in the form of obsession. Arnie Cunningham's fixation on Christine. Jack Torrance's mania with the hotel, his job, and the play he's trying to write. Ben Mears's preoccupation with the Marsten House. (Of course, in the latter case, Ben turned his obsession to positive action, rather than descending into insanity, as do Arnie and Jack.)

Yet another similarity is that each of these characters' obsessions reflects, in some way, the warped passion of a predecessor. Arnie takes the place of Roland LeBay. Jack takes the place of Delbert Grady, former caretaker of the hotel, who murdered his entire family with an ax. Both of them still exist as ghosts within the respective man-made hosts. In the third case, things are different. Ben Mears does not replace Hubie Marsten, the obsessed, evil man who killed his wife and himself in his home. Rather, he sets himself against Marsten's heinous legacy.

Another element that is prevalent throughout *Christine* is that of the horrors of high school. Arnie is a loser on the scale of the title character in *Carrie*, and suffers many of the same injustices from his peers. Like Carrie's callous tormentors, *Christine*'s Buddy Repperton and his cronies represent the worst that high school has to offer. In both novels, the cruelty of the teens feeds into the seemingly inescapable horrors that occur at the climax of each book.

With its mix of pop culture and King's special brand of evil, *Christine* is a classic American ghost story.

CHRISTINE: PRIMARY SUBJECTS

ARNIE CUNNINGHAM: As a senior at Libertyville High School, Arnie is the quintessential sidekick. He speaks softly and minds his own business, trying not to get picked on by his peers and hoping to live long enough to survive high school. He loves Leigh Cabot, though he doesn't have the guts to even ask her out until he buys Christine, a red 1958 Plymouth Fury.

Arnie's new car changes him, in more ways than one. At first he seems more confident. He asks Leigh out, and they date for a bit. A nice car has given Arnie the boost he needs to feel good about himself. Or so it seems.

But Christine has wrought other changes on Arnie. His appearance changes. His face clears up, and he carries himself differently. His best friend, Dennis Guilder, notices the alterations immediately. He finds, over time, that he doesn't really like the new Arnie, and eventually, neither does Leigh.

Arnie is not himself. Quite literally. He has been manipulated and at times even possessed by the malignant ghost of Roland LeBay, the first owner of Christine. In the end, Arnie sees what he has done to his life, and how much he has hurt the people he loves the most. He wrests control of himself from LeBay one final time, and attempts to save his mother's life. It is a failed attempt, and both Arnie and his mother are killed.

CHRISTINE: A 1958 red-and-white Plymouth Fury, Christine was built on the assembly line in Detroit, and she was born bad. There was something evil about her from the beginning, a supernatural force that reached out to hurt those it came into contact with.

Christine's first owner was Roland LeBay, an Army veteran. LeBay was a cruel man, though he prized his car more than anything. Upon his death—shortly after selling Christine to Arnie Cunningham—his spirit merges with the car, combining his cruelty with Christine's already considerable evil.

Then Arnie begins to be tainted by Christine's evil, and LeBay's presence as well. After local toughs, led by Buddy Repperton, vandalize the car to get at Arnie, the car sets out on its own at night, hunting them down and killing them. Eventually, in an effort to put an end to that evil, Dennis Guilder and Leigh Cabot use an enormous sewage truck to crush Christine until she is useless scrap. Later, she is destroyed in a compactor at a junkyard.

However, that may not be the end. For out in California, a kid named Sandy Galton, who had once attacked Christine with his friends, is struck and killed by a car. Dennis Guilder wonders if this murderer is Christine, and still fears that she might be coming for him.

DENNIS GUILDER: The most valuable player on the football team at Libertyville High, Dennis Guilder isn't the average jock. His relationship with Arnie Cunningham proves that. Everything Dennis is, Arnie isn't. Where Dennis is handsome and athletic and outgoing . . . Arnie isn't. And yet they remain friends, as they have been since grade school. Dennis is Arnie's protector, and tries to be his voice of reason when things in Arnie's life get out of control.

Nobody understands why Dennis always defends Arnie, and in time, Dennis comes to realize that he *can't* save Arnie anymore. Despite their outward differences, they're both intelligent young men, and their friendship means more than the prejudices of high school, the cruelties of teenage life.

But it has always been easier for Dennis than for Arnie. They are both enamored of the same girl, Leigh Cabot, but Arnie doesn't believe he stands a chance with her if Dennis is his competition. Yet when Arnie begins to change, thanks to Christine's influence, he finds the courage to ask Leigh out, and she says yes.

Over time, however, both Leigh and Dennis have to deal with the further changes in Arnie, and the way his obsession with Christine has twisted him. As a result, the two of them are drawn together, and eventually fall in love.

Together, Dennis and Leigh destroy Christine—or at least believe they have.

Presently, Dennis Guilder remains in Libertyville, where he is a high school teacher. He still fears that one day Christine may return to unleash her vengeance upon him.

ROLAND LeBAY: Born and raised in Libertyville, Pennsylvania, Roland LeBay was a misanthrope all his life. He was a cruel individual who didn't ever see the need to get on well with people. But he knew cars. In the Army, he was a mechanic known for his ability to fix anything.

When he bought Christine in 1958, it was a match made in Hell. The car itself was already evil, somehow, and LeBay's natural hatred of people fed the auto, just as it fed him.

Some twenty years later, Roland sells Christine to a local teenager named Arnie Cunningham. Shortly thereafter, he dies. At least, physically. His spirit, however, merges with Christine, and together, the two of them—car and owner—change and possess Arnie Cunningham. In the end, however, when Christine is being destroyed, LeBay's spirit flees the vehicle in an effort toward self-preservation. He tries to fully possess Arnie himself, but Arnie fights him. The struggle takes place in a speeding car, and an accident ensues that takes Arnie's life and that of his mother, Regina Cunningham.

It is presumed that without a host, Roland LeBay's spirit has gone to its final reward. Or final punishment, as the case may be.

LEIGH (CABOT) ACKERMAN:

As a senior at Libertyville High, Leigh has the misfortune to briefly become the girlfriend of Arnie Cunningham and the object of Roland LeBay's obsession. Leigh cares for Arnie a great deal, but soon comes to realize that his fixation on his car is very unhealthy. In fact, along with Arnie's best friend, Dennis Guilder, Leigh realizes that there is something supernatural at work here. Together with Dennis, she aids in the destruction of Christine.

For a time afterward, Leigh and Dennis remain together as a couple. Eventually, however, they split and Leigh marries another. She settles in Taos, New Mexico, where she still lives with her husband and their twin girls.

WILL DARNELL:

The owner of Darnell's Garage, where Arnie restores and garages Christine, Will Darnell is a common criminal. He uses his operation to smuggle drugs—among other things—inside cars. When Arnie Cunningham is arrested for working for him, Darnell lets him take the fall. In vengeance, Christine kills Darnell.

BUDDY REPPERTON:

The most notorious member of Arnie's class at Libertyville High, Buddy is the leader of those students who frequently abuse Arnie. When Arnie begins to change and grow more confident—and more importantly, less afraid of Buddy—Repperton and his friends attack and vandalize Christine.

For that act, Christine later forces Buddy's car off the road, and Buddy and several of his friends die in the ensuing crash.

SANDY GALTON:

Though Sandy Galton doesn't participate in the assault on Christine, he is the one who tells Buddy where the car can be found, and lets them into the airport parking lot where the attack occurs.

Though for a very long time it appears that Sandy has escaped Christine's vengeance, it is later reported that he has been struck and killed by a hit-and-run driver in California. It is Dennis Guilder's belief that Christine has somehow returned and is responsible for Sandy Galton's death.

VERONICA and RITA LeBAY: The wife and young daughter of Roland LeBay, both of them die while inside Christine. Rita chokes to death. Veronica's death appears to be suicide, but Dennis Guilder believes that Christine murdered her.

CHRISTINE: ADAPTATIONS

Just in time for Christmas, in 1983, Columbia Pictures released the motion picture version of *Christine*. Oddly enough, despite the marquee value of the Stephen King name, and the fact that the story was, of course, his, the film was marketed as "John Carpenter's *Christine*." Carpenter, director of *Halloween* (1978), *The Fog* (1980), and *Escape from New York* (1981), among many others, clearly had his own box office appeal, but the billing seemed awkward nevertheless.

Produced by long-time Carpenter collaborator Richard Kobritz and adapted by Bill Phillips, the 111-minute movie remained relatively faithful to the original novel (except for the change of making Christine inherently evil rather than possessed), despite the title billing. Keith Gordon, who would later become a director himself, played the doomed Arnie Cunning-ham, with John Stockwell as Dennis Guilder and Alexandra Paul as Leigh Cabot.

The film version of King's novel met with mediocre reviews and unimpressive box office, but continues, as with just about everything these days, to survive in the eternity of video.

CHRISTINE: TRIVIA

• Alexandra Paul, who plays Leigh Cabot in the film, went on to become the costar of the most-watched television series in the world, *Baywatch*, in the 1990s.

- Actress Kelly Preston plays the relatively minor role of Roseanne, a girl Dennis Guilder briefly dates. In an odd confluence of events, the book features Dennis and Roseanne going to see the movie *Grease* (1978), which starred John Travolta, who happens to be married, in real life, to Kelly Preston. Travolta also had an early role in a King film, as Billy Nolan in *Carrie* (1976).

43

SKELETON CREW

(1985)

Seven years after the publication of *Night Shift*, Stephen King released a second short story collection entitled *Skeleton Crew*. He penned both an introduction and a chapter of story notes for the volume, both of which give readers valuable insight into the mind of the author. As King states in his introduction, the tales span a long period in his life. The oldest, "The Reaper's Image," was written shortly after he graduated from high school in 1966. The newest, "The Ballad of the Flexible Bullet," was composed in 1983.

The volume's contents reflect King's change in fortune since his first collection, especially in the markets now available to him. The majority of the entries in *Night Shift* had first appeared in slick men's magazines like *Cavalier, Penthouse,* and *Gallery.* Some of the stories featured in *Skeleton Crew* were first published in men's magazines as well, but in more reputable and better-paying publications such as *Playboy.* An examination of the copyright page reveals King's growing influence on the horror genre: several of those included here had also appeared in Kirby McCauley's landmark *Dark Forces: New Stories of Suspense and Supernatural Horror* (1980), *Rod Serling's The Twilight Zone Magazine*, the revived *Weird Tales*, and assorted volumes of Charles L. Grant's critically acclaimed *Shadows* anthologies from the early 1980s.

The collection, which features twenty stories and two poems, contains an epigram that reads, "Do you love?" This phrase shows up three times in the collection, first in "Nona" (the title character poses the question to the narrator as he stands over the corpse of an ex-girlfriend), then in "The Raft" (Randy somewhat absurdly asks this query of the "oil slick" creature), and finally, most poignantly, in "The Reach" (as the narrator inquires, "Do the dead sing? Do they love?").

"Here There Be Tygers"

A chilling short story, this piece is all the more effective because King never explains how a tiger came to be in the boys' bathroom at the Acorn Street Grammar School. The horror is just simply there.

"HERE THERE BE TYGERS": PRIMARY SUBJECTS

CHARLES: A third grader who first encounters the tiger in the boys' restroom but manages to escape back to his homeroom.

KENNY GRIFFIN: A third grader who is eaten by the tiger in the boys' restroom after being instructed by Miss Bird to check up on Charles.

MISS BIRD: Charles's third-grade teacher, Miss Bird scoffs at his assertion that there is a deadly tiger in the boys' restroom. Entering the restroom, she, too, is presumably killed by the imaginary tiger.

"The Monkey"

This story is a perfect example of taking a commonplace object—a toy—and making it utterly terrifying. In this narrative, the object of terror is a mechanical monkey, the kind that clashes a pair of cymbals together when you wind it up. (King has told similar stories since, namely "Chattery Teeth," which appears in *Nightmares & Dreamscapes*, and "Chinga," a teleplay he cowrote for *The X-Files* in the late 1990s. The first features a set of novelty windup teeth; the latter showcases a haunted doll.)

Hal Shelbourne was abandoned by his father at a young age. Searching through his father's effects one day, Hal discovers a mechanical monkey. Hal winds it up, its cymbals clash, and, shortly thereafter, their babysitter, Beulah, is accidentally killed in a shootout. Then, in rapid succession, Hal loses the family dog, a best friend, and, tragically, his mother. Each time, the monkey's clanging preceded the death. Deathly afraid of the toy, he throws it in a well. The toy resurfaces years later, scaring Hal out of his wits. Knowing its presence threatens the well-being of his family, Hal weighs the toy down and throws it into Crystal Lake, presumably destroying it forever. One sign that the deadly toy monkey may still be with us is the fact that hundreds of fish die in the lake soon thereafter.

"Cain Rose Up"

Originally published in the Spring 1968 issue of *Ubris* (the University of Maine at Orono literary magazine), this story was inspired in part by Charles Whitman's Texas tower massacre. This type of story soon became a subgenre—stories like Harlan Ellison's "Thrillkill" cover similar terrain. Sadly, acts of violence like those in these stories have become a fact of life in modern-day America.

Shortly after finals, Curt Garrish starts shooting people from his dorm window. His motivation for doing so is never explained.

"The Raft"

A tragic coming-of-age story, one in which all the principals succumb to the hypnotic callings of a carnivorous oil slick that makes its home in a Pennsylvania lake. King originally submitted this story to *Adam*, a men's magazine that published horror fiction at the time. The tale—then titled "The Float"—was accepted, and King was duly paid. Because it was *Adam*'s policy to pay on publication, King assumes the story was published, even though the magazine folded soon thereafter and he never saw the story in print. Rewritten years later, its first official publication was in yet another men's magazine—*Gallery*.

"THE RAFT": PRIMARY SUBJECTS

RANDY: The narrator of the events that occurred on the raft, Randy usually follows the whims of his best friend, Deke. So when Deke suggests they commemorate the end of summer (and the end of classes at Horlicks, of "The Crate" fame) by taking a dip in an isolated Pennsylvania lake, Randy reluctantly agrees. The two pals take their girlfriends, Rachel and Laverne, with them. Diving into the lake, they swim out to a raft, where they are cornered by a sentient oil slick. Rachel, who makes the mistake of trying to touch it, is consumed when the creature surges onto her arm and pulls her in. Deke goes next, literally pulled through a crack in the boards that make up the raft's surface. After Laverne is taken, Randy is left with only the creature for company. He is slowly hypnotized by the colors that swirl in the living oil slick. Presumably, he succumbs and is consumed by the creature.

[NOTE: *As adapted by George A. Romero, this story was the most effective tale in* Creepshow 2 *(1987). That particular segment starred actors Daniel Beer, Jeremy Green, Page Hannah, and Paul Satterfield.*]

"Word Processor of the Gods"

This story came about because of King's fascination one day with what he could do with the DELETE button on his keyboard.

An English teacher, Richard Hagstrom always wondered how his sister-in-law, Belinda, could have married a worthless, abusive drunk like his deceased brother, Roger. Further, he marvels at how such a disjointed union could have produced such a wonderful child as his beloved nephew, Jonathan. Married to the shrewish Lina, father of the loathsome Seth, Richard wonders how fate had screwed things up. Richard is heartbroken when Jon and Belinda are killed in an automobile accident caused by his drunken brother—all he has are his memories and the homemade word processor Jon built for him before his death.

Richard is aghast to discover that the DELETE and EXECUTE buttons on his keyboard actually work in the most literal sense: Experimenting with a portrait, Richard makes it disappear, then brings it back, merely by typing a phrase on his keyboard. Realizing the machine's potential, he next deletes his repulsive son and wife, then types "I AM A MAN WHO LIVES ALONE EXCEPT FOR MY WIFE, BELINDA, AND MY SON,

JONATHAN," and hits EXECUTE. Although the machine is destroyed in the process, it once again manages to alter reality, thereby providing Richard with a new, and much happier, home life.

[NOTE: *This story was adapted by Michael McDowell (who would later co-write the screenplay for 1996's feature version of* Thinner) *and appeared in 1985 as an episode of* Tales from the Darkside, *a television series produced by George A. Romero and Richard Rubinstein.]*

"The Man Who Would Not Shake Hands"

This tale is narrated by George Gregson, a member of a poker club that meets at a brownstone located at 249B East Thirty-fourth Street, New York City, a locale King readers will recognize from the novella *The Breathing Method* in 1982's *Different Seasons*. Gregson relates the curious events that took place in the club in 1919.

"THE MAN WHO WOULD NOT SHAKE HANDS": PRIMARY SUBJECTS

HENRY BROWER: Brower is the man referred to in the title of the story. Cursed to cause the death of anyone he touches by an Indian holy man who blames him for the death of his son, Brower usually shuns human contact. Playing poker one night in the club, he wins a round, upon which one of his opponents, a man named Jason Davidson, grabs his hand and shakes it. Brower pulls away and runs out into the night. Following Brower, Gregson confronts him and hears his story. When Gregson laughs, Brower demonstrates his power, killing a dog merely by touching its paw. Gregson remains unconvinced until Davidson passes away suddenly and Brower commits suicide, apparently just by grasping one of his hands with the other.

STEVENS: Stevens, or someone who very much resembled Stevens (he himself claims it was his grandfather), has worked as a butler at 249B for as long as anyone can remember. Stevens has the uncanny ability to choose the club member who is most in need of relating a tale.

"The Reaper's Image"

This story has the distinction of being King's second professional sale after "The Glass Floor." It originally appeared in the Spring 1969 issue of *Startling Mystery Stories*.

"THE REAPER'S IMAGE": PRIMARY SUBJECTS

THE DelVER LOOKING GLASS: An enchanted mirror displayed in the Samuel Claggert Memorial Museum, designed by John Delver, "an English craftsman of Norman descent who made mirrors in . . . the Elizabethan period of England's history." His mirrors are collector's items because of their fine craftsmanship and because he used a "form of crystal that has a mildly magnifying and distorting effect upon the eye of the beholder." Over the centuries, many have looked into the mirror and seen the image of the Grim Reaper in the upper left-hand corner of the glass. All those who have done so, including a judge named Crater, then vanished off the face of the earth.

MR. CARLIN: The current guardian of the Delver Glass, and the curator of the Claggert Museum. He explains the strange history of the mirror to the curious Mr. Spangler.

JOHNSON SPANGLER: Johnson visits the Claggert Museum for the express purpose of studying the Delver Glass, only to become its latest victim.

"Survivor Type"

As King explains it, he got to thinking about cannibalism one day, wondering if a person could eat himself. This particularly unpleasant account, reminiscent of King in his Richard Bachman (or George Stark) storytelling mode, was the result.

A surgeon turned drug dealer, Richard Pine finds himself stranded on a desert island with only meager supplies (including two kilos of heroin) to sustain him. Pine survives a month or so on these provisions, and on the birds he can catch, but soon must resort to his only remaining food source—himself. Using the heroin as anesthetic, he amputates, then eats, his right foot, then his left, then his right leg to the knee, then . . . well, you get the picture.

"Morning Deliveries (Milkman #1)" and "Big Wheels: A Tale of the Laundry Game (Milkman #2)"

These tales were plucked from King's abandoned novel *The Milkman*. They are interesting mostly because they seem to be King's first attempt at developing ideas that eventually appeared in *Needful Things* (1991).

In "Morning Deliveries," readers join milkman Spike Milligan as he makes his predawn rounds. In addition to dairy products, however, Spike delivers such items as spiders, deadly nightshade, and bottles of acid gel to his customers.

The second story follows the misadventures of two drunken laundry workers, Johnny "Rocky" Rockwell and Leo Edwards, as they visit a gas station to obtain an inspection sticker. We learn that Rocky is being cuckolded by Spike Milligan. Leo has worse problems, however: he has a gaping hole in his back, caused by water dripping from a hole in the laundry's roof.

"The Ballad of the Flexible Bullet"

A story about storytellers, it is one of King's earliest examinations of the relationship between madness and writing.

"THE BALLAD OF THE FLEXIBLE BULLET": PRIMARY SUBJECTS

HENRY WILSON: The narrator of the tale, Wilson tells how he fell under the spell of Reg Thorpe, a writer who believed that a tiny creature called a fornit lived in his typewriter, and acted as his muse. At first Wilson goes along with Thorpe's mad ideas out of respect. But as they continue to

King in 1998　　BETH GWINN

exchange letters, he catches Thorpe's madness, actually validating the writer's obsession and paranoia. Wilson has since regained his sanity, but still wonders just how crazy Thorpe really was.

REG THORPE: The author of *Underworld Figures* and the story that Henry Wilson championed, "The Ballad of the Flexible Bullet," Reg kills himself after shooting his wife, Jane, their housekeeper, Gertrude, and

Gertrude's son Jimmy. Reg goes off the deep end when he discovers Jimmy shooting his fornit Rackne with "death rays" from a toy ray gun.

THE FORNITS—RACKNE and BELLIS: Rackne is Reg Thorpe's fornit, a tiny elflike creature who lives inside his typewriter. Reg believes that Rackne is the true creative force behind his writing and becomes enraged when he discovers that his housekeeper's son has been torturing the creature. The discovery comes too late, however—Jimmy zaps Rackne with a toy ray gun, exploding the creature's body. Bellis is the name of Henry Wilson's fornit. Whether this is all in Reg's twisted imagination is a matter for debate; true, his typewriter is found drenched in blood, but the blood is Type O—Reg's blood type.

"Paranoid: A Chant" and "For Owen"

Skeleton Crew also contains two poems. The first, "Paranoid: A Chant," takes readers inside the mind of a man both mad and completely paranoid. In the second, "For Owen," a father walks his son to school. In spite of the millions of words King has published in his career, in an impressive variety of mediums and forms, he has for reasons unknown published only a handful in his entire writing career in the medium of poetry.

[NOTE: *"Mrs. Todd's Shortcut"* and *"The Reach"* are discussed in section four. *"The Jaunt," "The Mist,"* and *"Beachworld"* are discussed in section eight. *"The Wedding Gig"* is discussed in section seven.]

SKELETON CREW: TRIVIA

- A signed, limited edition of *Skeleton Crew* was published by Scream/Press in 1985. It reportedly sold out before the trade edition was published.

44

CAT'S EYE

(1985)

The film *Cat's Eye* was produced during an extraordinarily prolific period in Stephen King's career, when there seemed to be almost as many movies made from his novels as there were books being published. During the preceding two-year period, no less than six motion pictures were produced based on his works: *Cujo* (1983), *The Dead Zone* (1983), *Christine* (1983), *Children of the Corn* (1984), *Firestarter* (1984), and *Silver Bullet* (1985).

What is perhaps most noteworthy about the relatively minor *Cat's Eye* is that it was only the second original screenplay of his to be produced, and that the author intentionally made fun of several established elements of his still-burgeoning Stephen King Universe.

The movie is also noteworthy in that King was not responsible for its genesis. Veteran producer Dino De Laurentiis, who would eventually be responsible for a half dozen movies based on the author's work, held the screen rights to several of the remaining short stories from *Night Shift* (1978). (King, of course, had already adapted some of them for his first produced screenplay, *Creepshow*, in 1983.) De Laurentiis had been so impressed with Drew Barrymore's work in the yet-to-be-released *Firestarter* that he flew to Bangor, Maine, to convince King to write a script that would not only be based on those unused stories from *Night Shift*, but would somehow feature rising star Barrymore in each episode. .

Intrigued by the challenge, King readily agreed, but with a hidden agenda—he would have as much fun in amusing his audience as he would in trying to frighten them. (He also agreed to work within the restrictions of a PG-13 rating. Typically a horror movie was produced with the understanding that it would receive an R, or "Restricted," rating.) What he also attempted—but largely failed in—was to conceal the fact that the movie, like *Creepshow*, would also be an anthology of unrelated stories. In theory, a cat was to be the connecting link between each of the tales, each of which take place in a different part of the United States.

Based on two previously published stories—"Quitters Inc." and "The Ledge"—and a new one called "The General," *Cat's Eye* is unquestionably and overtly an anthology film. It shares much in spirit with the adaptations that were used in *Creepshow* in that King purposely attempted to blend a satisfying mixture of humor and horror, of gore and guffaws.

To a large degree, the ninety-three-minute feature succeeds on that intended middle ground—especially considering the MPAA rating and the mainstream audience for which it was intended. Unfortunately, in the form that the picture was finally released, audiences were immediately confused by, rather than drawn into, the story line. Who was the anonymous cat? Why was this ghostly vision of a little girl speaking to him as if he might be a former pet? What is the cat traveling across America in search of? For what is not widely known is that the first part of the wraparound story to the entire movie, although shot, was removed from the completed film after being seen by only a handful of preview audiences.

The way King originally wrote the movie, the narrative opens with the funeral of a little girl who has died in her sleep for reasons never clearly explained. Her mother, insane with grief, believes that somehow the girl's pet cat had "stolen her life's breath" (as was believed in ancient times by some European cultures) and was the cause of her sudden demise. Going berserk, she attempts to kill the cat with an Uzi machine gun. The cat manages to escape, and the ghost of the little girl urges the feline to find the supernatural creature that actually stole her life—a hideous little troll that secretly lived in the walls of her bedroom.

Studio executives at MGM were concerned that audiences wouldn't respond favorably to a movie that opened with the funeral of a child, nor would they react well to seeing a harmless cat being put in such extreme peril. And so the prologue was deleted, which meant that anyone who did see the film would wonder why star Drew Barrymore (who plays multiple roles) would first appear as a ghost, and why this seemingly ordinary cat was wandering in and out of each different plot line. (Of course, the fact that this was promoted as "the latest Stephen King thriller" should have tipped off potential audiences that they weren't going to see *Terms of Endearment*.)

If we disregard the crippled wraparound story, what remains is certainly entertaining enough—albeit not particularly memorable or distinctive. *Cat's Eye* is perhaps only important as an affectionate send-up of what was already recognizably the Stephen King Universe. For besides the considerable novelty and suspense inherent in the stories themselves, King demonstrates from the outset (with the full cooperation of director Lewis Teague, who had previously helmed *Cujo*) that the world's bestselling horror author was not above poking fun at himself. Consider that:

- Early on, an obviously rabid St. Bernard chases the cat. *(Cujo)*

- The cat is nearly run over by a red '58 Plymouth Fury. *(Christine)*

- Morrison complains, "I don't know who writes this crap!" while watching a horror movie starring Christopher Walken and Herbert Lom on television. (It's *The Dead Zone*.)

- Morrison's daughter attends a private school appropriately called "Saint Stephen's School for the Exceptional."

- Amanda's mother is reading an appropriately scary novel in bed. (It's *Pet Sematary*.)

Unlike *Creepshow*, in which the stories that were adapted for the screen were relatively obscure, the stories adapted for *Cat's Eye* are familiar to most long-time King readers from their appearance in *Night Shift*. Therefore, we have chosen to consider the original stories as published in *Night Shift* to be "in continuity." They are covered in that section, and thus only the original story "The General" will be dealt with here.

"The General"

Here we follow the trail of the apparently indestructible cat (who made fleeting appearances in the previous two episodes) to the home of another little girl, this time in Wilmington, North Carolina. (It's now irrelevant whether this is the same child whom the cat had been seeing in ghostly visions previously throughout the story line.) There the cat—now named "the General"—battles a deadly little troll that intends to steal the life force of this young girl while she sleeps. Naturally, her unsuspecting father (James Naughton) and mother (Candy Clark) have no idea what kind of mortal danger their daughter is truly in after they go to bed. They mistakenly believe that the General is the cause of their daughter's vivid nightmares. Ultimately, good triumphs over evil in this overt tale of the supernatural, as both the youngster and the cat (even though it has no doubt used up most of its nine lives) survive the final attack of the horrid little monster. To keep the bizarre incident a secret, Amanda sweetly blackmails her still-perplexed parents into letting the General join their little family.

"THE GENERAL": PRIMARY SUBJECTS

AMANDA: A precocious little girl who suffers from bad dreams about a tiny monster coming into her room late at night when everyone else is asleep and trying to steal her life force through her breath. Of course, Amanda is correct in her wild belief that it is more than just a bad dream, even if she can't convince her understandably skeptical parents. Fortunately for her, she is able to convey her fears to the stray cat she calls the General, and this brave feline is instrumental in the destruction of the deadly troll.

HUGH: Amanda's sympathetic dad, he doesn't believe her story of a monster hiding inside the walls of her room, but fortunately for her, he does share her innate love of cats. He sides with Amanda every time her mother tries to convince them that the General is the monster in the child's nightmares.

SALLY ANN: Amanda's less than sympathetic mom, who does not believe in monsters lurking in the closet or skulking about under her daughter's bed. Worse still, she is definitely not a cat lover, and at one point captures the General and brings him to an animal shelter to be put to sleep.

Of course, once she realizes that the animal has somehow truly saved her only child's life, she finally relents on her firm anti-feline policy.

THE TROLL IN THE WALL: This nameless creature invades the home of Amanda and her parents. True to legend, the little monster comes out only at night, and scampers close to the face of the sleeping child. Then it tries to suck out the youngster's very life force by magically stealing the breath from her body. Although armed with a tiny dagger, it still cannot survive a wild battle to the death with the faithful cat known only as "the General."

CAT'S EYE: TRIVIA

- Country-and-western singer Ray Stevens sings the original theme song "Cat's Eye" over the movie's end credits.

- The prop department made a bed for "the General" sequence that was later cited in the *Guinness Book of World Records* as the world's largest bed.

- The screenplay for "The General" was later published in *Screamplays* (Del Rey, 1997), edited by Richard Chizmar and Martin Greenberg.

45

MISERY

(1987)

Although Stephen King would make writers the protagonists of some of his most intriguing novels (*The Tommyknockers, The Dark Half, Bag of Bones*), it is *Misery* that remains his most memorable examination of that profession. When you think about it, who would be better qualified to write a story about a bestselling author who is stalked by an insane fan than a bestselling author who has in real life been stalked by an insane fan?

Paul Sheldon is a very popular novelist with an unusual dilemma. His problem is that he has become successful due to the creation of a single character—one who has in many ways taken over his entire career. That character is Misery Chastain, star of a series of historical romances that have made Sheldon a household name and a minor celebrity. But Sheldon desires to be more than a writer of popular genre fiction; he wants to produce a novel that will keep his name alive long after he has passed on. To serve that end, he has just completed a mainstream novel, *Fast Cars*, about his rough-and-tumble life growing up on the mean streets of an urban landscape. The second step in his carefully conceived plan is to publish *Misery's Child*, in which Misery Chastain dies during a difficult childbirth. By doing so, Paul hopes to free himself from the literary shackles with which success has burdened him.

But fate is not going to allow Sheldon to change gears so quickly and painlessly. As has been his custom for many years, the novelist retreats to a small resort hotel in the Colorado Rockies to finish his new book—of which he has yet to make a copy. Leaving the rural hotel, Sheldon finds himself driving in a sudden blizzard. When he loses control of his car and crashes, his life is saved by a mysterious stranger who takes him to her secluded farm. The new woman in his life is Annie Wilkes, and fortunately for Sheldon, she just happens to be a former nurse. She also happens to be his "number-one fan." She owns every Paul Sheldon book—and every Misery Chastain novel—that has been published. She has even named her pet pig Misery.

As the days pass, Sheldon comes to realize that his hostess is not altogether sane. Unfortunately, there is not much he can do about this unsettling realization. He is her prisoner, and he has a multitude of injuries, including a dislocated pelvis and two broken legs. He's not only completely bedridden and totally at her mercy, she has also hooked him on a potent brand of painkillers.

Annie Wilkes, it turns out, is a female Dr. Jekyll and Mr. Hyde. Her mood swings are abrupt and unpredictable—sweet and solicitous one moment, furious and violent the next. Sheldon later learns her anger found unfortunate outlets. It seems that many of Annie's charges have died over the years, usually under mysterious circumstances. Somewhat brazenly, Annie has kept a scrapbook detailing these incidents.

Speaking with Paul, Annie is dismayed to discover that his new novel is *not* the new chapter in the Misery saga. Possessed of a peculiar temperament that includes a strong revulsion to obscenities, Annie is further shocked when she reads Sheldon's new mainstream novel. How could her beloved creator of Misery Chastain be the writer of such utter filth? Convinced that he has been delivered to her by the hand of God, Annie demands that he burn the only existing copy of *Fast Cars*. If he does not, he will suffer the consequences personally.

But Paul's suffering does not end even after he reluctantly complies with his captor's wishes. Annie, who only can afford paperbacks and has thus not yet heard of Misery's "retirement," becomes totally enraged when she learns that her beloved heroine dies at the end of *Misery's Child*, which she only recently purchased. Threatening further psychological and physical torture, Annie buys Sheldon a used typewriter and several reams of typing paper and instructs him to write a new Misery novel, to be titled *Misery's Return*. And the Lord have mercy on Paul Sheldon's slowly healing legs if he doesn't deliver a book that meets her expectations.

Trapped in his room, addicted to the painkillers he must take to bear up to the constant pain, and totally cut off from the rest of the world, Paul employs his creative as well as his physical powers to stay alive.

Plotting his escape, Paul takes perverse pleasure in devising the best Misery novel ever, as he is literally writing as if his life depends on how the tale pleases his number-one fan.

Misery fits well into the Stephen King Universe in that it deals with several themes that appear repeatedly in other works, most predominantly the idea of life not being fair and how accidents control our lives—not our will or desires. Although Annie Wilkes is a sadistic monster, she is also a tragic figure who, on one level, realizes that she is ill. Annie has accepted that she is destined to lead a miserable existence filled with loneliness and despair. Although life has treated her poorly, she finds solace in reading the Misery saga. To have her favorite writer kill off her beloved Misery is a blow she can barely stand.

Paul Sheldon, meanwhile, has found great success in writing in a genre he really doesn't respect and secretly wishes he could escape. But if he doesn't create the ultimate Misery novel for his number-one fan, he will never live to write anything else. It's an ironic situation of having to appease one's fans before you can be allowed to please yourself as a creative individual. Of course, if his Misery saga hadn't been commercially successful, then he also might never have had a chance to write something as potentially financially risky as another "serious" mainstream novel.

It is a situation to which Stephen King surely can relate, as he has been asked by critics repeatedly throughout his career when he was going to abandon the "scary stuff" and write something "serious" and "literary." To his credit, King has always been proud to be a horror writer—but he has also never wished to be typed as someone who can perform successfully only in that genre.

Yet it can certainly be argued that the fame, fortune, and acclaim he has received as "the world's most popular horror writer" has been a double-edged sword. For a time, King must have wondered if the only way he would be accepted by his hundreds of millions of fans would be in the role of literary boogeyman. (This is, of course, part of the reason he created the alter ego of Richard Bachman, so that he could publish novels that were clearly not in the horror genre, with the obvious exception of 1984's *Thinner*.) In many ways, King was addressing several issues in *Misery* that only a celebrated writer would ever have to deal with, in terms of fame, fortune—and the occasional deranged fan.

Misery is also a gripping psychological study in which former nurse Annie Wilkes is not the only monster Paul Sheldon must combat. The novelist has his share of inner demons and personality quirks. He is not quite "all there" either, at least in the sense that he almost exclusively defines himself by what he does for a living—writing, creating characters out of whole cloth, then living in their imaginary worlds until the story or novel is done.

Misery was clearly inspired by events in King's own life—he has been stalked by obsessive fans, and his home has been invaded by someone claiming to have a bomb. In 1980, he reportedly signed one of his books for a stranger who actually did call himself King's "number-one fan." That lost soul was Mark Chapman, who would later earn his place in history by shooting John Lennon shortly thereafter.

Once asked what he thought about being a world-famous writer, King curtly replied, "Being famous sucks."

Signing at Betts Bookstore   BETH GWINN

MISERY: PRIMARY SUBJECTS

PAUL SHELDON: A successful novelist with few friends or acquaintances outside the publishing industry, Paul has reached the top of the bestseller lists by writing a series of historical romances starring the plucky heroine Misery Chastain. Feeling stifled by his genre work, Sheldon decides to free himself of the character by having her die in the latest saga, *Misery's Child*. While trapped at Annie Wilkes's farm near Sidewinder, Colorado, he writes his best Misery novel even while desperately trying to find a means of escape. When his captor purposely cripples—"hobbles" is the old slave term—Sheldon by first mutilating his foot and then one of his hands, the writer realizes it is only a matter of time before she will eventually kill him. Surviving the ordeal by killing the woman in a brutal fight, he suffers the irony of becoming a better writer for enduring the horrible experience by publishing the Misery novel he wrote for Annie Wilkes. Of course, he also finds himself more typecast and potentially vulnerable to the next "number-one fan" he might encounter one day. Paul Sheldon currently resides somewhere in New York City.

ANNIE WILKES: Large, unattractive, and obese, Annie is also hopelessly insane. In her midforties when she kidnaps Paul Sheldon, her homicidal tendencies have been with her since she was a teenage babysitter, when she apparently set fire to the home of the three children she had been hired to watch. Keeping a scrapbook called Memory Lane, she fills it with various accounts of the people she has known, and the places around the country where she has been employed as a nurse. Unfortunately, almost every account deals with a sudden and violent death—but all of them are dismissed by the local authorities as tragic accidents. The deceased include her own father, a roommate at nursing school, and literally dozens of patients at the various hospitals where she has been employed.

An avid reader to pass the lonely hours, Annie has read all eight of Paul Sheldon's novels, but had reread his four Misery titles dozens of times. In her madness, she sees herself as Sheldon's lover, mentor, and muse. As she swings back and forth between sanity and insanity, she displays a venomous temper that can quickly morph into a murderous rage. When she realizes that Sheldon is trying to escape her rural home, she hobbles him.

Annie is killed after a desperate battle with Paul Sheldon. But her death was not in vain—without her, Misery Chastain would never have come back from the dead, to the delight of her millions of fans.

MISERY: ADAPTATIONS

The 107-minute movie version of *Misery* was released in 1990, and has the distinction of being the first adaptation of a Stephen King novel to win an Academy Award. The Oscar went to actress Kathy Bates, who did a masterful job of playing the Jekyll/Hyde character of Annie Wilkes. James Caan, best known for his tough-guy roles in such films as *The Godfather* (1972) and *The Killer Elite* (1975), turned in an equally strong performance in the role of Paul Sheldon.

The R-rated picture was directed by Rob Reiner, who had already done a superior job in 1986 with an earlier King story, *Stand by Me* (based on the novella *The Body* from 1982's *Different Seasons*). The author was reportedly extremely pleased with the way the second screen production with Reiner turned out, as he had been with *Stand by Me*. (In an article for *Entertainment Weekly* published in 1999, the author listed the movie as one of his ten personal favorite screen adaptations.)

What is most interesting is how Academy Award–winning screenwriter William Goldman (*Butch Cassidy and the Sundance Kid*, *All the President's Men*) deftly modified the novel to bring it to the big screen. Except for the last few pages, when Sheldon is seen back in New York trying to get a new novel under way, virtually the entire story takes place inside the home of Annie Wilkes. In many ways, the novel is set up like a two-character play on a single claustrophobic set. What Goldman did was to purposely open up the story by creating the characters of Sidewinder's Sheriff Buster (Richard Farnsworth) and his deputy-wife Virginia (Frances Sternhagen), who spend much of their time searching for the missing novelist. He also opened and closed the story with Sheldon's meetings with high-powered literary agent Marcia Sindell (Lauren Bacall).

In addition, Goldman toned down some of the extreme physical tortures that Annie Wilkes puts Sheldon through, most notably in the scene where she breaks his ankles with a sledgehammer so he can't walk again. (In the novel, she practically shears off a foot with an axe and then cauterizes the gaping wound with a blowtorch.)

Goldman also has Paul Sheldon destroying his only copy of *Misery's Return* in his climactic fight with Annie Wilkes. Therefore, when he returns to New York to recuperate, he spends his time writing the mainstream literary novel he had always been hoping he would write again someday. Finally he is freed of the "curse" of Misery and can realize his career goal of being a serious novelist. In King's novel, however, Paul Sheldon had *not* destroyed the only copy of the manuscript, and so when it is published, it makes him only richer and more famous than ever before as the creator of Misery.

In an odd way, one could justifiably say that bestselling author William Goldman had chosen a more plausible fate for bestselling author Paul Sheldon than even Stephen King may have thought possible.

MISERY: TRIVIA

- On the original paperback edition, a second, interior cover is actually a lavishly rendered version of *Misery's Return*, in which the intrepid suitor is cradling Misery lovingly in his arms. The distinctive face on that dashing hero belongs to none other than Stephen King!

- A Mrs. Kaspbrak was a neighbor of Sheldon's family when he was a child. This may mean that Sheldon may have known Eddie Kaspbrak, a character who appears in *It* (1986).

- Due to its realistic themes and dark ending, Stephen King originally intended *Misery* to be published as a Richard Bachman novel.

46

FOUR PAST MIDNIGHT

(1990)

I't's inevitable that *Four Past Midnight* be compared to *Different Seasons* (1982). The comparison is not very apt, however. It's true that, like the prior collection, *Four Past Midnight* gathers four of Stephen King's longer, novella-length works together. But unlike *Different Seasons*, which contained three more or less mainstream stories, *Four Past Midnight* features four terrifying journeys into the fantastic, and the truly horrific.

[NOTE: Secret Window, Secret Garden *is discussed in the Jerusalem's Lot and King's Maine section,* The Sun Dog *is discussed in the Castle Rock section, and* The Langoliers *is discussed in the Tales of The Shop section.]*

The Library Policeman

In his Note preceding *The Library Policeman*, King reveals that this entry had its genesis in an exchange he had one morning with his son Owen. The boy needed a book for school; his father quite naturally suggested a visit to the library. Owen was reluctant to do so, because he feared the Library Police, maniacal enforcers who actually come to patrons' houses if they fail to return their loaned-out books on time. This story delighted

King, who had heard similar tales in his youth. Starting to craft a story around the idea, the author realized that the Library Police were mere stand-ins for other, darker fears; thus, *The Library Policeman* developed into a tale about childhood trauma and secret shame.

Like *The Sun Dog*, the novella *The Library Policeman* is about growing up. In *The Sun Dog*, Kevin becomes an adult in a moment of stress and terror. Sam Peebles differs from Kevin, however, in that his moment of stress and terror actually retards his growth into a mature adult, keeping him from trusting those around him. Like *Secret Window, Secret Garden*, however, it's also a tale about repressed memory. This was a hotly debated topic at the beginning of the 1990s—when real-life horror stories about unspeakable memories began resurfacing decades after the alleged incident, producing a psychiatric cottage industry in uncovering so-called "repressed" memories. In this story, at least, King seems to be saying we should extend to these children the benefit of the doubt.

The Rock Bottom Remainders relaxing   SUSANNE MOSS

THE LIBRARY POLICEMAN: PRIMARY SUBJECTS

SAM PEEBLES: Everything, Sam Peebles decides later, is the fault of "the god damned acrobat." The acrobat, who is scheduled to perform at a Rotary Club meeting, breaks his neck, leaving a hole in the schedule. Strong-armed by a friend, realtor Sam Peebles agrees to substitute as a guest speaker. Finishing a draft, he shows it to his secretary, Naomi Higgins, who, suggesting he punch it up with quotes, sends him to the library. There he meets an odd librarian, Ardelia Lortz, who recommends *Best Loved Poems of the American People* and *The Speakers Companion*. A grateful Sam checks those books out. As he leaves, Miss Lortz admonishes him to return the books on time—after all, she wouldn't want to be forced to send the Library Policeman after him.

His speech is a rousing success. Basking in the glow, Sam forgets all about the library books. After receiving threatening calls from Ardelia, he searches for the books, and, to his dismay, determines that they must have accidentally been tossed out with the recycling. Traveling to the library to make amends, Sam is surprised when he enters—it's the same place, but with a more modern feel. Inquiring after Ardelia, Sam is informed that nobody by that name is employed there.

Doing some research, Sam realizes he has had an encounter with a ghost, the spirit of a vicious woman who committed a handful of murders several years before. Ardelia also has a powerful ally; she sends the Library Policeman to terrorize Sam.

Ardelia is actually a creature who feeds on fear. Sam discovers that the only way to combat her is by confronting his fear. This realization allows him to battle, and eventually defeat, Ardelia.

NAOMI HIGGINS: Sam's part-time secretary, she sets the events of *The Library Policeman* in motion by suggesting Sam visit the library. Naomi later provides Sam with much-needed background information on Ardelia Lortz, data that allows Sam to eventually uncover the truth.

ARDELIA LORTZ: The Junction City librarian who, sensing Sam's vulnerability, appears to him many years after she supposedly died. Ardelia is a shape-shifter; like a cicada, she emerges every few years to gorge herself on human fear. Although she could appear as a human being, her real form is disgustingly horrific—her most prominent feature being a huge funnel-shaped proboscis that can suck the fear out of a person through the tear ducts. Ardelia manufactured fear by telling horrid versions of classic fairy tales to her children's story hour group. Mesmerizing the children, she would then feed on their traumatized emotions.

Ardelia is nearly slain after Sam, in a symbolic rejection of his childhood fears, sticks a wad of red licorice in her snout. She survives the encounter, however, then attaches herself in embryonic form to Naomi's neck. Fortunately, Sam realizes what has happened, and finally destroys the parasite for good. Ardelia Lortz is quite durable, however, and may yet haunt the Stephen King Universe.

"DIRTY" DAVE DUNCAN: Ardelia's lover and accomplice in the 1950s, Dave turned to drink after she "killed" herself. Dave is homeless, and makes a living off of other people's recyclables. Perhaps still under the influence of his old girlfriend, Dave accidentally takes Sam's library books to the recycling center along with his old newspapers, providing Ardelia with an excuse to terrorize the realtor. Dave at least gives Sam insight into Ardelia's true nature. Even so, he still dies at the hands of the loathsome "Ardelia thing."

"THE LIBRARY POLICEMAN": The name by which Sam knew the child molester who traumatized him. Also, the imaginary character featured in a sinister wall poster created for Ardelia Lortz by Dave Duncan. Using Sam's fear to power her minion, Ardelia gives the Library Policeman life and sends him after Sam.

JUNCTION CITY, IOWA: The small Iowa town where realtor Sam Peebles meets Ardelia Lortz and the Library Policeman. According to the epilogue of *Needful Things* (1991), Sam and Naomi Higgins marry and leave Junction City soon after the events recorded in *The Library Policeman*. Readers also learn that Leland Gaunt has come to occupy Sam's old office.

47

SLEEPWALKERS

(1992)

While not by any means the first Stephen King screenplay to be produced as a motion picture (*Creepshow, Cat's Eye, Silver Bullet, Maximum Overdrive*, and *Pet Sematary* all preceded it), only 1992's *Sleepwalkers* could claim the distinction of being his first truly *original* screenplay, that is, one that was not based on a previously published short story or novel. It was also the first feature film in which the bestselling author would work with a talented young director named Mick Garris, who would later be selected by King to direct television miniseries adaptations of *The Stand* (1994) and *The Shining* (1997).

Although not tied to any previously published source material, King nevertheless chose to work with some of his favorite supernatural themes and monsters—werewolves, vampires, and, in particular, cats (you may recall that 1985's *Cat's Eye* featured a feline in all three story lines, and 1989's *Pet Sematary* revolved to a large degree around the unholy resurrection of a family cat named Church). Even though *Sleepwalkers* may not be the most memorable movie ever dealing with the topic of shape shifters, the R-rated feature makes for a suitably scary and fast-moving ninety-one-minute thriller.

The narrative is essentially a twisted love triangle—an outrageous blending of the supernatural with the forbidden erotic. Charles Brady

(Brian Krause) appears to be a handsome high school student who has just moved to a quiet, small town in Indiana with his beloved mother Mary (Alice Krige) from yet another quiet, small town in Ohio. But in truth, Charles is an ancient and apparently immortal shape shifter—a "sleepwalker"—who can instantly change from human to animal form when angered, and render himself and other objects invisible, at least briefly. Except for his mother, he is also apparently the last of his species, a species that survives via a unique process. Charles, you see, is the food gatherer who feeds both himself and his mother. But Charles doesn't eat meat or vegetables—rather, he feeds on the life force of virgin girls, transmitting what he doesn't need to his mother through sexual intercourse.

King takes great pains to show that these two creatures are human only in appearance—whenever they look into mirrors, they see their true identities as hideous demonic entities. But apparently even demons have emotions, as Charles develops genuine feelings for his next intended victim, a beautiful student named Tanya (Mädchen Amick).

This leads to a twisted love triangle, for Charles, drawn to Tanya much like any human male would be, knows he must kill her if his mother is to survive. Although this premise would have made for a fascinating story line in its own right, King fails to go any further down that particular path. Rather, after Charles and Tanya go to a local cemetery to obtain gravestone rubbings, his barely controllable animalistic tendencies take over. He attempts to date-rape the girl, and in doing so reveals that he is in fact a predatory shape shifter.

When a deputy sheriff, who just happens to have his pet cat with him on patrol, arrives on the scene, the officer's feline instinctively attacks Charles after he kills her owner. Apparently, even though the "sleepwalkers" appear to be part feline themselves, they are mortal enemies of all cats— the only creatures, it seems, that can do them harm.

Although grievously wounded, Charles manages to return home and collapse in Mary's arms. Now it's up to his enraged mother to return to town and kidnap an already traumatized Tanya so her now-bedridden son can finish the job he started in the cemetery. If he is unable to do so soon, he will die from his wounds, and Mary, in turn, will die of starvation.

Even as dozens of cats begin to gather outside her house, Mary kidnaps Tanya and drags her home. The police, however, also gather there, eager to avenge their comrade. Before this night of incredible horror is over, nearly everyone involved is either terribly injured or killed, including the two mysterious "sleepwalkers."

Cemetery, Durham   DAVID LOWELL

In *Sleepwalkers*, women play the pivotal roles of both heroine and main villain. With the exception of Charles, all the other men presented herein are either arrogant fools or inherently weak. The most developed and vital figures are clearly Tanya and Mary. Even Tanya's mother is shown, in her brief time on screen, to be a more complex and stronger character than her husband. King clearly enjoyed creating a new species of supernatural monsters whose incestuous sexual habits are their most shocking and memorable characteristic. The early scene of the erotically charged Mary being playfully "seduced" by the young man whom we have just learned is her offspring never fails to strike an unsettling chord in viewers.

Unfortunately, the author raises too many unresolved questions in his intriguing if not fully developed premise. Why does he call them "sleepwalkers"? Why have we never heard of this species of shape shifter before? Why are there apparently only two of them left in the world? Why can't the female of the species herself take the life force from young virgin males? Why are they so afraid of cats when they have such immense power? And how did these beings develop the incredible ability to temporarily turn huge objects (such as moving automobiles!) invisible, as well as themselves?

Of course, even though Charles and Mary Brady appear to be destroyed, that certainly doesn't rule out more of their species from appearing somewhere down the road. Perhaps the answers to all these questions will one day be made known in a sequel.

SLEEPWALKERS: PRIMARY SUBJECTS

CHARLES BRADY: One of the last surviving members of a species of shape shifters called "sleepwalkers," Charles Brady appears to be an excessively charming young man in his late teens. In reality, he is actually a creature who feeds on the life force of virgin girls, and who can make himself (and other objects) temporarily invisible. Although humans cannot perceive his true visage, it can be seen if he passes a mirror, which would reveal a loathsome creature, a horrid blend of human, reptilian, and feline features. Apparently immortal, his kind greatly fears cats, which inexplicably have the power in number to destroy them. After being attacked by a cat, Charles Brady ultimately dies from his wounds, even though his mother tries valiantly to save him.

MARY BRADY: The lovely mother of Charles Brady, she is also an immortal shape shifter. She, too, needs the life force of virgin girls on which to feed. It is up to her son to suck the life force from "nice girls" he meets in school so that he can in turn feed his mother via sexual intercourse. But after the death of her beloved Charles, Mary Brady is destroyed by the latest "nice girl" whom she had earlier hoped Charles would bring home for dinner . . . with the chosen young lady as the main course.

TANYA ROBERTSON: The pretty high school student who finds herself attracted to the new kid in school after hearing him read a self-composed fantasy tale entitled "Sleepwalkers" in class. From the way she speaks and carries herself, it appears she is still a virgin, and Charles sets his sights on making her his next meal. After Charles attacks her in a cemetery in his animalistic state, Tanya quickly realizes that no one will believe the wild story she has to tell. Returning home, she is later kidnapped by Mary and dragged to the Brady house. Escaping her captor, Tanya employs all her youthful resources to combat the two supernatural creatures.

With the assistance of a large pack of cats that have surrounded the Brady home, Tanya kills both "sleepwalkers" and escapes. Her current whereabouts are unknown.

DEPUTY SHERIFF SIMPSON: Deputy Simpson has the unfortunate assignment of being on the lookout for speeders when Charles Brady's vehicle roars past his patrol car on the main road out of town. Chasing madly after Charles, Deputy Simpson eventually tracks him down at the local cemetery. There he encounters a hysterical Tanya, who tries to warn him that something inhuman is after her. While bravely trying to protect her, Simpson is mauled, stabbed, and finally shot to death by an animalistic Charles. However, his pet cat, Clovis, fearlessly attacks this ancient enemy and gravely wounds the shape shifter.

SHERIFF IRA: The local sheriff, he doesn't understand what is going on in his peaceful community, but he knows his job is to protect the innocent—no matter what the price. After repeatedly wounding Mary Brady, he is slain by her when she impales him on a picket fence.

SLEEPWALKERS: TRIVIA

- Stephen King had a cameo appearance as a cemetery caretaker who complains to anyone within earshot, "You can't blame this one on me!"

- Popular horror film directors Tobe Hooper (forensic technician), Joe Dante (lab assistant), John Landis (lab assistant), and Clive Barker (forensic technician) also appeared in cameo roles.

- Although the story is set in Travis, Indiana, at one point Sheriff Ira calls to the police station dispatcher to ask for more police backup from the township of Castle Rock. Although certainly not Castle Rock, Maine, the reference to King's fictional town is an amusing in-joke.

48

NIGHTMARES & DREAMSCAPES

(1993)

In the introduction to 1985's *Skeleton Crew*, Stephen King wrote: "Writing short stories hasn't gotten easier for me over the years; it's gotten harder. The time to do them has shrunk, for one thing. They keep wanting to bloat, for another (I have a real problem with bloat—I write like fat ladies diet). And it seems harder to find the voice for these tales . . . the thing to do is keep trying, I think. It's better to keep kissing and get your face slapped a few times than it is to give up altogether."

King did indeed keep trying; the sheer size (816 pages in the hardcover version) of *Nightmares & Dreamscapes*, his third major short story collection, pays mute testament to that. In the introduction to that book, a slightly more militant King again discusses how hard it is for him to write short stories: "These days it seems that everything wants to be a novel, and every novel wants to be approximately four thousand pages long. A fair number of critics have mentioned this, and usually not favorably. In reviews of every long novel I have ever written, from *The Stand* to *Needful Things*, I have been accused of overwriting. In some cases the criticisms have merit; in others they are just the ill-tempered yappings of men and women who have accepted the literary anorexia of the last thirty years with a puzzling (to me at least) lack of discussion and dissent."

Despite these concerns, King was delighted to find he had at hand sufficient short stories to issue a third major collection. Perhaps for the reasons stated above, his short fiction output has indeed dwindled since then, but he continues to work in the form as the mood strikes him. (Evidence of this is found most recently in 2002's *Everything's Eventual*, which featured the multiple-award-winning tale "The Man in the Black Suit.")

Although *The Stephen King Universe* is primarily concerned with King's fiction, it should be noted that *Nightmares & Dreamscapes* also contains an excellent nonfiction work entitled "Head Down." This essay/memoir chronicles the triumphs and travails of the Bangor West All-Star Team as it battled for the Maine State Championship in Little League in 1989. King characterizes "Head Down" as "the opportunity of a lifetime," stating that his editor, Chip McGrath of *The New Yorker*, "coaxed the best nonfiction writing of my life out of me."

So who are we to contradict him?

The book also contains a poem about Ebbets Field and the Brooklyn Dodgers, entitled "Brooklyn August." The piece, a departure from his usual oeuvre, has since been reprinted several times in various baseball-related anthologies.

[NOTE: "Suffer the Little Children," "The Night Flier," "Popsy," and "The Rainy Season" are discussed in the section on Jerusalem's Lot and King's Maine. "The End of the Whole Mess" and "Home Delivery" are discussed in the section entitled Tales from Beyond. "The Fifth Quarter," "My Pretty Pony," and "Dolan's Cadillac" are discussed in the section entitled The World of Richard Bachman.]

"Chattery Teeth"

A bizarre tale that recalls to some degree an early King tale, "The Monkey," especially as it features a cheap novelty toy in a major role.

"CHATTERY TEETH": PRIMARY SUBJECTS

BILL HOGAN: A traveling salesman, Hogan purchases a set of windup chattery teeth at a diner. The false teeth, which seem to have a life of their own, come to his rescue when he is threatened by a psychopathic hitch-hiker. The teeth attack and kill his assailant. Hogan believes he was deliri-ous, as he thinks he saw the teeth dragging the hitchhiker's body into the desert. Returning to the diner a year later, Hogan finds that the proprietor has a package for him—a paper bag containing the supernaturally endowed chattery teeth. Struck dumb, Hogan takes the teeth back, concluding they would be a nice gift for his son in case someone ever tried to attack him.

BRYAN ADAMS: A young long-haired drifter who accepts a ride from Hogan. Although he appears harmless enough, he pulls a knife during the course of their trip and threatens to kill the salesman. After a fight in the van in which it appears that Adams is going to carry out his threat to slay the innocent driver, the supernatural chattery teeth viciously bite and tear the drifter to death.

Shop in Auburn that appears in "Chattery Teeth"   DAVID LOWELL

"Dedication"

King has often stated that he isn't afraid of grossing his readers out if that is what it takes to make an effective story. This tale most definitely falls into that category, for reasons that will be made all too clear below.

An African-American, Martha Rosewall has worked as a maid at the LePalais, one of New York's finest hotels, for decades. In "Dedication," she tells how her contact with a famous resident of the hotel drastically altered her life. Pregnant by her shiftless husband Peter, Martha is stunned when a neighborhood *bruja* woman tells her she must find the child's "natural father." Although surprised by this statement, a name immediately springs to Martha's mind who would be far better suited to be that father. And that is the man who resides at the hotel where she works, a Caucasian writer named Peter Jeffries. While cleaning Jeffries's bedroom each morning, Martha, under the influence of a spell cast by the witch, swallows the deposits Jeffries leaves on his sheets after masturbating each night.

As far as Martha is concerned, the spell works. Her son, Peter Rosewall, grows up to be an author. His first novel, about the ravages of war, is called *Blaze of Glory*, echoing the title of his "natural" father's first book, *Blaze of Heaven* (also a war novel).

"The Moving Finger"

The question not answered in this surrealistic story is that if there can be one gigantic finger waiting to attack us, where are the others? And what about that killer thumb? There are no answers in response to that query—and King in his notes states that "my favorite sort of short story has always been the kind where things happen just because they happen."

One day, mild-mannered accountant Howard Mitla discovers a finger poking up out of his bathroom sink drain. The only one who can see it, Howard tries to rid himself of the pest by pouring Draino on it, then by attacking it with a pair of electric hedge clippers (the mangled finger grows to a length of over seven feet before disappearing). Howard is later found by police who have been summoned by angry neighbors. He is all alone in the corner of the blood-splattered bathroom, mumbling incoherently to himself.

"Sneakers"

Another entry whose main action takes place in a bathroom, "Sneakers" revolves around a haunted toilet stall. Once again, King is not above examining the "gross-out" when he finds it appropriate to make his literary point. John Tell, the narrator of this strange tale, relates his experiences as a record producer. Visiting a men's room at a recording studio, he notices a pair of sneakers poking out from under a stall door. Unremarkable in and of themselves, the sneakers are surrounded by dozens of dead flies. He dismisses the strange sight and leaves. Subsequent visits over the next few days reveal that the sneakers haven't budged—the only thing that has changed is the increasing number of dead flies around the high-tops. Tell, who was also facing some questions about his own sexuality, steels himself and opens the door, confronting the specter inside the stall. The spirit, finally able to tell his story, gratefully abandons the stall.

"You Know They Got a Hell of a Band"

One of two stories (the other is "The Rainy Season") in *Nightmares & Dreamscapes* that deal with what Stephen King terms "a peculiar little town," "You Know They Got a Hell of a Band" is also reminiscent of "Children of the Corn," an early story that was collected in *Night Shift* (1978). It would also make for a hell of an episode for any revival of *The Twilight Zone*.

Mary and Clark Willingham get lost on the back roads of Oregon, ending up in a small town named Rock and Roll Heaven. The doomed couple quickly realize that the residents don't merely look like various deceased rock stars (such as Jim Morrison, Janis Joplin, Otis Redding, Rick Nelson, and of course Elvis Presley), but are in fact the real thing. Because performers require an audience, people who wander into town are never permitted to leave—for here the cliché "rock and roll will never die" is taken literally.

"Sorry, Right Number"

This is an original half-hour teleplay King originally wrote for Steven Spielberg's *Amazing Stories* (1985–1987) network series, but ended up being produced by George Romero and Richard Rubenstein's syndicated series

Tales from the Darkside (1984–1988). It is a rare example of a published teleplay by the author. (King has also published the scripts for 1985's *Silver Bullet* and his 1999 "novel for television" *Storm of the Century*.)

One evening, Katie Wiederman receives a hysterical phone call from a caller with an oddly familiar voice. Cut off before she can identify the caller, Katie's attention is diverted shortly thereafter by the death of her husband. Years later, she accidentally dials her old number, and hears the events of that fateful night being played out on the other end of the line. Distraught, she attempts to warn her past self of impending disaster, but can only utter a few meaningless phrases. After being cut off, Katie finally realizes why the voice sounded so familiar all those years ago—it was her own.

"The Ten O'Clock People"

A group of smokers are inexplicably able to see a horrible race of aliens who, planning to take over the world, have infiltrated positions of power all over the globe. This one reads as homage to classic science fiction shows like *The Invaders* (1967–1968), or paranoia movies like John Carpenter's *They Live* (1988); it can also be seen as a dry run for concepts King later used in *Insomnia* (1994). An ex-smoker himself, King in late 1999 would release an audio-only book entitled *Blood and Smoke*, containing three tales in which smokers or smoking was a central element to the plot.

"THE TEN O'CLOCK PEOPLE": PRIMARY SUBJECTS

BRANDON PEARSON: Walking to his ten o'clock cigarette break, bank employee Brandon is stunned to see a hideous "bat creature" dressed in an expensive suit walking toward him. He almost screams, but is pulled away by an associate, an African-American man named Duke Rhinemann, before he can attract attention to himself. Duke explains to Brandon why he can see the usually masked aliens (something to do with his many attempts to quit smoking), and the bat people's motivations (like most aliens, they naturally want to take over the world). Brandon becomes involved in the antibat resistance movement, spending the rest of his days combating the monstrous creatures.

DUKE RHINEMANN: An African-American who works in Computer Services, he is the first to realize that Brandon Pearson also has the ability to see the otherwise invisible alien bat-creatures. He introduces Brandon to other smokers who are combating the aliens, convincing him to join their cause to save the human race.

"Crouch End"

This contemporary "Cthulhu Mythos" story was inspired by events when King and his wife, Tabitha, became lost in London while on their way to visit their new friend, author Peter Straub, in 1977. Straub, of course, would later collaborate with King on the epic novels *The Talisman* (1984) and *Black House* (2001). "Crouch End" originally appeared in the 1980 anthology edited by Ramsey Campbell, *New Tales of the Cthulhu Mythos*, a collection of original stories inspired by the writings of horror legend H.P. Lovecraft (1890–1937).

Like the unfortunate couples in "The Rainy Season" and "You Know They've Got a Hell of a Band," Doris and Lonnie Freeman are American tourists who are destined to take a side trip straight into hell after getting lost searching for a friend's home. That side trip leads them into London's creepy Crouch End, where loathsome Lovecraftian demons—like the Goat with a Thousand Young—lie in wait for fresh victims.

"The House on Maple Street"

This story once again demonstrates author Ray Bradbury's profound influence on Stephen King, from the last name and age of its heroes to the subject matter of the tale itself. It appears for the first time in the collection, and King states in his Notes that it was actually inspired by an illustration from Chris Van Allsburg's wonderfully strange 1984 picture book, *The Mysteries of Harris Burdick.*

The Bradbury children discover that their residence hides the contours of a spaceship, a craft that is counting down to takeoff. Able to pinpoint the launch, they lure their evil stepfather into the house just as it lifts off into space.

Tabitha King   PHOTOGRAPHER UNKNOWN

"Umney's Last Case"

First appearing in print in *Nightmares & Dreamscapes*, "Umney's Last Case" was also later reissued as a Penguin Single, an elite group of paperback specials published by Penguin Books in 1995 to celebrate its sixtieth anniversary. A Raymond Chandler/Ross McDonald pastiche, "Umney" is yet another of King's journeys into the mind of a writer, this time exploring the relationship between an author and a character he has created. In his Notes, King states that this tale is a personal favorite in the book.

"UMNEY'S LAST CASE": PRIMARY SUBJECTS

CLYDE UMNEY: In 1938, private investigator Clyde Umney is faced with a serious dilemma—in the course of a single day, his entire world comes crashing down around him. His problems, he learns, are caused by a visitor to his office named Samuel D. Landry. Landry not only looks like an older version of himself, but claims to have created Umney and the entire world he inhabits in a series of gritty, violent novels such as *Scarlet Town*—which was first published in 1977! Landry informs Umney that he has grown tired of his unsatisfying and complicated life in the 1990s, and wants to change realities with him. Before Umney can stop him, Landry accomplishes the deed, trapping Umney in the real world of today. The hard-boiled detective does his best to cope, even teaching himself to be a writer, living for the day when he can turn then the tables on Landry.

SAMUEL D. LANDRY: A successful writer of crime and private eye novels, Landry finds the fictional world he has created of Los Angeles in the Great Depression more vibrant and real to him than the world he is inhabiting in 1994. He possesses a futuristic device that permits him to switch realities with one of his favorite characters, a hard-boiled shamus named Clyde Umney. In spite of Umney's stunned disbelief that the author has created his entire world, Landry is still able to usurp his place back in the more exciting past of the 1930s. Here Landry can make all his childhood dreams of being a private eye literally come true.

"The Beggar and the Diamond"

Included almost as an afterthought, this is King's retelling of a Hindu parable told to him by a man named Surrendra Patel (King later dedicated *From a Buick 8* to Mr. Patel and his wife, Geeta); King westernizes the tale by substituting God and his angel Uriel for Lord Shiva and his wife, Parvati.

Ramu begins to curse his lot in life after he trips over something in the road. (Ironically, it is a massive diamond that God has sent down at the insistence of the angel Uriel to provide Ramu with enough money to live out the rest of his days in comfort.) Ramu's anger quickly dissipates; counting his blessings, he picks himself up and walks away, most likely to find the sturdy stick God has left in his path, a gift that will prove far more useful to him than any diamond.

49

ROSE MADDER

(1995)

In retrospect, it seems as if Stephen King had been building toward *Rose Madder* his whole career. The theme of spousal/child abuse, touched on in early novels like *'Salem's Lot* (1975), *The Shining* (1977), and *Cujo* (1981), emerged more prominently in *It* (1986). The notion of men as the enemy became more explicit in *Gerald's Game* (1992); the insensitive Gerald Burlingame was only the first in a depressingly long line of abusive males King would introduce to readers over the course of his next four novels.

In *Gerald's Game*, readers watched in disgust as Jessie Burlingame was sexually molested by her father; in *Dolores Claiborne*, they saw another child abuser, the loathsome Joe St. George, hit his wife with a piece of firewood. King also pursued this track in *Insomnia* (1994), when the increasingly erratic Ed Deepneau beat his wife, Helen, putting an end to their marriage.

To date, however, *Rose Madder* stands as King's most unflinching look at abuse. It is the account of Rose Daniels and her monstrous husband, Norman. He is King's scariest psychopath since Greg Stillson of *The Dead Zone* (1979). Norman is not satisfied with merely hitting his wife, or degrading her verbally. No, Norman takes abuse to a new level, burning Rose and sodomizing her with foreign objects. He's also what psychologists call a "biter," and Rose bears the scars of his strange pathology.

The brutal realities of *Rose Madder* are balanced by a fantasy element, a subplot involving a world accessed through an otherwise unremarkable portrait Rose discovers in a pawnshop. This world seems to be the same one inhabited by Roland, the Gunslinger. An inhabitant of this world, alternately known as Wendy Yarrow and Dorcas, tells Rosie Daniels: "I've seen wars . . . heads by the hundreds poked onto poles along the streets of the City of Lud. I've seen wise leaders assassinated and fools put in their places . . ."

Dorcas speaks of Lud, a city that has been shown in King's *Dark Tower* saga, and the reference to the assassination of wise leaders and fools being put in their places could be a veiled reference to events in *The Eyes of the Dragon* (1987). Both Wendy and Rose Madder also mention "*ka*," a concept familiar to readers of *The Dark Tower* saga.

More so than in other works, King spends time in *Rose Madder* referencing classic works of fantasy and mythology. Lewis Carroll's Alice in Wonderland adventure *Through the Looking-Glass* (1872) is mentioned as Rosie enters the world of the painting. In naming the bull in the temple Erinyes, the author evokes Greek mythology. In having Rosie pass through a maze in the temple, he recalls the legend of the minotaur.

ROSE MADDER: PRIMARY SUBJECTS

ROSE DANIELS: Rose leads a miserable existence with her savagely abusive husband, Norman. Subsequent to one particular beating, a distraught Rose miscarries the baby she's come to think of as "Caroline." Rose remains with her police detective husband for nine more years, and the constant beatings take a physical and mental toll. One day, as she is making her bed, a single drop of blood falls from her nose, landing on a pillow. Seeing the blood triggers an uncharacteristic response in the usually docile Rose. Acting almost on instinct, she drops everything and flees the home that had been her prison for nearly fourteen years.

Rose decides she will not go by the name Rose Daniels any longer, and reinvents herself as Rosie McClendon, the hopeful young woman she was before she met Norman.

The newly minted Rosie travels to Liberty City, a town some 800 miles west, and ends up at Daughters and Sisters, a private shelter for battered women. There she meets Anna Stevenson, the shelter's strong-willed founder, who finds Rosie an apartment and a position as a maid at a local hotel.

Needing cash, Rosie visits Liberty City Loan and Pawn, offering her wedding ring for sale. The owner, Bill Steiner, informs her that the stone is only zirconium, not a diamond as Norman had led her to believe. Rosie is shaken, but not surprised—it is just one more slap in the face from the deceitful Norman.

Entering that store changes her life. The pawnbroker, Bill Steiner, falls in love with Rosie. Overhearing her voice, Robbie Lefferts, a producer of recorded books who is in the shop at the time, becomes convinced she would be perfect as a reader, and later offers her a job. Finally, while browsing through the store, Rose comes across an oil painting in a wooden frame, a portrait of a blonde woman in a rose madder toga standing on a hill, her back to the viewer, facing the ruins of what appear to be a Greek temple. Written on the back of the painting are the words "Rose Madder."

Titillated by the connection to her own given name, Rose is seized by a desire to own the artwork. Even though she recognizes that it isn't very good, the image portrayed on the canvas speaks to her on an almost primal level. Bartering her ring, Rosie acquires the painting and leaves.

Rosie hangs the painting on a wall in her apartment, where it blends in as if it belongs there. Rosie starts hearing things that are alien to her urban environment, such as the sounds of crickets chirping, or wind blowing through grass. At times, the vista in the painting seems to expand. Sometimes, Rosie believes items are actually moving within that vista. The painting comes to exert an influence on her daily life—Rosie dyes her hair blonde and has it done in the style of the woman in the portrait.

One evening, Rosie awakens to find the painting covering the entire wall. Strangely unafraid, she enters the world of the painting, and encounters a woman she recognizes as Wendy Yarrow, another (fatal) victim of her husband's rage. Wendy serves as Rosie's guide, introducing her to the woman in the toga, whose name is Rose Madder. Rose is an imperfect double of Rosie; her skin is mottled, her voice harsh, her state of mind near madness.

At her request, Rosie retrieves Rose's baby from a temple guarded by the blind bull Erinyes. When Rosie returns with the infant, Wendy tells her about the importance of forgetting the past, of getting on with her life. After expressing her disdain for men, Rose promises Rosie she will repay the act of kindness. Rosie returns to the real world with three seeds from the tree of forgetfulness and Rose's golden armlet as keepsakes.

Rose's promise to repay becomes important to Rosie when Norman, a gifted tracker with almost telepathic abilities, reenters Rosie's world with a trail of corpses in his wake. Finding her apartment, Norman follows her into Rose Madder's world. Mistaking Rose for his wife, Norman attacks her and is killed. Rosie returns to the real world and marries Bill Steiner. Soon thereafter, she bears a child whom she names Pamela Gertrude, after her friends Pam Haverford and Gert Kinshaw.

Rosie, Bill, and Pamela Gertrude Steiner are alive and well, presumably still living in Liberty City.

ROSE MADDER: Rosie's mad doppelganger, Rose inhabits the world of the painting from the pawnshop. Although Rose's features are the same as Rosie's, she is radically different; in fact, she can be viewed as the embodiment of all the rage Rosie suppresses. This fury has driven her mad, and has even disfigured her. As recompense for the favor Rosie does for her, Rose draws Norman into the world of the painting, confronts him, and eventually kills him.

After killing Norman, Rose leaves her station in front of Erinyes' temple, presumably to travel in the world of the portrait. Rose is accompanied in her travels by her infant daughter and Dorcas. Their present whereabouts are unknown.

NORMAN DANIELS: When she was fifteen, Rose McClendon met Norman Daniels at a varsity basketball game. Norman wooed, won, and finally wed young Rosie, marrying her after her graduation, then proceeded to make her life a living hell. Over the course of their fourteen-year union, the police detective beat Rosie regularly. In 1985, he beat her so severely that she miscarried. Norman's temper is always quick to flare—besides beating his wife, he also brutalizes suspects. In fact, in 1985 Norman and his partner accidentally beat an innocent young black woman named Wendy Yarrow to death.

After Rose leaves him, Norman becomes even more volatile, killing a hooker who resembles her. He then embarks on a murderous rampage in search of his spouse. Utilizing his uncanny ability to get into the minds of those he is tracking (he calls it "trolling"), Norman traces Rose to Liberty City, where his murder spree continues, extending to many of Rose's friends and protectors.

Norman comes into possession of a Ferdinand the bull mask (no doubt a likeness of the character in the children's book *The Story of Ferdinand*, created by Munro Leaf and illustrated by Robert Lawson), which he impulsively steals. The mask begins to talk to Norman in the voice of his deceased, abusive father. Perhaps reflecting a latent telepathic ability of Norman's, the mask provides information about Rosie, eventually leading him to her apartment. There, after donning the mask, Norman follows Rosie into the painting, where he in effect becomes the embodiment of Erinyes, the bull god of the temple. Still wearing the mask that has somehow grafted itself to his face, Norman meets his fate at the hands of the vengeful Rose Madder.

ERINYES: In Greek mythology, the Erinyes, or Furies, punished sinners. Known as "those who walk in darkness," they had snakes for hair and wept tears of blood. Erinyes comes from the Greek word meaning "hunting down" or "persecuting." Thus it is fitting that a skilled tracker like Norman, whose only real emotion seems to be anger, becomes Erinyes in the world of the painting.

In the world of the painting, Erinyes is the one-eyed, blind bull inhabiting the temple therein. Rosie braves that temple and its dangers to save Rose Madder's child. Just as Rosie and Rose are linked, so are Erinyes and Norman. They connect when Norman finds the Ferdinand the bull mask in the real world. The mask guides Norman to Rosie's apartment, where Norman follows Rosie into the art piece. There he dons the mask and in effect becomes Erinyes.

WENDY YARROW: A young woman who falls victim to Norman's anger in the real world, Wendy is seemingly reincarnated in the world of the painting as Dorcas (sometimes translated as "Tabitha"), Rose's companion. Dorcas acts as Rosie's mentor in the strange world of the artwork, telling her what she must do there, giving her the tools and the information she needs to survive. She later lectures Rosie on the importance of forgetting the past. At present, she is wandering the world of the painting with Rose Madder.

BILL STEINER: The owner of Liberty City Pawn and Loan, he meets Rosie when she comes in to pawn her wedding ring. It falls to Bill to tell her that the diamond in the ring is not real, and thus only worth a small amount. Smitten with Rosie, Bill asks her out, becoming the first man Rosie has ever had a romantic relationship with besides Norman. Norman's polar opposite, Bill helps Rosie in her transformation from submissive victim to confident adult. After Norman's death, Bill and Rosie marry and have a child, Pamela Gertrude.

DAUGHTERS AND SISTERS: A shelter for battered women, Daughters and Sisters becomes Rosie's home for a short time following her escape from Norman.

ANNA STEVENSON: The formidable administrator of Daughters and Sisters, Anna reminds Rosie of Beatrice Arthur, the acerbic actress who played Maude on the sitcom of the same name. Anna takes Rosie under her wing, enabling her to start a new life under the name of Rosie McClendon. Anna is later slaughtered by the rampaging Norman.

ROBBIE LEFFERTS: A producer of books on audiotape, Robbie hires Rosie to read hard-boiled mysteries penned by women writing under male pseudonyms. The first book Rosie narrates is *The Manta Ray*, written by Christina Bell under the name of Richard Racine. Robbie is lucky in that he never meets Norman Daniels. He presumably still makes his home in Liberty City.

ROSE MADDER: TRIVIA

- The character Cynthia Smith of *Rose Madder* also appears in 1996's *Desperation*. An alternate universe version of the same character also appears in *The Regulators*, published that same year.

- Rosie McLendon and Anna Stevenson are fans of Paul Sheldon, the fictional author who is the main character of King's novel *Misery* (1987).

50

THE GREEN MILE

(1996)

W hen *The Green Mile* was originally published, it surprised many people, particularly long-time readers of Stephen King. He had most recently written several books about women in jeopardy (though that's simplifying matters considerably), and for the most part, those had not been very well received. The last thing anyone would ever have expected from the author at the time was a serial novel about prison guards and inmates on Death Row in 1932, published in six thin monthly installments.

It was an idea, and a book, that seemed to fit more comfortably with some of the works he had produced much earlier in his career. And yet, as written, it is obviously a story only the middle-aged King could create with the degree of subtlety that is present in the narrative.

Serial novels, of course, are a dead publishing format. It hadn't been done successfully in decades, and it hadn't been done by a pop culture icon since Charles Dickens wrote in serial form in nineteenth-century England. But in March 1996, the first part of *The Green Mile*, "The Two Dead Girls," appeared and was an immediate critical and popular success. The idea of such a series of cliffhangers from the undisputed "Master of Horror" (though this is hardly a horror story in that sense) appealed to a vast number of readers. Anyone who had ever read King, and probably a great many who never had, picked up the first part and were hooked.

But it wasn't just the promotional gimmick that did it. A gimmick is, after all, only effective once. The truth of the matter was that *The Green Mile* was King's best writing in years. Interesting, since the author plainly admitted to not having had the ending fully fleshed out even as the first installments were being published.

The story is a deceptively simple one. Paul Edgecombe is the senior guard working on E Block at Cold Mountain Prison in the southern United States in 1932. E Block is, for all intents and purposes, Death Row. A new prisoner, John Coffey, is brought into E Block, and changes the lives of everyone with whom he comes into contact. A simpleton with a supernatural healing gift, Coffey is set to be executed for a crime he didn't commit. The interaction of the guards and inmates is both a chilling and tragic plot and a wonderful morality play. The fact that it is all bookended by the story of the 104-year-old Edgecombe looking back on the events adds texture that is surprising in a book as short (in comparison to most of King's works) as this.

On the other hand, since the long-term effects of exposure to John Coffey are really what the book is about—along with mortality, and the fragility of the human condition, both physical and emotional—the book could not have worked successfully without that framing sequence.

King had, of course, already successfully done a prison novel (or, in this case, novella) called *Rita Hayworth and Shawshank Redemption*. It appeared in 1982 in the collection *Different Seasons*. More dauntingly, perhaps, by the time King was working on *The Green Mile*, the novella had been made into an extraordinarily good (and very faithful) film called, more simply, *The Shawshank Redemption* (1994).

Of course, calling both stories prison novels and expecting them to be the same is sort of like expecting *'Salem's Lot* (1975) and *Christine* (1983) to be identical simply because they each deal with small-town horror. Certainly, the atmosphere of prison life (and lest we forget, both of the tales are period pieces, which adds a certain texture) was something King had proven he could do. But the stories themselves are very different. There are instances in *The Green Mile* when it seems about to turn into a caper or escape yarn. It never does.

While the two tales share a focal character who is apparently innocent of the crimes for which he has been imprisoned, there is little similarity beyond that. *Shawshank* is about the prison experience, and finding a way to triumph over a system that has malfunctioned and destroyed an individual's life. It is about escape.

The Green Mile, on the other hand, is about suffering the tragedy that ensues because of a malfunction in the system (here, of course, the system is not merely prison, but society as a whole, given that racism is one of the keys to Coffey's wrongful imprisonment). It is not about beating the system. Instead, it focuses on what the characters around John Coffey learn from the wrongs that have befallen him, and the benevolence with which he faces them. Finally, more than anything, *The Green Mile* is about transcendence, both for John Coffey and for the other characters involved in the narrative.

Also unlike *Shawshank*, *The Green Mile* surprised readers by including a supernatural element. Though the presentation of the supernatural is subtle throughout the story, it is there, nevertheless. John Coffey's empathy and healing touch aren't merely the alleged God-given gift of a faith healer. It is a real, tangible thing, where Coffey pulls the pain and suffering and disease of others into himself, feels the agony of it, and then expels it in a horrid, visible form, not unlike the demon rising from the ruins of the Overlook Hotel in *The Shining* (1977).

But beyond Coffey's "touch"—which, let's not forget, manages to make both Paul Edgecombe and Mr. Jingles, the mouse, almost immortal—there's that damned mouse. Mr. Jingles is *no* ordinary rodent, even before Coffey gets his hands on him. It may be possible that a mouse is just a mouse, but it's clear that King doesn't think so. Neither does Paul Edgecombe.

Which brings us to another element of the supernatural, something even more subtle than the others, which also ties in with John Coffey. Or, more accurately, with Coffey's execution. Paul—and, we are led to believe, the other characters in the story—can feel the almost electrical current running through the air as Coffey is about to be executed. The weather changes, the air itself is altered, as if some preternatural force is disturbed by what is about to occur. But there is no *deus ex machina*, much as Paul, and the readers, might have hoped for it. If some cosmic force has empowered John Coffey, or is bothered by the notion of his execution, it does nothing to save him.

But in Paul Edgecombe, and in Mr. Jingles, the "magic" legacy of John Coffey lives on for a very long time.

THE GREEN MILE: PRIMARY SUBJECTS

PAUL EDGECOMBE: As the senior guard on E Block at Cold Mountain penitentiary, Paul Edgecombe has a job no one would envy (save, perhaps, for the sadistic Percy Wetmore). E Block is where prisoners are sent after they are sentenced to die on Old Sparky, Cold Mountain's electric chair, and Paul is frequently required to strap the convicts into the chair.

During that period in 1932 when John Coffey is on E Block, Paul has one of the strangest and most tragic experiences of his life. Coffey has been convicted of murdering two young girls, but from the moment he is brought into the prison, Paul believes there is something just a little different about John Coffey.

Over time, experiencing Coffey's ability to heal firsthand, and realizing the large black man is fairly simple-minded, Paul begins to believe that Coffey is innocent of the murders. He sets out to prove exactly that, but racial issues prevent anyone from reopening the case, even though Paul believes he has the actual killer, Billy Wharton, right there on E Block.

Eventually Coffey is executed. None of the other guards will give the order to throw the switch, and Paul is forced to do that himself. Not long thereafter, Paul retires, never participating in another execution.

However, Coffey's legacy does not die along with him. The influence of his healing power remains in Paul Edgecombe's life, as well as in the "life" of the mouse, Mr. Jingles. Paul experiences flashes of telepathy, an ability that eventually fades, and is perfectly healthy all his life, up to his present age of 104.

In 1956, Paul and Janice Edgecombe are in a horrible bus accident from which only four people walk away. Janice dies, but Paul emerges without a scratch.

Finding himself a resident of the Georgia Pines retirement home, he begins to write the story of John Coffey and the events at Cold Mountain. There he meets a woman named Elaine Connelly, who becomes his companion, and he gives her the account to read. Though Elaine finds it difficult to believe, particularly Paul's advanced age, she believes when Paul shows her the pet he has been keeping—Mr. Jingles. The mouse has survived all that time, just like Paul, thanks to John Coffey's lasting power.

Eventually, though, Mr. Jingles expires. Elaine passes on as well. For his part, Paul continues on in good health at Georgia Pines.

JOHN COFFEY: A black migrant worker, John Coffey was born with something extra. He has a special empathy with people, and the ability to heal them, to take their pain into himself for a time, and then release it into the ether. Fate is not kind to John Coffey, however. While traveling through the woods, he comes upon the bodies of two young white girls who have just been murdered. Coffey does his best to revive the victims, to heal them, but cannot. When the bodies are found, Coffey is still there, crying over them, a large black man with blood on his hands at the site of the murder of two small white girls.

Simple-minded, Coffey does not have the wits or the will to defend himself, and is convicted of the crime and sentenced to death. While on E Block, awaiting execution, he meets and heals senior guard Paul Edgecombe and others. Edgecombe and several other guards try to help Coffey, but to no avail.

Much to Edgecombe's dismay, Coffey seems almost relieved to face his execution. His empathy—feeling the pain of those around him so constantly—has become an almost unbearable burden. Coffey is executed on November 20, 1932, for crimes he did not commit.

EDUARD DELACROIX: Delacroix lands on E Block after he raped a girl and then set a fire to cover it up that took the lives of six people. While in prison, the skittish inmate keeps mostly to himself, with the exception of Mr. Jingles, a mouse who becomes his pet. However, the guards on E Block have some questions, mostly in jest, as to who is the owner and who the pet. Delacroix claims that Mr. Jingles speaks to him, whispers in his ear, and it seems as though the tricks the inmate "trains" the mouse to do might not have required very much training at all.

It is Delacroix's ill fortune that a sadistic guard named Percy Wetmore takes an instant dislike to him. Percy brutalizes Delacroix and, when preparing him for execution, purposely does not properly wet the sponges that go into the helmet of the electric chair. As a result, Delacroix is not so much electrocuted as he is burned alive in the chair.

MR. JINGLES: The guards on E Block originally call this mouse "Steamboat Willie," after the famous Mickey Mouse cartoon. However, the mysterious rodent, who always seems a bit more intelligent than any mouse ought to be, eventually becomes the pet of inmate Eduard Delacroix. Delacroix claims that Mr. Jingles speaks to him, and has told him his "real" name. In order to hurt Delacroix, the sadistic guard, Percy Wetmore, kills Mr. Jingles, but the mouse is revived and healed by John Coffey.

Coffey uses enough of his power in this instance to infuse Mr. Jingles with a miraculous health and life span (just as Coffey does with Paul Edgecombe). Mr. Jingles later shows up, almost as if he'd been searching the man out, on the step of Paul Edgecombe's Georgia retirement home. It seems an unlikely coincidence, and one can only assume that there is, indeed, more to the mouse than would be considered natural. However, whether that comes from John Coffey's power or, as seems to be indicated, was always inherent in Mr. Jingles, remains a mystery.

Mr. Jingles dies in the care of Paul Edgecombe at Georgia Pines.

BILLY "THE KID" WHARTON: A nineteen-year-old serial killer, William Wharton fancies himself a modern-day Billy the Kid. Upon his arrival at E Block, he tries to kill a guard named Dean Stanton. It becomes obvious to the jailers, after a time, that Wharton is likely responsible for the murders of the two little girls for which John Coffey is facing execution, but they can do nothing about it.

Coffey, on the other hand, could. After healing the wife of the warden, Coffey holds onto her pain and sickness until he returns to the prison. There he sends all that dark pain into Percy Wetmore, a sadistic guard whom he hates, and somehow manipulates Percy into turning that pain on Wharton. Wetmore shoots Wharton six times.

So Billy the Kid never makes it to Old Sparky.

PERCY WETMORE: A born sadist, Percy Wetmore won his job on E Block by virtue of being the governor's nephew. That connection also allows him to make a great deal of trouble for Paul Edgecombe and the other keepers on E Block. He brutalizes inmates, both physically and emotionally, and purposely interferes in Eduard Delacroix's execution so the man will not be electrocuted, but instead burned by the electricity. After that event, he is intimidated into requesting a transfer to Briar Ridge Mental Hospital.

After Percy murders an inmate (though his will is not entirely his own at the time), he is sent to Briar Ridge as a patient, and dies there in 1965.

BRUTUS HOWELL: A guard on E Block along with Paul Edgecombe, Brutus also believes in John Coffey's innocence and participates in the trek with Coffey that leads to the healing of the warden's wife. His nickname is "brutal," though perhaps more because he is physically intimidating than because of any actual brutality. Brutus dies in 1957 of a heart attack.

HAL MOORES: The warden of Cold Mountain penitentiary, Hal Moores is reluctant to see John Coffey executed after Coffey heals his wife's brain tumor. He is helpless, however, to stop the execution. Warden Moores dies of a stroke.

MELINDA MOORES: The wife of Cold Mountain's warden, Hal Moores, Melinda is dying of an inoperable brain tumor before she is miraculously healed by John Coffey. She later expires of a heart attack, in 1943.

JANICE EDGECOMBE: Paul's wife, she keeps after him to find a way to prove John Coffey's innocence or to help him escape. She dies in a bus accident in 1956.

ELAINE CONNELLY: A resident of the Georgia Pines retirement home, Elaine becomes Paul Edgecombe's companion in his (very) old age. Though both Paul and Elaine are tormented by a sadistic orderly (not unlike Paul's old co-worker, Percy Wetmore) named Brad Dolan, Elaine manages to intimidate Dolan somewhat with her connections at the Georgia state house.

Elaine dies of a heart attack three months after reading Paul's story about John Coffey and Cold Mountain.

THE GREEN MILE: ADAPTATIONS

King's groundbreaking serial novel was adapted for the big screen in 1999 by writer/director Frank Darabont, who had previously performed the same miracle with *The Shawshank Redemption* (1994, the screen version of King's other period prison story, adapted from the 1982 novella *Rita Hayworth and Shawshank Redemption*).

The film featured Hollywood's favorite leading man, Tom Hanks, as Paul Edgecombe, but also sported a marvelous supporting cast. Michael

Clarke Duncan (*Armageddon*) manages the challenging role of John Coffey with quiet dignity and aplomb. James Cromwell (*L.A. Confidential*) is a perfect Warden Moores, and Bonnie Hunt (*Jumanji*) portrays Janice Edgecombe, Paul's wife, with a wonderful twinkle in her eye and confidence not often found in such roles. Chameleonlike actor Michael Jeter achieves great pathos as Delacroix, and Doug Hutchison and Sam Rockwell are gloriously evil in their respective roles as Percy Wetmore and Billy Wharton. Barry Pepper and Jeffrey DeMunn are equally adept in their parts as Paul's fellow prison guards, Dean Stanton and Harry Terwilliger. Perhaps the film's best performance, however, can be attributed to character actor David Morse (*The Rock*), who gives prison guard Brutus Howell amazing range and texture of emotion.

Darabont's adaptation is extremely faithful to King's original text. The only major deviation concerns the wraparound story that the author included mainly as a necessity of the serial publishing format. The film opens and closes with the elderly Paul Edgecombe and Elaine Connelly, and includes Mr. Jingles—all of the elements that are pertinent to the themes of the narrative—but the Percy Wetmore–like orderly, Brad Dolan, has been excised completely.

THE GREEN MILE: TRIVIA

- A pair of E Block guards are named "Harry" and "Dean Stanton," and veteran character actor Harry Dean Stanton appears in the film as inmate trustee Toot Toot. The actor also appeared in the film version of King's *Christine*. It is highly doubtful that this is a coincidence.

- Director Darabont has joked that after his first two films he's firmly established himself as the major force in a sub-sub-subgenre: lengthy period prison dramas based on the works of Stephen King. However, the auteur has also been working for quite some time on an adaptation of King's novella *The Mist*.

- Jeffrey DeMunn, who portrays Harry in the film version of *The Green Mile*, was also in King's 1999 television miniseries *Storm of the Century*, as Robbie Beals. DeMunn also appeared in *The Shawshank Redemption*. David Morse is also a regular in King-related films, having appeared in *The Green Mile, The Langoliers*, and *Hearts in Atlantis*.

51

SIX STORIES

(1997)

Published by King's own Philtrum Press, this signed, limited edition of 1,100 copies became an instant collector's item, quickly appreciating from its original sales price of $85. Designed by Michael Alpert, this handsome trade paperback featured two previously unpublished works, "L.T.'s Theory of Pets" and "Autopsy Room Four." The other four stories—"Lunch at the Gotham Café," "Luckey Quarter," "Blind Willie," and "The Man in the Black Suit"— were previously published in *Dark Love* (1995), an anthology edited by Nancy A. Collins; *USA Weekend; Antaeus;* and *The New Yorker* respectively.

Six Stories is comparable to the novella collection *Different Seasons* (1982) in that the stories don't quite fit within the normal King mode. However, the author's very distinctive voice and astounding storytelling ability make this a memorable collection. More odd than horrific, these tales highlight King's extraordinary ability to create believable, three-dimensional characters to which readers can relate and sympathize.

[NOTE: "The Man in the Black Suit" is discussed in the Castle Rock section. "Autopsy Room Four" is discussed in the Derry section. "Lunch at the Gotham Cafe, "Luckey Quarter," and "L.T.'s Theory of Pets" are discussed in the section on the collection Everything's Eventual, as that collection was a mass-market release.]

"Blind Willie"

"Blind Willie," the most intriguing story in this collection, follows mild-mannered businessman Bill Teale on his commute to work in New York City. Bill arrives at his office and then proceeds to another room in the same building, where he changes clothes, becoming Willie Teale. He departs, only to switch outfits again in a posh Manhattan hotel. Willie then goes to his real place of employment—Fifth Avenue, just outside of St. Patrick's Cathedral, where he earns a living as Blind Willie, Vietnam vet and panhandler. Despite its unique take on the phenomenon of street people, this narrative has a lot to say about the plight of the homeless.

[NOTE: *The character of Bill Teale is not considered to be part of the Stephen King Universe, as an altered and expanded version of this story is incorporated into 1999's* Hearts in Atlantis, *which must be considered the preferred and therefore, for our purposes, "official" text.*]

SIX STORIES: TRIVIA

- In 1999, "Lunch at the Gotham Café" was released in an audio version along with two other smoking-related tales. The package was entitled *Blood and Smoke.*

- An altered version of "Blind Willie" is included in King's 1999 experimental novel/collection, *Hearts in Atlantis.*

52

FROM A BUICK 8

(2002)

Like 1983's *Christine*, *From a Buick 8* is ostensibly about a vintage automobile, but that's where any similarity between the two novels ends. Unlike the former, which featured a demonic car out for blood, the latter features something that looks like an auto, but is actually a doorway to another reality.

The aforementioned doorway takes the approximate shape of a 1954 Buick Roadmaster; said car is impounded by troopers of Pennsylvania State Patrol Troop D in 1979, after its apparent owner, a tall man dressed in black, abandons it at a local gas station. Examining the vehicle, the responding officers realize that it contains far too many anomalies to actually be a car. Intrigued by its utter strangeness, they tow it back to their barracks, where it becomes a source of wonderment to them for the next two decades.

Why? Well, strange things happen around the Buick, which is kept in a storage shed on the grounds. The first night it is there, the temperature in the shed drops twenty degrees. Then the car begins to emit intense bursts of light. Finally, a trooper disappears—subsequent investigation leads the troop to conclude that, strange as it may seem, the car was somehow responsible.

Over the years, any number of strange plants and creatures appear in the shed, seemingly emerging from its trunk. Objects placed in the shed for experimental purposes disappear. The light shows continue, but are separated by greater and greater intervals. During this time, the troop manages to keep the car a secret, revealing its presence and proclivities to only a select few.

The troopers relate the Buick's history over the course of an evening to young Ned Wilcox, son of Curtis Wilcox, a trooper who died a year earlier in an accident eerily similar to the one that befell King in 1999 (even eerier, King wrote the novel before his accident). Curtis was obsessed with the car, studying and recording its activities, even going so far as to autopsy one of the creatures that emerged from its "womb." Despite this, he never found definitive answers.

If *From a Buick 8* is "about" something, it is about the fact that life itself rarely yields definitive answers. As one character says, "Life rarely finishes its conversations." Why do some people survive accidents when others perish? Why are some successful and others failures? Why? Real life is not orderly, nor is everything that occurs easily explainable. Human beings can look for patterns, for explanations, but they very rarely manifest themselves. The book also makes the point that despite the tragedy or wonderment that appears in our lives, life, indeed, does go on. King's characters go to great pains to emphasize that to Ned, who, being in his teens, does not have the perspective that the older troopers have.

The tone of this novel is a hybrid between King's "own" voice and that of his pseudonym, Richard Bachman, a tightrope walk between optimism and cynicism. The story slowly builds momentum, drawing the audience into the narrative so subtly that you find yourself a good two hundred pages into the book before looking up. Of course, like most of King's novels, it features well-realized characters that evoke readers' sympathies. Although King set the story in rural Pennsylvania, these characters resemble the native New Englanders with which King usually populates his tales, "keeping themselves to themselves," accepting what life throws at them with preternatural calm and stoicism. It is their all-too-human reactions to the strangeness that has entered their lives, rather than the special effects (which are plentiful), that make this book the subtle triumph that it is.

FROM A BUICK 8: PRIMARY SUBJECTS

SANDY DEARBORN: As of 2002, the commanding officer of Pennsylvania State Patrol Troop D. It is Sandy who narrates the majority of *From* *a Buick 8;* he steps aside only to let others relate the pieces of the story that he was not directly privy to. Sandy is unique among the members of Troop D in that he's actually had a glimpse of the world on the other side of the Roadmaster's trunk.

CURTIS WILCOX: Along with fellow trooper Ennis Rafferty, Curtis Wilcox answers the call that brings the Buick Roadmaster into the lives of Patrol Troop D. Impounding the car, they remove it from the gas station where it was abandoned by a man in black and bring it to their barracks. After stowing the car in Shed B, they start to move on with their lives. But strange things start to happen at the barracks, and they all center on Shed B. The troopers soon realize that the car, which appears to be a doorway between this reality and another, is something extraordinary.

Curtis becomes obsessed with the Buick, performing experiments to test his theories about its nature and origins. Unfortunately, the mystery of the car is not one that lends itself to easy solution. Wilcox is forced to accept the fact that he will never understand anything about the car besides what he has directly observed.

Curtis is killed in 2001 by a drunk driver who hits him while he's inspecting the rear outside wheel of a semi he had just pulled over.

NED WILCOX: Curtis's son, Ned becomes part of everyday life at Troop D's barracks after the death of his father. The troop is glad to have the boy around, first because he reminds them of Curtis, and second because he is part of their extended family.

Making himself useful around the barracks by cleaning up, Ned discovers the car that is being stored in Shed B. Ned asks Sandy Dearborn about the car. Sandy, who has been dreading this moment, decides to tell Ned the entire story. Like his father, Ned, too, becomes obsessed with the car. Thinking he can destroy the vehicle, Ned embarks on a risky plan that nearly costs him his life. Luckily, he is saved when Sandy Dearborn intervenes.

THE BUICK ROADMASTER: Actually, this "not-of-this-world" object only resembles a midnight blue 1954 Buick Roadmaster. In reality, it is a doorway from this world to another world that proves lethal to humans; likewise, the strange creatures from the other side that enter this world from the object's "trunk" do not survive long on Earth.

The object is left at a gas station in 1979 by its driver, a man in black. The officers who respond quickly realize that the car is not really a car, and tow it to their barracks. A forensic examination (which is never filed) reveals the following:

1. The odometer was set at zero, which is appropriate, as the car would never drive. In fact, no one involved has ever seen it move under its own power.
2. Pebbles placed between the knuckles of the tread of the car's tires do not remain there, even when placed so far up along the curve of the tire that gravity should have held them in.
3. There are three portholes on one side of the "vehicle" instead of the customary four.
4. The "car's" exhaust system is made of glass.

The object is stored in Shed B of Troop D's barracks. The temperature in that shed is usually normal, but often starts to drop precipitously. The drop in temperature is often followed by a phenomenon the troopers call "lightquakes," fantastic displays of bright light emanating from the "Roadmaster." Over the years, many members of Troop D have felt a mysterious "pull" emanating from the object in the shed.

The Buick remains in Shed B to this day. Although it has exhibited little sign of aging from the time it arrived, the car developed a crack in its windshield in 2002, perhaps indicating its eventual deterioration.

THE MAN IN BLACK: The "driver" of the "car." He tells Brad Roach, the attendant at the gas station where the car appears (Brad has his nose in a magazine when the bell in the garage dings, so he doesn't actually see it pull up), to "Fill 'er up." When Brad asks him if he wants the oil checked, he replies "Oil's fine," then disappears around the corner of the station, presumably on his way to the men's room. He is never seen again.

BRAD ROACH: The attendant on duty the day the man in black leaves the "Buick" at the gas station. Also the "veteran county drunk" driver who accidentally kills Curtis Wilcox in 2001.

SHIRLEY PASTERNAK: The dispatcher for Troop D. Sandy Dearborn says that law enforcement would "fall apart in western Pennsylvania" without Police Communications Officer Pasternak. Shirley takes a liking to Ned and trains him in the art of dispatching.

ENNIS RAFFERTY: Besides his partner, Curtis Wilcox, Ennis Rafferty is the first member of Troop D to see the Buick Roadmaster. He is also its first victim, as he disappears shortly after the state troopers impound the car. Many years later, Sandy Dearborn glimpses Ennis's hat on the other side of the portal contained in the Roadmaster's trunk.

MISTER DILLON: The Troop D mascot, this friendly German shepherd instinctively fears the Buick Roadmaster. He will not enter Shed B. The dog gives up his life protecting his masters from a creature that emerges from the trunk of the Roadmaster.

TONY SCHOONDIST: Sergeant Commanding at the time the Buick Roadmaster entered the lives of the members of Troop D. Per Sandy Dearborn, Tony, along with Curtis Wilcox, became a Roadmaster (instead of Rhodes) scholar over the years, becoming especially sensitive to the warning signs the car gives off before something strange occurs in Shed B.

ARKY ARKANIAN: Troop D's custodian is the first to see one of the creatures that emerge from the trunk of the Buick, a batlike monstrosity that makes most people sick just looking at it.

BRIAN LIPPY: Pulled over by a patrol car manned by troopers George Morgan and Eddie Jacubois for reckless driving, Lippy is arrested by the duo and brought to the Troop D barracks. Escaping during a moment of confusion, Lippy is apparently drawn to the Roadmaster and enters its trunk. Although he's never seen again, Sandy sees a swastika Lippy wore when he briefly peers across the void into the other world.

HUDDIE ROYER: A member of Troop D, Huddie accompanies Arky Arkanian into Shed B the day the bat thing appears.

FROM A BUICK 8: TRIVIA

- In publicity for *The Dark Tower VI: Song of Susannah*, King stated that *From a Buick Eight* was an explicit part of the *Dark Tower* continuity. Due to obvious connections within the text, some speculate that the Man in Black might have in fact been one of the Crimson King's Low Men, and the Buick one of the flashy but subtly wrong automobiles that the Low Men favor. Certainly, a link to the *Dark Tower* continuity exists in that the Buick itself is a door to another reality—a mobile thinny, perhaps? Another, more tenuous connection lies in the name Dearborn. Sandy Dearborn is the primary narrator of *Buick 8*. When the young Roland travels to Mejis in *Wizards and Glass*, he assumes the alias Will Dearborn.

- The title, *From a Buick 8*, brings to mind the Bob Dylan song, "From a Buick 6," featured on his album *Highway 61 Revisited*.

- According to King's Author's Note at the end of the book, his fictional town of Statler is just down the road from Rocksburg, "the town which serves as the locale for K. C. Constantine's brilliant series of novels about small town police chief Mario Balzic." King also points out in his Author's Note that "liberties" have been taken with the Buick that appears on the hardcover's dust jacket, noting that "*Eight*'s cover girl is several years older than the Buick in the story." When asked if this bothered him, he said absolutely not—he was bothered more by the sneermouth grille, which he said looked "almost ready to gobble someone up."

53

ROSE RED

(2002)

Filmed in Seattle over a four-month period in 2000, this six-hour mini-series premiered on ABC in January 2002. Written by King, it is said in the publicity materials for the show that *Rose Red* was the first script the author worked on "after the devastating accident that nearly ended his life." Directed by Craig R. Baxley and produced by Mark Carliner (King's collaborators on the 1999 miniseries *Storm of the Century*), it was presented over three nights, receiving respectable ratings.

Featuring a cast anchored by veteran actors Nancy Travis (playing Joyce Reardon), David Dukes, and Julian Sands (playing Professor Miller and Nick Hardaway, respectively), *Rose Red* tells the story of a decaying mansion located in Seattle, Washington. Built in 1907 by oil magnate John P. Rimbauer, the house, which is said to be haunted, has known its share of tragedy.

Believing the strange stories told about the house, Professor of Paranormal Studies Joyce Reardon wishes to study it. In order to "wake" the dormant haunted house, Reardon assembles a team consisting of six individuals, all possessing extrasensory skills. Reardon and her team enter the building and, to their dismay, succeed in their goal of rousing the spirits who haunt the mansion.

Rose Red had its beginnings in a project involving King and Steven

Spielberg, the 1999 remake of *The Haunting*. Due to creative differences between the writer and director, King withdrew from that project. King, however, continued to pursue his idea of a "Moby Dick haunted house story." The way King envisioned it, the story "would take off from the point of the Winchester House in San Jose, in which the widow of the Winchester Rifle magnates was told by a psychic, 'As long as you're not done building the house, you'll stay alive.'"

The plot of the story resembles that of the classic novel *The Haunting of Hill House* by Shirley Jackson; *Rose Red*'s basic story line, that of a team of researchers entering a haunted house, stirring up supernatural forces, is obviously derived from the Jackson classic. King's cast of characters also bears a resemblance to Jackson's. Standing in for intense Dr. John Montague is the intense Dr. Joyce Reardon. Standing in for Luke Sanderson, nephew of Hill House's owner, is Steven Rimbauer, the last surviving Rimbauer. Standing in for Eleanor Vance is Annie Wheaton. Like Eleanor, Annie has also caused stones to rain from the sky. Elements of the story also bring to mind elements of other King stories. Constant Readers will recall that King paid homage to Jackson once before in *Carrie*, when the title character caused a rain of rocks to fall on her home.

The companion volume to the series, *The Diary of Ellen Rimbauer: My Life at Rose Red*, thought originally to have been penned by King, was actually revealed to have been written by Ridley Pearson, who has appeared with King as part of the Rock Bottom Remainders. Telling the "backstory" of *Rose Red*, it, too, was later made into a miniseries. As additional publicity, the producers created a Web site for Beaumont University, Dr. Reardon's place of employment.

Sadly, veteran character actor David Dukes (Professor Miller) died shortly before filming was completed.

ROSE RED: PRIMARY SUBJECTS

ROSE RED: According to Dr. Joyce Reardon, this Seattle mansion was "born bad." The house, which has claimed many victims over the decades, is now in a coma of sorts. Hoping to wake it up, Reardon assembles a team composed of members with wild talents to explore it with her.

Awakening Rose Red proves a bad idea. The hostile homestead, capable of shifting its architecture and floor plan, attacks its visitors, resulting in several gruesome deaths.

JOHN RIMBAUER: A Seattle oil magnate, Rimbauer used his vast wealth to build the Seattle mansion he named Rose Red. Abusive and unfaithful, Rimbauer made his wife Ellen miserable.

ELLEN RIMBAUER: The mistress of Rose Red, she was told by a psychic that Rose Red "isn't finished until you say it is." The unhappy Ellen becomes obsessed with reworking the house, adding room after room. She disappeared in 1952. Some say she disappeared into the house.

STEVEN RIMBAUER: The last surviving Rimbauer, he is heir to the estate. He has a relationship with Joyce Reardon; it's not clear whether she actually feels anything for him or is just using him to gain access to Rose Red in hopes of furthering her career. The house has a special interest in Steven, but he resists its call. He survives his visit to his ancestral home, subsequently entering into a romantic relationship with Rachel Wheaton.

SUKEENA: Ellen Rimbauer's African servant, she shares a deep bond with her mistress, one that persists even after death. Proud and mysterious, Sukeena holds great sway over her mistress. Her influence seems supernatural at times.

JOYCE REARDON: A professor of paranormal studies at Beaumont University, she assembles a group of individuals who have psychic gifts to enter the haunted mansion known as Rose Red, hoping to wake up whatever supernatural force resides there. Her experiment succeeds; the results prove lethal to her and several members of her team.

ANNIE WHEATON: Fifteen years old and autistic, Annie possesses enormous telekinetic powers. Annie's wild talents are the key to Joyce Reardon's plans to wake Rose Red. Annie feels the pull of Rose Red, but resists; she is the primary reason any of Joyce Reardon's team survives their expedition to the mansion.

RACHEL WHEATON: Annie Wheaton's older sister and protector, she manages to sneak the young girl away from their overbearing father so that Annie can join Joyce Reardon's team. Rachel survives her trip to Rose Red, finding romance with Steven Rimbauer.

NICK HARDAWAY: The handsome, easygoing Nick has a talent for mind reading. Nick is among those who accompany Reardon on her expedition to Rose Red. Nick, unfortunately, falls victim to the evil forces inhabiting the house.

CATHY KRAMER: An automatic writer, she is part of the team Joyce Reardon assembles to explore Rose Red. Like Nick Hardaway, she loses her life while inside Rose Red.

EMERY WATERMAN: A whiny, obnoxious henpecked Mama's boy, Emery experiences gory visions. Also part of the team Joyce Reardon assembles to probe the secrets of Rose Red, Emery loses several fingers in a desperate attempt to escape the confines of the mansion. Despite his injuries, he survives his visit to the haunted house, eventually developing a deep friendship with Annie, her sister, and Steven Rimbauer.

VICTOR KANDINSKY and PAM ASBURY: Two additional members of the Reardon team, they are killed off by the house on the first evening the team spends there.

PROFESSOR MILLER: The obnoxious head of the Department of Paranormal Studies at Beaumont University, he seems to live to torment Joyce Reardon. Attempting to make contact with his flunky, Kevin Bollinger, Miller dies on the grounds of Rose Red.

KEVIN BOLLINGER: One of Professor Miller's students, he assists the professor in harassing Joyce Reardon and her team. Sneaking into the mansion ahead of the team, Kevin falls victim to the house before the team arrives. They find his cell phone on the premises, leading them to believe he is in the house with them. He is, in a way, as his spirit has been captured by Rose Red.

ROSE RED: TRIVIA

- Joyce Reardon's employer, Beaumont University, is almost certainly named after one of King's favorite writers, Charles Beaumont, author of many famous short stories, among them "It's a *Good* Life," which formed the basis of one of the most famous episodes of Rod Serling's *The Twilight Zone*.

- The promotional Web page for Beaumont University included a link to HistoryLink.org's Web site (http://www.beaumontuniversity.net/links .html). The site was inundated with e-mail from people who believed that Joyce Reardon, Beaumont University, and Rose Red were all real. Many of these writers could not be convinced otherwise.

54

EVERYTHING'S EVENTUAL:
14 DARK TALES

(2002)

Ling's first collection of the new millennium gathered together work from three primary sources, his 1997 collection *Six Stories* ("Autopsy Room Four," "The Man in the Black Suit," "Lunch at the Gotham Café," "L. T.'s Theory of Pets," and "Luckey Quarter"), his audio book *Blood and Smoke* ("In the Deathroom" and "1408"), and *The New Yorker* ("All That You Love Will Be Carried Away," "The Death of Jack Hamilton," "That Feeling, You Can Only Say What It Is In French"). "Riding the Bullet" was originally offered via the Web. The remainder came from *The Magazine of Fantasy and Science Fiction* ("Everything's Eventual"), and the anthologies *Legends* ("The Little Sisters of Eluria") and *999* ("The Road Virus Heads North").

In the table of contents, King tells his Constant Readers that he used a deck of cards to select the order in which the stories appeared; based on our reading, the choices were uniformly excellent.

[NOTE: "Autopsy Room Four" and "The Road Virus Heads North" are discussed in the section concerning Derry, and "The Man in the Black Suit" is discussed in the section on Castle Rock. "The Little Sisters of Eluria" and "Everything's Eventual" are covered in the section on the Dark Tower. "Riding the Bullet" is discussed in the section concerning Jerusalem's Lot and King's

Maine. "The Death of Jack Hamilton" and "In the Deathroom" are discussed in the Richard Bachman section.]

"All That You Love Will Be Carried Away"

Alfie Zimmer, a traveling salesman, and thus constantly on the road, writes down interesting bathroom graffiti he's seen in rest stops all over the United States. As the story begins, Alfie is checking into a Motel 6 on I-80 just west of Lincoln, Nebraska. Alfie, sadly, is contemplating suicide. At the end of the story, Alfie is seen standing on the edge of a farmer's field, still undecided about doing himself in.

"L. T.'s Theory of Pets"

"L. T.'s Theory of Pets" deals with the broken marriage of dog lover Lulu DeWitt and cat lover L. T. DeWitt. Lulu DeWitt abruptly leaves her husband, and is never heard from again. Some folks think she has been slaughtered by the serial killer known as the Axe Man, others think L. T. might have had something to do with it. L. T.'s devotion to Lulu and his sadness at his abandonment is poignant, almost pitiful, but never maudlin. King keeps this sad, gently humorous tale on track without making L. T. the object of ridicule he is to his peers. This story of pet ownership and failed marriages is either sad or macabre, depending on your thoughts about L. T.'s possible involvement in his wife's death.

And what *is* L. T.'s Theory of Pets? Simply this: "If your dog and cat are getting along better than you and your wife, you better expect to come home some night and find a Dear John note on your refrigerator door."

"L. T.'S THEORY OF PETS": PRIMARY SUBJECTS

L. T. DEWITT: L. T., an employee of the W. S. Epperton Processed Meats Plant of Ames, Iowa, is happy to tell his tale of woe to anyone who will listen. The breakup of his marriage begins shortly after his wife, Lulubelle, buys him a dog, a Jack Russell terrier that he names Frank. Instead of being man's best friend, however, Frank takes to Lulubelle in a big way.

Lulu responds to his affections, and the two form a deep bond that makes L. T. jealous. Hoping to put a wedge between the two, L. T. buys Lulu a kitten. Since turnabout is fair play, the kitten, named Lucy (LuLu calls her "Screwlucy"), develops a crush on L. T.

Shaky to begin with, the DeWitts' marriage is further strained by the presence of the jealous pets. One day L. T. returns home to discover a Dear John letter on his refrigerator door—LuLu has left, taking Frank with her. L. T. respects her request for privacy, and never attempts to follow her. He remains at the meat packing plant, trotting out his sad story every time a new recruit comes to work at the factory. L. T. DeWitt still resides in Ames, Iowa.

LULUBELLE DeWITT: Lulu, the wife of L. T. DeWitt, disappears for good the day she leaves L. T. Her car is found splattered with animal blood, which turns out to belong to her dog, Frank. Police discover Frank's body near the scene, but Lulu is still missing. Some suspect she is the sixth victim of the serial killer known to authorities as "the Axe Man."

"Lunch at the Gotham Café"

First and foremost, this is a tale about smoking, a companion piece to King classics like "Quitters Inc." and "The Ten O'Clock People." It is also a story about perceptions: Steven's and Diane's differing viewpoints about the state of their marriage, Steven's change in outlook after giving up cigarettes, and the maitre d's warped concept of reality.

"LUNCH AT THE GOTHAM CAFÉ": PRIMARY SUBJECTS

STEVEN DAVIS: Steven returns home one evening to discover that his wife has abandoned him. Painfully aware that his marriage is troubled, Davis is nevertheless stunned by this development. He sleepwalks through the next few weeks, clinging to the hope that he and his wife might reconcile. During this troubled time, he manages to give up cigarettes, which can be viewed as either an act of penance or as Steve's attempt to gain control over at least one aspect of his life. His hopes for reconciliation are dashed by a call from his wife's attorney, requesting a luncheon meeting at Manhattan's

Gotham Café to discuss the terms of their divorce. Davis reluctantly agrees, and attends despite feelings of disorientation (primarily due to nicotine withdrawal) and the fact that his lawyer isn't available to accompany him.

Arriving at the restaurant, Davis is greeted by a high-strung maitre d', who, while showing the patron to his table, keeps muttering about Davis's umbrella, which he apparently mistakes for a small dog. The conference, which quickly turns bitter, is interrupted by the maitre d', who attacks and kills lawyer Humboldt with a huge butcher knife. He then turns to Davis, who, accompanied by his wife, flees to the kitchen. The maitre d' follows him in, ranting, and kills the chef. Davis manages to subdue the maitre d', who is taken away on a stretcher, still raving.

Steven Davis is presumably alive and well, at large in the Stephen King Universe.

DIANE DAVIS: It is obvious that Diane feels that Steven has greatly wronged her. Even after Steven saves her from the maitre d', Diane still hates her spouse. Diane Davis is presumably alive and well, at large in the Stephen King Universe.

WILLIAM HUMBOLDT: Diane's divorce attorney, this tough customer is eliminated by the Gotham Café's mad maitre d'. Humboldt's last word is "boot."

GUY (THE MAITRE D' FROM HELL): Little is known about the madman who is maitre d' at the Gotham Café. His first name is Guy. Apparently in the grip of potent hallucinations, Guy stabs William Humboldt in the head, then guts a co-worker in the kitchen. Steven Davis manages to disable him before he can kill again. When last seen, Guy is being taken away on a stretcher by paramedics. He is presumably still alive, but certainly not well. His whereabouts are unknown, but one would hope he is incarcerated in a place where he can do no further harm.

"That Feeling, You Can Only Say What It Is In French"

First appearing in the June 22, 1999, Summer Fiction Issue of *The New Yorker*, this is a tale concerning marriage and *déjà vu*. King does a great job of depicting how good and bad memories bind a couple together, and also conveys feelings of *déjà vu* to his readers, repeating sequences from different angles throughout the story.

On a second honeymoon to celebrate her silver anniversary with her husband, Bill, Carol Shelton reflects on their life together during the flight. On their way to their honeymoon hideaway, Carol experiences vague feelings that she's been in this situation before, even though that's not possible. At times she's able to predict exactly what's around the bend; but just as often, her guesses are inexact or outright wrong. Throughout, she wonders where she heard the name Floyd before, and why she associates it with disaster. Floyd, she finally discovers, is the pilot of the plane she's on.

And readers are left to wonder if some of the terrifying visions she's had throughout the story are about to occur, or whether they are merely flights of fancy.

"1408"

This is the second of three recent tales read aloud by the author in *Blood and Smoke*, and it is truly one of King's creepiest.

"1408" is the number of one of the most infamous haunted hotel rooms in the world, located in an otherwise ordinary establishment, somewhere off Fifth Avenue in New York City; at the least, it's probably unlucky (just add the digits in the room number and see what you get). Skeptic Mike Enslin has demanded to spend the night in that room, despite the hotel manager's extreme reluctance. He is not afraid to tell Mike that the room is truly haunted and that perhaps thirty people have mysteriously died or disappeared in that room since the hotel opened in 1910. But that is precisely why Mike has to have the room for the night.

Mike, you see, is the author of three *New York Times* bestsellers: *Ten Nights in Ten Haunted Houses*, *Ten Nights in Ten Haunted Graveyards*, and *Ten Nights in Ten Haunted Castles*. His current work in progress is no doubt going to be published as *Ten Nights in Ten Haunted Hotels*. The brash writer is finally allowed into the room—a room he truly believes cannot be haunted. For in spite of his chosen subject matter, the author has never seen a real ghost, nor does he believe in their existence. But very shortly the incredible supernatural events that occur in Room 1408 will change Mike's views on the subject of haunts and evil spirits forever.

"1408": PRIMARY SUBJECTS

MIKE ENSLIN: A cynical writer of "true" ghost stories, Mike writes the books because he knows he can make a good living from them, not because he believes in the supernatural. But after spending only seventy minutes in Room 1408, Mike nearly loses his life after being assaulted by the evil presence that inhabits the suite. Completely shattered by the experience, he gives up his writing career completely, and lives in constant fear of being assaulted again by dark forces.

MR. OWEN: A short, round man, Mr. Owen tries to talk Mike out of staying in Room 1408. He tells Mike of the room's grim history, but this doesn't dissuade the writer. Since Mike has reminded the hotel manager that he cannot, by state and federal law, prevent him from renting any specific room in a hotel that is not currently occupied, the man reluctantly allows the writer to have the room. It is presumed that Mr. Owen is still working at the hotel in spite of the legacy of Room 1408.

RUFUS DEARBORN: The sewing machine salesman who saves Mike's life by dousing him with the contents of an ice bucket after he observes the author making a mad dash from Room 1408 with his upper torso ablaze.

"The Luckey Quarter"

"The Luckey Quarter" unravels the account of Darlene Pullman, a woman who lives off the tips she earns as a maid at the seedy Rancher's Hotel. One morning, Darlene finds an unimpressive quarter in the gratuity envelope she left in Room 322. The tip is accompanied by a note that reads, "This is a Luckey quarter! Its true! Luckey you!" A practical woman, Darlene is nevertheless taken with the possibility that the coin may indeed be a good luck piece, as demonstrated by a gripping fantasy sequence in which she beats the odds at a local casino. Darlene ultimately realizes that she is already blessed with outrageous luck, and gives the quarter to her son.

SECTION SEVEN

The World of
Richard Bachman

ust who was—or is—Richard Bachman?

Was he really just a New Hampshire dairy farmer who wrote novels of science fiction and psychological terror in between tending to his cows? Or was he the pseudonym of the world's most popular contemporary author, Stephen King?

Of course, as the world now knows, "Richard Bachman" was indeed a pen name for King, one he might still be using to this day if the literary deception had not been discovered in the spring of 1985. Questions still remain, however. Just *why* did the author create him in the first place? And how do the Bachman titles, both those written pre and postdisclosure, relate to the rest of the known Stephen King Universe?

As readers will see after delving into the various entries in this section, King, very early in his career, faced a dilemma that plagues many bestselling authors. Traditionally, publishers prefer that a highly successful writer release only *one* novel or short story collection each calendar year. This preference is based on the logic that the publisher is then better able to promote sales (first in hardcover and later in paperback) of the individual title throughout that time period. In theory, if a major author wanted to publish more than one title a year, he would have to do it under a pseudonym, as members of the supposedly literate public for some reason were not likely to purchase more than one new book per annum from the same author.

Of course, King has since completely shattered that unwritten rule of publishing—a look at his career chronology will show that in certain years the author would introduce three or four new books, *all* of which were successful.

King also had another dilemma to solve. By the time of the publication of his third novel, *The Shining*, in 1977, he was already universally recognized—and marketed—as a bestselling writer of horror. But the prolific author had *other* books that he wanted to see in print—works that were not as readily marketable as new titles from "the undisputed master of modern horror." These included some of his earliest efforts, such as *Getting It On* (a.k.a. *Rage*) and *The Long Walk*, both written before *Carrie*, which saw print in 1974, as well as such later mainstream works as *Roadwork* and another overtly science fictional tale, *The Running Man*. Besides the understandable urge to publish what he had written, King, as an admitted "brand-name" author, was also curious to see if he could repeat his success as a bestselling writer strictly on literary, rather than marketing and advertising, terms.

In 1977, King asked his editor at New American Library, Elaine Koster, if she would consider publishing *Rage* as a paperback original. More importantly, he asked if she would agree to publish it under a pseudonym. Koster agreed, and *Rage* was published in 1977 with King's secret closely guarded.

According to Douglas E. Winter's *Stephen King: The Art of Darkness* (1984), King's first choice for a pen name was that of his maternal grandfather, Guy Pillsbury. But NAL, fearing that someone might trace the family lineage, called the author and requested another pseudonym. Reportedly King was listening to the rock 'n' roll band Bachman-Turner Overdrive at the time of the publisher's call. On his desk at that moment was a novel by "Richard Stark" (a pseudonym for novelist Donald E. Westlake). Seizing on these disparate elements for inspiration, King opted to use the name "Richard Bachman."

Not surprisingly, each of the Bachman novels provided clues to their readers as to the true identity of its author (for people in the know, the dedications alone were a dead giveaway). So with the publication of each Bachman title, King had to repeatedly deny rumors that surfaced in the horror community that he was, in fact, Richard Bachman. Although he was able to successfully deny the speculations with the first four titles (all of which were published as mass-market paperback originals with little or no fanfare or acclaim), his denials became less and less plausible with the 1984 release of *Thinner*.

For not only was this novel clearly a tale of the supernatural, it was written precisely in the style that the bestselling author's millions of fans could readily recognize as being "brand-name Stephen King." The book's in jokes at his expense (as when one of the characters notes "You were start-ing to sound a little like a Stephen King novel . . .") further indicated that the author himself was sooner rather than later going to let the proverbial cat out of the bag. It did not help the deception any that NAL, for the first time, brought out this latest Richard Bachman novel in a hardcover edition and heavily promoted it (advance copies were given away to hundreds of readers and reviewers at the American Booksellers Association convention that year). Again, anyone who was familiar with King's writing style would have had very little trouble recognizing the new work of Bachman as being by one and the same author.

For some time, specialty book dealers such as Robert Weinberg and L. W. Currey had been stating in their catalogs that the Richard Bachman entries could only have been written by King, openly selling these titles to their customers as "Stephen King writing as Richard Bachman." Despite this, the general public was not yet aware just how many "unknown" King novels were actually in print, if they only knew where to look.

The truth was finally publicly revealed in the spring of 1985 when a Washington, D.C., bookstore clerk named Steve Brown went to the Library of Congress to examine the copyright forms that had been issued for the Bachman novels. Unfortunately for King, someone at NAL had inadver-tently identified him as the author of *Rage* on those documents, rather than the registered pseudonym of Richard Bachman. (As the publisher filed these forms, it's highly unlikely King ever saw them to insure there were no such revelations.) In short order, it was revealed to the world that, yes, King and Bachman were one and the same.

Even though Bachman was now for all intents and purposes dead—the author would state in later interviews how "Dickie" had died early of "can-cer of the pseudonym"—that wasn't to be the case for long. In the Stephen King Universe, just because you kill someone, that doesn't always mean they stay dead.

The idea of writing under a pseudonym obviously appealed to King, as demonstrated by his comments in various forums. His bitterness at Bach-man's apparent demise was evident, likely inspiring his fictional treatment of the subject in *The Dark Half* (1989). Indeed, as is so aptly stated in the Author's Note at the beginning of that novel: "I'm indebted to the late Richard Bachman for his help and inspiration. This novel could not have been written without him."

As King explained in his introduction to the second edition (1996) of *The Bachman Books*, he had learned that Donald E. Westlake had written his exceedingly grim and violent "Richard Stark" novels on what he termed his "rainy days." On "sunny days" he authored books as Westlake. This was how King felt as Bachman: "Bachman—a fictional creation who became more real with each published book which bore his byline—was a rainy-day sort of guy if there ever was one."

So when it came time to write *The Regulators* (1996), King decided it was also the right time to bring Bachman back from the dead. At that time, King revealed that Bachman had conveniently "left" a stack of unpublished manuscripts in his home that had been unearthed by his widow, Claudia Inez Eschelman. This information, related in the second edition of the omnibus collection *The Bachman Books*, published as a trade paperback in 1996 to coincide with the publication of the new Bachman novel *The Regulators*, strongly suggests that *The Regulators* is only the first of many "unpublished" works of Richard Bachman. As King states, "I have to wonder if there are any other good manuscripts, at or near completion, in that box found by the former Mrs. Bachman in the cellar of their New Hampshire farmhouse. Sometimes I wonder about that *a lot*."

Other indications of how King has come to perceive Bachman can be found in the subtle differences between the various omnibus collections of Bachman's novels. The first, published in 1985, was called *The Bachman Books: Four Early Novels by Stephen King*. The title of the original introduction, "Why I Was Bachman," is openly confessional. The latest edition, first released in 1996, was called *The Bachman Books: Four Early Novels by Richard Bachman*. Note that it says by Bachman—*not* King. And as for the new introduction, the only place King is mentioned in the book? Well, King called it "The Importance of Being Bachman." At one point, Bachman "was" clearly part of Stephen King. And now, with the publication of *The Regulators*, Bachman clearly still "is" a vital part of the imagination of Stephen King.

But to what end in the overall Stephen King Universe? Clearly the "early Bachman" titles (*Rage, The Long Walk, Roadwork, The Running Man*) were never meant to be identified as books by Stephen King. They do, however, contain certain elements that link them to the Universe. Most of these elements are subtle—for instance, *Rage* and *The Long Walk* are set in Maine, and *Roadwork* mentions the Blue Ribbon Laundry chain, which is also mentioned in King's short story "The Mangler" (a supporting character in that novel is clearly identified as hailing from Portland, Maine, as well) and in his first published novel, *Carrie*.

Perhaps most intriguingly—particularly since the town in question would not become a significant part of the Prime Reality of the Stephen King Universe for some years—a large part of the action of *The Running*

Man takes place at a regional airport located in a small Maine town called Derry. This may indicate a nightmare future for the Derry of Bachman's mirror-image reality.

Although Bangor, Maine, features prominently in *Thinner,* and King was also mentioned by name, the major connections to the Stephen King Universe in that book lie in the use of "trademark" characters and themes, most notably in the fact that it is clearly a horror novel, rather than one of science fiction or suspense. However, it is clear that those connections may have indeed become more explicit, in that King has stated that *Misery,* with its numerous ties to the Universe, was originally slated to be the next "Bachman" book.

It was only with the publication of the "mirrored" volumes of *Desperation* (by King) and *The Regulators,* both released in 1996 after his pseudonym had become almost as well known as his own name, that the author consciously chose to incorporate the Bachman books into the Stephen King Universe. Here we do indeed have heroes and villains fighting a cosmic battle of good versus evil. The references are infrequent (such as Ellen Carver in *Desperation* being a fan of Paul Sheldon's "Misery" novels) and the connecting characters minor (Cynthia Smith from *Rose Madder* appears in *Desperation*), but King is at last consciously allowing the world of Richard Bachman to interact with his other parallel realities.

It seems clear that as far as King is concerned, Richard Bachman is indeed alive and well, lurking in the darkest recesses of the author's imagination, just waiting for the next rainy day.

As far as the relationship between the world of Richard Bachman and the rest of the Stephen King Universe is concerned, there are parallels to be drawn other than the coincidences noted above. However, in order to do so, one must examine the King novel *Desperation* and its mirror image in the Bachman novel *The Regulators.* Both books feature a powerful being from beyond our familiar reality known as Tak. Tak is described as being an "outsider," a word used to describe the evil force in King's *Bag of Bones,* and indeed the two creatures—along with It from the novel of that name—seem to have a great deal in common.

In both of these mirror-image books, King has returned to the cosmic battle between chaos and order, or the Random and the Purpose, though on a microcosmic level. Clearly, though, the connection between the Bachman corner of the Universe and its other facets is strongest and clearest there.

55

RAGE

(1977)

Although technically the third novel King published, *Rage* was the first issued by the author using the pseudonym of Richard Bachman. More to the point, it has since been learned that *Rage* was in fact the very first novel-length work ever completed by King. Begun in 1966 while still in high school, King would not complete the work until 1971, when he was in college. Prior to the book's initial publication, King updated the story by inserting mentions of bestselling books and popular movies of the mid-1970s.

Regardless of when it was originally written, *Rage* remains to this day one of King's darkest, most pessimistic, and, unfortunately, most chillingly plausible works. But as to where this extremely early novel fits within the Stephen King Universe, it's crucial to realize that by the time he had first reached the hardcover bestseller lists with *The Shining* in 1977, King was already firmly established in the public's mind as a writer of supernatural horror. Of course, this was to be expected, given the clearly "horrific" content of novels such as *Carrie, 'Salem's Lot,* and *The Shining,* not to mention the numerous short stories he had penned with supernatural themes. It would not be much longer before reviewers would brand him as "the King of Modern Horror" or "King of the Boogeymen" as he quickly attained brand-name status in the literary field.

But King knew—even if his readers would not for several years—that he was capable of writing vital and important works of suspense outside the genre as well. He also knew that due to his incredible success with his current novels, he had enough leverage to rescue his earliest works from the traditional writer's "trunk" where they had been languishing and publish them, albeit under a pen name and only as mass market paperback originals.

By creating Richard Bachman, the author believed he could best serve his desire to see *all* of his early fiction published and, even more liberatingly, break free of readers' expectations. Not only would King get to see his early novels in print, but he also gave himself the freedom to create new works on any topic, and in any style, he cared to experiment with—and no one but Bachman fans would be impressed or upset with the published results.

"The morning I got it on was nice," is how this quiet time bomb of a novel begins. The young man planning to "get it on" (a popular phrase of the 1970s meaning to get something accomplished—no matter what the consequences) is Charlie Decker. An average student, Charlie outwardly appears no different from the others in his class, except for the fact that he's taken to carrying a handgun to school with him. Before this "nice," sunny day is over, people will be terrorized and humiliated. Some will be shot. Some will die.

Charlie is a classic "troubled youth," a teenager who has big problems with authority, problems that manifested themselves a few months earlier when he attacked a teacher with a wrench. Shortly after a troubling encounter with his overbearing father, something inside Charlie snaps, as he first sets fire to his school locker, then proceeds to shoot two teachers. Holding his classmates hostage, Charlie forces his terrified peers to examine where each of them belongs in this world, trying to decide who is worthy to live through this ordeal and who is not.

Although Charlie is portrayed at all times as an unrepentant killer, King manages to evoke sympathy for the teenager, such that the reader often finds himself thinking, "You know, I might have done the same thing if I had walked a mile in his shoes." Even as he's taken away into custody, we're left with the unsettling impression that there are a lot more young people like him just waiting for something to set them off. Something will someday—for no apparent reason—trigger a murderous urge to "get it on." And as recent tragic events in schools across the country have shown, there are troubled students who have in fact forsaken everything to unleash their murderous rage against their teachers and peers.

Not too surprisingly, this novel bears a number of striking similarities to *Carrie*, another novel about a troubled high school student (it must be remembered that although not published until 1977, *Rage* was written several years before *Carrie*). Like Carrie White, Charlie Decker is someone who doesn't fit in with any established clique or group. Similar to Carrie, he finds the only way he can resolve his personal conflicts is to lash out against others in a violent and deadly manner. Both novels deal with young individuals trying to survive in what for them is a very harsh and brutal environment—contemporary public high school.

The major difference between the two works is that *Carrie* is basically "science fiction," featuring a young woman with a so-called "wild talent." *Rage*'s premise, however, is all too believable, although in one sense, it, too, almost falls into the category of "science fiction" in that the novel predicted— decades before it would occur in reality—the scenario of young, fresh-faced killers stalking the classroom.

In terms of its place in the Stephen King Universe, if we use the term broadly, *Rage* is indeed a contemporary horror novel; it's a tale that deals with strictly plausible horrors, such as the author would later explore in such works of suspense as *Cujo* (1981), *Gerald's Game* (1992), *Misery* (1987), and *Apt Pupil*. (*Apt Pupil*, a brilliant novella originally published in the 1982 collection *Different Seasons*, is especially significant, as King again explores the idea that sometimes the best place for true evil to fester and grow is within a high school student.)

From the very beginning of his career, King reminded readers that perhaps the greatest horror in life is that sometimes good people die unexpectedly. And just as unfairly, sometimes very bad and evil people go on living. He is also telling us, of course, that the scariest monsters in this world are not vampires or zombies, but the one we may encounter one day staring back at us from a mirror.

Due to the unfortunate circumstance of young people claiming to have been inspired by *Rage* to carry out their own violent acts in school, King has decided to allow the book to go out of print. He details his concerns in the second edition of *The Bachman Books* (1996), in the new introduction "The Importance of Being Bachman." There King relates the many sleepless nights he has spent wrestling with the idea that something he has written, however remotely, may have been part of what he terms "a triggering mechanism" to later acts of violence.

The author himself does not know the answer. He does realize that *Rage* is a book about the consequences of extreme anger, and it shows on every page that someone who was also inwardly frustrated and resentful at the world composed it. King can barely recall what kind of person he was at the time he wrote *Rage*, which may be another reason why he is reluctantly but willingly letting it go.

King in campus protest   YEARBOOK PHOTO

RAGE: PRIMARY SUBJECTS

CHARLIE DECKER: A lonely misfit, Charlie Decker is a young man who resents most adults and authority figures, especially his brutish father. After various altercations with his father, his teachers, and the school principal, Charlie can no longer contain his growing feelings of resentment and rage. Shortly after he is expelled from Placerville High School, Charlie retrieves a gun from his locker and proceeds to shoot two teachers, taking a class of his peers hostage in the process. After he is captured, Charlie is judged unfit to stand trial by reason of insanity and sent to the Augusta State Hospital in Augusta, Maine.

TED JONES: One of the most popular boys in school, Ted Jones is one of the students Charlie holds hostage for the day. Publicly humiliated during the course of a violent "encounter session" instigated by Charlie, Ted has a nervous breakdown. He is eventually committed to a mental institution, where it is presumed he still resides.

CAPTAIN FRANK PHILBRICK: The man in charge of the Maine State Police unit who responds to the hostage crisis, it is his task to try and talk Charlie Decker into surrendering to the authorities without further violence. He is also responsible for giving the order to a sharpshooter to try and kill Charlie.

DANIEL MALVERN: A member of the Maine State Police, he is considered the state's best sharpshooter. He fires one shot at Charlie using a Mauser rifle with a telescopic lens. The bullet hits Charlie directly in the area of the heart, but the young man is spared a fatal injury when the bullet is deflected by a padlock he had placed in his shirt pocket earlier in the day.

RAGE: TRIVIA

- The original title for the novel was *Getting It On*.

- Charlie's father admires the crime novels of Richard Stark. That name is in fact a pseudonym of one of King's favorite writers, Donald E. Westlake. King, of course, was using Bachman as a pseudonym to write *Rage*. Later in his career, King would write *The Dark Half* (1989), in which author Thad Beaumont uses "George Stark" as a pseudonym.

56

THE LONG WALK

(1979)

One of what have become known as the "early Bachman" books *(Rage, The Long Walk, Roadwork,* and *The Running Man)*, *The Long Walk* is in fact the second-earliest novel-length work ever completed by Stephen King. Written in 1966 during his freshman year at the University of Maine in Orono, it was also one of his earliest attempts at what could be termed a work of science fiction rather than the horror novels and short stories on which his initial fame would rest. (Interestingly, King himself considered *Carrie* [1974], *The Dead Zone* [1979], and *Firestarter* [1980] to be more in line with what he would himself consider science fiction, as he felt these explorations of fantastic paranormal talents were but variations on classic science fiction themes.)

Like the previous Bachman novel, *Rage* (1977), this entry also concentrates solely on young people as its primary characters—the action is seen only through the rudely awakened eyes of adolescents. *The Long Walk* takes place in an unspecified near future, in a bleak, ultraconservative Amerika (note the spelling for a then-popular representation of a fascist state), in which the country seems to have fought and lost a major energy crisis and the former democracy has been replaced by a police state.

King never states precisely why or how these events have come to pass, but it is clearly a parallel world where joy and hope are two emotions that have long since been lost, along with most of our customary constitutional rights. Given similarities to the future world presented in *The Running Man*, we have posited for the purposes of this book that the future presented in both books is simply the dark future of the more contemporary world of the other Bachman novels. Thus, despite the difference in time periods, it is feasible to think they all take place in the same reality, at different times.

To buoy the sagging spirits of the citizenry, the powers that be have created a pseudospectacle/sporting event called the Long Walk, a grueling 450-mile marathon trek down through the state of Maine.

One hundred of the nation's best young men (with one hundred alternates) are selected to enter this marathon through means of a national lottery. Whomever wins the race—there can be only one champion—will be rewarded with whatever his heart may desire for the rest of his life. His one great wish will come true, no matter what it may be.

For reasons of which not even he is certain, sixteen-year-old Ray Garraty enters the contest. It is truly a case of winning a grand lottery for life—all he has to do to win is to complete the Long Walk. Unfortunately, there are no stops, no rest periods, no breaks of any sort. If you want to eat, you must do so while walking. If you must eliminate body waste, you have to do it while walking. And there's a simple incentive to obey the rules once you begin. Those who do not keep up with the pack are given three separate warnings by the soldiers/observers accompanying the Walkers. After issuing the third warning, the soldiers are authorized to shoot to kill. No excuses. No exceptions. No mercy.

Quite obviously a crude allegory about the military selective service carried to its extreme, King's tale is always grimly compelling, if undeniably narrow, in its vision. Like *The Running Man* (1982), there are also several elements of *The Long Walk* that were likely inspired by television game shows. For instance, nearly every chapter opens with epigraphs from a host or creator of a classic television game show, including *Jeopardy!*, *Let's Make a Deal*, and most tellingly, *You Bet Your Life*. Perhaps the book's most explicit quote is attributed to *Gong Show* creator Chuck Barris at the opening of Chapter 4, in which he states that "The ultimate game show would be one where the losing contestant was killed," which is the basic premise for both *The Long Walk* and *The Running Man*.

The Long Walk is a game of winner-take-all, with a live audience of thousands of bystanders cheering from the sidelines in every town the Walkers pass through. These spectators are just as thrilled with the carnage that takes place as they are to cheer for their favorites to reach the finish line. In this future, King suggests that human nature has changed very little since the era of the ancient Romans when slaves were fed to the lions in the barbaric games played out in the coliseums. And even though Garraty survives the marathon, it's hinted that he's been driven insane by the experience, and thus is unable to enjoy his spoils. The cruel satire is that there is really no point to participating in the Long Walk—everyone loses in the end.

As he did in *Rage*, King's Bachman alter ego posits a much grimmer world than readers might expect from the average Stephen King novel. Except for the science fictional element of the lethal race, *The Long Walk*, like *Rage*, focuses on human beings under extreme pressure, detailing the horrors that can occur when people are pushed to their limits.

The Long Walk, like the author's other early works, is extremely linear in its focus, with no major subplots or digressions from its main narrative. Indeed, there is very little diversion from the hopeless situation of one hundred young men who have been selected to live and die on their fateful journey through Maine. The narrative radiates an unrelentingly angry and pessimistic worldview—as with *Rage*, the young author was writing during a period in his life when the literary cliché of "angry young writer" more than likely applied.

Much of the novel's extreme pessimism is a product of the era in which it was written, an era in which King and his contemporaries faced the grim prospect of being drafted to fight in the Vietnam War. After one went off to fight in the jungle war, it was largely fate that dictated if a combatant would survive his term of service without being grievously wounded or killed. Just as many people of King's generation believed that the Vietnam War—indeed, *all* wars—made no sense, nor served any meaningful purpose, this is also the case with the Long Walk itself. Ultimately, the government-run ordeal serves no purpose other than to insure that the young men involved in the process suffer horrible and violent deaths.

We never learn exactly why the Long Walk is so important to the interests of this parallel Amerika. It's never suggested that women become involved in the Long Walk, though one can safely assume that the futuristic premise was undertaken before the concept of women's liberation in the military had become as well known as it is today.

It is also hinted by the Walkers themselves that it's very possible that *no one* truly survives the Walk to become a winner—that whoever survives the marathon is ultimately rewarded by being taken behind some building and shot in the head. In this Amerika, it just doesn't matter if you support or oppose the conservative politics of the nation—either way, you are just so much target practice for the Establishment.

King makes several veiled references to Shirley Jackson's classic short story "The Lottery" (1948) in furthering a major point of *The Long Walk*, namely, that life is unfair. At the chilling climax of that story, an innocent person is unexpectedly sacrificed by a crowd of people simply because someone *has* to die—the outsider just happened to be in the wrong place at the wrong time. In Jackson's tale, that victim could be any one of us. No one denies it may not be fair, but it's a system that works for those in control— for those who make the rules.

In *The Long Walk*, King's young victims—who sometimes cry out "It's not fair!" before being shot—could be any innocent person chosen in the national lottery of the government's selective service process. Forced to embark on a deadly journey of self-discovery, they hope against hope that they can somehow reach the end of their tour of duty—their long walk— without being shot by nameless, faceless enemies.

The Long Walk fits well into the Stephen King Universe in that it reveals King's long-standing distrust of the government (i.e., "the Establishment"), and of how little control most of us have over our own lives, even in a free society. No matter what Garraty's comrades/competitors say or do to protest their impossible situation, after three warnings they are snuffed out by the soldiers obeying the faceless, nameless men who control the country. Three strikes, you're out.

Permanently.

THE LONG WALK: PRIMARY SUBJECTS

RAY GARRATY WALKER: Number 47, he is only sixteen years old. Ray isn't sure why he didn't try to get out of participating, even though he had several chances to do so, and considering that his father had already been taken into custody for speaking up against the ghastly practice. At one point in the grisly marathon, he goes out of his way to embrace his mother and his girlfriend—the action very nearly costs him his life. Despite the odds, Garraty somehow completes the Long Walk, emerging as its sole winner (and survivor). Garraty's whereabouts in the Stephen King Universe are unknown—it is strongly suggested that he has been driven insane by his experiences.

JIM GARRATY: Ray's father. When he dared to speak out against the inhumane Long Walk, he was taken away in the middle of the night by one of the government's special Squads. His current whereabouts are unknown, but he is presumed dead.

PETER McVRIES: Number 67 of the Walkers. One of the very last to fall, he gets to know Ray more intimately than any of the other Walkers. The two young men repeatedly save each other's lives before all their warnings from the soldiers are used. Unfortunately, McVries receives his final "ticket" just as the end of the Long Walk is in sight.

STEBBINS: Number 88 of the Walkers, he almost makes it to the very end of the Walk before being terminated. While possibly gripped by madness, Stebbins claims that the mysterious major, an important member of the oppressive governing body, is his father, and that he is one of his many illegitimate sons.

THE MAJOR: The mysterious military man in charge of the Long Walk, he never appears in public without reflective sunglasses. There at the beginning of the Walk to tell the young men how proud he is of them, and to wish them all good luck, he then disappears for most of the remainder of the arduous contest. He may or may not be Stebbins's father. Before the Squads took him away, Garraty's father called the major "the rarest and most dangerous monster any nation can produce, a society supported sociopath."

THE DARK FIGURE: At the very end of the Long Walk, Garraty spies a figure who seems to be taunting him to keep on walking, to continue playing this ultimately fatal game, a nameless figure who may merely be the specter of death, but whose obscene actions suggest he may instead be a pawn, or maybe yet another incarnation of the dark man, Randall Flagg.

THE LONG WALK: TRIVIA

- The fact that the novel is dedicated to three of King's teachers at the University of Maine (Jim Bishop, Burt Hatlen, and Ted Holmes) was a major clue in solving the mystery of the "Richard Bachman" pseudonym.

- A character named Raymond (Ray) Garraty appears in Mike Noonan's novel *My Childhood Friend* in *Bag of Bones*.

57

ROADWORK

(1981)

Certainly one of the bleakest, if not *the* bleakest, of the Richard Bachman books, the argument could be made that *Roadwork* is truly the darkest of all of Stephen King's writings. Created at a time when the author was already enjoying considerable success as a bestselling author, the decidedly mainstream novel was written between *'Salem's Lot* (1975) and *The Shining* (1977), a depressing time in recent U.S. history. More to the point, it was also composed a year after the author's mother had died painfully from cancer.

King has had mixed feelings about this book over the years. In the introduction to the first omnibus edition of *The Bachman Books* in 1985, King states that "I suspect *Roadwork* is probably the worst of the lot simply because it tries to be good and to find some answers to the conundrum of human pain." However, in his second, new introduction to a later edition of *The Bachman Books*, issued in 1996, King says that it is "my favorite of the early Bachman books." Whether it is the best or the worst of the early Bachman titles is still open to debate. But like *Rage*, it remains one of the few books by King where not a hint of the supernatural nor the bizarre is to be found—the horrors of everyday life are more than enough to drive some of us mad, thank you very much.

Roadwork tells of the imminent destruction of one man's life.

Barton George Dawes has spent all of his adult life living in the same average house, living on the same ordinary street, married to the same plain woman, working for an undistinguished company, the Blue Ribbon Laundry. All of that is about to radically change, as the state government decides to build a freeway extension in his small city that will not only pass right through the Laundry's current location, but also through Dawes's neighborhood. In subsequent months, everything that has held Dawes's life together will be plowed under and covered over—in other words, methodically erased.

But Barton Dawes isn't going to let his world be taken from him without a fight, nor allow his life and livelihood to be stripped away for no ostensible reason. Thus, Dawes decides to do everything in his power to prevent the extension from being constructed. It doesn't matter that the cards are stacked completely against him, that whatever he does to hinder the roadway, the extension *will* be built. Dawes single-mindedly pursues his goal, continuing even when he knows it's hopeless. One example of this is when Dawes secretly firebombs the construction site, burning down the construction hut and damaging most of the heavy equipment. Turning on the evening news, he learns, to his utter disbelief, that the project is only going to be delayed by a few months at most. Dawes is no better than an ant foolishly trying to hold back a tidal wave.

Roadwork starts on a shrill note of unwanted change, and doesn't let up until Dawes's entire world dissolves in a nerve-shattering wail of loss, mistrust, and pain. Subtitled *A Novel of the First Energy Crisis*, the majority of the plot occurs between November 20, 1973, and January 20, 1974, the time of the United States' nationwide energy shortage due to the Middle East oil crisis. In that brief time span we witness Dawes's rapid disintegration, as he first loses his livelihood, then his marriage, and finally his cherished home. Distraught, Dawes concludes that he has no other choice than to literally go out in a blaze of glory.

Finally realizing he can't permanently stop the freeway extension, he instead wires his empty home with high explosives, arms himself with high-powered weapons, and waits for the police—and the bulldozers—to arrive. His home—his little castle—is the last part of his special world where he can exist safely; if he can't live there, he won't live anywhere.

Tellingly, King makes a point of never saying precisely what small city or state Barton Dawes does calls home (although one could make an educated guess that the story is set in the Midwest, probably lower Wisconsin). His point? That this could happen anywhere, to anyone.

Never has King written a more earnestly mainstream novel. There are no fantasy or supernatural elements whatsoever in *Roadwork* to soften the blows, and yet it quickly becomes surreal in the sense that everything that befalls Dawes is like a personal solar eclipse. In short, everything just gets increasingly blacker and blacker until he finally becomes totally consumed by the darkness all around him. There are no joyful sequences to balance the unremitting series of small catastrophes that are steadily burying Dawes alive, one brick at a time. The nation, rocked by an energy crisis, is still licking its psychic wounds from the recent end of the Vietnam War, and no one seems to know what tomorrow may bring.

There are no heroes to be found in *Roadwork*. Most of the characters introduced are unlikable, untrustworthy, or immoral. Oddly enough, one of the few relatively likable figures is a small time Mafia hood. In *Roadwork*, decent people die in senseless car accidents. Or they drop dead in supermarkets of a brain hemorrhage. Or they are fired from their jobs for no good reason. Most tellingly, Dawes's only child, a boy named Charlie, expires from a brain tumor that his doctors couldn't explain.

Dawes himself feels he is dying of "soul-cancer" and so believes his criminal actions are his only way of striking back against the world that has so terribly wronged him. Yet King never allows us to do more than pity Barton Dawes, as we only see his dark, obsessive side. His obsession with maintaining his rapidly disappearing lifestyle cannot have any other outcome than to ultimately lead to his violent and meaningless death.

King tells us time and again in *Roadwork* that life is not fair, that it doesn't matter that you tried to live your life honestly—we are all going to die sooner or later, and when we do, it probably won't be at the right time. And it probably won't be very pleasant. Most frightening of all, it's likely that no one else is going to notice your passing, or really care if you were ever here in the first place.

ROADWORK: PRIMARY SUBJECTS

BARTON GEORGE DAWES: A middle-aged, low-level businessman who has worked all his adult life for a local laundry firm. He is married to Mary Dawes, who, even though she loves him, leaves him as his behavior becomes increasingly erratic. Desperate to stop the progress of a road extension that is slated to go through his home, he goes to a local used car salesman, who is actually a criminal, to purchase high explosives to blow away the impending invader. After first temporarily halting construction by firebombing a work site, Dawes uses the explosives he has purchased to wire up his home. After being cornered by the police in a violent shootout, Dawes puts himself out of his misery by setting off the dynamite.

MARY DAWES: A local woman who has lived her life through her husband, Barton Dawes. She has given birth to two children by him, both with tragic results. The first was born dead, while the second, Charlie, dies from an inoperable brain tumor. She leaves him when she realizes that he is too inflexible to cope with any further hard blows from life. Mary Dawes's current whereabouts are unknown.

CHARLIE DAWES: The young son of Barton and Mary Dawes, Charlie Dawes dies of a brain tumor—a cancerous growth about the size of a walnut, according to his doctor—leaving his parents childless and alone. Before he kills himself, Barton Dawes frequently holds imaginary "conversations" with his dead boy.

OLIVIA BRENNER: A native of Portland, Maine, Olivia is a twenty-one-year-old woman who is hitchhiking to Las Vegas when Barton Dawes gives her a lift. Although he deeply regrets the act later, Barton gives in to the temptation and sleeps with the attractive young stranger. He later uses monies from the sale of his home to set up a trust fund for her. She apparently uses it to get her life together and enrolls in business school, an achievement Dawes will never live to see.

SAL MAGLIORE: A local criminal who uses a used car lot as a cover for his extralegal activities, Sal is an obese, vulgar, and unattractive individual who has the ability to get anything for anyone—for the right price. Although he at first refuses to sell Barton Dawes the high explosives he asks for, he later decides to do so out of a grudging respect for him. Sal realizes that Dawes, crazed though he clearly must be, is operating out of his own code of honor. As such, the criminal finds himself perversely drawn to the doomed man, despite his better judgment.

DAVE ALBERT: A reporter for the local television station WHLM who first encounters Barton when they both attend the official ground-breaking for the highway extension. By a quirk of fate, Albert is also the first journalist on the scene when Dawes makes his last stand in his home. After giving the reporter an exclusive, Barton advises him to leave the scene before it is too late. Dawes tells the reporter he'll probably earn the Pulitzer Prize for being in the right place at the right time, and as fate would have it, that's precisely what happens.

THE BLUE RIBBON LAUNDRY: This is the small family business that Barton Dawes has been working for his entire life, before it is taken over by a company that no longer has any concern for anything but the bottom line.

ROADWORK: TRIVIA

- The Blue Ribbon Laundry chain figures prominently in the short story "The Mangler," from *Night Shift*. Carrie White's mother, Margaret, also worked for the chain.

- On the original paperback edition of *Roadwork*, the main character is misidentified on the back cover copy as George Bart Dawes.

- *Roadwork* is the only Bachman novel to have a subtitle ("A Novel of the First Energy Crisis"), but it was not carried over for the later omnibus editions.

58

THE RUNNING MAN
(1982)

An earnest attempt at writing a spare, fast-paced novel squarely set in the science fiction genre, *The Running Man* was also Stephen King's second work—after *The Long Walk* (1979)—to be directly inspired by television game shows.

Indeed, in the epigram that opens Chapter 4 of *The Long Walk*, game show creator Chuck Barris is quoted as saying: "The ultimate game show would be one where the losing contestant was killed." Clearly, that statement was the trigger for this grim satire of a North American police state where there is no hope for the masses—except to watch and bet on the ultraviolent games shown continuously on "Free-Vee." As was also the case with *The Long Walk*, the setting here is an even more corrupt vision of an ultraconservative police state—an "Amerika" spelled with a fascist "k."

The book is set in the year 2025, when the most popular game show on the planet is *The Running Man*. It is also the most deadly: if a contestant successfully eludes the police and the specially trained government Hunters for thirty days, he wins the game. Of course, no one has long enough to collect the staggering one-billion-dollar prize.

But Ben Richards (whose name might be a nod to the comic book characters Ben Grimm and Reed Richards of *Fantastic Four* fame), a sullen outsider whose stubborn streak of independence and relative high intelligence keep him from accepting the status quo, decides to take that suicidal risk and enters *The Running Man*. He feels he has no other options: he is chronically unemployed, his wife has to work occasionally as a prostitute to support the family, and their only child may die unless they get the necessary finances to secure the proper medical care.

Of course, the game is rigged, and it's all but impossible for anyone to last for more than a few harrowing days. Portrayed as a killer and a thief to millions of television watchers by the program's unscrupulous producers, Richards finds the odds stacked against him. Now perceived as a ruthless criminal, it seems only a matter of time before he is spotted by one of his fellow citizens and turned in for a monetary reward.

With the aid of the members of a small underground movement (seemingly the only ones aware of how the Establishment is poisoning the very air the common citizens must breathe), Richards manages to stay one step ahead of the Hunters, at one point kidnapping a wealthy citizen to deter the police from firing upon his car. After a harrowing cross-country chase, he ends up at an airfield in Derry, Maine. Pretending he has a bomb, he hijacks an aircraft and has it flown toward the city where the Games Headquarters is situated.

In the meantime, the powerful men who run the game decide that it would be better for the government if, instead of killing Richards, they fake his demise and give him a fresh identity and a new job for which he would be perfectly suited—as their new Chief Hunter. They make their proposal to him, but make the tactical error of informing him that his wife and child have been murdered by "vandals." Devastated, Richards decides to strike back at his tormentors by crashing the huge aircraft directly into their headquarters (a plot development that seems eerily prophetic in light of the events of 9/11). Hopefully, the act might inspire the masses to rise up against their oppressors. Then again, maybe no one will even notice.

According to King's own note in *The Bachman Books* omnibus, issued in 1985, "*The Running Man*, for instance, was written during a period of seventy-two hours with virtually no changes." It was conceived over a long weekend stint in 1971, shortly after writing the first draft of *Carrie*. King believed at the time that *The Running Man* was a more commercial prospect than his tale of a high school misfit endowed with paranormal abilities. He submitted it to both Doubleday & Co. and Ace Books (a leading paperback publisher of science fiction and fantasy), and both promptly passed on it.

The reasons for the rejection may have had as much to do with the dark tone of the novel as with the quality of the writing itself. The novel is unrelentingly bleak—Ben Richards is presented as a doomed figure, someone who is selected from the masses to provide a few hours of entertainment on "Free-Vee" and then be trashed. Richards knows he is a marked man, and the way he deals with the individuals who are hunting him can only be resolved in one of two ways: either through their violent termination or his own.

Although written several years after *The Long Walk*, *The Running Man* shares many themes with that novel. Both Ben Richards and Ray Garraty of *The Long Walk* enter a government-controlled game in which they both appreciate from the outset that they have a very small chance of winning—or surviving. Both men, when they realize they are going to win, no longer care about the outcome. In spite of the great personal ordeal, their ultimate fate is meaningless. Just because you survive the Long Walk or *The Running Man* doesn't mean you're safe. Life still remains horribly unfair—for most, hopelessness remains the status quo.

In both novels, King presents us with grim dystopian societies where, no matter what the final scorecard might say, there are never any real victors. You might survive the games imposed upon you by the government, but you will still never make any lasting mark or change upon the rest of the world. That doesn't mean, however, that the battle is not worth fighting—in the Stephen King Universe, there will always be a Ray Garraty or Ben Richards who will try to overcome seemingly impossible odds.

THE RUNNING MAN: PRIMARY SUBJECTS

BEN RICHARDS: The longest-surviving contestant to ever play the national game *The Running Man*. Twenty-eight years old, he has no family beyond his wife and child. Essentially a loner, he has never believed in any causes or shown allegiance to any political movement or cause. Never comfortable with authority, he was fired from his last six jobs due to gross insubordination.

Tired of being stuck in abject poverty, hoping to be able to afford the medicine his child needs for her debilitating illness, he takes the suicidal risk of becoming a contestant on the government-sponsored show *The Running Man*.

While traveling across the country in the run of his life, Richards realizes how the government is purposely keeping the majority of the population downtrodden and ill. After hijacking an airplane, he purposely directs the craft into the Games Building in Co-Op City, giving his life to make his first and last political stand.

SHEILA RICHARDS: The wife of Ben Richards, she is among the millions of stricken citizens kept in poverty by the government. Just as Richards's mother had done, she is often forced to sell her body to help put food on the table. She is murdered by persons unknown shortly after her husband begins his stint on *The Running Man*.

CATHY RICHARDS: The eighteen-month-old infant child of Ben and Sheila Richards, she is very ill with the flu. Because medicine is prohibitively expensive, her father becomes a contestant on *The Running Man* to obtain the funds to purchase the necessary drugs. She is murdered with her mother by persons unknown, though these nameless intruders may in fact have been under the employ of the Games Authority.

DAN KILLIAN: The executive producer of *The Running Man*, he is the puppetmaster, the man who controls everything that goes out over the airwaves. Ben Richards hates him from the moment they meet. Killian later tries to convince him to stay on as the new Chief Hunter, but his offer is refused. Killian presumably dies when the aircraft carrying Richards crashes directly into the Games Building.

BOBBY THOMPSON: The on-air host and emcee of *The Running Man*, it is his job to incite the studio audience—and the millions of people watching in their homes—to turn against Ben Richards. He dies in the resulting explosion and fire caused when Richards's aircraft smashes into the Games Building.

EVAN McCONE: The unflappable head of the Hunters, he is aboard the aircraft that Richards uses against the Games Authority. Before he dies, he learns that the Authority is quite willing to let Richards kill him and become the new Chief Hunter. He expires in a shoot-out with Richards on the plane, even though Ben has no intention of ever taking his place on *The Running Man*.

ELTON PARRAKIS: An automatic vending machine serviceman, he is instrumental in assisting Ben Richards in his cross-country flight. Part of an underground movement trying to inform the public how the government is killing them with unchecked environmental pollution, he is shot to death by the police after a car chase.

AMELIA WILLIAMS: The well-to-do woman whom Ben Richards kidnaps near the end of his fateful journey. Because she is a clearly a member of the upper class, the police and those hunting Richards are afraid to eliminate him while she remains his prisoner. Also, her innocent death would be watched by millions on the global television system, and would not be good for ratings. Although she is terrified by Richards and all that he represents, Amelia inexplicably finds herself going along with the desperate man's requests. Amelia survives Richards's suicidal act of defiance when her captor allows her to parachute from the plane shortly before impact.

THE RUNNING MAN: ADAPTATIONS

Released in 1987, the film version of *The Running Man* was the first screen adaptation of a Richard Bachman novel. King reportedly insisted that the credits on the movie reflect that fact—"based on the novel by Richard Bachman"—despite the fact that the world already clearly knew that he was the true author of the novel. It is interesting to note, though, that the movie rights to the paperback original were purchased *before* it was known that King was in fact Bachman.

In terms of the basic plot, the movie is faithful to the source material: if Ben Richards (Arnold Schwarzenegger) and his reluctant companion Amber (Maria Conchita Alonso) can escape a band of professional Stalkers, he will win the grand prize on the planet's most popular television game show, hosted by the flamboyant Damon Killian (Richard Dawson). It's yet another, futuristic version of the classic short story "The Most Dangerous Game," with a man on the run from a pack of vicious hunters.

Of course, Schwarzenegger's presence influenced the final version, as the story was extensively revamped to serve as a vehicle for the international action star. Rather than a sullen, desperate man trying to win the merciless competition to purchase medicine for his sick child, Ben Richards is now a rogue policeman who has been betrayed by the corrupt government. There really isn't much suspense, as viewers are never really in doubt that Richards will ultimately triumph in the end. Schwarzenegger capitalizes on the larger-than-life roles he had already played in *The Terminator* (1984) and *Commando* (1985). The movie even showcases the brutal one-liners that were to become a signature part of his career in action movies.

To increase the odds against Richards, screenwriter Stephen E. de Souza created a group of professional hit men—cartoonlike villains called "Stalkers"—for him to dispatch in imaginative and darkly humorous ways. The actors in these bizarre roles are appropriately larger than life: professional wrestlers Jesse "the Body" Ventura and Professor Toru Tanaka, and athlete-turned-actor Jim Brown, among others. Richard Dawson—himself a long-time television game show personality—clearly has the most fun as the man who controls these hit men, the ruthless yet jovial game show host Killian.

In the end, this extremely violent, R-rated feature shares little in common with the book other than the original title and basic concept. Perhaps Stephen King was wise to let the world remember it as a movie based on an early work by Richard Bachman.

THE RUNNING MAN: TRIVIA

- *The Running Man* is the only novel by Richard Bachman not to carry a dedication.

59

THINNER

(1984)

As noted in the introduction to this section, the public at large learned of King's Richard Bachman pseudonym shortly after the publication of this novel in the fall of 1984. Ironically, King had at one point considered issuing the book under his own name. This is not surprising in hindsight, given that *Thinner* reads very much like an archetypal Stephen King novel.

Thinner remains true to the spirit of previous Bachman titles in that it is exceedingly bleak and downbeat. None of the characters are particularly likable, and their ultimate fates are not particularly pleasant. From the very first page there is a sense of dread, of inevitability, that gives the reader the immediate impression that the author wants to show us humanity at its worst and most vengeful. *Thinner* grapples with the concepts of guilt, responsibility, justice, and retribution. If "revenge is a dish best eaten cold," then nearly all the characters in *Thinner* get their fill.

Billy Halleck is a successful attorney who resides in suburban Connecticut and practices law in New York City. At age thirty-six, he has it all: a great career, a pretty wife, and a wonderful daughter. His one flaw is that he enjoys eating too much—he is fifty pounds overweight, and has been warned by his doctor that he risks a heart attack if he doesn't cut back a little.

Billy's girth ceases to be an issue after he accidentally hits and kills an old Gypsy woman, Susanna Lemke, with his car. Taking advantage of his good standing in the community, and of his close ties to the local police and judge, he gets off with the proverbial slap on the wrist. Enraged by this miscarriage of justice, the Gypsy woman's father, a Gypsy elder named Taduz Lemke, places a curse on Billy as he is leaving the courthouse, whispering a single word:

"Thinner."

From that day forward, Billy loses two pounds every day. At first overjoyed, he later turns fearful, as it appears that he can do nothing to reverse the process. Judge Cary Rossington and Police Chief Hopley, who assisted Billy in avoiding punishment in the death of Susanna Lemke, are also victims of Gypsy curses, suffering terribly from unknown and incurable afflictions that are rapidly disfiguring their bodies. These curses are, of course, metaphors for the many terrifying maladies that can inflict themselves upon us at any time in our lives: cancer, heart disease, even mental illness.

The fact that nearly two out of every three Americans suffers from a weight problem makes Billy Halleck's dilemma extremely easy to relate to. The real-life horror of losing too much weight—anorexia nervosa—was a psychological disorder just becoming known to the general public at the time of the book's initial publication. The cruel irony presented in *Thinner* is that although being overweight can kill you, being underweight can do the same.

King delights in showing us the numerous ironies inherent in the lives of these characters. He explores the thin line between hate and love, between justice and vengeance, between denying and accepting responsibility. With the exception of the ruthless gangster Richard Ginelli, a former client whom Billy hires to put "the curse of the white man from town" on Taduz Lemke and his extended family of Gypsies, none of the characters in *Thinner* choose to accept responsibility for their actions. Unlike Billy, Ginelli has no problem with facing up to the possibility that his own illegal actions might lead to his violent death. What is important to him is that he is true to his own personal moral code, and that he live up to his promises.

King has always displayed a grudging admiration for gangster and Mafia types. He has demonstrated this in several early stories ("The Man with a Belly," "The Wedding Gig," "The Fifth Quarter") and, most significantly to the world of Richard Bachman, in the character of Salvatore Magliore in *Roadwork* (1981). In that novel, Magliore is the only person who can perceive the futility of the protagonist's actions to change the inevitable.

Ginelli can also see "the big picture," how no one is going to "win" this blood feud. Ginelli may be an unsavory character, but at least he has a defined moral code that clearly can distinguish black from white. Whether "white" always represents Good and "black" always represents Evil is not the question. What matters is that his actions are carried out through a clear sense of moral responsibility. He alone can accept the fact that in this lawless situation, the only code is an eye for an eye and a tooth for a tooth. But justice—whether that of the "white man from town" or the pagan Gypsy's—is not achieved in the end. As occurs so often in the Stephen King Universe, and seemingly always in The World of Richard Bachman, everyone loses. *Life is not fair*, King constantly reminds us, and we can do nothing but accept that fact.

Ginelli carries out a campaign of terror against Lemke and his family, forcing the old man to lift the curse. Lemke does so, but the power of the curse is strong. Transferring the curse to a pie, Lemke tells Billy that he must get someone else to eat it to insure that the spell will be lifted from him. Angry with his wife for her actions during his ordeal, Billy decides to feed it to her. He later repents, but only after both his wife and daughter eat a piece of the cursed pie. Realizing that the only people he loved are now cursed, Billy resignedly cuts himself a piece and sits down to eat it. The circle of vengeance is complete: everyone remotely involved with the accidental death of an old Gypsy woman is dead or will soon perish.

THINNER: PRIMARY SUBJECTS

BILLY HALLECK: A successful lawyer whose main problem in life is his tremendous appetite. When he accidentally hits and kills a Gypsy woman with his car, the leader of the clan puts a one-word curse on the man: "Thinner." Halleck begins to lose two pounds each day. After ruling out cancer and a host of other, equally terminal illnesses, he eventually comes to realize that he is the victim of a supernatural curse.

Billy learns that the only way he can be free of the curse is if he passes it on to someone else. Suspecting that his wife has been unfaithful to him (at one point she tries to have him committed to an asylum), Halleck tricks her into eating a piece of a strawberry pie that contains the essence of the curse. Unfortunately, his beloved teenage daughter also has a piece of the pie, dooming her to a nasty death. In the end, Billy realizes there is no escape from the Gypsy's vengeance, and also partakes of the deadly dessert.

HEIDI HALLECK: Billy's devoted wife, she is partially responsible for the automobile accident with the Gypsy woman (she was performing oral sex upon her husband while he was driving). Heidi comes to believe that Billy is starving himself out of guilt, and at one point tries to have him institutionalized as mentally ill. There are rumors that she is having an affair with the family doctor, but they are never proven. In her husband's growing paranoia, he believes she is against him, and so brings home a cursed strawberry pie for her to unknowingly ingest. She presumably perishes soon afterward.

LINDA HALLECK: Billy and Heidi's only child. A normal, attractive fourteen-year-old girl, she suffers as she watches her parents' marriage deteriorate. She is thus thrilled when her dad, who left when his malady became too much for him to handle, calls her to say he is coming back home to stay. Eager to take his revenge on his wife, however, he asks Linda to go stay at a friend's home for a few days until that last bridge can be mended. Returning home unexpectedly, Linda joins Heidi in a midnight snack, eating part of the cursed pie. Like her mom, she no doubt soon dies a painful and totally undeserved death.

SUSANNA LEMKE: The Gypsy woman who died when she stepped out from between two parked cars and was hit by the vehicle driven by Billy Halleck.

TADUZ LEMKE: The elderly leader of the Gypsy clan who puts the curse on Billy Halleck and his associates. How elderly? Official records place his age at well over one hundred. Possessed of supernatural powers, he takes his revenge against all who were responsible for the death of his daughter Susanna, including Billy, the police chief who looked the other way, and the judge, who has a long-standing hatred for all Gypsies. Taduz's current whereabouts are unknown, but presumably he is still with extended family traveling somewhere along the coast of New England.

RICHARD GINELLI: The small-time gangster who succeeds in getting the curse lifted from Billy Halleck. Billy had been successful in the past in keeping Richard out of prison, and the gangster feels he owes Halleck a personal debt. When Halleck decides to put "the curse of the white man from town" on the Gypsy clan that had targeted him, he employs Ginelli as his dark angel of vengeance. Ginelli mounts a campaign of terror against the Gypsies, leaving messages that they must take the curse off of Halleck. Although he gets the curse lifted, it is at the price of his own life. (Halleck finds Ginelli's head on the front seat of the gangster's car.)

POLICE CHIEF DUNCAN HOPLEY: He investigates the accident in which Billy Halleck struck and killed the Gypsy woman. A friend of Halleck, he has no trouble assuming that the attorney is completely blameless in the death of the old woman. Taduz Lemke curses Hopley, however, creating a worsening skin condition that transforms the police officer into a hideous freak. Unable to cope with the suffering any longer, he commits suicide with his own service revolver.

JUDGE CARY ROSSINGTON: An old friend of Billy Halleck's, he is the judge in charge of the court case involving the automobile accident. An elitist and a racist, he hates the Gypsies who occasionally pass through his district. At the hearing regarding the accident, Rossington wastes no time in clearing Halleck of any possible liability. But the judge, like Halleck, is touched by Taduz Lemke, and has one word spoken to him: "Lizard." Immediately afterward, Rossington develops a spreading skin growth that rapidly transforms his skin into lizardlike scales. He visits the world-famed Mayo Clinic, but to no avail. Like the police chief, he kills himself to end his suffering.

THINNER: ADAPTATIONS

In spite of the novel's commercial success, the film adaptation of *Thinner* did not appear until more than a decade later, perhaps due to the dearth of likable characters, or to an inability to create convincing special effects. Despite the fact that adapter Michael McDowell's and director Tom Holland's screenplay is remarkably faithful to the plot of the original novel, the ultimate result was similar to the fate of *Firestarter*. In other words, the plot and the characters were all there, but little of the spirit or mood of the author's original vision was successfully translated. Although Robert Burke *(Robocop 3)* and Joe Mantegna do a credible job of portraying Billy Halleck and Richard Ginelli, there is still nothing in any of the characters as portrayed that leads the viewer to care about the fate of any of them; considering how petty and self-centered everyone is, there is very little sympathy we can develop for anyone we meet.

THINNER: TRIVIA

- The original title for the novel was *Gypsy Pie.*

- The unabridged audio adaptation of this novel was read by Joe Mantegna, who also starred in the movie version.

- *Thinner* was the first Richard Bachman title to be published in hardcover and given strong promotion by its publisher, New American Library.

- In the film version, Stephen King has a cameo role as a pharmacist named Dr. Bangor.

60

DESPERATION

(1996)

In addition to the paperback serial novel *The Green Mile*, 1996 saw another unique publishing event devised by Stephen King—the simultaneous publication in late September of two mammoth hardcover novels, *Desperation* and *The Regulators*. Companion novels, the two entries share interlocking cover art (a truly unforgettable piece created by Mark Ryden), a nasty villain (an ancient demon named Tak), and a shared cast of characters who exist in parallel realities.

The hook here is that *Desperation*, published by Viking, was written by King, and *The Regulators*, published by Dutton, was written by King's alter ego, Richard Bachman.

In *Desperation*, King returns to themes he first visited in *The Stand* (1978), namely man's relationship with God, and His divine intervention in human events. The God reflected in both books resembles the God of the Old Testament, the God who worked through intermediaries like Moses to achieve his agenda. Like that God, King's deity seems content to sit on the sidelines and observe, unless forces beyond human ken come into play. In *The Stand*, that force was the Dark Man, Randall Flagg; in *Desperation*, it is the ancient demon Tak.

In both cases, God never acts directly, but through human vessels like *The Stand*'s Mother Abagail and *Desperation*'s young David Carver. As depicted here, despite his active role in events, God remains a mystery; both his part in the universe and his motivations are unknown.

The parallels to *The Stand* go beyond the religious. For instance, David's speech in *Desperation* to the rest of the Collie Entragian Survival Society echoes the words Mother Abagail spoke to the members of the Free Zone. David tells his friends that "if we leave Desperation without doing what God sent us here to do, we'll pay the price." In other words, God wants them to take a stand. When the evil is dispatched in *The Stand*, Tom Cullen witnesses the fist of God in the sky over Las Vegas. In *Desperation*, Tak's passing is marked by a gigantic cloud of dark gray dust: "It hung in the sky, still connected to the [China] pit by a hazy umbilicus of a mountain rising into the sky like poisoned ground after a nuclear blast." The cloud takes the shape of a giant wolf.

Biblical allusions abound as well here. Wondering why Tak chose them and killed others, his former prisoners conclude that they were selected, that Tak acted like the Angel of Death in Egypt, only in reverse. David's battle with Tak is reminiscent of the conflict between David and Goliath. David's first encounter with God recalls Moses on Mount Horeb: When Moses asks "Who are you?," God replies, "Who I am."

In a flashback to the early days of his religious conversion, David recalls the story of Daniel in the lion's den. Marinville later cites the phrase, "And a little child shall lead them." David also performs miracles: he gets Steve's cell phone to work in the midst of a vicious sandstorm; later, he feeds his unfortunate band much like Jesus fed the multitude with the loaves and fishes. Similar to Jesus, he pleads with God to lift the burden placed on his shoulders.

Let's not forget the links with *The Regulators*, which should become a little bit clearer in the next chapter. Kirsten Carver is wearing a Moto Kops 2200 T-shirt when Tak kills her (*Moto Kops 2200* is a popular TV show in both realities). The Carver family hails from 248 Poplar Street, Wentworth, Ohio, the setting of *The Regulators*. Several supporting characters in *Desperation* bear the same names as leading characters in *The Regulators*, among them Jim Reed, Brad Josephson, and Cary Ripken.

Finally, there are the links to the overall Stephen King Universe. Ellen Carver is described as preferring novels with titles like *Misery in Paradise*. Cynthia Smith, a supporting character from *Rose Madder*, shows up in *Desperation*, providing Steve Ames with a capsule version of the events of that novel.

Publishers Weekly reported that the idea for *Desperation* came to King in 1991. Driving across the Nevada desert in his daughter Naomi's car, the author passed through the apparently abandoned town of Ruth. At this point, the internal Voice that King has often written about (his muse, perhaps) began speaking to him. His first thought was, "They're all dead," then, "Who killed them?" The Voice shot back, "The sheriff killed them all."

The book's opening scene, featuring Mary and Peter Jackson, sets the eerie tone for the rest of the novel. Peter, an English professor at New York University, has recently published a scholarly article entitled "James Dickey and the New Southern Reality," ironic in light of what subsequently happens to the couple (think *Deliverance*, only in the desert). Traveling on Route 50 through the Nevada desert, they get their first hint that something might be wrong when they spy a cat nailed to a speed limit sign on the outskirts of Desperation. Soon thereafter, they are pulled over by a cop who stands six feet five inches tall, easily tipping the scales at 300 pounds; the policeman seems to be bursting out of his skin.

King, expertly playing on the fear many of us have of authority, raises the tension notch by notch—like Mary and Peter, readers quickly discern that the cop is not quite right. As he reads the Jacksons their rights, the unfortunate couple see just how far gone their persecutor is. "You have the right to remain silent. If you do not choose to remain silent, anything you say may be used against you in a court of law. You have the right to an attorney. I'm going to kill you. If you cannot afford . . ."

DESPERATION: PRIMARY SUBJECTS

DESPERATION: A small Nevada mining town. Located off Interstate 50, Desperation is inhabited by approximately 260 people, at least until an ancient evil living beneath the earth's crust is released. Then it quickly becomes a ghost town, haunted by its lone surviving resident, police officer Collie Entragian. Collie has been possessed by a demon named Tak. Tak likes his new host, but knows he can't use him indefinitely, and thus is looking for another. Having slaughtered the entire town, Tak/Collie takes to pulling people off the highway, seeking an adequate vessel to contain his essence. Collie's body is worn by Tak, its energy sucked out until it is only a shell or husk.

TAK: The ancient evil entity that possesses Collie Entragian. Tak has lived under the earth, near the vicinity of the mine called the China Pit, for eons.

At first, David tells his friends that Tak is some kind of deity. Later, he tells them he believes it is more like a disease than something ethereal like a demon or spirit. As to where Tak actually lives, David is a little vague. The creature is referred to as an outsider, existing somehow beyond the reality we know. David manages to seal Tak in his tomb, where he remains to this day, presumably waiting for a chance to rise again.

CAN TAH: Tak, or Can Tak, is a "big god" (a translation of Can Tak). He has minions, or little gods, called Can Tah. They inhabit small stone carvings of wolves, coyotes, snakes, spiders, rats, and bats found inside the China Pit. Merely touching one of these carvings is enough to drive humans crazy with lust and hate.

THE CHINA PIT: Also known as Rattlesnake Number One, the China Mine, the China Drift, or the old China Shaft, the pit has been home to Tak and the Can-Tah for thousands of years. In September 1859, miners (57 Chinese and 4 whites) broke into a cave containing thousands of small stone carvings, the Can Tah. When the miners picked up these statues, they went crazy. Before they could escape the mine and spread their evil, the mine was sealed by the heroic efforts of the Lushan brothers. The mine remained sealed until a fateful day in 1996 when employees of the Desperation mining company accidentally reopened it, unleashing Tak and his minions on Desperation.

COLLIE ENTRAGIAN: The big blond police officer possessed by Tak, who uses his body first to decimate the population of Desperation, then to collect new candidates to host his essence. Tak uses Collie up, then casts his ravaged body aside like a child would toss away a candy wrapper.

PETER and MARY JACKSON: Driving a borrowed car across Nevada, this unfortunate couple is pulled over by Tak/Entragian and subsequently arrested. Arriving at the Desperation police station, Peter is fatally shot by the lawman. Mary is imprisoned along with the Carver family and Tom Billingsley. Tak, who has left Entragian's body and moved into that of Ellen Carver, intends to possess Mary next, but is foiled when she escapes from her makeshift prison deep in the China Pit mine. Mary

Jackson survives her encounter with Tak. She is last seen driving away from Desperation, accompanied by David Carver. Her present whereabouts are unknown.

JOHN EDWARD MARINVILLE: Winner of the National Book Award, author of the novels *Delight* and *Song of the Hammer*. This Norman Mailer-esque bad boy is touring the United States on his motorcycle, searching for material for his new nonfiction book (working title: *Travels with Harley*). Passing by Desperation on Route 50, Marinville decides to relieve himself on the side of the road. Finishing, he looks up to find a giant cop waiting for him at the top of the gulley.

At first fawning over the famous author, Tak/Entragian soon reveals his true ugly nature. He beats and arrests Marinville, then throws him into jail with Mary Jackson, Tom Billingsley, and the Carvers.

After David frees the group, Marinville struggles with his inherently selfish nature, eventually emerging as one of the group's leaders. Never a religious man, Marinville is somewhat contemptuous of David, referring to him at one point as "the Jesus Scout." Needless to say, he is overwhelmed when he himself receives a message from God, instructing him that he must be the one to finally destroy Tak. The scales fall from the writer's eyes as he suddenly realizes he has been a part of God's plan since a near-death experience he had in Vietnam.

During that interlude, he actually speaks with David in a sort of limbo, giving the boy instructions as to how to dispatch Tak. Marinville accepts God's will. Entering the China Pit, he detonates enough explosives to reseal the mine, giving his life to save the others, a selfless act of redemption for a man who until then had rarely thought of anyone else.

STEVE AMES: Accustomed to working with rock stars, this Texan is hired by John Marinville's publishers to guard him during his tour. Steve follows Marinville at a discreet distance, and thus is not close by when Marinville is abducted by Tak/Entragian. Marinville does contact Steve briefly on his cell phone, a clue that eventually leads him to Desperation. Accompanied by hitchhiker Cynthia Smith, Steve eventually links up with the group that escapes the Desperation town prison. Steve survives the encounter with Tak. He is last seen in the company of Cynthia Smith, driving down Route 50. His present whereabouts are unknown.

CYNTHIA SMITH: Cynthia is hitchhiking back home for a reunion with her parents when Steve Ames picks her up just outside Ely. Present when Steve gets his garbled message from John Marinville, Cynthia becomes embroiled in the trouble plaguing the town of Desperation. Cynthia survives, and departs with Steve Ames for destinations unknown.

RALPH, ELLEN, and KIRSTEN "PIE" CARVER: The members of the Carver family are the first victims of Tak/Entragian after he wipes out the population of Desperation. The Carvers are forced to stop on Highway 50 just outside of Desperation when their RV runs over a carpet of nails left in the road by the marauding policeman. There they are approached by Tak/Entragian, who makes them his prisoners.

The Carvers endure much tragedy over the next few hours. First, young Kirsten is brutally murdered by Tak, thrown down the jailhouse stairs. Ellen dies also, but only after suffering the indignity of being possessed by Tak. Ralph is terminated as he, his son, David, Mary Jackson, and John Marinville descend into the China Pit; he is executed by Tak, who has been forced to occupy the body of a vulture.

DAVID CARVER: Some say you cannot petition the Lord with prayer, but don't tell that to young David Carver. A year before the events in Desperation, David faces another tragedy—his best friend, Brian, is critically injured after being struck by a drunk driver. Near death, Brian lies in the hospital as his distraught friend wanders the streets.

For some reason, David is drawn to the Bear Street Woods, where he and Brian often played. While walking in the woods, David hears the voice of God. At first scared, David begs God to help his friend, promising that he will be God's servant in return. Shortly thereafter, God works a miracle on Brian, bringing the boy out of his coma.

David receives guidance from God through prayer; the faith instilled in David on the day Brian returns to health becomes deeper with each passing day. God instructs the boy to seek out Reverend Martin, the Methodist minister who eventually becomes his spiritual guide. The reverend tells David that he has been chosen by God. David feels that God is preparing him for something, but has no idea what.

When David's family is captured by Tak, he quickly realizes it is no accident—God has sent him to do His work. After Tak kills his sister and imprisons his family, a divinely inspired David wriggles free from his cell and releases his fellow inmates. Later, David informs them that God has chosen them to battle Tak.

David mistakenly believes that God has called him to be the main architect of Tak's return to his prison in the China Pit; he later learns that John Marinville is God's chosen one. David survives his encounter with Tak—the battle leaves him without family, but with the conviction that his God is indeed a loving God, not the cruel, pitiless deity he has always perceived him to be.

David is last seen leaving Desperation in a car driven by Mary Jackson. His present whereabouts are unknown.

AUDREY WYLER: Visiting Desperation shortly before Tak/Entragian's killing spree, Audrey unwittingly falls under Tak's power. Posing as the last survivor in town, Audrey later makes an unsuccessful attempt on David's life. Audrey, consumed by the power of a Can Tah, dies from injuries sustained in her struggles with the Collie Entragian Survivors Society.

TOM BILLINGSLEY: This retired veterinarian is one of the last survivors of Desperation; Tak throws him in a holding cell, then goes out to look for other potential hosts. Tom tells the group of Entragian's rampage through town. Tom is killed by a panther sent by Tak to distract the group while Audrey Wyler makes her attempt on David's life.

DESPERATION: TRIVIA

- The audio version of *Desperation* was read by actress Kathy Bates, a veteran of several King film and television projects.

- The words David uses to describe Tak recall those King employed to describe It in the 1986 novel of the same name. Tak is also referred to as an "outsider," a word used to describe an evil being from beyond our reality that merges with the spirit of Sara Tidwell in the pages of *Bag of Bones* (1998). *Can-tah* and *can-tak* also show up prominently in the later books of the *Dark Tower* series.

61

THE REGULATORS

(1996)

As mentioned in the previous chapter, *The Regulators* contains many connections to its companion novel, *Desperation* (1996). Some of the characters from the latter appear in major roles in *The Regulators*; others do not. People survive the events of one novel and die in the next, expire in both, or survive in each. Some appear as children in one book and adults in the other; one book's shining hero may be somewhat tarnished in the other. The interplay is fairly complex: both texts are salted with insider jokes and pieces of similar-sounding dialogue, no doubt providing much grist for Stephen King enthusiasts to debate.

According to various published interviews with King, the idea for *The Regulators* came to him near "the three-quarter mark on *Desperation*." He jotted down the idea, which consisted of a single word on a scrap of paper: it read "Regulators." At the time, he only knew that his idea had something to do with "toys, guns, TV and suburbia."

Soon thereafter, another thought burst forth. King decided to take the characters from *Desperation* and place them into *The Regulators*, using them "like the members of a repertory company acting in two different plays." As the idea evolved further, King realized that what worked with the characters might work with the plot as well; that is, he could use many of the elements of *Desperation* in a different configuration, creating a kind of mirror world in the new book.

One last hurdle existed. Even though the books shared many elements, he didn't want it to sound or feel as if the same writer had created both works. Then it occurred to King that he'd had the answer all along—his alter ego, the pseudonymous Richard Bachman, could write *The Regulators*. There was only one problem with this: King had already declared that Bachman had died of "cancer of the pseudonym" in 1985, shortly after the publication of Bachman's breakthrough novel, *Thinner*.

King's office bookshelf   BETH GWINN

King's solution was rather ingenious. An Editor's Note at the beginning of *The Regulators* states that the manuscript was found in Bachman's effects by his widow, Claudia Inez Eschelman. The manuscript was then validated by Bachman scholar Douglas Winter, Elaine Koster at New American Library, and Carolyn Stromberg, editor of the earliest Bachman novels. After making minor changes to correct for anachronisms (e.g. substituting the name of younger actor Ethan Hawke for that of performer Rob Lowe in the first chapter), E. P. Dutton editor Charles Verrill pronounced it fit for publication.

The tongue-in-cheek publicity materials stated: "Stephen King, who had an advance look at *The Regulators* manuscript, said: 'The most interesting thing about *The Regulators* is that Bachman and I must have been on the same psychic wavelength. It's almost as if we were twins, in a funny way.'" King continued to say in the PR materials that he had found similarities between *The Regulators* and his upcoming novel *Desperation*. "It's a little bit like the similarities between *Alice in Wonderland* and *Through the Looking Glass*. It's like everything's been turned on its head."

The two books benefited from all the publicity their combined two-million-dollar marketing budget could buy. One of many gimmicks was a "limited" (200,000-copy) edition two-for-one gift pack in which both volumes were shrink-wrapped together with a keep-you-up-all-night book light.

The Regulators itself had a five-hundred-copy limited edition (selling at $325) published by Dutton, available on a first-come, first-served basis via phone order. Each copy contained a fake check signed by the non-existent Bachman, each made out to a friend or associate of King's or one of his fictional characters. (For instance, one check was made out to The Overlook Connection, an independent bookseller specializing in "all things King." Another was made out to Quitters Inc., the anti-smoking organization immortalized in King's short story of the same name.) The book came in a cloth-covered box featuring artist Alan M. Clark's conception of a Power Wagon—the vehicles driven by the Regulators.

The Regulators is dedicated to two "legendary shadows," hard-boiled novelist Jim Thompson (1906–1977) and groundbreaking film director Sam Peckinpah (1925–1984). Although Thompson (*The Grifters, The Getaway*) certainly influenced the Bachman style, he doesn't cast a large shadow over *The Regulators* (he does, however, influence *Desperation*, which nods toward the Thompson classic *The Killer Inside Me*). *The Regulators* does, however, owe a deep debt to Peckinpah. The novel had its genesis in "The Shotgunners," an original screenplay King wrote specifically for Peckinpah. Unfortunately, the film was never produced (it was in preproduction when Peckinpah passed away in 1984).

It seems that King also drew inspiration from Peckinpah's classic western, *The Wild Bunch* (1969), which also almost certainly inspired King's fictional Western film *The Regulators*, a movie that plays a key role in the plot of the novel. *The Wild Bunch* gained almost instant notoriety for its bloody, almost poetic action scenes. Set in 1913, the plot centers on a group of aging outlaws who, realizing that time is passing them by, decide to retire after one last score. *The Regulators* features a character named Major Pike, after the role played by William Holden in *The Wild Bunch*.

Another fictional precursor is Jerome Bixby's classic 1953 short story, "It's a Good Life," a tale that was adapted for both *The Twilight Zone* television show (in 1961) and for the feature film *Twilight Zone—The Movie* (1983). This narrative, about a small boy who controls reality, is evoked within *The Regulators* when suburban Poplar Street is transformed by Seth Garin into a surreal Western landscape, a panorama that resembles a child's cartoon-influenced perception of the old West.

As King has noted, *The Regulators* is also a sly commentary about "the god of suburbia, television." The author was most assuredly commenting on the influence TV has on children, especially recent broadcast phenomena like *Mighty Morphin Power Rangers* and *Teenage Mutant Ninja Turtles*, which were extremely popular at the time the book was first published. In this case, the *Power Rangers/Turtles* analog in the Bachman book is *MotoKops 2200*, an ultraviolent cartoon that captures young Seth's imagination.

The book begins innocently enough. It's summertime and, as the old song goes, the living is easy. On Poplar Street, a paper boy delivers this week's edition of *The Wentworth Gazette*. People are barbecuing, washing their cars, throwing Frisbees. But up the street, right where Poplar intersects with Bear Street, sits a futuristic-looking red van with what looks like a radar dish on top. Soon it will start its deadly journey down Poplar Street, changing the lives of its residents forever.

THE REGULATORS: PRIMARY SUBJECTS

POPLAR STREET: Poplar Street is located in Wentworth, Ohio. It's abutted on its northern end by Bear Street and by Hyacinth Street on the south. There are eleven houses and an E-Z Stop convenience store on the street, odd-numbered houses on the west, even-numbered on the east. On the afternoon of July 15, 1996, Poplar Street is cut off from the rest of the world and transformed into a surreal killing ground, a combination of the Old West as it exists on TV and movies (the homes on the block change into log cabins and adobe haciendas; buzzards, wolves, and wild boars, looking as if they are created by a child, roam through back yards) and a place called the Force Corridor, which only exists in a TV cartoon version of the twenty-third century. Poplar Street returns to normal after the death of Seth Garin, whose young body serves as a vessel for an ancient demon named Tak.

CARY RIPTON: Cary is the local paper boy and, unfortunately, the first to fall victim to the Regulators on the fateful day of July 15, 1996. Cary is shotgunned to death by the occupants of a red van.

THE GARIN FAMILY: A Toledo family of five, they are the victims of a senseless drive-by shooting while vacationing in San Jose, California. Killed in the July 31, 1994, incident were William Garin, his wife, June, and two of their three children, John and Mary Lou. The only survivor is six-year-old Seth, who was playing in a sandbox behind the home where the shooting took place. Witnesses reported seeing a red van in the vicinity shortly before the shooting, with what looked like a radar dish on the roof.

SETH GARIN/TAK: At the age of six, autistic, telepathic Seth Garin is possessed by a demon named Tak who, sensing the boy's hidden abilities, lures him to an abandoned mine located in Desperation, Nevada. After Tak kills his family (see above), Seth goes to live with his aunt and uncle, Audrey and Herb Wyler, at 247 Poplar Street. Tak has an odd kind of symbiosis with Seth, both augmenting and feeding off the little boy's latent powers.

Tak also seizes on the boy's preferences in animated cartoons, combining Seth's devotion to *MotoKops 2200* with his own love of television and movie Westerns to create the futuristic Regulators who terrorize the Poplar Street residents. This symbiosis is not total, however. Tak, disgusted by the human's need to void its bowels, departs his unwilling host whenever the boy goes to the bathroom.

Under his autistic shell, Seth has a more "normal" personality, one that is considerably more alert and mature. Able to communicate with his Aunt Audrey on a psychic level, Seth conspires with her to rid himself of the demon, an act they accomplish at the cost of both their lives. Although his body is dead, it appears that Seth and Audrey's spirits live on, inhabiting a gazebo at the Mohonk Mountain House in New York State.

BRAD and BELINDA JOSEPHSON: The owners of 251 Poplar, they are the only African-American family living on Poplar Street. Brad is gored by Seth/Tak's cartoon version of a wild boar, but both he and his wife, Belinda, survive the Regulators' attack. It is presumed that they still reside at 251 Poplar Street.

JOHN MARINVILLE: The owner of 250 Poplar, Johnny Marinville, winner of the National Book Award for his adult novel, *Delight*, got rich in the 1980s writing children's books about a character named Pat the Kitty-Cat, a feline private detective, then "retired" to Wentworth. Johnny is the first resident of Poplar Street to put together the available clues, realizing that Seth, a wild fan of *MotoKops 2200*, must somehow be behind the strange events. Johnny is at the Wyler home when Tak is defeated. It is presumed that he still lives at 250 Poplar Street.

GARY and MARIELLE SODERSON: Thought of as the Poplar Street Bohemians, the Sodersons of 249 Poplar are an odd couple. Gary is a helpful soul, though he drinks too much. The neighbors do not think as kindly of Marielle. She loses an arm in one of the Regulators' early attacks, and later dies from the trauma. Gary is killed by a cartoonlike gila monster later that same day.

THE CARVERS: The residents of 248 Poplar, the Carver family is composed of David and Kirsten "Pie" Carver; their daughter, Ellen "Ellie" Margaret; and her little brother, Ralph. Ellie and Ralph are orphaned by the Regulators; their present whereabouts are unknown. Their father, David, is killed in the Regulators' second attack; their mother, Kirsten, is wounded in a subsequent assault, and expires shortly thereafter.

AUDREY and HERB WYLER: They live at 247 Poplar. William Garin's sister, Audrey Wyler, takes Seth Garin in after his family is slaughtered in a drive-by shooting. Audrey and Herb, who come to love Seth as if he were their own child, conclude that something is desperately wrong with him as Tak emerges from hiding. First, Seth/Tak drives their neighbors, the Hobarts, from Poplar Street. Then he takes control of their very lives, forcing Audrey to injure herself and draining the life force from Herb as if he were a human battery.

Herb eventually commits suicide, leaving Audrey at the mercy of Tak. Although he keeps her alive (Seth wouldn't let him eliminate her), he makes her life a living hell. Audrey retains her sanity by mentally retreating to the past, to a time when she and a friend visited the Mohonk Mountain House in New Paltz, New York. Audrey is killed when Cammie Reed fires on Seth, whom she is holding at the time.

Audrey's spirit lives on, however, and is often seen haunting a gazebo at Mohonk. Audrey is not alone, however. She is accompanied by a little boy, presumably the spirit of Seth.

TOM BILLINGSLEY: The owner of 246 Poplar, this retired veterinarian is forced to treat Poplar Street's wounded, but is largely ineffective due to the severity of their traumas. Tom survives the onslaught, but it seems unlikely that he remains a resident of Poplar Street.

THE REED FAMILY: The neighbors residing at 245 Poplar, Charlie and Cammie Reed, have twin sons, Jim and Dave. Although Charlie is not present on Poplar Street on the fateful day of July 15, 1996, his wife plays a key role in the action. During a lull in the carnage, Mrs. Reed sends her two sons out for help from the outside world. While on this trek, a shaky Jim accidentally shoots and kills Collie Entragian. The distraught Jim subsequently kills himself, an action precipitated by Tak. A shaken Cammie later tries to avenge his death by shooting Seth and, incidentally, Audrey Wyler. Tak, robbed of his host, tries to possess Cammie, but her body is not strong enough to contain his life force. Cammie dies in this attempt. Unable to contain the power of Tak, her body literally explodes.

Charlie and Dave Reed's present whereabouts are unknown. It seems unlikely that they still live on Poplar Street.

THE GELLER FAMILY: The residents of 243 Poplar, Frank and Kim Geller have one child, their daughter, Susi. Frank is not there the day the Regulators attack. Kim is killed in the Regulators' final assault. Frank and Susi's present whereabouts are unknown.

PETER and MARY JACKSON: The residents of 244 Poplar, Peter Jackson is a professor at Ohio State University. His wife, Mary, is an accountant. Returning from an adulterous rendezvous, Mary Jackson is rear-ended by a futuristic yellow van at the beginning of the Regulators' second assault. Leaving her car, she is gunned down by the van's occupant. Peter Jackson is murdered by Tak, who sucks the life force out of his victim after forcing him to watch Seth's video of the movie *The Regulators*.

CYNTHIA SMITH: A clerk at the E-Z Stop, she is one of a small group of people who survive the Regulators' bloody assaults.

STEVE AMES: Driving his rented Ryder truck down Poplar Street, Steve witnesses Cary Ripton's death at the hands of the Regulators. Acting instinctively, he and Cynthia Smith protect Ellie and Ralph Carver from injury during the Regulators' first attack.

COLLIE ENTRAGIAN: The owner of 240 Poplar and an ex-cop, Collie is fired from the Columbus Police Department after a positive drug test for cocaine and heroin. Collie believes that he was framed, since he never took either drug. His police training kicking in, Collie tries to restore order after the Regulators' first attack. He is later shot and killed by Jim Reed.

MOTO KOPS 2200: A popular Saturday morning cartoon, *MotoKops 2200* chronicles the interstellar adventures of Colonel Henry, Snake Hunter, Bounty, Major Pike, Rooty the Robot, and Cassandra Styles as they battle archenemies No Face and Countess Lili Marsh. Each character pilots a futuristic Power Wagon, essentially vans equipped with fold-up wheels and stubby extendable wings. Colonel Henry's vehicle is the yellow Justice Wagon, No Face's is called the Meatwagon, Snake Hunter, Rooty the Robot, and Cassandra Styles the red Tracker Arrow, the silver Rooty-Toot, and the "Mary Kay" pink Dream Floater, respectively.

THE REGULATORS: Premiering in 1958, this American International Pictures release starred John Payne, Ty Hardin, Karen Steele, and

Rory Calhoun, and was directed by Billy Rancourt. The movie, based on a screenplay written by Craig Goodis and Quentin Woolrich, tells the story of a Colorado mining town that is terrorized by vigilantes who first appear to be supernatural beings but turn out to be post–Civil War baddies "of the Capt. Quantrill stripe." According to reviews, the movie includes some scenes and effects that are "surprisingly gruesome for a late-fifties oat opera."

THE REGULATORS: Tak's kill squad, they represent a strange blend of characters from the 1958 Hollywood movie and the *MotoKops 2200* TV cartoon. Also among Tak's hit squad are characters from classic TV Westerns such as *Bonanza* and *The Rifleman*.

THE REGULATORS: TRIVIA

- Tak's use of creatures whose appearance is based upon characters from film and television recalls the same sort of activity by It (from the 1986 novel of the same name). Both beings are revealed as "outsiders" by King, indicating that they are likely of a related breed of extradimensional monster.

- The novel *The Regulators* contains a script excerpt from *MotoKops 2200* episode entitled "The Force Corridor," a segment that Seth/Tak is particularly enamored of. The script was penned by Alan Smithee. Movie aficionados know that the name Alan Smithee is a Hollywood in joke. Often, when directors want to disassociate themselves from a film or TV program, they substitute that name for their own.

- The King-created film *The Regulators*, which is mentioned in the novel, is also referred to in the author's 1999 release *Hearts in Atlantis*.

62

RELATED TALES

Although King has never stated that *all* his crime stories were composed while in a "Richard Bachman frame of mind," several seem to have been written in that mode. While perhaps not exhaustive of every non-supernatural tale King has composed, the following stories certainly *feel* like Bachman stories, even if King hasn't explicitly identified them as such. Also, none of them are specifically connected to the Prime Reality. Thus, we have taken the liberty of assigning them to the World of Richard Bachman. One read-through of the tales below reveals why each was deemed more appropriate for this section.

"The Fifth Quarter"
(from 1993's *Nightmares & Dreamscapes*)

Reminiscent of Donald E. Westlake's pseudonymous "Richard Stark" novels featuring professional criminal Parker, this hard-boiled crime story was first published in *Cavalier* magazine in 1972 under the byline "John Swithen" (the sole time to date the author has used this particular pseudonym). King himself states in his Notes to *Nightmares & Dreamscapes* that this story was written in his Richard Bachman mode.

"THE FIFTH QUARTER":
PRIMARY SUBJECTS

JERRY TARKANIAN: An ex-con (he spent time in Shawshank Prison) out to revenge the death of a comrade known only as Barney, Tarkanian accosts Barney's double-crossing partners, Sarge, Jagger, and Keenan. He is seeking their pieces to the map showing where their loot has been stashed.

"The Ledge" (from 1978's *Night Shift*)

A tennis pro who has fallen in love with a mobster's wife is forced by the man to take a bet: walk around the windswept, five-inch-wide ledge of his building and receive a pile of money and the freedom to leave with the criminal's wife, or go to prison, framed on drug charges. The story originally appeared in *Penthouse* magazine in 1976, and was later part of 1985's motion picture anthology scripted by King, *Cat's Eye*.

"THE LEDGE": PRIMARY SUBJECTS

STAN NORRIS: A tennis pro and an ex-con, Stan meets and falls in love with Marcia Cressner. Much to his misfortune, Marcia is already married to a man tied to the mob. Forced to accept Cressner's wager, Norris manages to make it around the building on the dangerous ledge, only to discover that Cressner has had Marcia murdered. In revenge, he makes Cressner walk the ledge. When last we see him, Stan is waiting for Cressner to fall or finish the walk, but intends to kill him in any case. The final outcome of this situation has yet to be revealed.

CRESSNER: An organized crime figure who loses his wife to Stan Norris, then has her killed. When last seen, he was out on the ledge. His eventual fate is as yet unknown.

MARCIA CRESSNER: After she has an affair with Stan Norris, her husband orders a killer in his employ to take her life.

"Quitters, Inc." (from 1978's *Night Shift*)

A man wants to quit smoking and inquires about a new program, only to discover that their methods are far more than drastic—they are violent and ultimately for keeps. "Quitters, Inc." was also part of the anthology film *Cat's Eye*, with James Woods effectively portraying Dick Morrison.

"QUITTERS, INC.": PRIMARY SUBJECTS

DICK MORRISON: When Dick visits Quitters, Inc., he is unaware that he is going to be forced to quit by threats against his own well-being, as well as the safety of his wife and his mentally challenged son. He does, however, give up his cigarette habit.

VICTOR DONATTI: An employee of Quitters, Inc., Donatti is in charge of Morrison's treatment. He torments Dick and tortures Mrs. Morrison, but he does gets results.

JIMMY McCANN: An old friend of Morrison's, it is McCann who first recommends that Dick try Quitters, Inc. with the words, "They'll cure you. Guaranteed."

"Man with a Belly" (1978)

Published in 1978 in *Cavalier* and never reprinted by King in any of his short story collections, this is a bleak crime tale dealing with unpleasant gangster figures and a twisted sense of revenge.

"MAN WITH A BELLY": PRIMARY SUBJECTS

JOHN BRACKEN: A ruthless hit man for the Mafia, Bracken is summoned by crime lord Don Correzente to perform a most unusual service.

He is to rape the Don's wife, who has a serious gambling habit and is humiliating him because of it. This will be her unique punishment.

DON CORREZENTE: The elderly crime lord who holds his honor above all. He is a "man with a belly," that is, someone who has an iron will. Although Bracken does the job as instructed, the Don will ultimately be the one who is the biggest loser.

NORMA CORREZENTE: Don Correzente's beautiful trophy wife, she accepts being raped by Bracken. But to get her revenge, she in turn hires the hit man to have sex with her repeatedly until she can become pregnant—with his child, not the Don's.

"The Wedding Gig" (from 1985's *Skeleton Crew*)

This decidedly hard-boiled crime story—and a period piece on top of that—first appeared in *Ellery Queen's Mystery Magazine* in 1980.

"THE WEDDING GIG": PRIMARY SUBJECTS

THE NARRATOR: The nameless narrator, a musician, tells of a jazz band that is invited to play at the wedding of Maureen, mob boss Mike Scollay's sister. Extremely overweight and homely, she is an easy target for unflattering jokes and comments. A loving brother, Mike wants her wedding to be perfect. Things don't quite go according to plan, however. One of Mike's rivals, the Greek, sends a lackey to the wedding to deliver an insulting message to the bride. An enraged Mike storms out of the wedding reception, straight into a deadly ambush.

MAUREEN SCOLLAY ROMANO: Mike Scollay's sister, she is the wife of Rico Romano. After her brother's murder, she seizes the reins of his operation and builds it into "a prohibition empire that rivaled Capone's." Rumors abound that Maureen later took revenge on the Greek by sticking a piece of piano wire through his eye into his brain, killing him even as he begs for mercy.

"My Pretty Pony" (from 1993's *Nightmares & Dreamscapes*)

According to King's Note in *Nightmares & Dreamscapes*, this is a section of an unfinished Richard Bachman novel about a hit man named Clive Banning. "My Pretty Pony" represents a flashback in that novel: the memorable day in 1961 when Clive's grandfather instructs him on the "plastic" nature of time. The story originally appeared in 1989 as a separate limited edition from the Whitney Museum of Art. It retailed for $2,200 each for the 150 copies available to the public, making it the most expensive limited edition King book ever.

"MY PRETTY PONY": PRIMARY SUBJECTS

GEORGE BANNING: The seventy-two-year-old grandfather of Clive Banning, he instructs (George never gives advice, he instructs) his grandson on the importance of time and what it means in a person's life. He dies in his sleep a month after the lesson.

CLIVE BANNING: A young boy who lives in the rural town of Troy, New York. He learns a great deal from his grandfather on the importance of time in a person's life, and that it is time that owns a person—none of us own time.

"Dolan's Cadillac" (from 1993's *Nightmares & Dreamscapes*)

This vivid tale of revenge in the Nevada desert is an update of Edgar Allan Poe's classic 1846 tale, "The Cask of Amontillado." For this story, King received technical advice on burying a Cadillac from his big brother, David King, "a child prodigy with a tested IQ of 150." "Dolan's Cadillac" originally appeared in issues #2 through #6 of *Castle Rock*, a subscription-only monthly newspaper that featured news on the author and his works in all mediums. The short-lived newspaper was the only effort of this type ever authorized by King. A revised version of this story was published as a limited edition by Lord John Press in 1989.

Dave King (Stephen's brother)   DAVID LOWELL

"DOLAN'S CADILLAC": PRIMARY SUBJECTS

DOLAN: A mobster, he has Robinson's wife, Elizabeth, killed to keep her from testifying against him. Dolan falls victim to Robinson's revenge; he is buried alive inside his Cadillac beneath a section of Interstate 71 in Nevada.

ROBINSON: A widower, Robinson blames Dolan for his wife's murder. After years of meticulous planning and preparation, Robinson traps Dolan's Cadillac in a car-sized hole and thus buries him alive.

ELIZABETH ROBINSON: Robinson's wife, she was there "at the wrong place and the wrong time" to accidentally observe Dolan engaging in some criminal act. "She went to the police, and the police sent her to the FBI, and she said yes, she would testify." Although promised protection, Elizabeth is killed by a car bomb.

"The Death of Jack Hamilton"
(from 2002's *Everything's Eventual*)

A tale narrated by Homer Van Meter, one of John Dillinger's gunmen, it tells the story of the lingering death of Jack "Red" Hamilton, and how Dillinger got the scar he bore on his upper lip.

"THE DEATH OF JACK HAMILTON": PRIMARY SUBJECTS

JACK (RED) HAMILTON: As the story opens, Red is wounded by police who are pursuing him, Dillinger, and Homer Van Meter after they pull off a job in Little Bohemia, Wisconsin. Although he initially shrugs off the wound, it eventually proves his undoing. Beyond pain, delirious, he dies while hiding out from the Feds in Aurora, Illinois.

JOHN DILLINGER: In this tale, readers see the softer side of the infamous Depression-era outlaw as he endeavors to save the life of one of his gang. Dillinger survives this incident, only to be gunned down later outside the Biograph Theatre in Chicago.

HOMER VAN METER: While doing time in Pendleton Reformatory, Van Meter taught himself how to rope flies. He uses this talent to distract Red Hamilton in the dying man's final hours.

"In the Death Room" (from 2002's *Everything's Eventual*)

Originally included in the audio book *Blood and Smoke*, a 1999 collection of three stories (the other two are "Lunch at the Gotham Café" and "1408") in which the act of smoking cigarettes is a central element, "In the Death Room" finds King dealing with horror of the most realistic sort.

Fletcher, an American reporter suspected of conspiring with a revolutionary group of insurgents to overthrow the current fascist regime of an unnamed South American country, finds himself held captive in a basement room of the Ministry of Information after being kidnapped off the streets in broad daylight. There are four other people in the room: a guard, Ramon; Escabar, the chief Minister of Information, who also just happens to be an experienced torturer; an unnamed older woman whose hairstyle reminds the reporter of the title character in the classic horror film the *Bride of Frankenstein*; and a small bespectacled man named Hinds. Although he looks harmless, Hinds is in charge of a electrical device specially designed to inflict incredible pain upon anyone he touches with the tip of its specially designed steel rod.

Fletcher figures he has "one or two chances in thirty" of surviving the interrogation if he says what he believes his captors want to hear. He soon realizes it doesn't matter whether he lies or tells the truth, he probably will not leave the aptly named Death Room alive. His only chance for escape lies in accepting a Marlboro cigarette offered to him by Escabar.

Against incredible odds, Fletcher not only kills all his captors, but also manages to escape the country all together. When he finally gets back to New York months later, looking like the survivor of a concentration camp, the first thing he does is treat himself to a single cigarette he purchases on Forty-third Street.

"IN THE DEATH ROOM": PRIMARY SUBJECTS

FLETCHER: A reporter for the *New York Times*, he realizes his only chance of escaping the torture room is by somehow employing the cigarette he is offered by his captors. After first being subjected to intense pain by a specially designed torture machine, he realizes he has to kill his captors before they kill him. When he is offered a lit cigarette, he plunges its burning tip into the eye of the guard, Ramon. Taking the guard's gun away, he shoots Ramon, Escabar, and the "Bride of Frankenstein." Believing that the punishment should fit the crime, he forces the chief torturer, Hinds, to subject himself to the pain of his own machine. Fletcher eventually escapes from the violent, fascist country but still suffers from his experience there.

ESCABAR: A fat, greasy man, Escabar is not only the Minister of Information in this small nation, he also acts as one of its chief torturers. He dies when Fletcher shoots him during a scuffle in the Death Room.

"THE BRIDE OF FRANKENSTEIN": This regal-looking woman, who does not speak with any Spanish accent, is in her sixties. Due to her dark black hair, which has streaks of white running through it, Fletcher thinks of her as "the Bride of Frankenstein." She dies while attempting to escape from the soundproofed torture room, shot by Fletcher.

HINDS: A small, bald, bespectacled man, he is the torture technician. It is his sadistic task to operate a machine he has apparently devised that sends electrical current through prisoners via the tip of a steel rod. The pain the device induces can be deadly—he almost kills Fletcher while using only one-quarter of the machine's potential charge. After Fletcher dispatches his three other captors, he insures that Hinds dies the most horrible death of all: Fletcher induces him to put the steel tip into his mouth, turns the dial to full power, then flips the switch.

RAMON: An obese prison guard who is there to watch over the ghastly proceedings. Fletcher jams a lit cigarette into his eye, then shoots him with his own gun.

Tales from Beyond:
Further Parallel Realities

63

RELATED TALES

In discussing the numerous definite, probable, and possible connections between one parallel reality and another in the Stephen King Universe, there are still a few threads left dangling. These are the handful of stories that stand alone in the sense that in each of them King posits a reality—often postapocalyptic—that exists for that tale alone. Even so, all of them share a similar theme: that of the protagonists believing they are in control of their world, only to slowly realize they have no control, and are likewise losing contact with the rest of the "real" world.

The Mist, for example, deals with a group of characters who suddenly find themselves in a world where they are increasingly cut off from reality as we define it. "Trucks" focuses on another small group of individuals who find that in their world man is no longer in control, but sentient machines are. "Home Delivery" takes place in a battered world dominated by zombies. In each story, man is presented as being the hunted, not the hunter.

Three of these stories have no overlapping connection with any other parallel realities, unless one imagines that the breach between worlds that takes place in *The Mist* is a "thinny" as those phenomena are conceived of in the Reality of the Dark Tower. "Beachworld" is a futuristic tale of doomed space explorers. "The Jaunt" presents us with another futuristic vision, while

"The End of the Whole Mess" is yet another grim examination of how the world might someday end.

"Trucks" (from 1978's *Night Shift*)

A group of people are trapped in a diner after all the world's trucks (and possibly planes as well) take on a mind of their own and start to randomly murder, and then systematically enslave, the human race.

"TRUCKS": PRIMARY SUBJECTS

THE STORYTELLER: The nameless main character of the story is the one who tries to keep the people inside Conant's Truck Stop & Diner from going insane and/or getting themselves killed. Several individuals die before he and the other remaining survivors realize that they are at the mercy of the trucks. Their bondage begins with their being forced to pump gas around the clock to feed their new masters.

THE COUNTERMAN: Another survivor, he is the short-order cook at Conant's before being enslaved by the trucks.

JERRY: He dies in a heroic attempt to protect those in the diner.

JERRY'S GIRLFRIEND: The third survivor.

"The Jaunt" (from 1985's *Different Seasons*)

A tribute of sorts to two classic science fiction novels, Alfred Bester's *The Stars My Destination* (1957) and Robert A. Heinlein's *The Door into Summer* (1956), "The Jaunt" is a futuristic tale of the discovery of a teleportation device capable of sending people and objects to other planets.

"THE JAUNT": PRIMARY SUBJECTS

THE OATES FAMILY: Mark; his wife, Marilys; their son, Ricky; and their daughter, Patricia. While preparing for their teleportation to Mars, Mark relates to his family the history of jaunting, focusing on the trials and tribulations of its inventor, Victor Carune. Although Mark tells his family how important it is for humans to be asleep during the Jaunt, his son, Ricky, holds his breath when the attendant administers his sleep gas. By being secretly awake during his Jaunt, young Ricky is unfortunately driven mad.

VICTOR CARUNE: The man who invents the teleportation process commonly known as "jaunting." Lionized due to his discoveries, Carune, a "rather peculiar man who showered perhaps twice a week and changed his clothes only when he thought of it," is remembered by the public at large as a "combination of Edison, Eli Whitney, Pecos Bill and Flash Gordon."

The Mist (from 1985's Skeleton Crew)

One of King's most popular novellas, this first appeared in *Dark Forces: New Stories of Suspense and Supernatural Horror* (1980), an outstanding volume of original works that many critics believe was *the* seminal anthology of the decade. The story of two universes colliding, *The Mist* reflects King's distrust of technology, a theme he would develop more explicitly in *The Tommyknockers*. It is also important to note that it seems very likely that the experiments in *The Mist* probably caused the creation of a thinny, a portal between worlds, a concept richly elaborated upon in the *Dark Tower* series.

THE MIST: PRIMARY SUBJECTS

THE ARROWHEAD PROJECT: Possibly the cause of the accident that unleashes the Mist. The group in the supermarket theorizes that the military may have created a door into another reality, allowing the creatures that live there to cross over to Earth.

DAVID DRAYTON: The narrator of the tale, Drayton tells of the coming of the Mist and its frightening aftermath. The Mist comes rolling across Long Lake, Maine, shortly after a terrific storm devastates the town. Accompanied by his son, Billy, and his neighbor, Brent Norton, David leaves his wife, Steffy, at home and travels into town for supplies. Once there, they become trapped in a Federal Foods Supermarket when hideous creatures emerge from the Mist (which by now has engulfed the town) and begin to slaughter those outside. After spending two days in the supermarket, David realizes he and Billy are no longer safe inside, as some of their number have clearly descended into madness. Along with several companions, David braves the Mist and gains his Jeep. When last seen, David was driving across the apocalyptic landscape toward Hartford, Connecticut, in hopes of meeting up with other survivors. It seems unlikely that he will.

STEFFY DRAYTON: Mother of Billy, wife of David, Steffy is presumed dead, most likely killed by the creatures that live in the Mist.

BILLY DRAYTON: David's son, he survives the siege on the supermarket. He is last seen in the company of his father, traveling toward Hartford, Connecticut.

BRENT NORTON: David's neighbor, he leads a group into the Mist and is never seen again. Brent and his followers are presumed dead—David asks one member of the group to tie a rope around his waist and tie it to something secure at the other end when it is played out. After screams erupt, the rope goes suddenly slack. The group in the supermarket pulls it back and sees that the blood-soaked end of the rope has been chewed through.

MOTHER CARMODY: Proprietor of the Bridgeton Antiquary, Mrs. Carmody is famous for her "gothic pronouncements and folk remedies" (which are always prescribed in God's name). Trapped in the supermarket, Mrs. Carmody begins preaching that the end of the world is at hand; not too surprisingly, she soon wins some converts. But when she begins to preach that a human sacrifice is needed to appease God, David Drayton takes it as a sign to leave to search for other possible survivors.

MRS. REPPLER: A third-grade teacher, she joins David and Billy in their quest to find other survivors beyond the supermarket. A practical woman, Mrs. Reppler battles the creatures that emerge from the Mist with weapons as varied as bug spray and a tennis racket.

MRS. TURMAN: Billy's babysitter, she takes charge of the boy as David, his father, deals with the situation in the supermarket.

AMANDA DUMFRIES: Seeking comfort in the midst of chaos, Amanda becomes David's lover. Amanda is the only one in the supermarket who is carrying a weapon—a gun that she keeps in her pocketbook.

[NOTE: "The Mist in 3D Sound" recording was produced in 1987; the script was written in part by acclaimed author Dennis Etchison. Produced using an audio technology called "Kunstkopf" ("artificial head") binaural sound, this dramatization does have the unique quality of seemingly placing the listener in the midst of the action. Mother Carmody emerges as a truly fearsome personality in this version, lending credence to Drayton's decision to face the horrors outside rather than dealing with the monsters inside the store.]

"Beachworld" (from 1985's Skeleton Crew)

Set in the future on a far-flung desert planet, this brief but effective science fiction/horror hybrid would not have been out of place in the EC Comics that King enjoyed as a child.

SHAPIRO and RAND: A spaceship crash-lands on a desert planet, killing one of the crew. By the time a rescue ship arrives, Shapiro is ready to leave, but Rand is not. Rand, you see, is insane, having been consumed by— and having consumed—the sentient sand of which the desert world is composed.

"The End of the Whole Mess"
(from 1993's *Nightmares & Dreamscapes*)

King mentions in his Notes that readers will "find reflections" of his brother, Dave, in Bobby Fornoy, Howard's genius brother. It is a cautionary science fiction tale, once again dealing with King's theme of the dire consequences of anyone possessing special powers or paranormal talents.

"THE END OF THE WHOLE MESS": PRIMARY SUBJECTS

HOWARD FORNOY: The narrator of the story, Howard tells of growing up with his genius brother, Bobby, opening his narrative with, "I want to tell you about the end of war, the degeneration of mankind, and the death of the Messiah . . ." Shortly after injecting himself with his brother Bobby's wonder drug, Howard tells the tale of Bobby's quest for world peace. Howard is a freelance writer, and his tale is told in a series of diarylike entries, which become increasingly incoherent as the story progresses.

BOBBY FORNOY: Howard writes, "People like my brother Bobby come along only once every two or three generations, I think—guys like Leonardo DaVinci, Newton, Einstein, maybe Edison." Bobby *is* a genius, but instead of pursuing wealth, he pursues a cure for man's inhumanity to man. Bobby finds his cure in an aquifer near Waco, Texas, and arranges to distribute it to the whole world. In an ironic twist of fate, the genius overlooks one thing—the water that pacifies people also causes a precipitous drop in their IQs. In essence, Bobby has turned the entire world into passive idiots.

"Home Delivery" (from 1993's *Nightmares & Dreamscapes*)

This tale of homicidal zombies, originally commissioned for a 1989 theme anthology entitled *Book of the Dead* and purposely set in writer/director George A. Romero's *Night of the Living Dead* (1968) universe, takes place on Little Tall Island, the setting of *Dolores Claiborne* (1993) and

Storm of the Century (1999). Clearly, however, this is *not* the Little Tall Island of the Prime Reality, but a nightmarish mirror image from some parallel dimension. Though focused on the ordeal of Maddie Pace, it's also a story about the stubbornness and sheer gumption of "Mainers" to never give up without a fight—no matter how daunting the odds.

"HOME DELIVERY": PRIME SUBJECTS

MADDIE PACE: Widowed when her husband falls off a fishing boat, Maddie still carries his baby. When the zombies attack humanity, Maddie, like the other citizens of Little Tall, determines to do what it takes to save their island, even if it means combating deceased family members and loved ones.

JACK PACE: Maddie's late husband, who has returned from the dead as a hideous zombie, seeks to make her his next victim. Although she had once truly loved Jack, she knows this monster is no longer her husband. To save herself and their unborn child Maddie takes an ax and chops Jack into little pieces.

"The Doctor's Case"
(from 1993's *Nightmares & Dreamscapes*)

This story was King's contribution to a 1987 anthology entitled *The New Adventures of Sherlock Holmes*, a group of original stories written in honor of the great Sir Arthur Conan Doyle (1859–1930).

"THE DOCTOR'S CASE": PRIME SUBJECTS

SHERLOCK HOLMES, DR. WATSON, and LESTRADE: If you don't know who these three gentlemen are, you have clearly failed Great Literary Characters 101. Suffice it to say that King indulges in a bit of role reversal here, allowing Dr. Watson to solve a locked room mystery instead of master British sleuth Holmes.

APPENDIX A

Recommended Further Reading

At last count, some forty-odd (some *very* odd) books have been published about Stephen King and/or his work in the United States alone, of which *The Stephen King Universe* will certainly not be the last word. At the risk of excluding a personal favorite, we have selected several titles that we feel are the most useful to both the casual King fan and the serious King scholar. (They are listed in order of their original publication. Many have since been reprinted in both hardcover and paperback editions by other publishers, often in revised form.)

Although some of the titles are currently out of print, they may be obtained through the usual services handling out-of-print and used books.

We recommend Betts Bookstore in Bangor, Maine, owned by Stuart Tinker, which handles "all things King" right in King's back yard. (Call 207-947-7052 or e-mail at bettsbooks@aol.com.) We also heartily recommend a search of the Overlook Connection, owned by Dave Hinchberger. He has been dealing in all things related to King since 1979, and his online bookstore carries many King rarities and oddities. (Call 770-926-1762 or e-mail at OverlookCN@aol.com.)

1. *Fear Itself: The Horror Fiction of Stephen King*, edited by Chuck Miller and Tim Underwood (Columbia, PA: Underwood-Miller, 1982). The first major collection of essays on King, written by such contemporaries as Fritz Leiber, Chelsea Quinn Yarbro, and Douglas E. Winter, with an introduction by Peter Straub and an afterword by George A. Romero. It's interesting that in the introduction to "Stephen King: A Bibliography," the compilers boldly observe: "It has been stated that Richard Bachman is a pseudonym of Stephen King. This is not the

case. Mr. Bachman lives in Bangor, Maine, and Stephen King has never used this name as a pseudonym."

2. *Stephen King: The Art of Darkness* by Douglas E. Winter (New York: NAL, 1984). The first and only authorized biography/overview/critical examination of Stephen King, written by noted critic and horror authority Douglas E. Winter. The first book one should turn to when wishing to know more about the man and his writings. An expanded and updated edition appeared in 1986, detailing the previously concealed subject of the Richard Bachman pseudonym. A further revised edition is long overdue.

3. *The Many Facets of Stephen King* by Michael R. Collings (Mercer Island, WA: Starmont, 1985). The first of many critical guides to the novels, short stories, and films of Stephen King by Professor Michael Collings. Although all his studies to date have been issued by academic or specialty publishers, and therefore have not been widely available to the general public, Collings would go on to become the most prolific critical writer on the subject at hand. (He has authored or co-authored more than a half-dozen volumes on Stephen King.) This initial volume is a comprehensive overview of the author, his work, and his critics.

4. *The Annotated Guide to Stephen King* by Michael R. Collings (Mercer Island, WA: Starmont, 1986). The first comprehensive bibliographic study. The author later expanded and updated the volume for Borgo Press as *The Work of Stephen King: An Annotated Bibliography & Guide*.

5. *Reign of Fear: The Fiction and Films of Stephen King* edited by Don Herron (Columbia, PA: Underwood-Miller, 1988). The third collection of original essays compiled by critic Herron for editors/publishers Underwood and Miller, who had previously released a second volume of essays entitled *Kingdom of Fear: The World of Stephen King* in 1986. This third volume is notable mostly for its tone in that although most of the essays look upon the work of King quite charitably and favorably, the editor himself does not.

6. *Bare Bones: Conversations on Terror with Stephen King* edited by Chuck Miller and Tim Underwood (Columbia, PA: Underwood-

Miller, 1988). The first collection of interviews, compiled from various sources and gathered together by theme. Nearly one-fifth of the book's contents is taken from interviews conducted by Stanley Wiater. Also published as a trade hardcover by McGraw-Hill (New York) in 1988.

7. *Feast of Fear: Conversations with Stephen King* edited by Chuck Miller and Tim Underwood (Columbia, PA: Underwood-Miller, 1989). A second collection of interviews, compiled from various sources and gathered together by theme. Also published as a trade hardcover by Carroll & Graf Publishers (New York) in 1992.

8. *The Stephen King Companion* edited by George Beahm (Kansas City: Andrews and McMeel, 1989). The first collection of articles, interviews, appreciations, reviews, and so forth to be issued by a major publisher. An interesting mixture of both new and reprinted material compiled by a recognized popular culture authority. (Beahm has also edited *The Unauthorized Anne Rice Companion* for the same publisher.) The same publisher issued a revised edition in 1995.

9. *The Shape Under the Sheet: The Stephen King Encyclopedia* by Stephen J. Spignesi (Ann Arbor, MI: Popular Culture Ink, 1991). A monumental work that reportedly took more than four years to write and compile. The book is both a companion volume (interviews, articles, reviews, fiction) and a concordance to everything (and we do mean everything) that King had written up until that time. A noted popular culture authority, Spignesi is also the author of two quiz/trivia books on King and, most recently, 1998's *The Lost Work of Stephen King* (Secaucus, NJ: Birch Lane Press), described as "a guide to the unpublished manuscripts, story fragments, alternative versions, and oddities," and 2001's *The Essential Stephen King* (New Page Books).

10. *The Stephen King Story* by George Beahm (Kansas City: Andrews and McMeel, 1991). A literary profile of the author, with emphasis on the manner in which King has become a celebrity and a worldwide publishing phenomenon. Given the rate at which King produces new work, the volume was revised and updated for its 1992 appearance in paperback.

11. *The Films of Stephen King* by Ann Lloyd (New York: St. Martin's, 1994). A heavily illustrated if woefully slender volume first published in England the previous year, it still remains one of the most accessible and entertaining of all the books written on the subject. Three other volumes covering much the same "pre-2001" territory: *Stephen King at the Movies* by Jessie Horsting (New York: Starlog Press, 1984), *The Films of Stephen King* by Michael R. Collings (Mercer Island, WA: Starmont, 1986), and *Stephen King Goes to Hollywood* by Jeff Conner (New York: NAL, 1987).

12. *Stephen King from A to Z: An Encyclopedia of His Life and Work* by George Beahm (Kansas City: Andrews and McMeel, 1998). An earnest attempt to look at the life and work of King through the format of an A-to-Z encyclopedic compilation, with entries ranging from "Ackerman, Forrest, J." to "ZBS Productions." According to the publisher, the volume is "the only book of its kind. Illustrated with seventy-five photos and twenty-six illuminated letters, the book includes hundreds of entries covering everything you wanted to know about King . . . but were afraid to ask."

13. *Stephen King Country* by George Beahm (Philadelphia, PA: Running Press, 1999). Subtitled *The Illustrated Guide to the Sites and Sights that Inspired the Modern Master of Horror*. A fascinating collection of photographs and text presenting the world of Stephen King from two viewpoints: first, the locations in Maine that show the "real" world of Stephen King, such as his home, the laundry where he once worked, and his old high school. It also has original photographs showing the actual sites, buildings, and locations that reportedly inspired corresponding locales in his fiction. These include the Shiloh Church in Durham, which may have inspired the Marsten House in *'Salem's Lot* (1975), and the Stanley Hotel in Estes Park, Colorado, the inspiration for the Overlook in *The Shining* (1977).

14. *Creepshows: The Illustrated Stephen King Movie Guide* by Stephen Jones (London: Titan Books, 2001). Inside you'll find a candid look at each and every Stephen King movie, sequel and spinoff through the end of the millennium, all complete with major cast and credit information, along with television adaptations, stage shows, radio plays, and computer games, plus details of upcoming projects. Another recent book of note regarding King cinema is *Hollywood's*

Stephen King by Tony Magistrale (New York: Palgrave Macmillan, 2003), which *Publishers Weekly* called "a useful elucidation of King's work through the skewed lens of Hollywood."

15. *Horror Plum'd: An International Stephen King Bibliography and Guide* by Michael R. Collings (Woodstock, GA: Overlook Connection Press, 2003). Exactly as billed by its subtitle, this is an exhaustive study of four decades of King's work.

16. *Stephen King's The Dark Tower: A Concordance, Volumes I and II*, by Robin Furth (New York: Scribner, 2003, 2005). In his foreword to Volume I, King says, "I found this overview of In-World, Mid-World, and End-World both entertaining and invaluable. So, I am convinced, will you."

17. *The Road to the Dark Tower* by Bev Vincent (New York: New American Library, 2004). Again, a King blurb says it all: "Wonderful . . . opens doors to Roland's world that not even I knew existed. If you like the Dark Tower books, you'll like this. Enthusiastically recommended."

[NOTE: *We would be greatly remiss if we didn't strongly recommend what remains the most personal and in-depth look at King's thoughts, feelings, and opinions on the subject of horror:* Stephen King's Danse Macabre *(New York: Everest House, 1981). Encouraged by editor William Thompson to write a nonfiction study so that he would never have to answer interviewers and fans about the topic again, King reluctantly but enthusiastically bent to the task. (The fact that what he had already said about horror filled no less than two volumes of interviews may also have had something to do with the undertaking.) As King explains in his introduction, "Writing this book has been both an exasperation and a deep pleasure, a duty on some days and a labor of love on others." As engaging and moving as his fiction,* Stephen King's Danse Macabre *remains an affectionate yet perceptive look at how horror in the mass media and the arts has affected our popular culture in general—and one little boy from Maine in particular.]*

APPENDIX B

Recommended Web Sites

As one might imagine, there are literally hundreds of Web sites devoted to the world's most popular author. For the sake of not writing another book just to discuss the subject of Stephen King on the Internet, we have chosen several Web sites that we feel will be the most useful—and most entertaining—to the devoted Stephen King fan. On most of these you will find book reviews, movie reviews, the latest news about Stephen King as an author and a celebrity, trivia games, discussions between fans, and so on.

OFFICIAL

1. The Official Stephen King Page
    (www.stephenking.com)
    Just as the title says, the only Web page authorized by King and maintained directly from his office.

UNOFFICIAL

2. Skemers
    (www.skemers.com)
    Started in 1995, it is the largest King fan club for those wanting to discuss and chat about their favorite author online.

3. The Stephen King Cover Galley
    (http://home5.swipnet.se/~55592/gallery.htm)
    An incredible site, fan Anders Jackson has scanned in more than a thousand different editions of Stephen King book covers from around the world.

4. The Stephen King Web Site
   (www.utopianweb.com/king/)
   A comprehensive King site, very well done.

5. David's Stephen King Page
   (www.lisp.com.au/~davidth/king/king.html)
   A comprehensive King site, more informal and purposely entertaining than most.

6. The Stephen King Page
   (http://malakoff.com/sking.htm)
   A very entertaining page, this site includes a Randall Flagg Homepage and a Richard Bachman Homepage.

7. The Last Gunslinger
   (www.geocities.com/Area51/Dimension/1004/gunslinger.html)
   A very impressive, visually dazzling site devoted exclusively to the *Dark Tower* epic.

8. The Unofficial Stephen King Website
   (www.stephenking.net)
   A very well designed and respectful site maintained by fan Ian Richardson, which has been in service since 1996.

9. Stephen King Information Site
   (www.eddog.com/sk/)
   One of the oldest and most reliable King sites out there, run by hardcore fan Ed Nomura.

10. Charnel House: The Stephen King Site for the Discerning Reader
    (http:/members.tripod.com/~charnelhouse/)
    A full-service information source for "all things King."

11. SkingWeb—Stephen King Fun and Information
    (http://skingweb.virtualave.net/)
    Just what the title indicates; this is part of the "official" series of Stephen King sites in the Stephen King webring.

12. IMDB—Stephen King
    (http://usidmb.com/Name?/King,+Stephen)

The International Movie Data Base listing of all movies associated with Stephen King. Complete and factual, but without any visuals to go along with the reams of data.

13. The Dark Tower.Net
    (http://thedarktower.net)
    As indicated by its address, this site is devoted exclusively to the object of the Gunslinger's quest.

14. Horrorking.com's Stephen King site
    (http://horrorking.com)
    A site created and maintained by David Rawsthorne, author of *Stephen King: Uncollected, Unpublished* (Forest Hill, MD: Cemetery Dance, 2006).

APPENDIX C

The Fiction of Stephen King, in Order of Publication

1. *Carrie* (1974)
2. *'Salem's Lot* (1975)
3. *Rage* (as by Richard Bachman) (1977)
4. *The Shining* (1977)
5. *Night Shift* (1978) (collection)
6. *The Stand* (1978)
7. *The Long Walk* (as by Richard Bachman) (1979)
8. *The Dead Zone* (1979)
9. *Firestarter* (1980)
10. *Roadwork* (as by Richard Bachman) (1981)
11. *Cujo* (1981)
12. *Creepshow* (1982)
13. *The Running Man* (as by Richard Bachman) (1982)
14. *The Dark Tower: The Gunslinger* (1982)
15. *Different Seasons* (collection) (1982)
16. *Christine* (1983)
17. *Pet Sematary* (1983)
18. *The Talisman* (with Peter Straub) (1983)
19. *Thinner* (as by Richard Bachman) (1984)
20. *Cycle of the Werewolf* (1985)
21. *Skeleton Crew* (collection) (1985)
22. *Cat's Eye* (original screenplay) (1985)
23. *It* (1986)
24. *The Dark Tower II: The Drawing of the Three* (1987)
25. *The Eyes of the Dragon* (1987)
26. *Misery* (1987)

27. *The Tommyknockers* (1987)
28. *The Dark Half* (1989)
29. *Four Past Midnight* (collection) (1990)
30. *Needful Things* (1991)
31. *Stephen King's Golden Years* (original television series) (1991)
32. *The Dark Tower III: The Wastelands* (1991)
33. *Sleepwalkers* (original screenplay) (1992)
34. *Gerald's Game* (1992)
35. *Dolores Claiborne* (1993)
36. *Nightmares & Dreamscapes* (collection) (1993)
37. *Insomnia* (1994)
38. *Rose Madder* (1995)
39. *The Green Mile* (1996)
40. *Desperation* (1996)
41. *The Regulators* (as by Richard Bachman) (1996)
42. *The Dark Tower IV: Wizard and Glass* (1997)
43. *Six Stories* (collection) (1997)
44. *Bag of Bones* (1998)
45. *Storm of the Century* (original miniseries) (1999)
46. *The Girl Who Loved Tom Gordon* (1999)
47. *Hearts in Atlantis* (1999)
48. *Dreamcatcher* (2001)
49. *Black House* (with Peter Straub) (2001)
50. *From a Buick 8* (2002)
51. *Everything's Eventual* (collection) (2002)
52. *The Dark Tower V: Wolves of the Calla* (2003)
53. *The Dark Tower VI: Song of Susannah* (2004)
54. *The Dark Tower VII: The Dark Tower* (2004)
55. *The Colorado Kid* (2005)
56. *Cell* (2006)

INDEX

Names listed in boldface refer to characters.
Page numbers in boldface refer to character biographies.

ABOUT THE AUTHORS

STANLEY WIATER has been called "the world's leading authority on horror filmmakers and authors" (*Radio-TV Interview Report*) and "the master journalist of the dark genres" (*World of Fandom*). He has recently begun production, as both writer and host, on a television series inspired by his award-winning series of Dark Dreamers books.

His first collection of exclusive interviews, *Dark Dreamers: Conversations with the Masters of Horror*, won the Bram Stoker Award for Superior Achievement from the Horror Writers Association. A companion volume, *Dark Visions: Conversations with the Masters of the Horror Film*, was a Bram Stoker Award finalist. *Comic Book Rebels: Conversations with the Creators of the New Comics*, co-authored with Stephen R. Bissette, was both an Eisner Award and a Harvey Award nominee. *Dark Thoughts: On Writing*, a "best of" compilation, also won the Bram Stoker Award. A collaboration with acclaimed photographer Beth Gwinn led to a unique collection of photographs and interviews in *Dark Dreamers: Facing the Masters of Fear*.

Wiater's first published short story, "The Toucher," was the sole winner of a 1980 competition judged by none other than Stephen King. He has been interviewing and writing about King for more than two decades.

Wiater was born and raised in Massachusetts, where he still lives with his family. He graduated from the University of Massachusetts with a degree in writing and cinema. He is presently completing work on a study of the films of Wes Craven. Please visit him at www.stanleywiater.com.

CHRISTOPHER GOLDEN is the award-winning, *Los Angeles Times*–bestselling author of such nonfiction works as *Buffy the Vampire Slayer: The Watcher's*

Guide, Buffy the Vampire Slayer: The Monster Book, and *CUT!: Horror Writers on Horror Film*, for which he received the Bram Stoker Award. As a journalist, his work has appeared in such publications as *Disney Adventures, The Boston Globe, Billboard*, and *Hero Illustrated*, and for several years he wrote a regular column for the international service *BPI Entertainment News Wire*.

Golden's teen thriller series *Body of Evidence* was recently optioned by Viacom Television, and he is currently developing a second series for teens with Pocket Books.

His novels include *Strangewood, The Shadow Saga* trilogy, and *Straight on 'til Morning*, as well as *Hellboy: The Lost Army*, among others. He has also written or co-written nine *Buffy the Vampire Slayer* novels.

As a comic book writer, his work has included *Batman Chronicles, Wolverine/Punisher, The Crow, Spider-Man Unlimited, Angel, Blade, Buffy the Vampire Slayer*, and the creator-owned *Thundergod*.

Before becoming a full-time writer, he was licensing manager for *Billboard* magazine in New York, where he worked on Fox Television's *Billboard Music Awards* and *American Top 40* radio, among many other projects.

Golden was born and raised in Massachusetts, where he still lives with his family. He graduated from Tufts University. Please visit him at www.christophergolden.com.

HANK WAGNER is a prolific and respected critic and interviewer. Among the publications where his work has appeared are *Cemetery Dance, Horror, Wetbones, Nova Express, Mystery Scene, Dark Echo, Hellnotes*, and *The New York Review of Science Fiction*. He lives in New Jersey with his wife and four daughters. He graduated from the University of Notre Dame in 1982, and received his J.D. from Seton Hall University in 1985 and an L.L.M. in Taxation from the New York University School of Law in 1991. Wagner is currently working on *Thrillers: 100 Must-Reads*, with David Morrell, author of *First Blood* (1972) and *Creepers* (2005).